Hutong Metabolism

Hutong Metabolism

ZAO/standardarchitecture

Table of Contents

8
Foreword
Farrokh Derakhshani

14
The Timeless Architecture of Zhang Ke
Kenneth Frampton

32
Micro Yuan'er Children's Library and Art Centre

86
Changing Character: China and the Idea of Contemporary Architecture
Mohsen Mostafavi

116
Micro Hutong

162
Hutong Metabolism: Silence Is the Power of Architecture
Martino Stierli

178
Fused Traditions: The Making of an International Contemporary Signature
Hans-Jürgen Commerell and Kristin Feireiss

184
Co-Living Courtyard

226
Hutong Living Conditions, Then and Now
Interview with Hai Daye, Wu A'yi and Wang Tong by Amanda Ju

236
Intimacies in Scale
Interview with Brenda Fang, Kuang He and Naiji Tian by Amanda Ju

248
In Conversation with Zhang Ke
Nondita Correa Mehrotra

254
Hutong Social Housing

282 Contributor Biographies
286 Image Credits
288 Imprint

Foreword
Farrokh Derakhshani

Several years ago, when I first entered the courtyard of the Micro Yuan'er Children's Library and Art Centre in the revitalised Dashilar neighbourhood, just south of Tiananmen Square in Beijing, I discovered a small space animated by a highly diverse crowd of young children, local elders and a few tourists, all of them seemingly mesmerised by an elderly storyteller clothed in traditional garments. He was playing the *erhu*, a traditional Chinese musical instrument, underneath a beautiful large tree. To me, his performance and the lively crowd testified to the many ways in which good architectural interventions can change and affect the daily lives of a community in a positive way. Architecture can give new purpose to old structures in the context of lifestyles and societal aspirations that are in a constant state of change, characterising the highly accelerated pace of our lives today. The purpose of my visit was to better understand why the Master Jury of the Aga Khan Award for Architecture had selected this small project to be honoured during the 2016 Award Cycle.

Being there in person, it was easy to see and appreciate the close collaboration between a visionary client and a talented architect. This relationship had characterised every aspect of the project, from conception through to realisation and subsequent use. Their keen ability to understand, acknowledge, and implement the project in the face of so many administrative, economic and social challenges, as was very evident throughout the entire process, guaranteed its high quality and continued success.

As well as demonstrating mutual understanding and collaboration between all the participants in good architectural interventions, the Micro Yuan'er project showcases other factors that the Aga Khan Award for Architecture perceives as essential in successful architectural solutions, elements such as the appropriate adaptation and reuse of existing urban fabrics, innovation, and enhancement of the quality of life.

Since the 1960s, and under the mantle of so-called progress, historic districts and neighbourhoods in large cities underwent erosion and continuing degradation that usually resulted in their demolition, and the destruction not only of the architectural legacy of these areas but also the socio-cultural components that characterised the essential vitality of societal life. In China as elsewhere throughout the world, area conservation and revitalisation projects have emerged as priorities for authorities responsible for built environments. Until the relatively recent past, conventional restoration efforts usually reflected nostalgic approaches aimed at promoting tourism, and most large-scale area conservation projects failed because they did not take consider the basic needs and aspirations that make urban communities thrive and provide the residents with a sense of inherent belonging to the inhabited areas. The projects presented in this volume – that in many ways serve as catalysts for other such efforts – directly counter earlier efforts at revitalisation and conservation by focusing on the lives of the residents as the most precious asset in the creation of architecture. These projects introduce new functions and programmes relevant to contemporary life-style in historic areas, and once again demonstrate the unique ability of architecture to enhance people's quality of life.

Architecturally, these projects also demonstrate the bold introduction of sculptural forms, and the use of new materials and construction technologies, in close juxtaposition to traditional building forms and methods. Once-neglected, these areas are now imbued again with a sense of vitality and contemporaneity that differs greatly from more typical approaches that, alas, most often result in a sense of community alienation and individual isolation.

The role of the Aga Khan Award for Architecture is to identify and encourage successful efforts in the built environment, and to share these outstanding achievements with others around the globe. This publication analyses the impact of Zhang Ke and his architectural practice, ZAO/standardarchitecture, within the context of the Aga Khan Award for Architecture, with a focus on the importance of the Micro Yuan'er Children's Library and Art Centre – studying and seeing it within the context of contemporary architecture in China, but also in the broader scope of international architectural discourse. The authors contributing to this volume help us to understand the evolution of architecture over the past century, during which society and culture in China underwent great change and upheaval. Also examined is the burgeoning, fast-paced evolution that characterises the country today. Additionally, interviews with residents of the Micro Yuan'er Hutong highlight the living experience of the innovative architectural project as seen by the actual users. This is complemented by the personal reflections and aspirations of the architectural team, who devoted great energy to ensuring the vitality and success of the project. An interview with the lead architect, Zhang Ke, is a unique window into his aspirations and view of the world.

In the late 1970s and early 1980s, the world became interested in discovering the various aspects of then-contemporary China following the post-revolutionary era, including architecture. This coincided with the establishment of the Aga Khan Award for Architecture in 1977 by His Highness the Aga Khan. The goal of the award, then as now, was to better understand all of our built environments and to expand the definition of architecture to encompass and highlight its unique ability to enhance the quality of the lives of all those who use it. Our search was conceived as a celebration of exemplary architectural achievements, and one important component of the ambitious programme was to bring together experts from around the world to discuss architectural issues in thematic seminars. The sixth of these international meetings, held in China in 1981, was entitled "The Changing Rural Habitat", a topic that was not generally within the scope of mainstream architectural discourse at that time. And the meeting took place in a country that was not yet open to international gatherings and visits. Architects, planners, economists, and historians from all over the world travelled to Beijing; they also visited other sites in China all the way to Kashgar in the westernmost part of the country, in order to see and visit local rural habitats first-hand. This was also a pioneering occasion for Chinese architects to discuss with their counterparts from around the world. The proceedings of the meetings and visits were published in Mandarin Chinese and widely distributed in China, as well as in English and French for the worldwide architectural community and others interested in China.

We are grateful to our friends and colleagues in China, and to all of the outstanding contributors to this volume, for the opportunity to discover and explore the many nuances of an Award-winning scheme that indeed speaks loudly and proudly to all of us throughout the world.

The Timeless Architecture of Zhang Ke
Kenneth Frampton

*All's well that begins well and has no ending,
worlds die but we stay young forever.*

—Aleksei Kruchenykh, *Victory Over the Sun*, Luna Park, Saint Petersburg, 1913

The term Hutong Metabolism, as ironic allusion to the short-lived Japanese Metabolist Movement of the late 1950s, is posited as a critical stratagem that seeks to open up a subversive space between the ruthless demolition and maximizing development of the time-honoured, decaying, single-storey residential fabric of Beijing and the occasional opportunity of restoring and converting into communal space a surviving fragment of this pitched-roof, tile covered, traditional carpet-housing.

As Zhang Ke, the founder of ZAO/standardarchitecture, has put it:

> Conservation and restoration of the old cities of China have always had a paradoxical relationship . . . After decades of development frenzy in the old city of Beijing the hutongs are on the verge of being either completely erased in order to make space for office towers, apartments and shopping malls or disfigured by kitsch restorations that take the image of a nostalgic past. The subtle complexity of the hutongs as authentic contemporary urban spaces have been overlooked by both the advocates of "tabula rasa" development and the defenders of historical restoration. In either case, the operation involves the relentless exodus of the hutong's traditional dwellers, resulting in the gradual disappearance of ethnic diversities in the Hutong communities and a rapid diminishing of hutong traditional culture.[1]

Under the slogan "Make New Hutong Metabolism", ZAO/standardarchitecture presents us with four different realised works: the Micro Yuan'er Children's Library and Art Centre in the Dashilar district of Beijing, as exhibited at the Venice Biennale in 2016; the Micro Hutong, close to the Ming City Wall Park; the Co-Living Courtyard in the Baitasi district; and the low-rise housing settlement realised, but seemingly as yet unoccupied, in the Shichahai district of the city.

Each of these works has a different programmatic agenda, and it is these subtle shifts in the scale and scope of each endeavor that concerns us in attempting to position this unique practice within the current upsurge of Chinese architecture.

It is clear that the Micro Yuan'er Children's Library and Art Centre sets the tone for the entire endeavour, above all because of its origins in the somewhat cryptic sketches and reflections that first came to Zhang Ke's mind as he sat on a riverbank in Berlin in 2014, when he wrote the following:

> Life is after all a tragedy. What really matters is how you are going to be remembered and what you did to this world during this ephemeral moment in history. Chinese intellectuals have always known that to create thoughts that could be eternal is much more important to have a glorious "now", only whereas sometimes the glorious "now" could overlap with a glorious "eternity". Therefore to live eternally becomes the goal and duty of life . . . Is this true?[2]

The Micro Yuan'er Children's Library and Art Centre displays all the attributes of an enigmatic, polemically poetic expression, predicated, first and last, on the pre-existence of a timeless "scholar tree" which serves as the spiritual centre of the site. This gnarled and tortured nexus plus its adjoining architectural analogue – a single cell diminutive pavilion, built of grey bricks with an integrated short spiraling stair leading up to its roof – jointly serve as the conceptual pivot for the entire complex with the various adjoining spatial components and their specific uses flowing out and in from and toward this point and looking back through wood-framed picture windows, on occasion doubling as showcases, faced in plate glass. These spaces extend out from the perimeter on all sides; first as a capacious drawing classroom to the south under a already present traditional, timber roof with its beams and rafters exposed, and second as a library/reading room to the east, partially housed in a reinforced concrete carapace beneath a similar pre-existing traditional roof. There are other contingent spaces opening on the alley adjoining the hutong, but clearly the action is focused here about the "scholar tree" and its pavilion and the interstitial courtyard, also paved in the same grey brick.

The quasi-narrative character of the complex is brilliantly orchestrated through a carefully edited and staged sequence of photographs that, in effect, document the consummation of the restored hutong by children of all ages, starting with the very young who gradually grow older into teenagers, so to speak, before our eyes. This all but cinematic photographic presentation begins with the empty hutong, shot at twilight, whereby the interiors lined in wood radiate out their warm reassuring light into the all-encompassing greyness of the brick, together with the grey concrete cast from a cement mix infused with Chinese ink. Thus the drama unfolds for the reader, step by step, around the nexus of the ancient tree.

Micro Yuan'er Children's Library and Art Centre by Zhang Ke, 2016

Micro Hutong Hostel at Yang-Mei-Zhu by Zhang Ke, 2016

By any standards this is a tectonic tour de force, with its all-enveloping poetics of construction beginning with the grey brick pavers, lining the earth underfoot, going onto the bonded grey brickwork of the pavilion with its own diminutive inner space and window answering to the overture of the corner display window of the library.

It is exactly the latter that is partially housed in a carapace of concrete and illuminated by protruding skylights, an invented self-contained image that haunted Zhang Ke as he traveled through Europe in September 2014. It is here, at a median scale, that we find tradition and innovation subtly juxtaposed in the Neo-Brutalist *béton brut* syntax of the library, with its own pitched roof set within and against the interior of a traditional timber-framed pitched roof covered with handmade clay tiles. And it is here that one finally and fully comprehends a

Co-Living Courtyard in the Baitasi district by Zhang Ke, 2016

latent ironic contrast between the technological palette of ZAO/standardarchitecture and the rudimentary pre-industrial substance of a typical hutong.

This contrast is never more evident than in the material synthesis of his new library, which is annotated in terms of millimetres; such as "12 mm single layer of tempered glass, 20 mm metal sheet, 18 mm solid wooden floor", and so on, evoking a precision that would be virtually unattainable in the United States.

The drama, enacted by children of all ages, is replete with countless images, flags, masks costumes, and shadow plays, the inexhaustibly exuberant vitality of *homo-ludens* as its pure beginning, as it builds to a crescendo in the photographic sequence, only to be transformed in the final images into the resigned sobriety of teenagers looking down from the roof of the pavilion into the empty mise-en-scène of the courtyard, where for a single instant one overlooks the mesmerising presence of the time-honoured mythical figure of the musician, magician-cum-storyteller, as he recounts momentarily the substance of a culture which is irretrievably lost.

Extraordinary as it may seem, the oneiric Micro Hutong, dating from 2013, is a trial run for the spatio-tectonic syntax which would be employed four years later in realising the Micro Yuan'er Children's Library and Art Centre. From the onset, the ZAO practice would identify the Micro

Hutong as an experimental building. Here modernity and tradition are handled as if they were interpenetrating moments with the Micro Hutong, assuming the improbable form of a concatenation of introverted boxed apertures, the whole being ingeniously cast in situ in concrete from a cement mix infused with Chinese ink. This cacophonous whole looks into a microcosmic angular courtyard paved in grey bricks; a singular space featuring a single sapling as an embryonic "scholar tree". Two encapsulated micro-volumes would prove essential to the everyday support of the Micro Hutong; in the first instance, a common kitchenette accessible from the alley as insisted upon by the surrounding community and, in the second, a public WC, also accessible from the alley. The other essential supplementary volume, looking into the angular courtyard and paved in brick, is a multipurpose exhibition room, with a wooden floor, which is separated from the introverted core by full-height, sliding/folding, steel-framed glass doors.

In the hollow, "thick" walls of the Micro Hutong, cast as *béton brut* from boarded formwork, there are two chambers at grade, comprising a dining alcove and a bathroom, and three chambers on the first floor above, comprising a study and two bedrooms. As Zhang Ke would write by the side of his original sketch of 2013, "We-Hutong 30 m², 5 rooms and a courtyard plus wood and steel construction. To make the new grow out of the old, to have a surprising at the same time humble coexistence, to open up new pathways, to make the old Hutong Daza Yuan a bit more public".

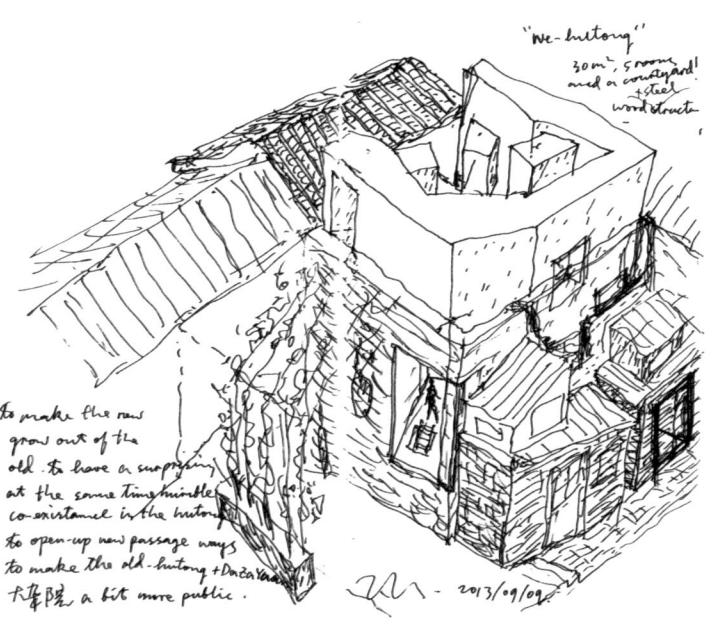

Original sketch of the Micro Hutong from 2013 by Zhang Ke

The Micro Hutong walls are cast as *béton brut* from boarded formwork

Most surprising in all this is the technical sophistication of the work, which as mentioned above was the prototype for the tectonic syntax adopted in the library and art centre of the Micro Yuan'er in Dashilar. Once again, we encounter the capacity to design and build in terms of millimetres, so that in the executive drawings we read in sequence such items as a 50 by 55 millimetre window frame, 25 millimetre double-layered tempered glass, 2 millimetre zinc flashing, 100 millimetre concrete walls, a 15 millimetre wooden floor on top of a 25 millimetre leveling screen, and an 80 millimetre concrete slab. In this way we are made aware not only of a new generation of architects but also of a new generation of builders. Not least among the concatenated shapes of the Micro Hutong are concrete skylights recalling similar apertures in the late work of Le Corbusier. Thus we discover the unusual conjunction of tool-making precision with an unusual topological imagination. And again, we read from the hand of Zhang Ke: "Inward space, to design the void versus to design the mass, inward space as the substance of making architecture".[3]

The technological sophistication of ZAO/standardarchitecture is even more evident in the Baitasi Co-Living Courtyard of 2017, where the design displays a "hi-tech" instrumentality capable of revitalising, piece by piece, sizable fragments of the existing hutong fabric throughout Old Beijing. As the architects put it:

Tibet Namcha Barwa Visitors' Center by ZAO/standardarchitecture, 2008

Main hall of the Tibet Namcha Barwa Visitors' Center

Yarlung Tsangpo Boat Terminal by ZAO/standardarchitecture, 2008

The 3-5 square metre service core, facilitated with kitchen, bathroom, laundry and storage and the prefabricated "Mini-House," a completely independent fully equipped living unit, provide amenities largely lacking in the Hutongs. Once propagated throughout the old city, the cores and the "mini-houses" may solve urgent infrastructural problems and dramatically improve the quality of life among Hutong residents, against both the "tabula rasa" approach and the possible gentrification phenomenon that is common in the old city renewal practices.[4]

At the same time, one is made forcibly aware, as one comes to the end of the Hutong Metabolist polemic, that the Yu'er Hutong Social Housing project in 2019 – ingeniously planned and partially realised on two separate sites – remains, as yet, not only unoccupied but also partially unfinished.

It is hard to imagine something more removed from Hutong Metabolism than the work of ZAO/standardarchitecture in Tibet, beginning in 2008 and amounting, to date, to two works of an exceptional topographic character, realised in that year on two equally remote and interrelated, spectacular mountain sites; the Yarlung Tsangpo Boat Terminal and the Tibet Namcha Barwa Visitors' Center, both being located in Pei Town in the Linzhi Prefecture. Where the first is the last stop on the Yarlung Tsangpo River at the foot of the Namcha Barwa Mountain, the second is essentially a retreat and a rest point along the road to Zhibai, the last village in the grand canyon at the foot of the mountain. Both buildings are made of thick, massive walls of local stone, coming from the site itself, and constructed by local craftsmen in a time-honoured vernacular manner. Both buildings are predicated on reinforced concrete substructures which surface here and there as slabs or lintels over wide-span windows. Of the two, the visitors' centre has the most cryptic character, for as the architects inform us, as one approaches the complex one remains uncertain as to whether this is a set of impenetrable retaining walls or even a Mani wall, erected as part of the local folklore of paying homage to the mountain, which is itself often shrouded in mist. Moreover, the virtually windowless stone walls of the centre appear as if they were fortifications in the midst of a rugged landscape. The core of this redout is hollowed out, for as the architects write:

> The main hall is lit by skylights and has a panoramic window that frames the view to the north towards the village and the Yarlung Tsangpo River. The public toilets and the luggage are placed behind one-metre thick stone walls, while further behind the next stone wall the internet café, medical clinic and the driver's rest space are located. Halfway between the two, a staircase leads to the second floor with the roof garden and meeting rooms . . .[5]

What is not accounted for in this description is the touristic parking lot, screened from view by a long, thick stone wall integrated into the contours of the landscape. Needless to say, we are totally removed here from the sophisticated millimetre precision of the various works projected by ZAO for the hutong fabric of Beijing. What we have here are cyclopean stone walls built by local craftsmen according to the most basic indications provided by the architect. It is clear that the masons are, or were, emerging like their craft out of the mists of time, when there is nothing left for the architect to envisage save the challenge of the inside space as opposed to the mass, which Zhang Ke has already alluded to as an aspiration for the content of a sublime yet unpredictable organic architecture.

Above all, on sites as remote and topographic as these, one cannot perceive with certainty what is new and what is old, nor what is the spiritual transaction between them.

---

1 Text written by Zhang Ke for the Venice Biennale exhibition in 2016.
2 Sketch drawn by Zhang Ke in 2014 for the Micro Yuan'er project.
3 Sketch of the Micro Hutong project drawn by Zhang Ke in 2013.
4 Description text written by Zhang Ke for the Co-Living Courtyard project for the Venice Biennale exhibition in 2016.
5 Description text written by Zhang Ke for the Yarluntzangbu Boat Terminal.

Hutong Development Area

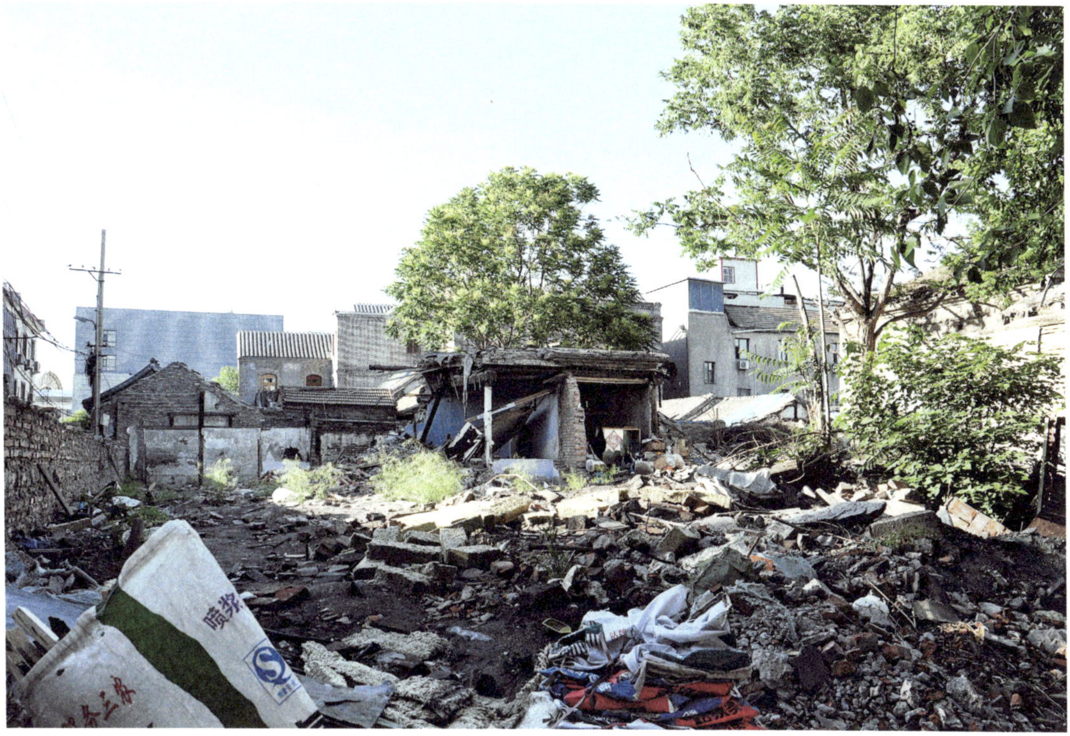
喷浆

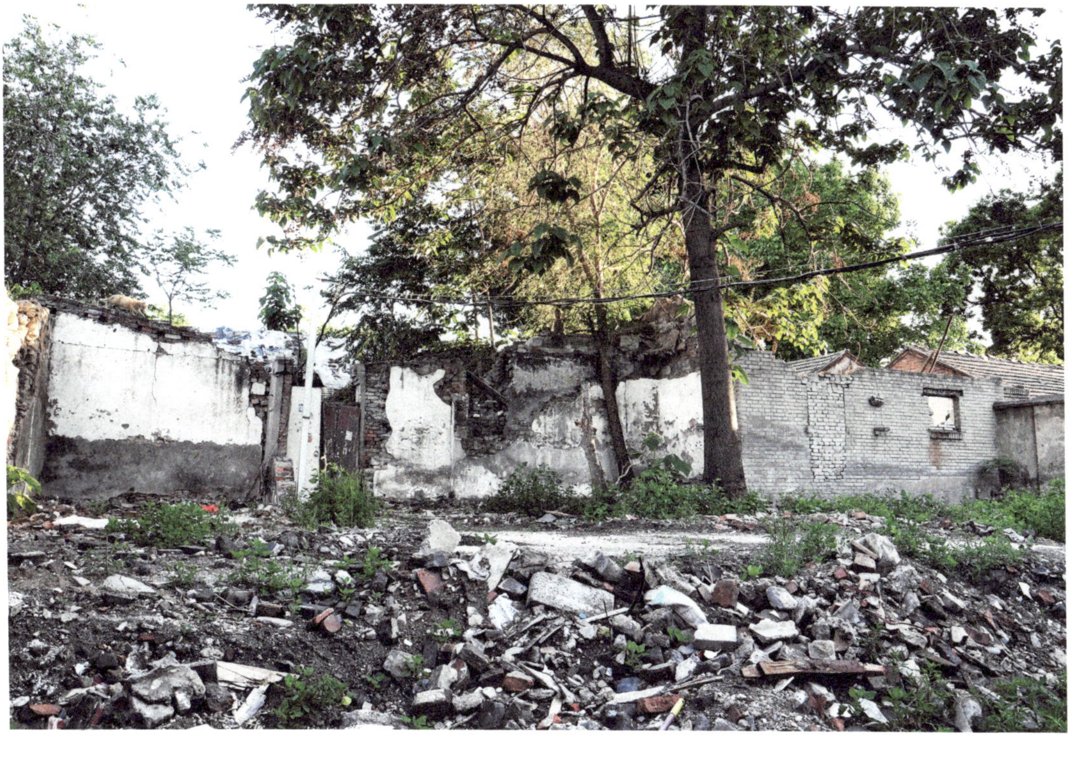

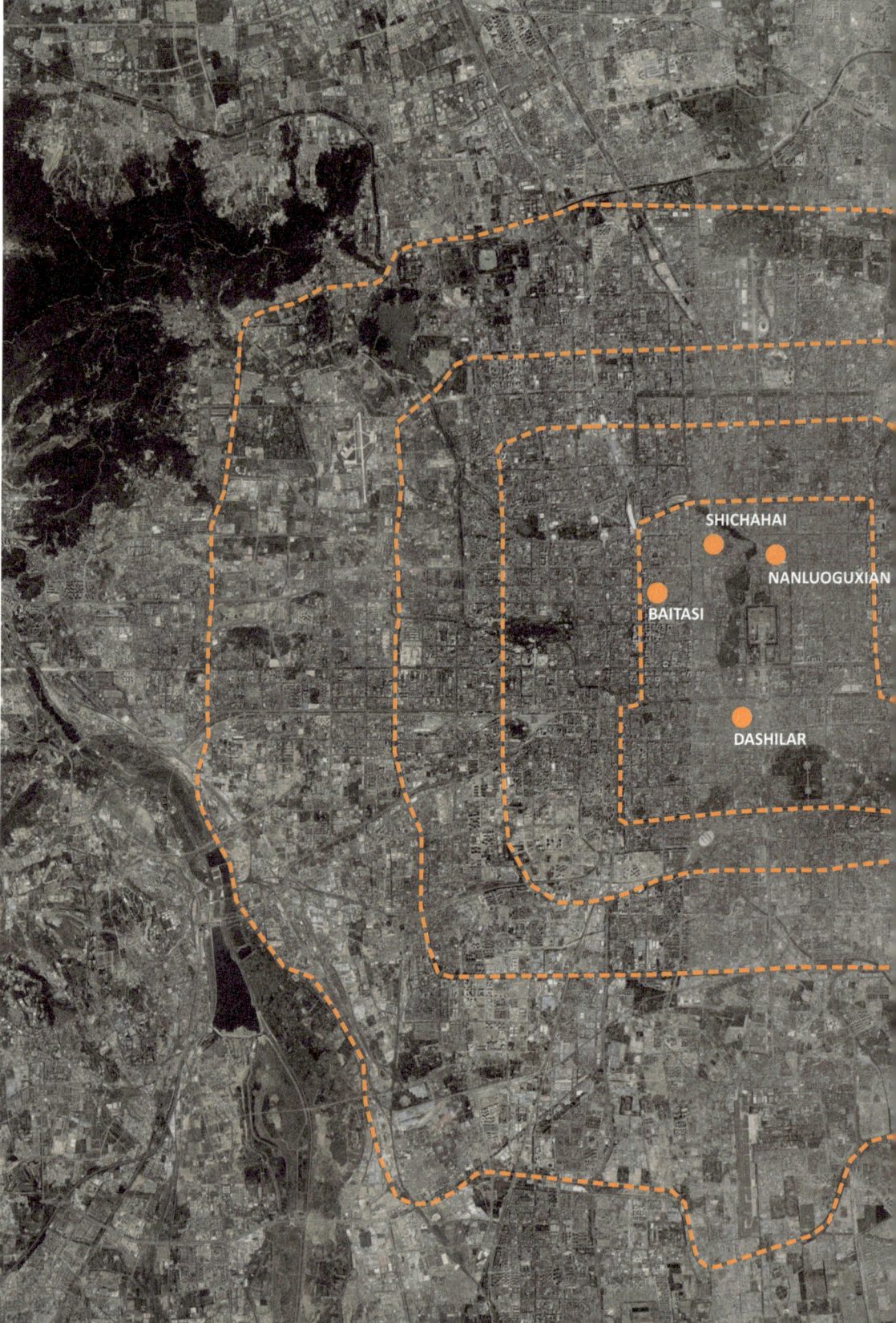

existing hutong area

existing hutong area   hutong conservation area   on-going demolition area

Micro Yuan'er Children's Library and Art Centre

Location: **Beijing, China**
Client: **Beijing Dashilar Investment Ltd.**
Design period: **2012-14**
Construction period: **June 2015-March 2016**
Site area: **300 m²**
Building area: **145 m²**
Total floor area: **145 m²**
Architect: **ZAO/standardarchitecture**
Project architect: **Zhang Ke**
Design team: **Zhang Mingming, Fang Shujun, Ao Ikegami, Huang Tanyu, Ilaria Positano, Wang Ping, Zhang Yifan**

Cha'er Hutong is a quiet spot within the busy Dashilar area, situated just a kilometre away from the Forbidden City in Beijing. It is located next to the Qianmen Mosque, first built in the late Ming dynasty. The hutong's courtyard is a typical *dazayuan* – big messy courtyard – once occupied by over a dozen families. The project originated from a two-year-long study searching for a more subtle and organic way to renew the endangered old hutong areas in the centre of Beijing. ZAO/standardarchitecture redesigned and reused the informal add-on structures instead of eliminating them, recognising them as an important historical layer.

This small-scale intervention aims to strengthen bonds between communities, to enrich the hutong life of local residents, and to enable local handicrafts to be passed on to the next generation.

The children's library, built of concrete mixed with Chinese ink, was inserted underneath the pitched roof of an existing building. Under the big Chinese scholar tree that may be as old as the courtyard itself, one of the former kitchens was redesigned into the mini art space. On its exterior, a trail of brick stairs leads up to the roof, where the residents can delve into the branches and foliage of the big tree.

By redesigning and renovating the add-ons in the hutong courtyards, the project allows Beijing citizens and government to see new and sustainable possibilities for how to put – the usually unvalued – add-on structures to good use.

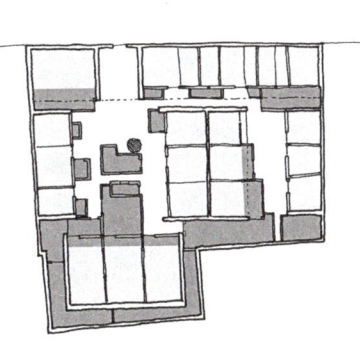

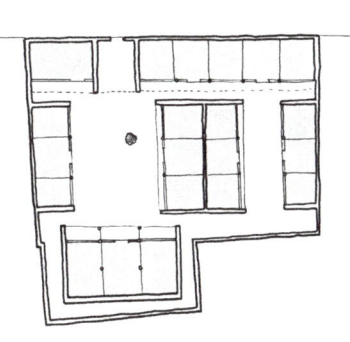

?

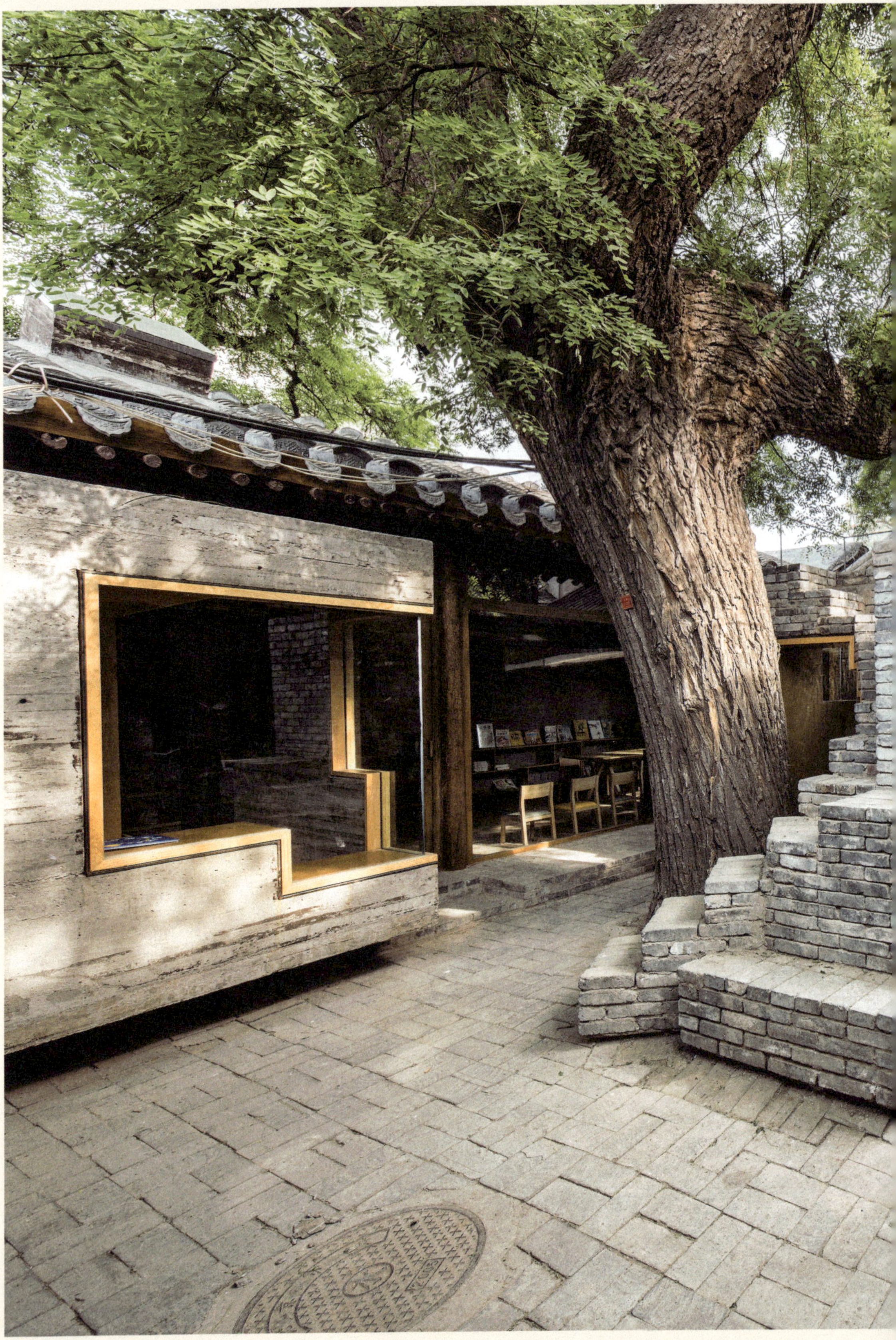

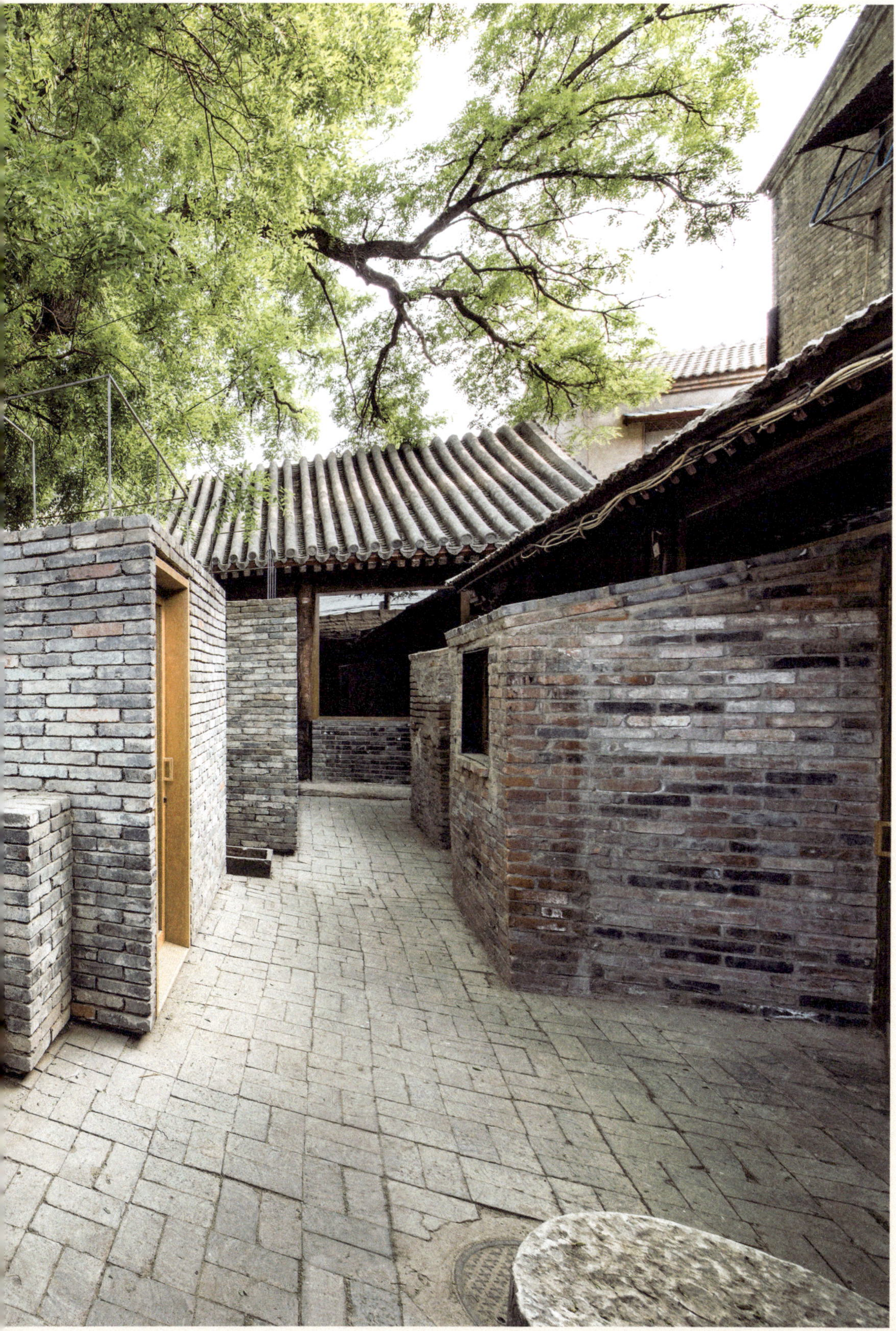

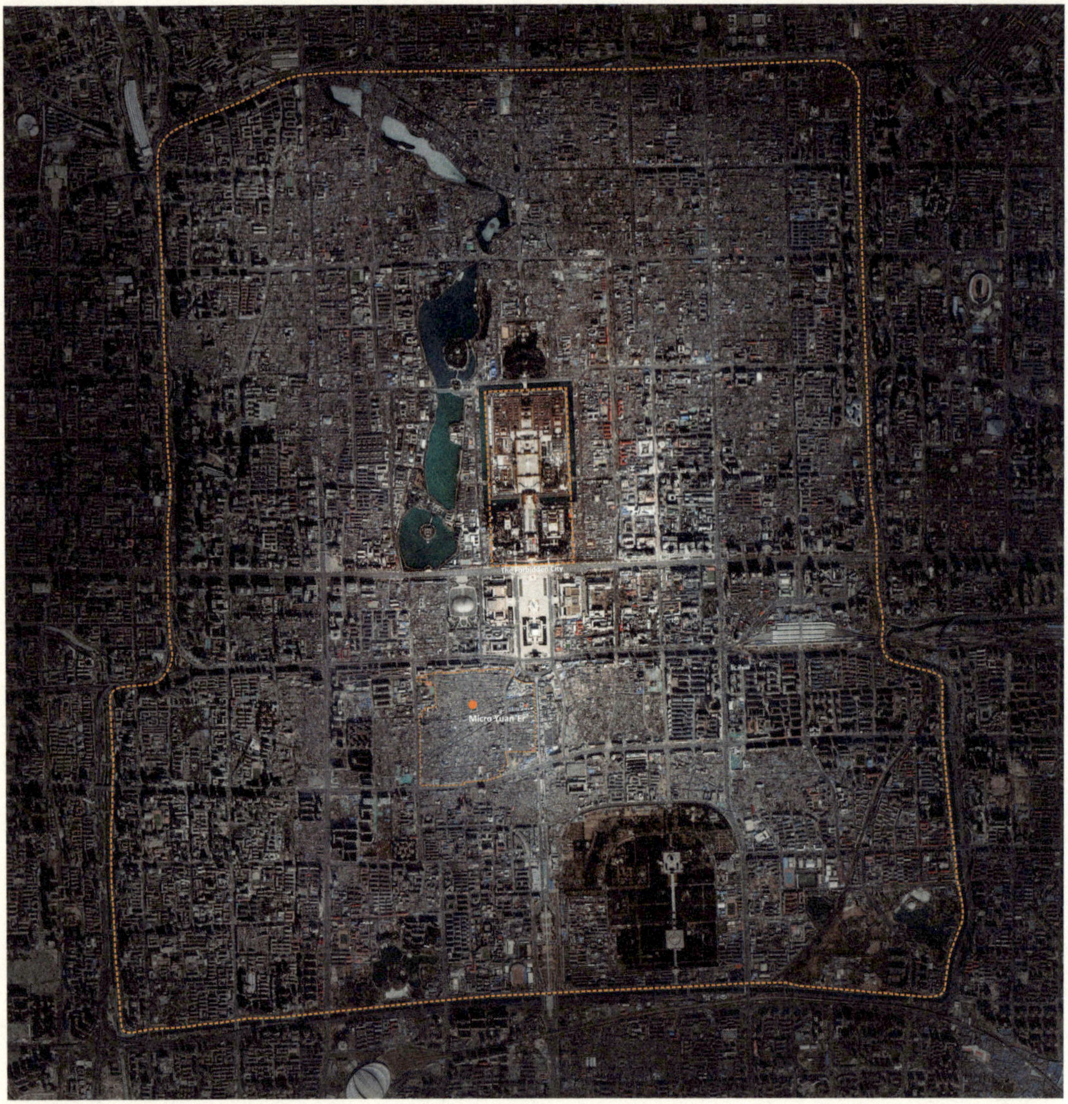

The Forbidden City

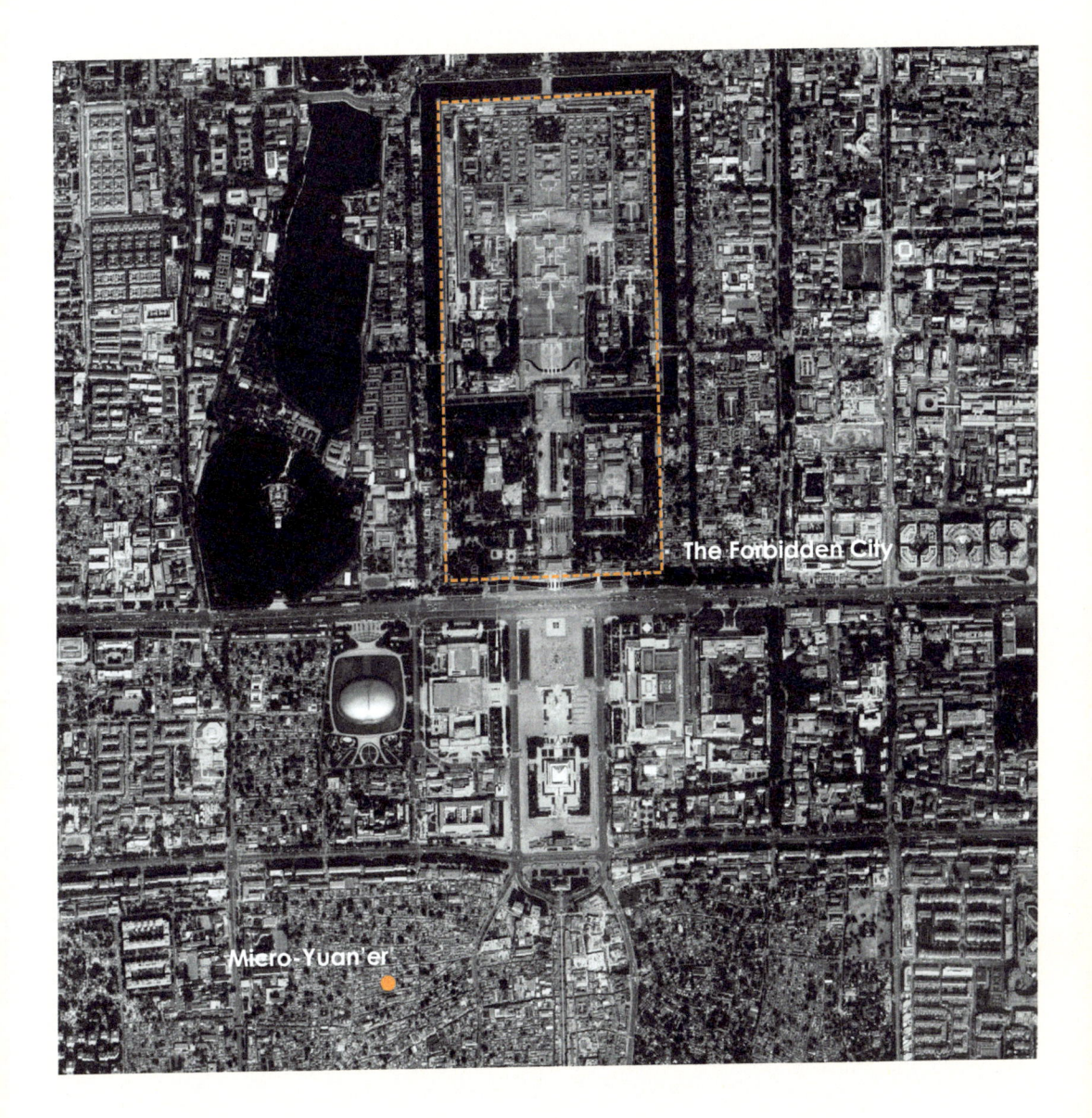

Micro-Yuan'er

耀武胡同 Yaowu Hutong

茶儿胡同 Cha'er Hutong Project Site

杨威胡同 Yangwei Hutong

笤帚胡同 Tiaozhou Hutong

炭儿胡同 Tan'er Hutong

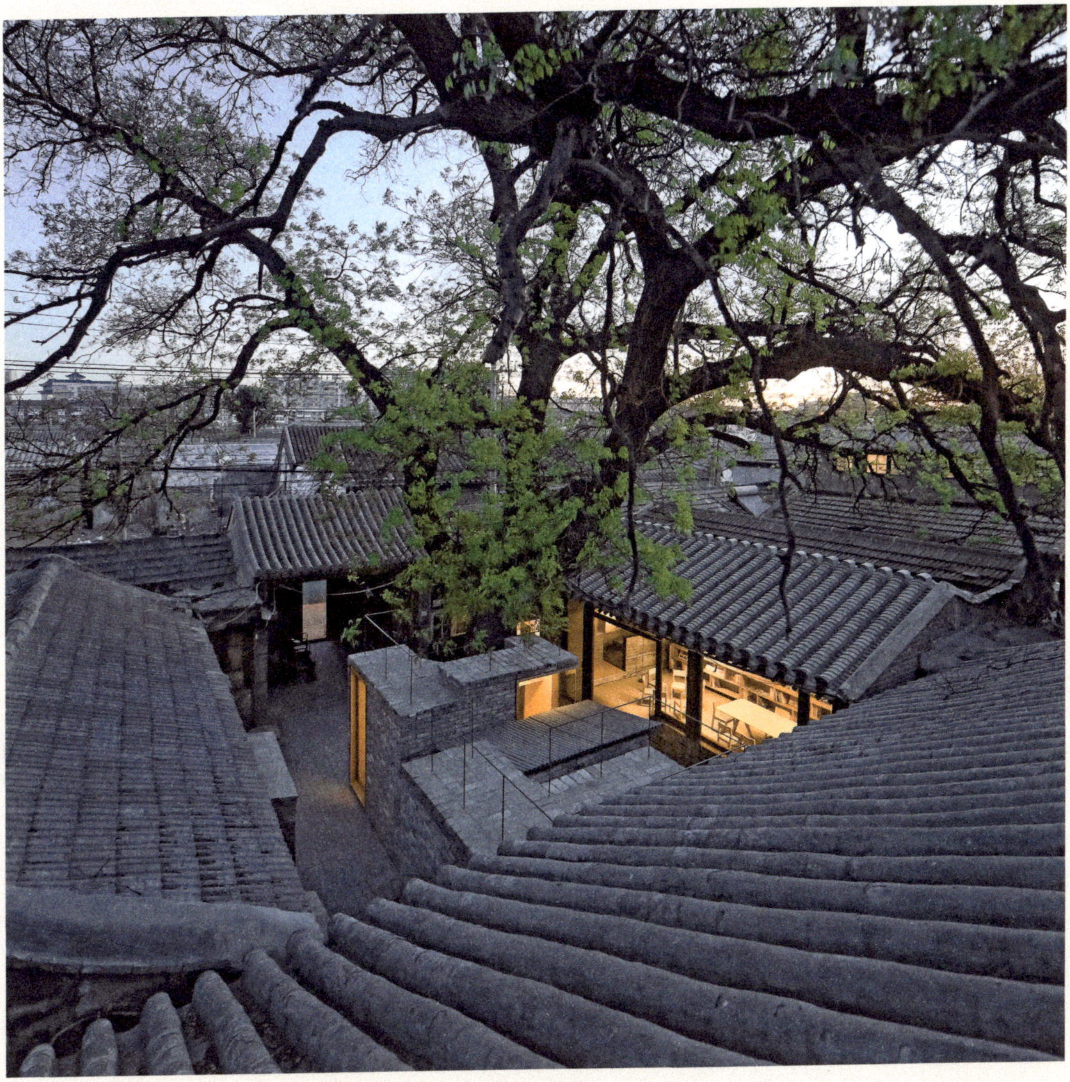

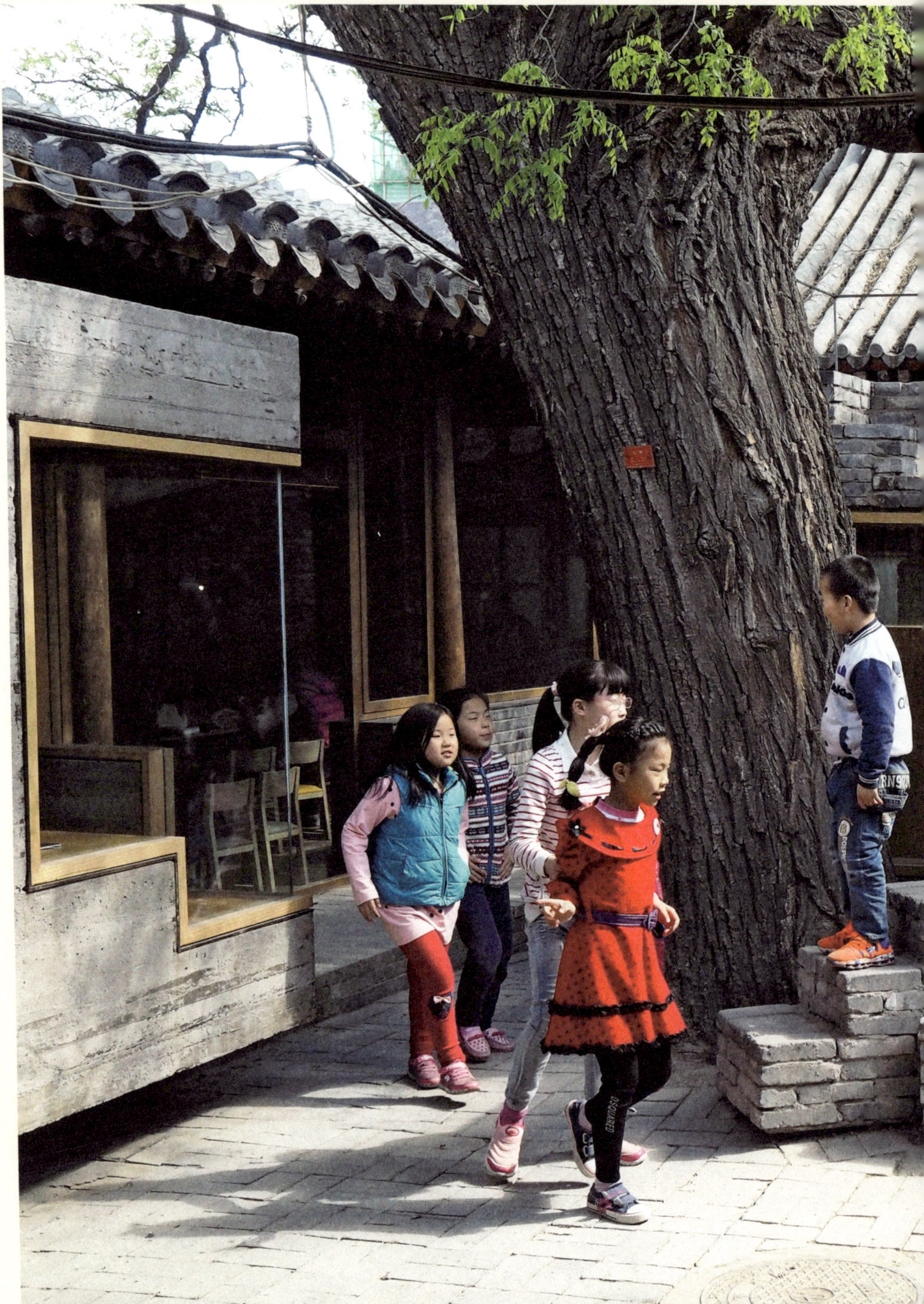

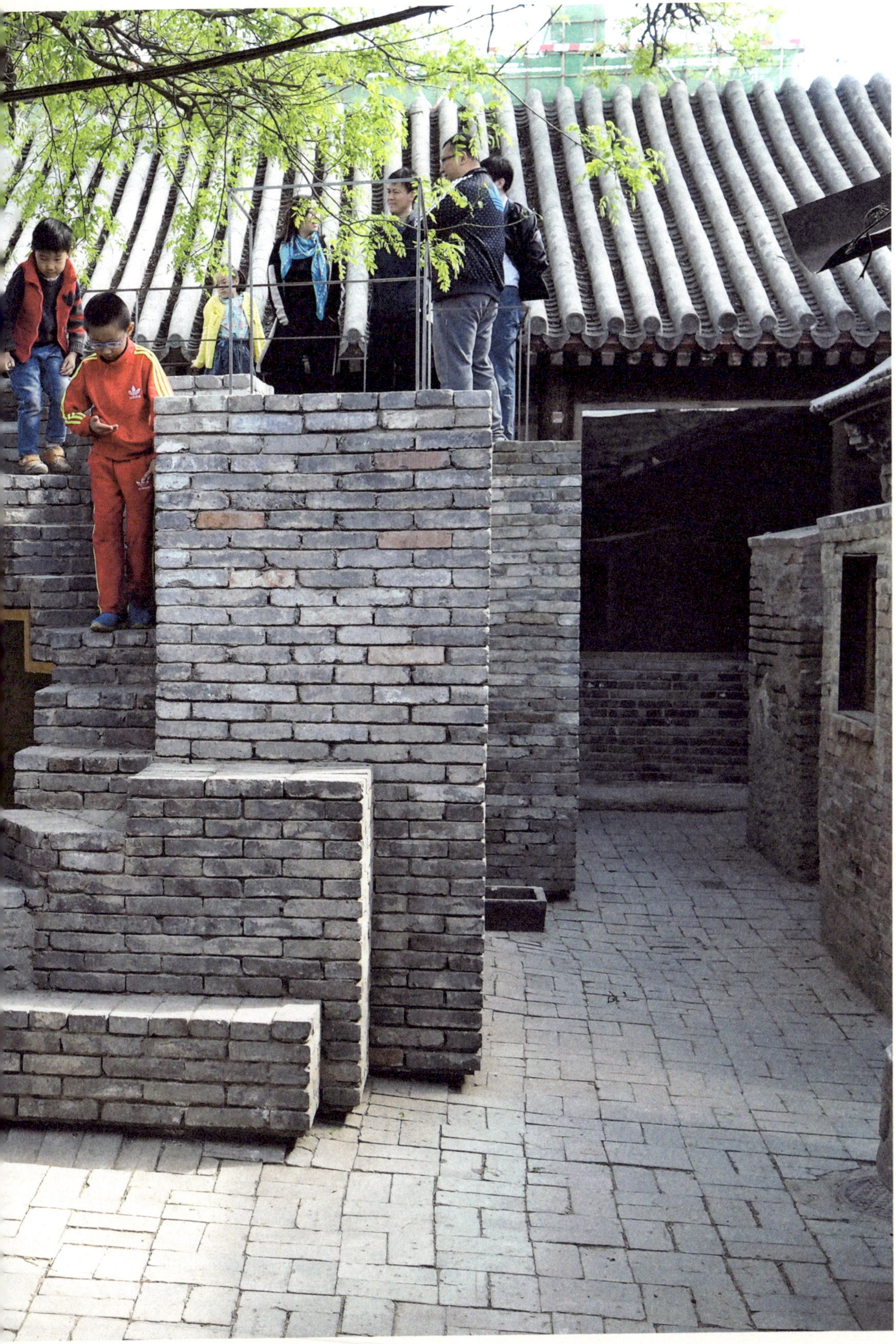

ORIGINAL GROUND FLOOR PLAN

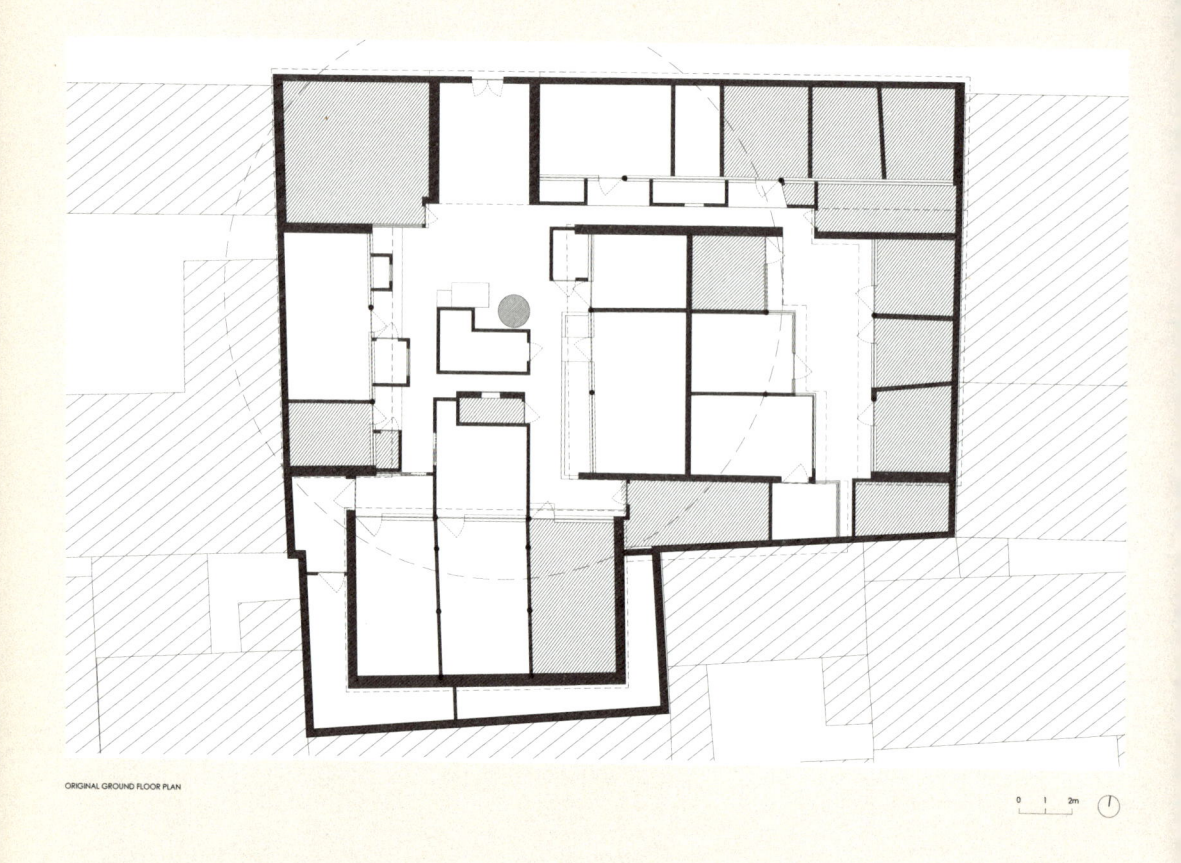

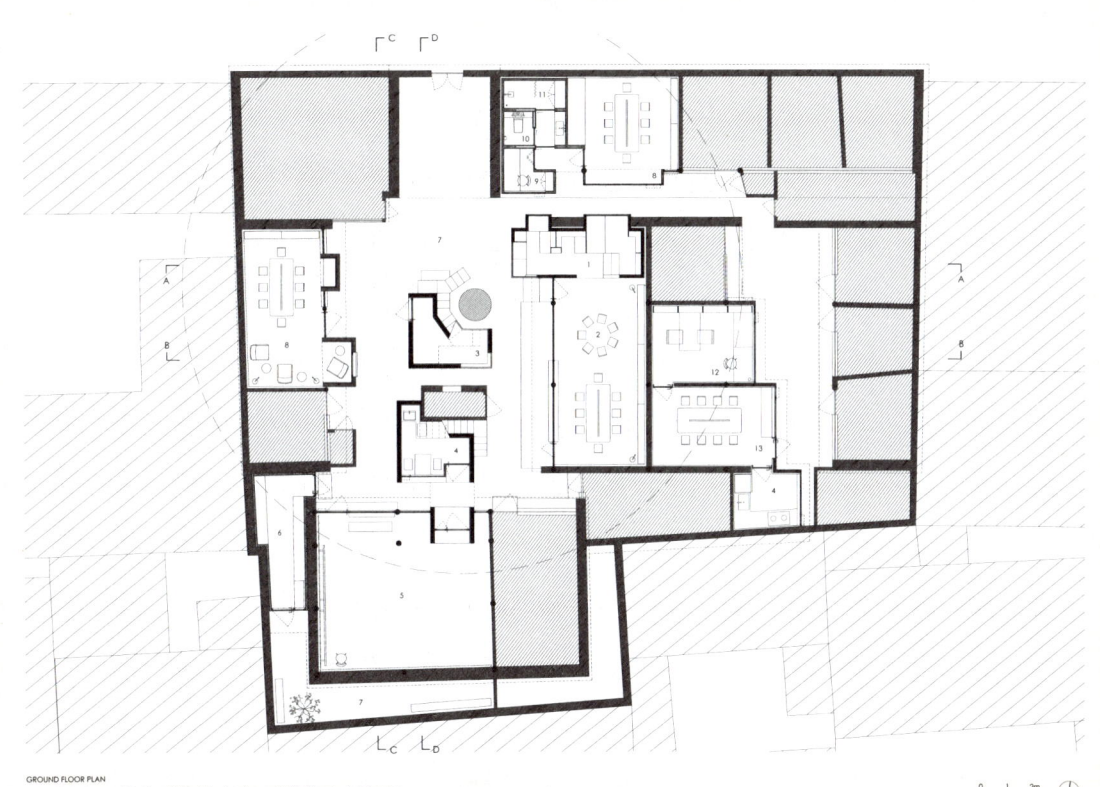

GROUND FLOOR PLAN
1. Library 2. Reading room 3. Pavilion 4. Kitchen 5.Dancing classroom/Multi-funtion room 6. Locker room
7. Courtyard 8.Art classroom 9. Guard room 10. Toilet 11. Bathroom 12. Office 13. Meeting room

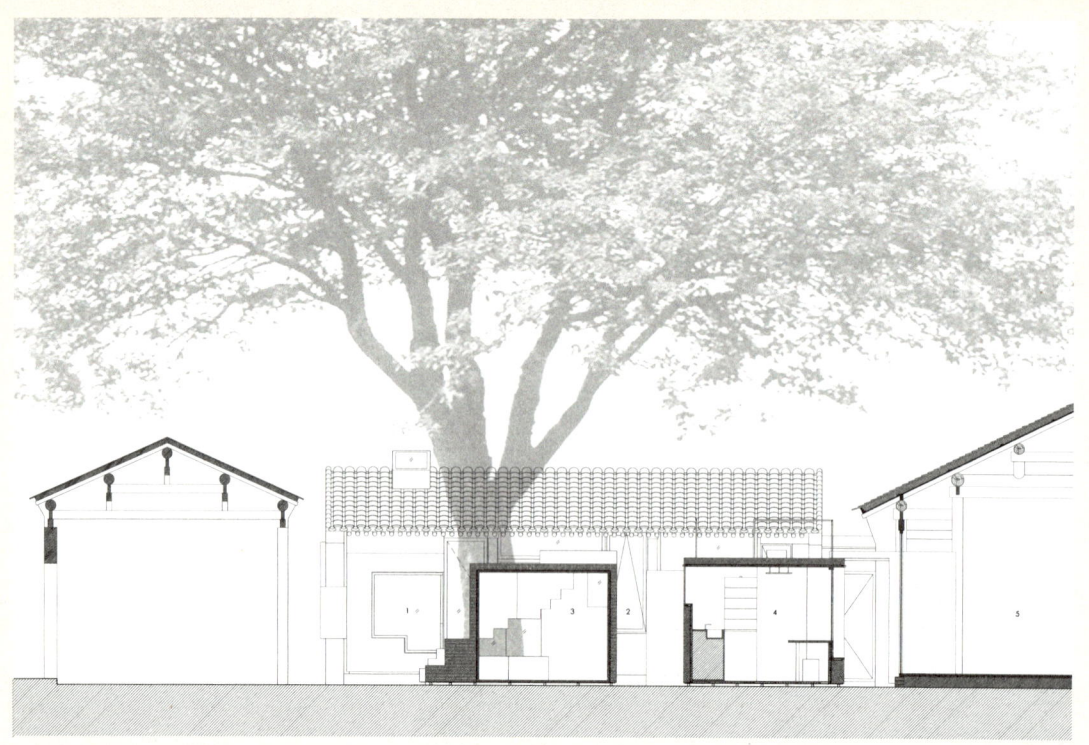

SECTION D-D
1. Library 2. Reading room 3. Pavilion 4. Kitchen 5. Dancing classroom/Multi-funtion room

0   1m

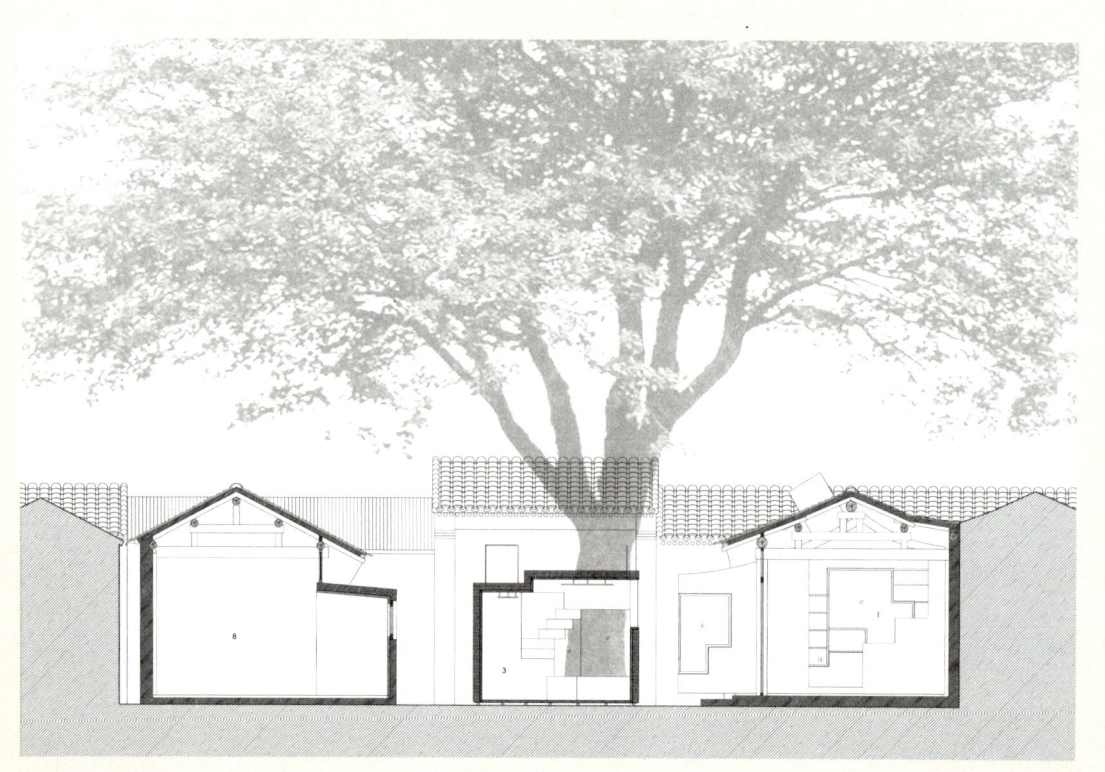

SECTION B-B
1. Library 3. Pavilion 8. Art classroom

0   1m

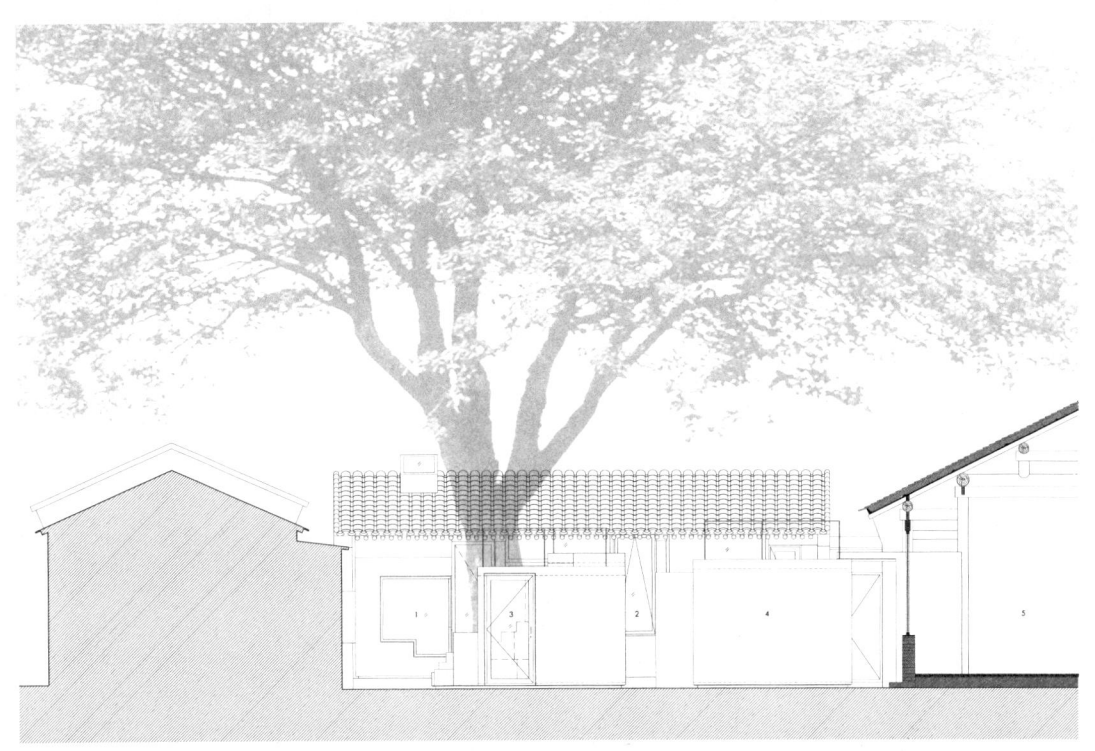

SECTION C-C
1. Library 2. Reading room 3. Pavilion 4. Kitchen 5.Dancing classroom/Multi-funtion room

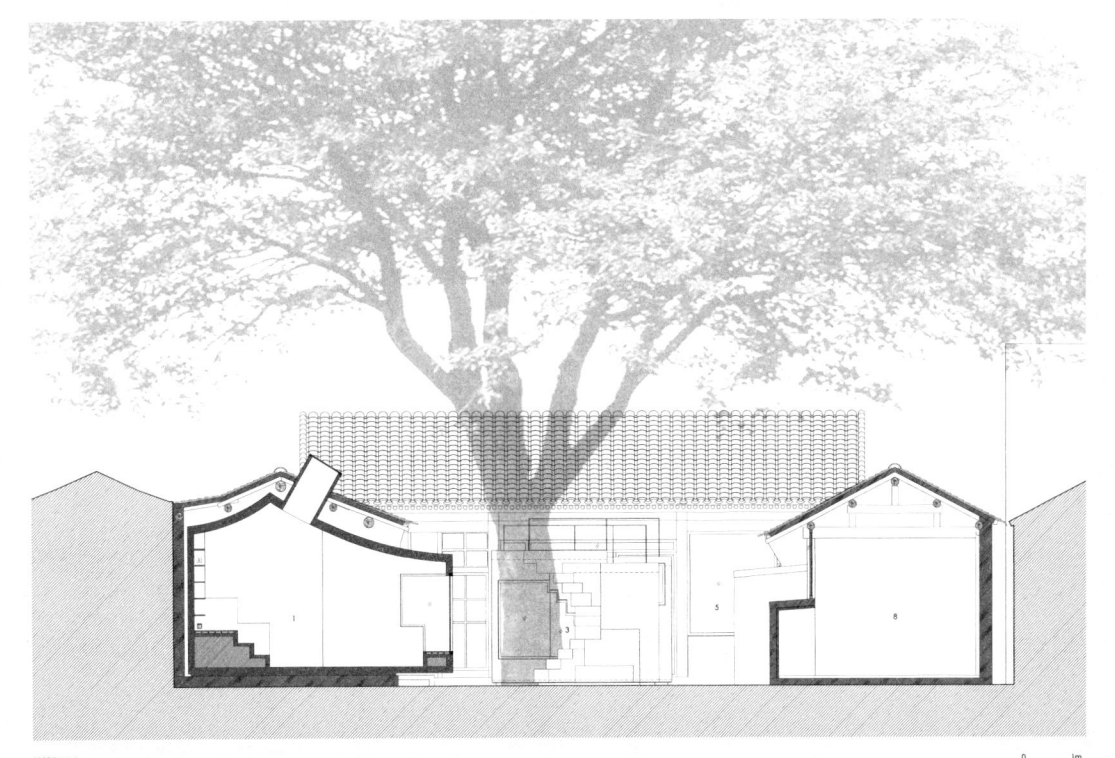

0   1m

SECTION A-A
1. Library 3. Pavilion 5.Dancing classroom/Multi-funtion room 8.Art classroom

0   1m

on the riverbank of Berlin

life is afterall a tragedy.
what really matters is how (we?)
are going to be rem(embered?)
and what you did (to the?)
world during this ephem(eral?)
moment of human histor(y?)
chine(se?) intellectually ha(ve?)
know that to creat(e something?)
that could be enternal is (more?)
important than to have a (mere?)
"now" only, whereas sometimes t(he?)
"now" could overlap with a g(reat?)
"enternity". therefore to l(ive?)
enternally is the goal (and?)
duty of becomes life .... is this

3/31/2014.

— bered
the
al

- always
thoughts
h more
lorious
"glorious
ious

and
ue?

zhongke. ~~standard archi~~
- comporens basics
- rethinking basics
- ~~basic urbanity~~
- playing with basics.
- intervention with ~~human~~ local
- absorbing basics? KV
- ZHANGKE / STANDARDARCHI
  2001-2015
  WORKS

Sketch of the Micro Yuan'er Children's Library and Art Centre, 2014

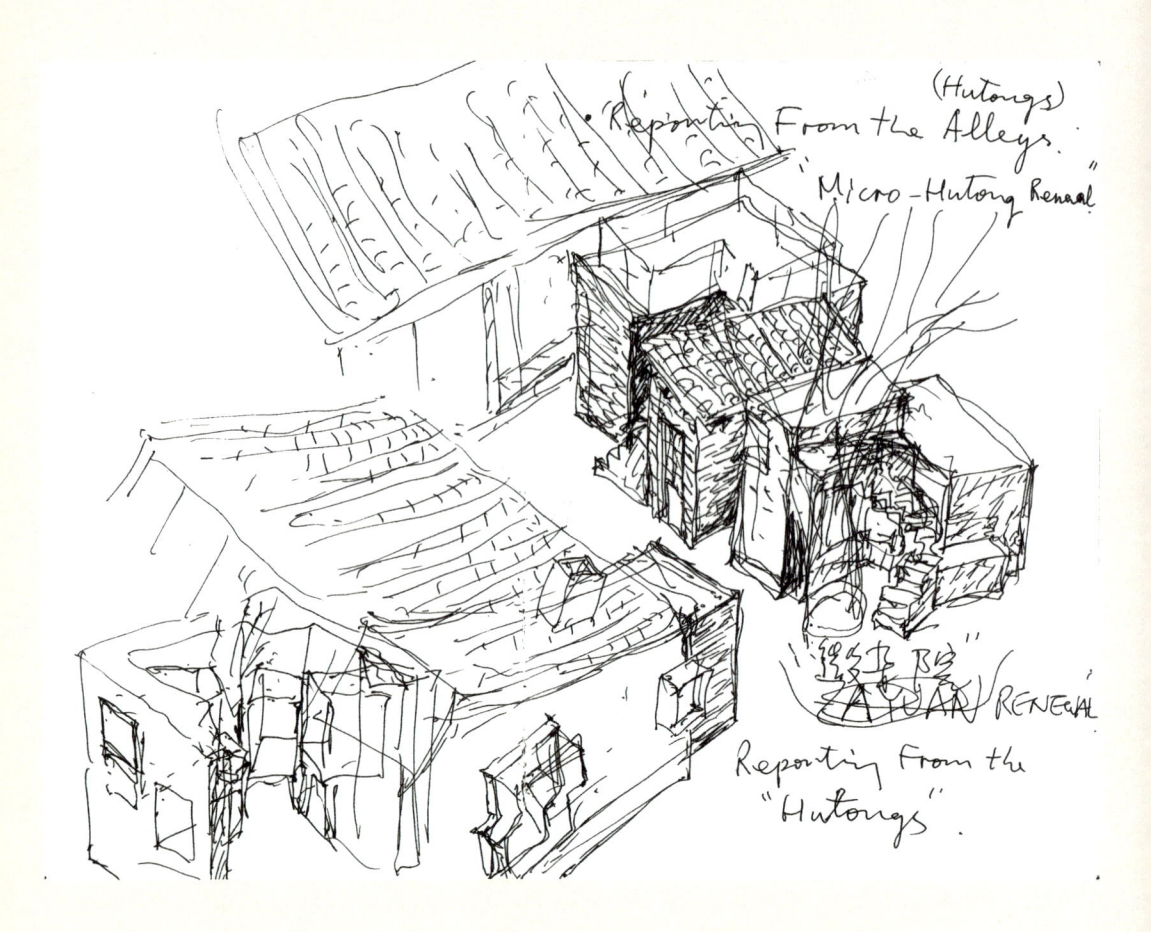

Reporting From the Alleys. (Hutongs)

"Micro-Hutong Renewal"

"ZA YUAN" RENEWAL

Reporting From the "Hutongs".

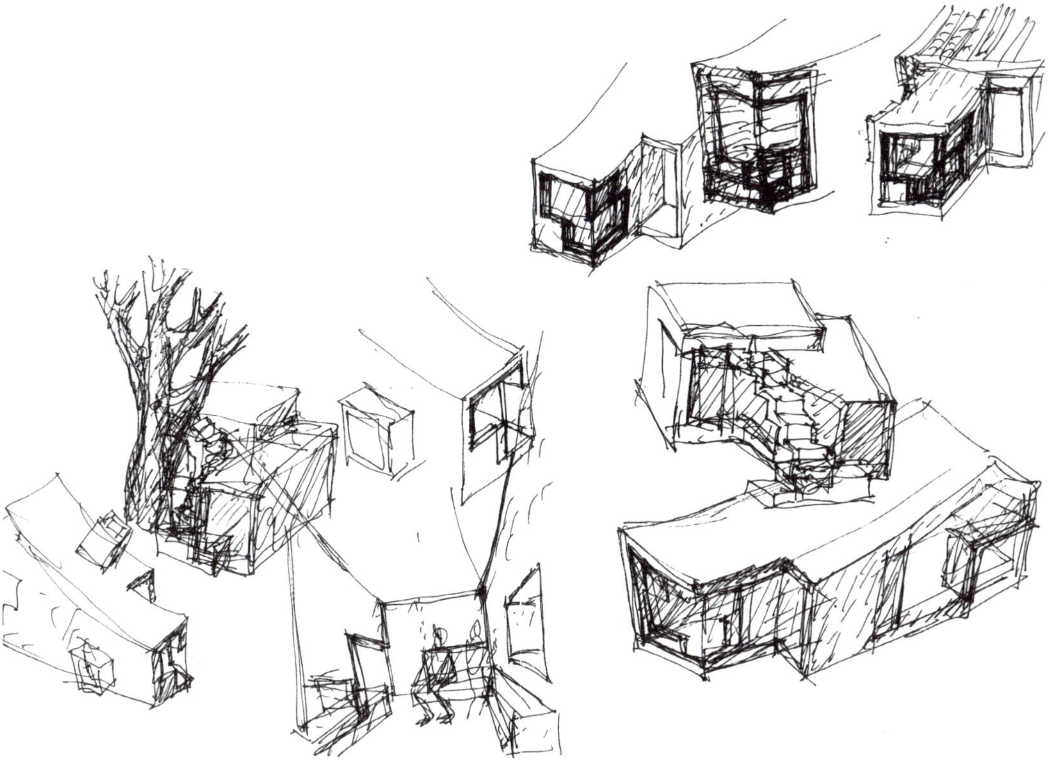

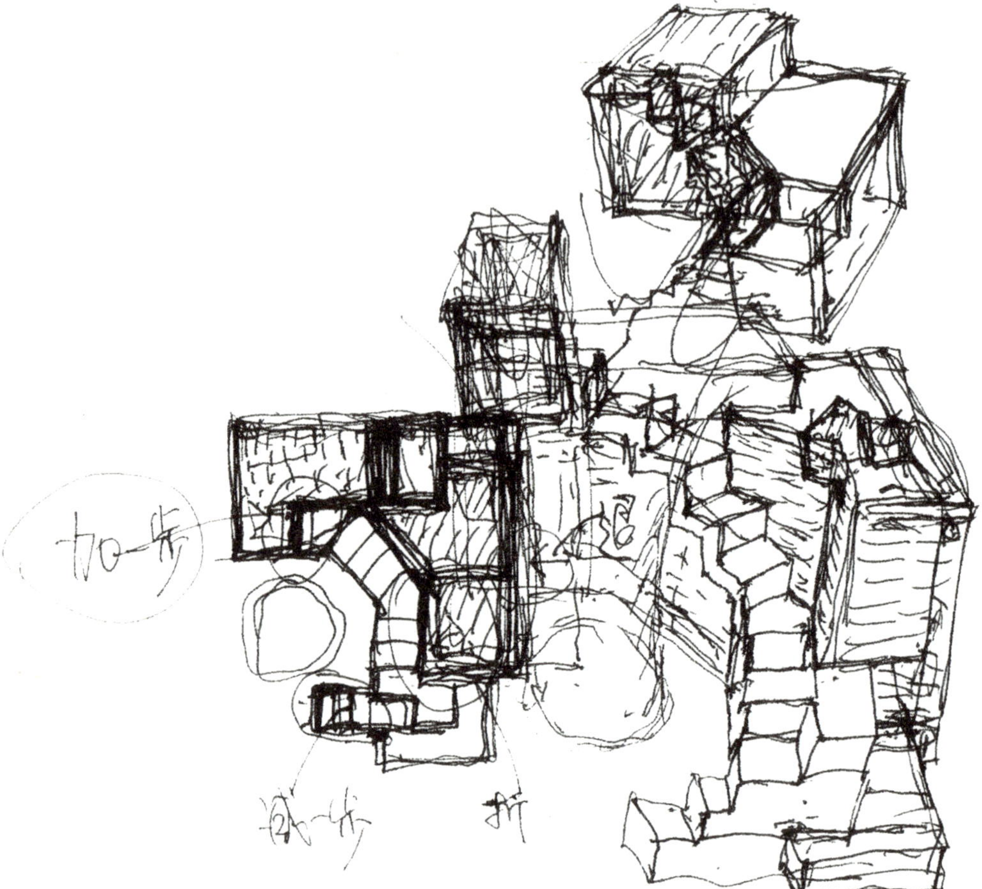
加一步
减一步
折

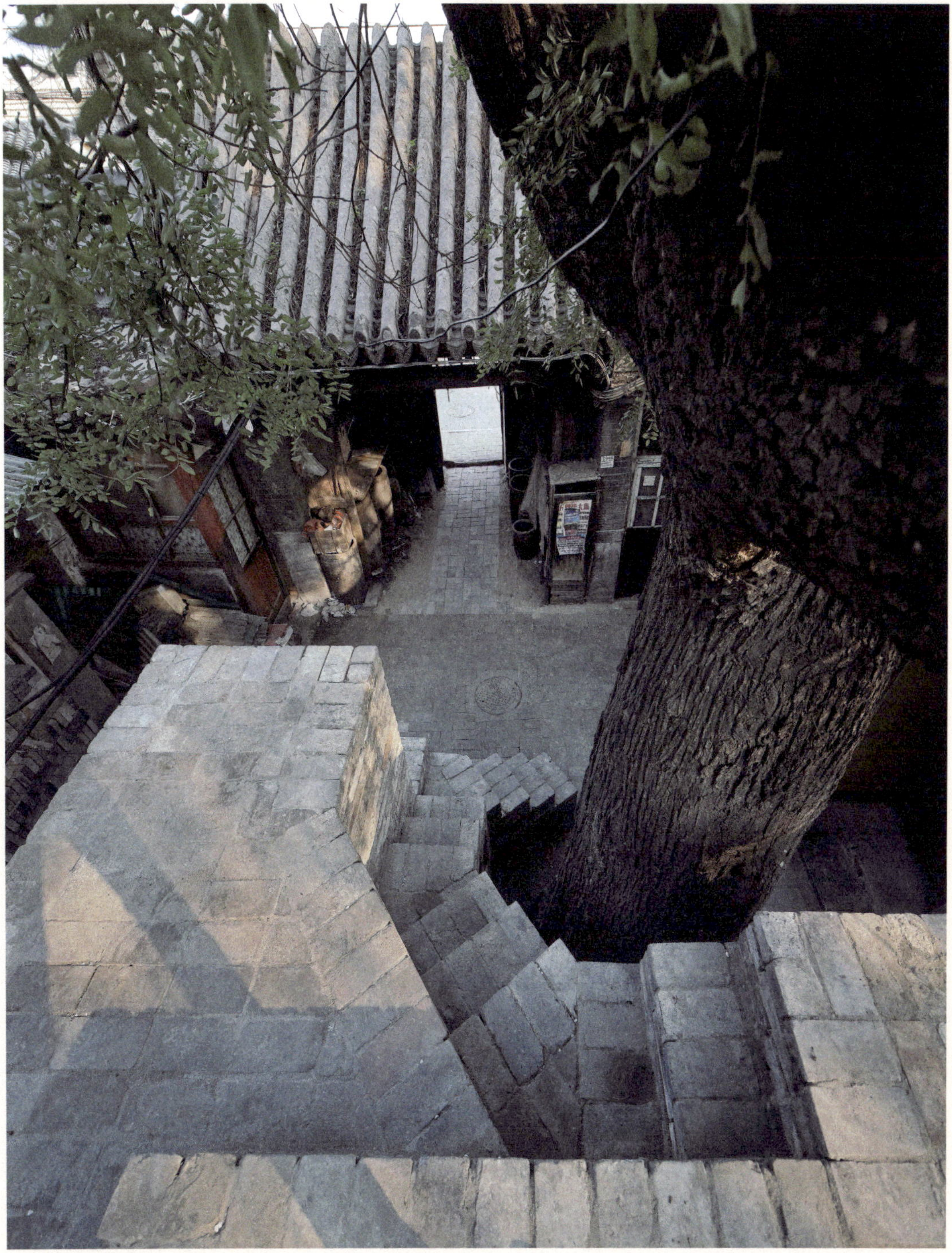

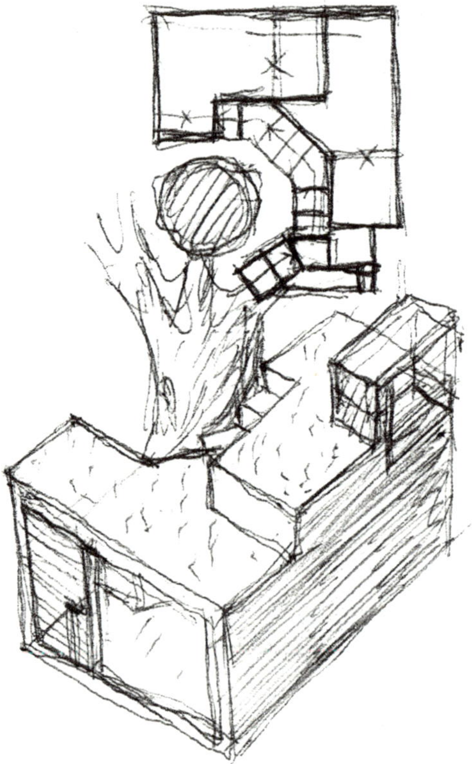

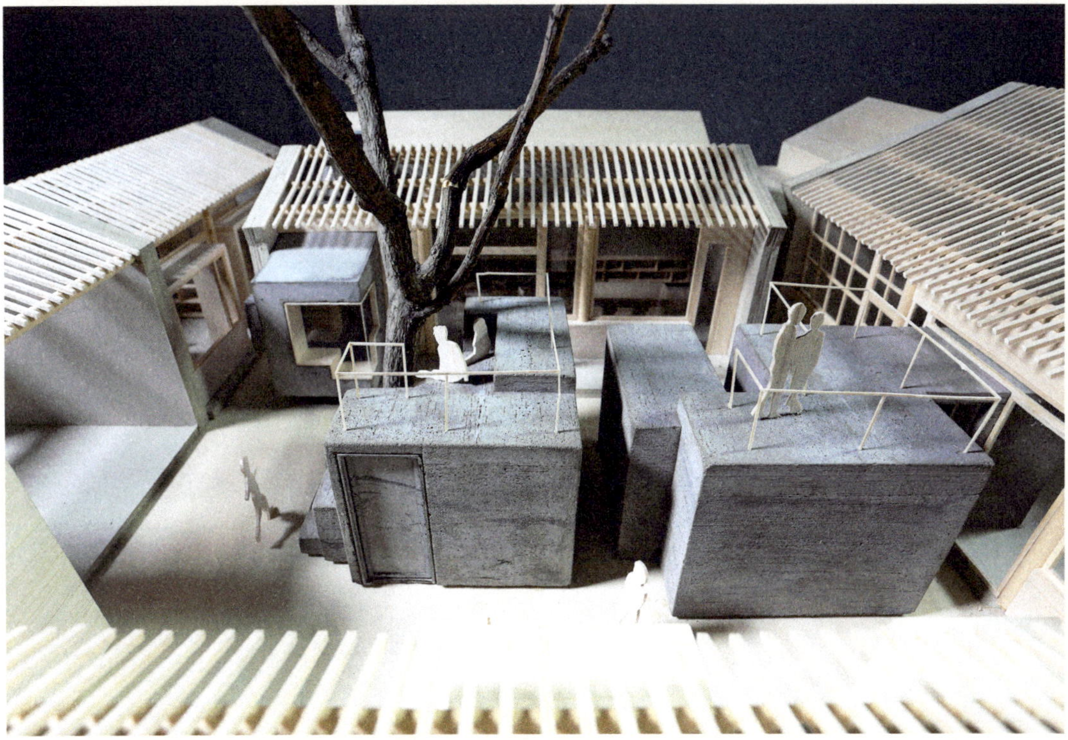

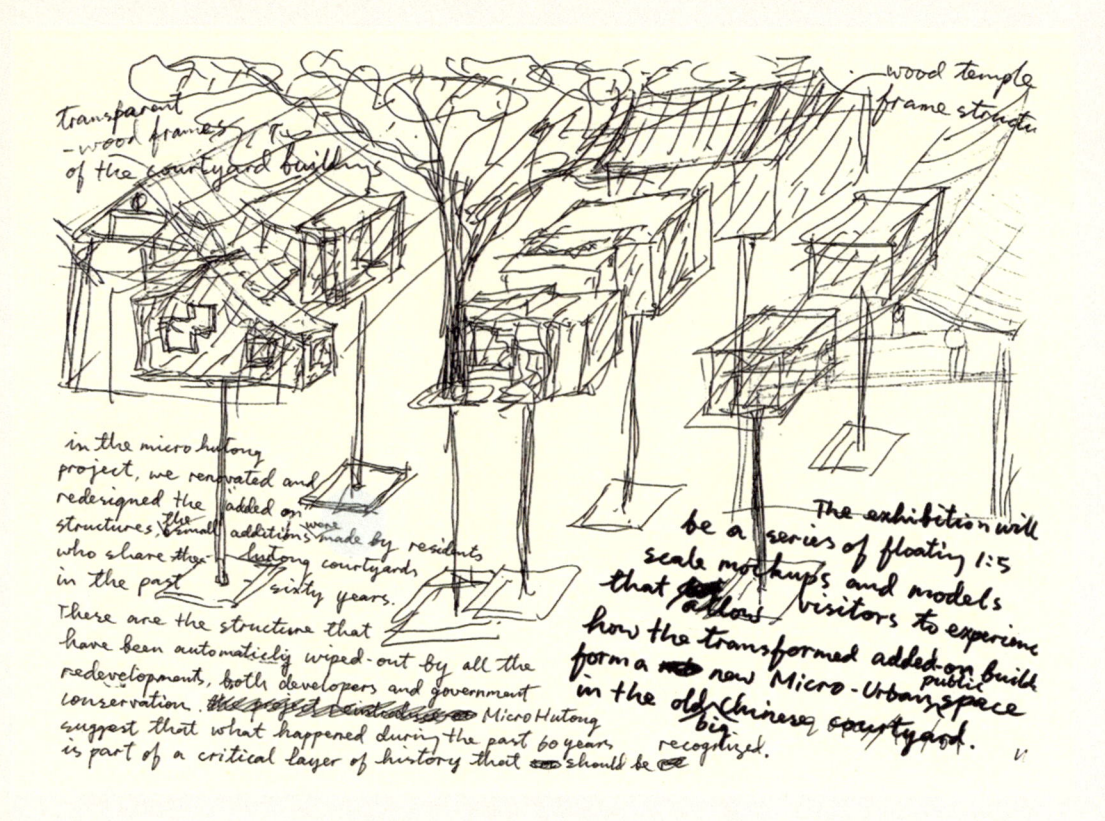

transparent — wood frames of the courtyard buildings

wood temple frame structure

In the micro hutong project, we renovated and redesigned the added on structures, the small additions were made by residents who share the hutong courtyards in the past sixty years. There are the structure that have been automaticlly wiped-out by all the redevelopments, both developers and government conservation. Micro Hutong suggest that what happened during the past 60 years is part of a critical layer of history that should be recognized.

The exhibition will be a series of floating 1:5 scale mockups and models that allows visitors to experience how the transformed added-on build form a new Micro-Urban public space in the old Chinese courtyard.

Library

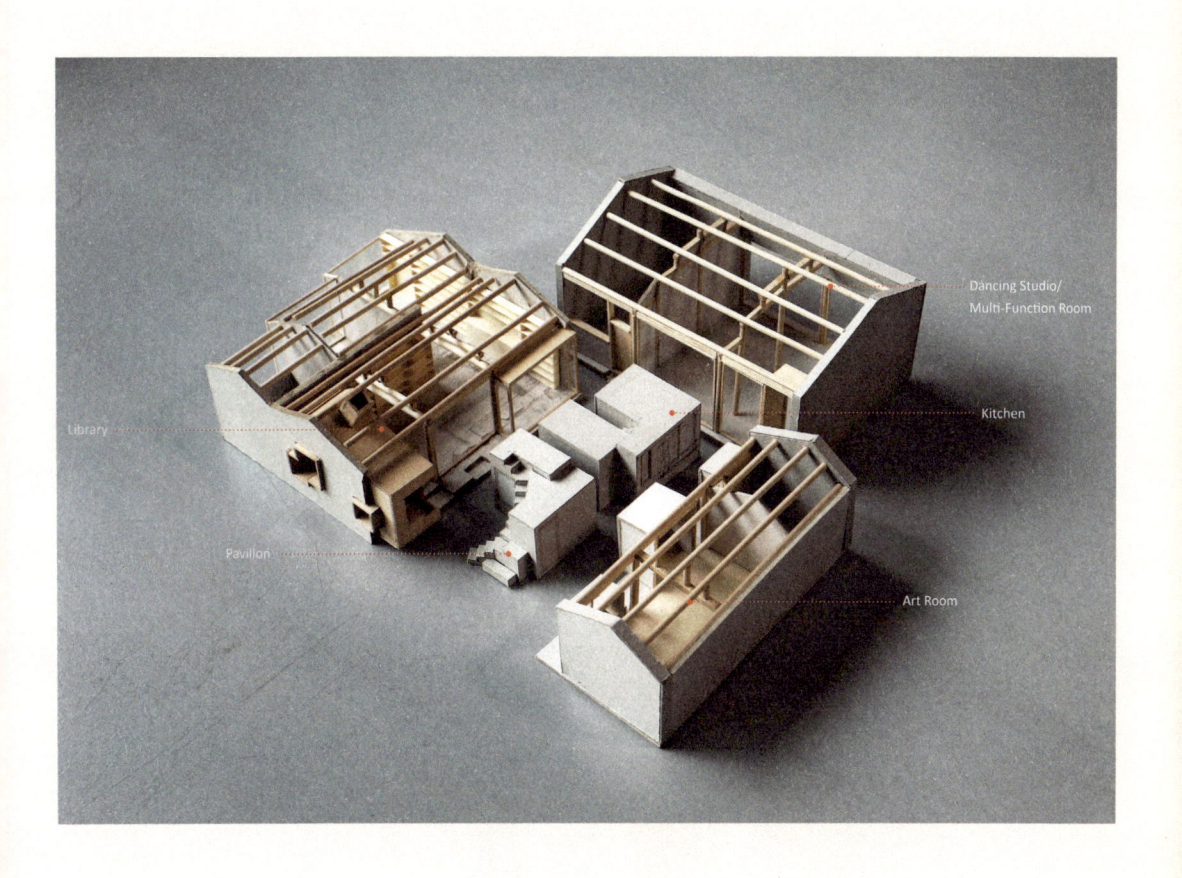

Pavillon

Dancing Studio/
Multi-Function Room

Kitchen

Art Room

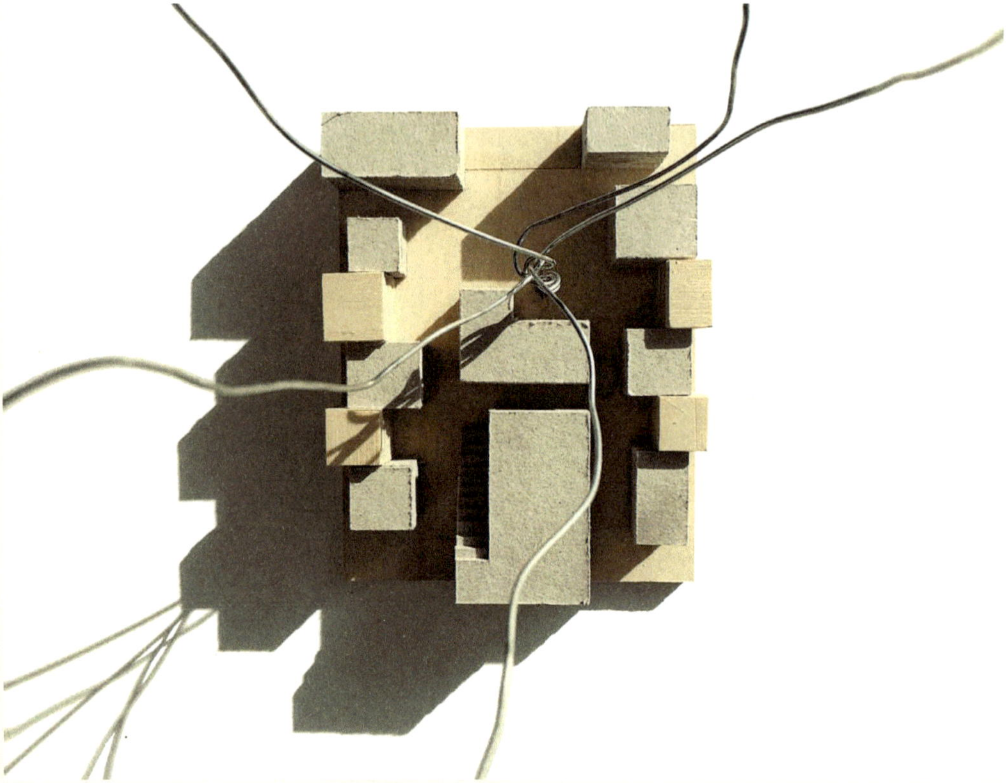

REPORTING FROM THE HUTONG OF BEIJING: "微杂院"
MICRO HUTONG (REVIVAL?/STORIES?) ZHANG KE

- Hutongs in Beijing (the traditional courtyard system of urban dwelling) have always been in the centre of battle ground between Redevelopment and conservation. After two decades of fast development in the old city of Beijing, the hutong is on the verge of being either completely replaced by taller buildings (offices, towers, apartments and shopping malls), or disfigured by kitsch fake restorations that immitate image of a nostalgic past. The subtle complexity of the Hutong as a authentic urban space has been overlooked both by developers who most of the time prefer to see it a tabula rasa so that they can build more square meters, and by the defenders of picturesque historic preservation. The MICRO HUTONG project, avoiding the usual methods of Hutong restoration, aim to explore the potential of the hutong and courtyards as a generator of communal space and as a catalyst of social interaction.

MILANO.
2014/09/03.

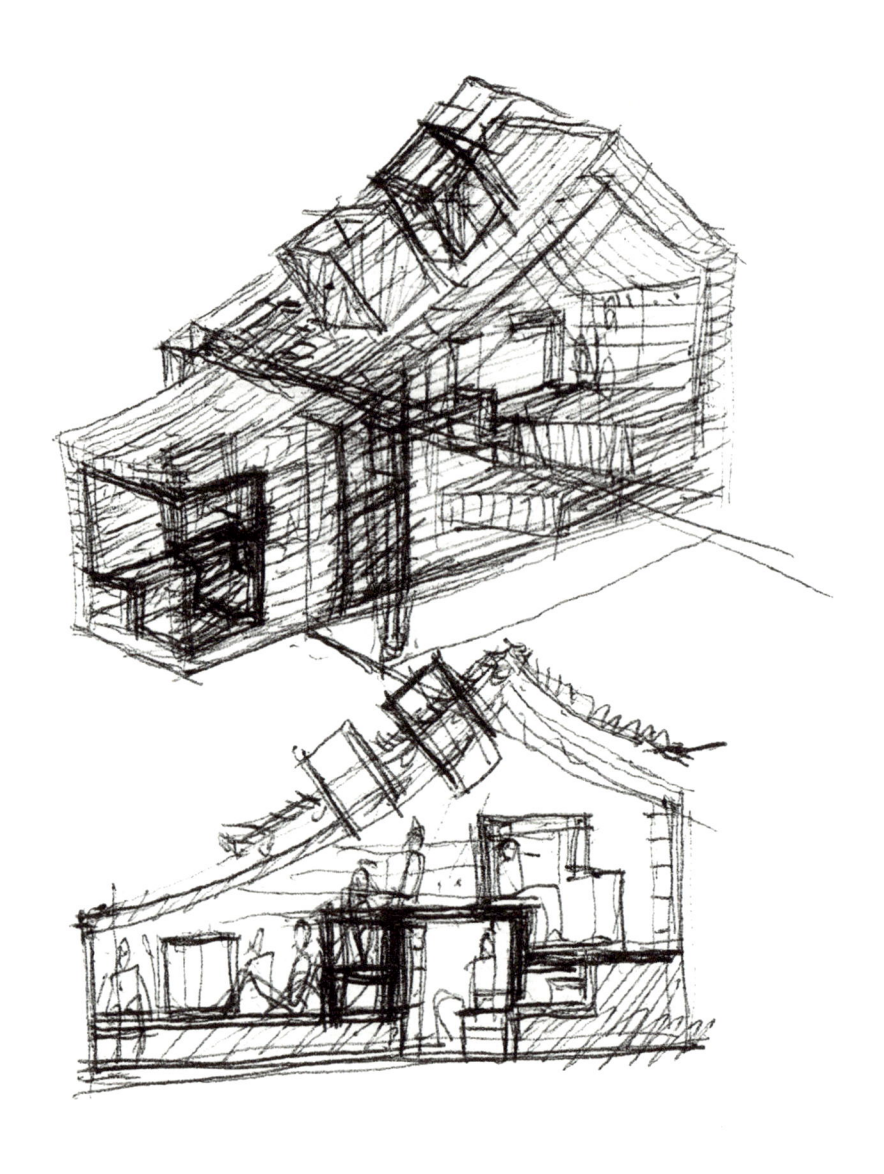

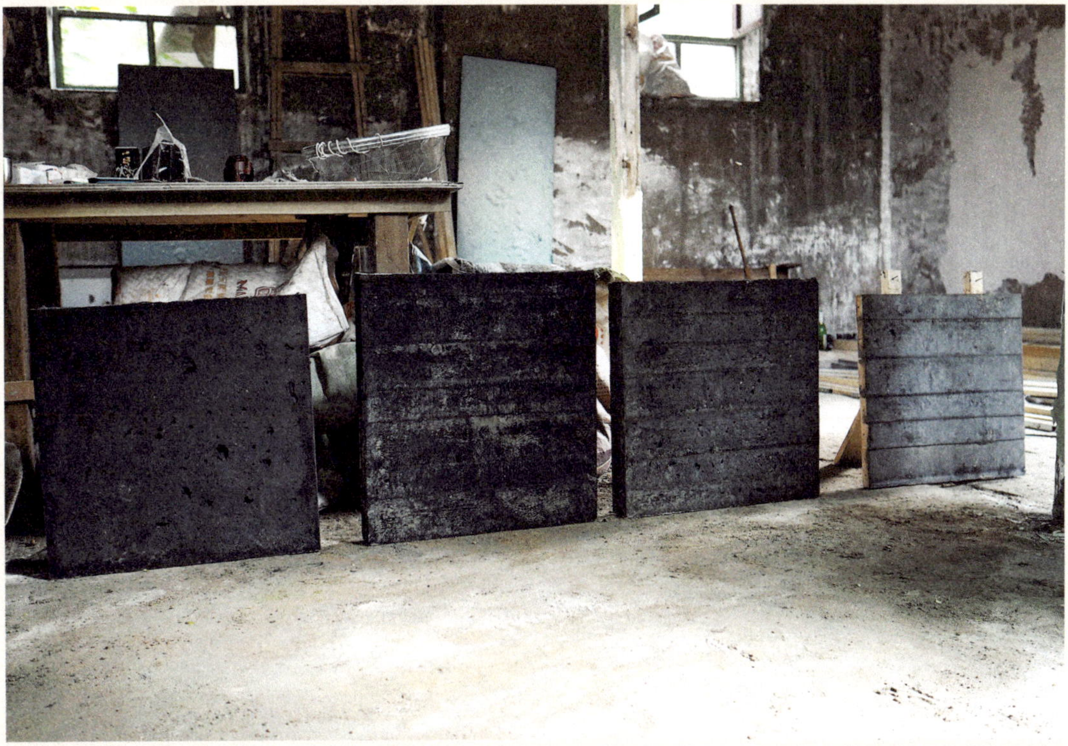

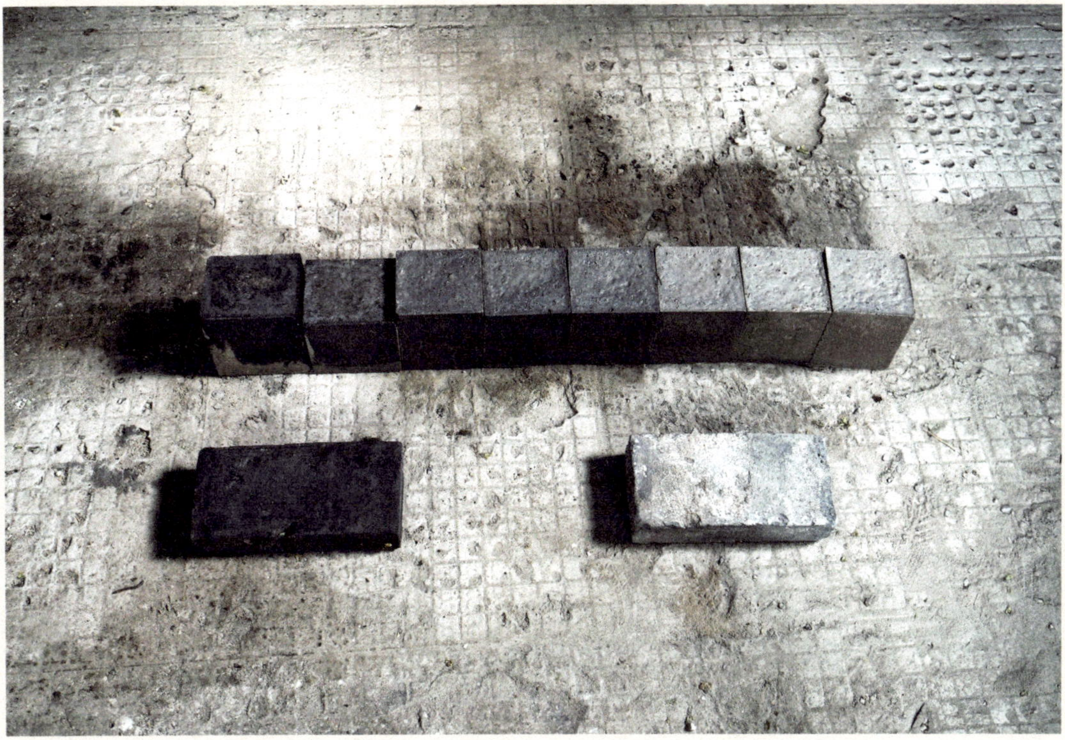

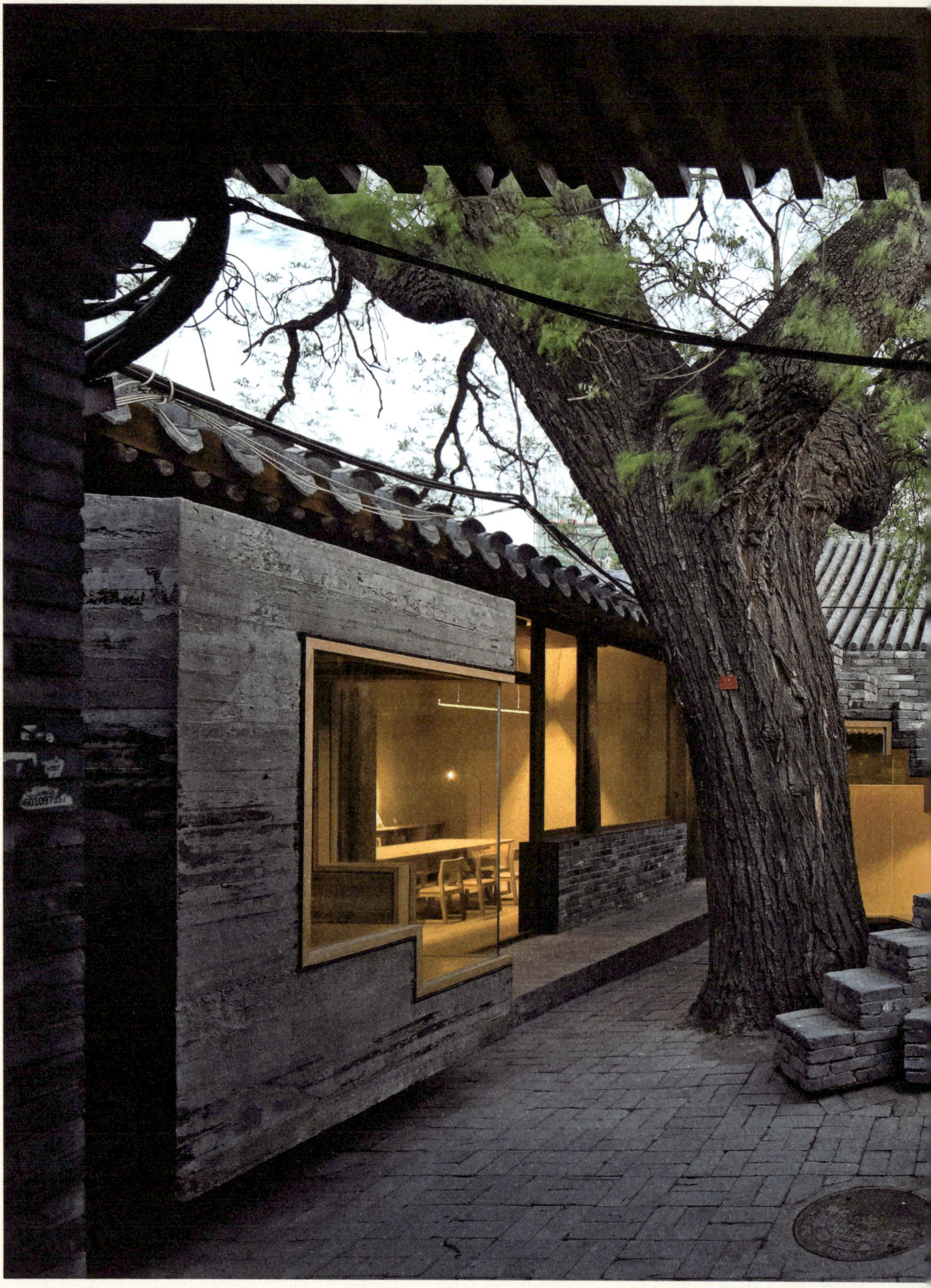

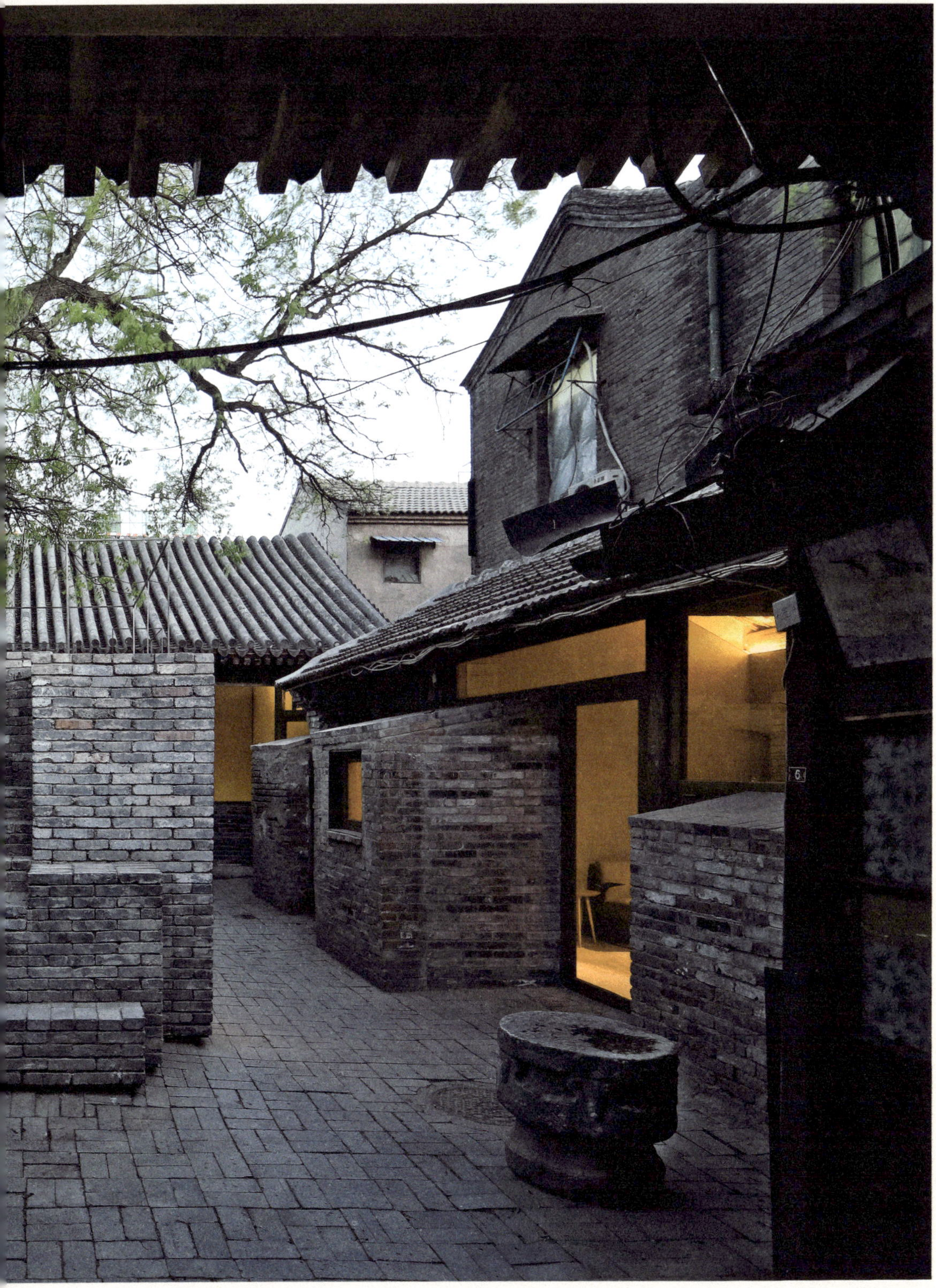
6

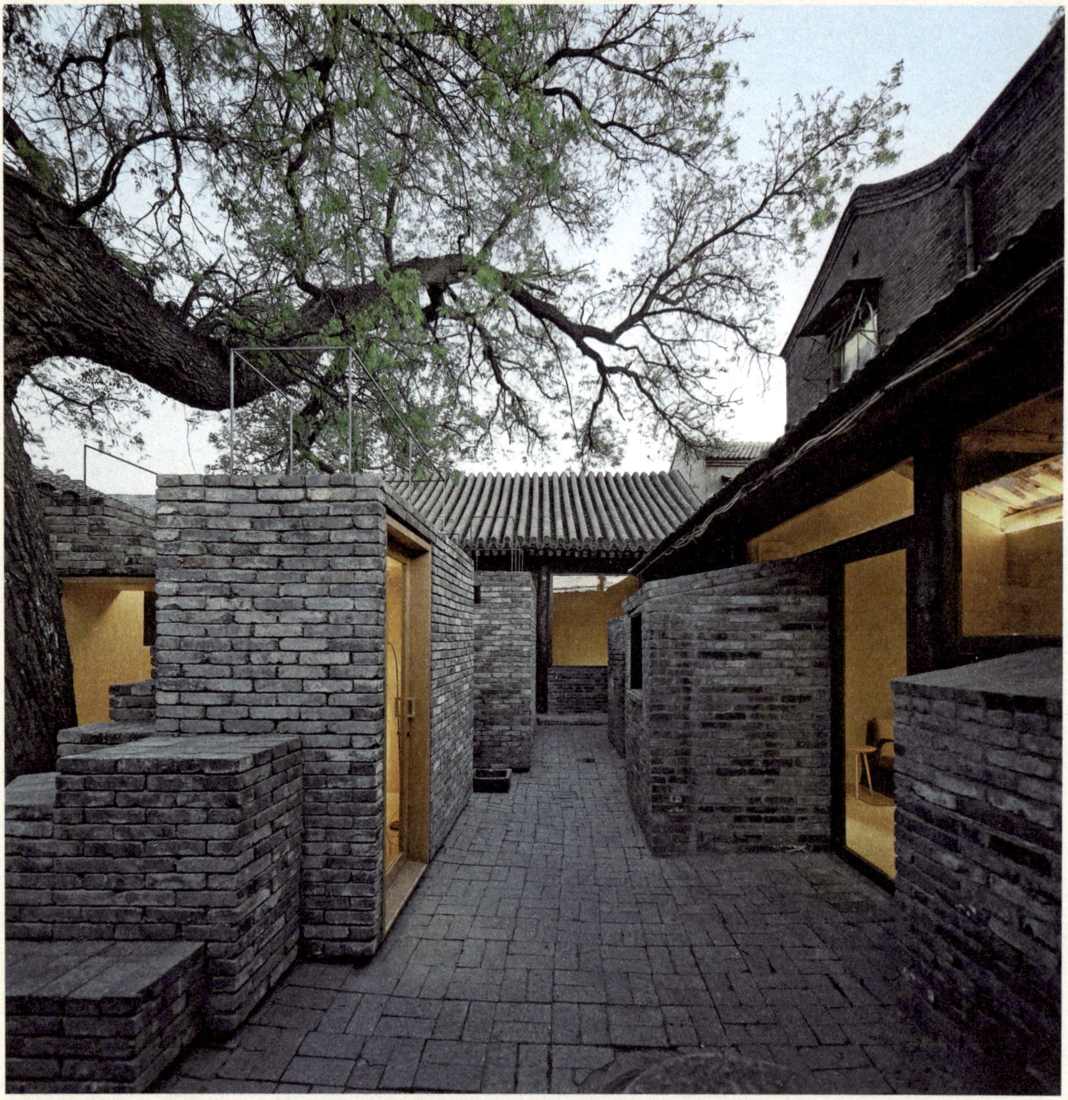

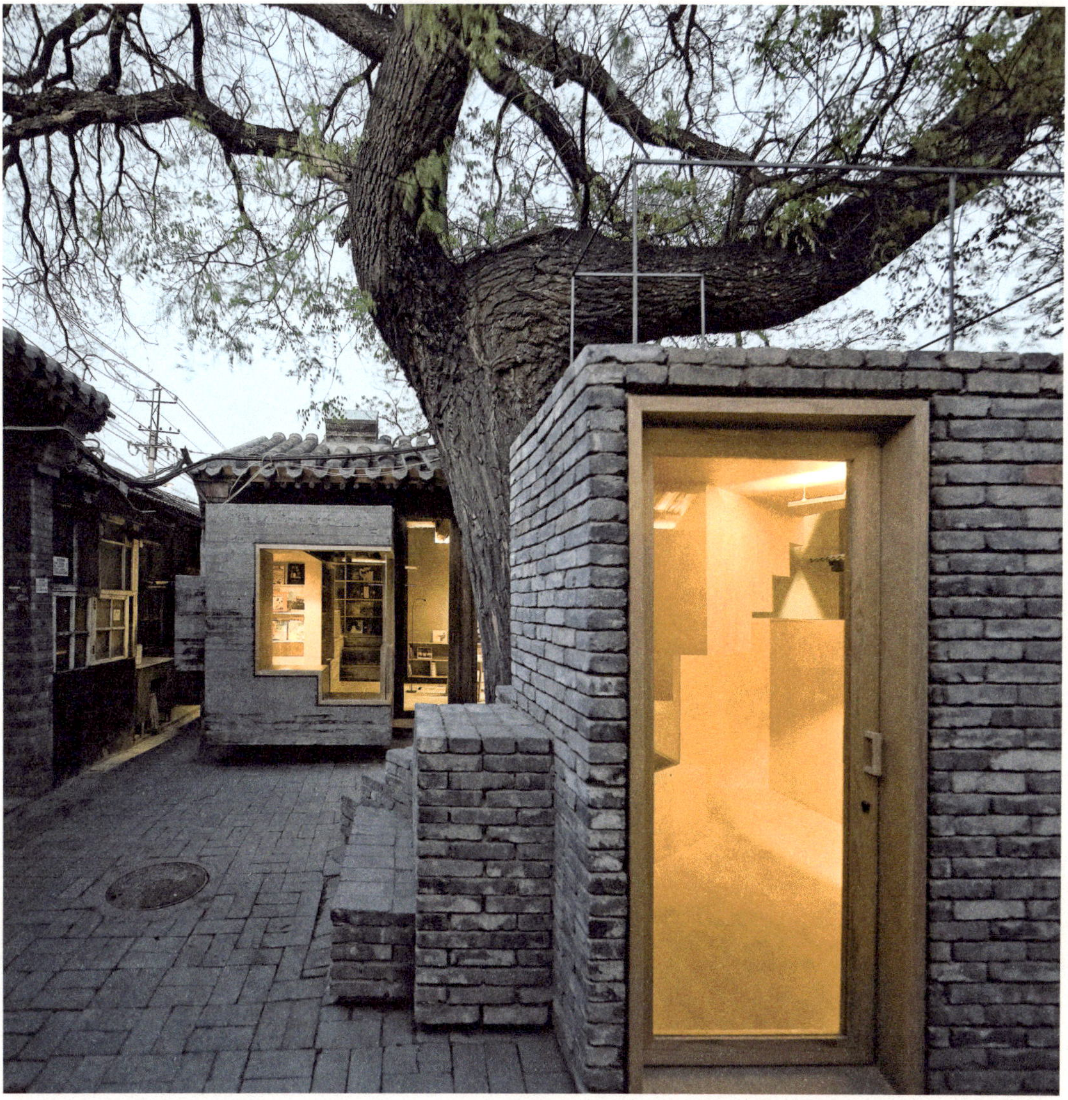

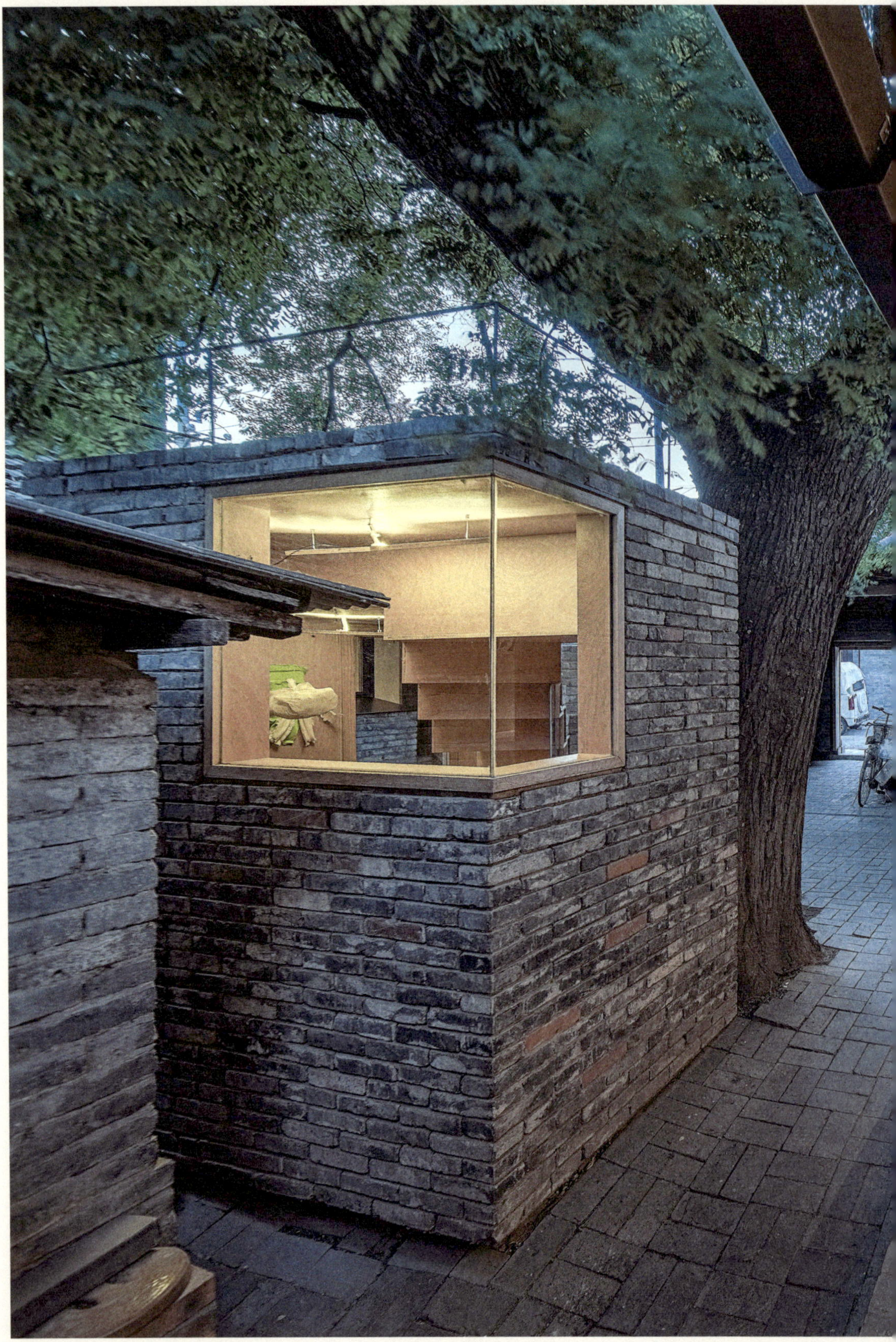

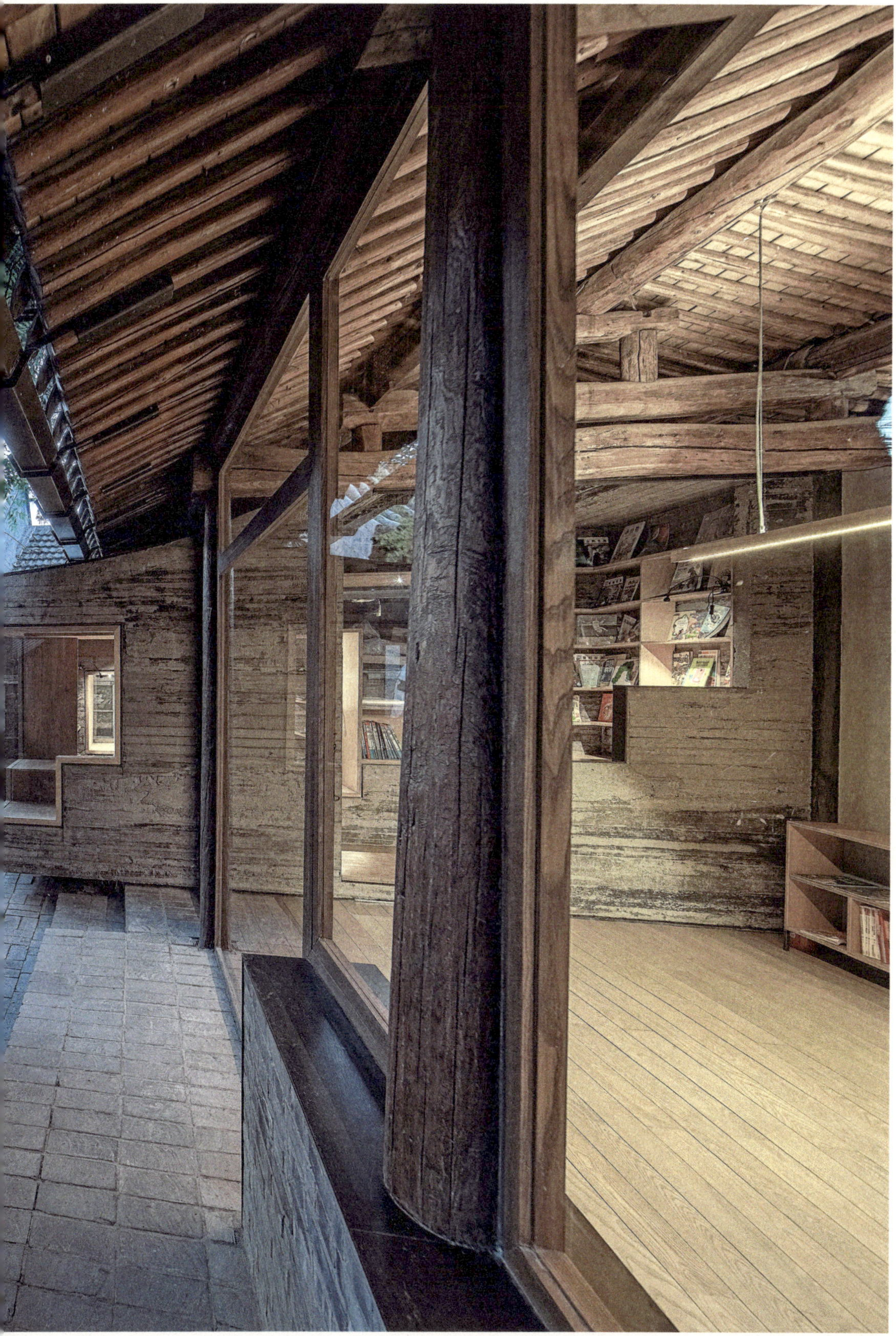

The brick stairs leading up to the roof, and the model
of the stairs at the Venice Biennale, 2016

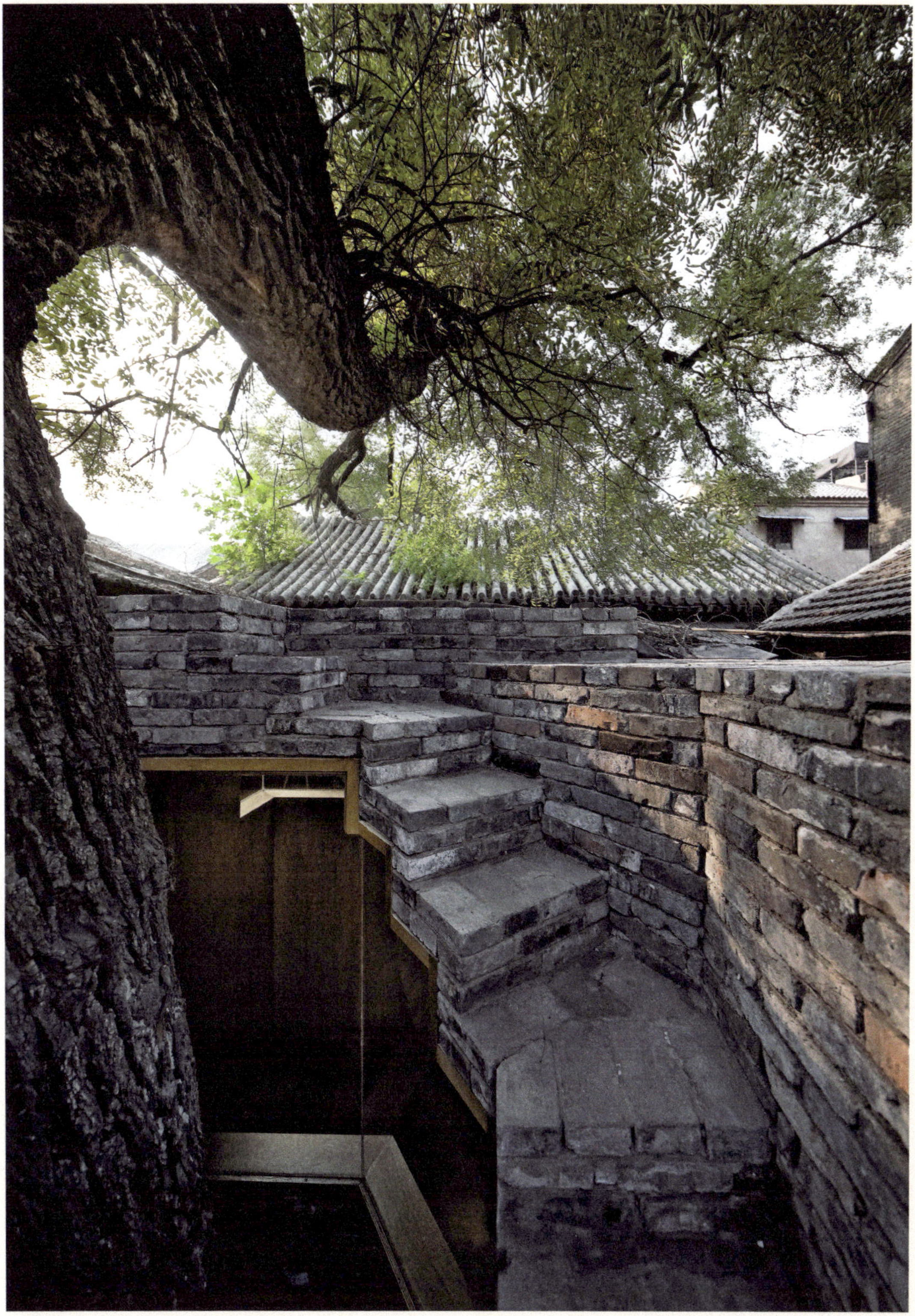

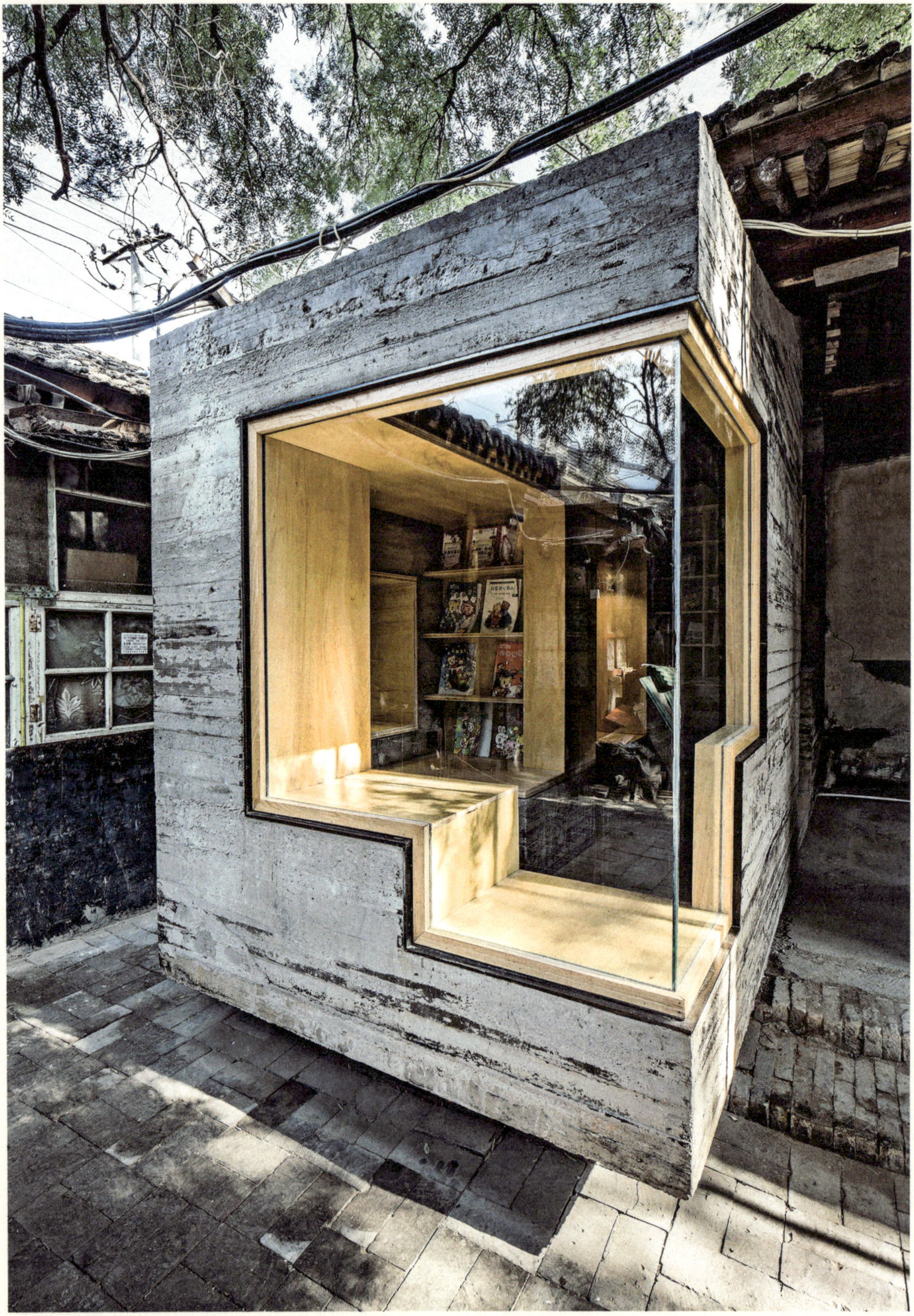

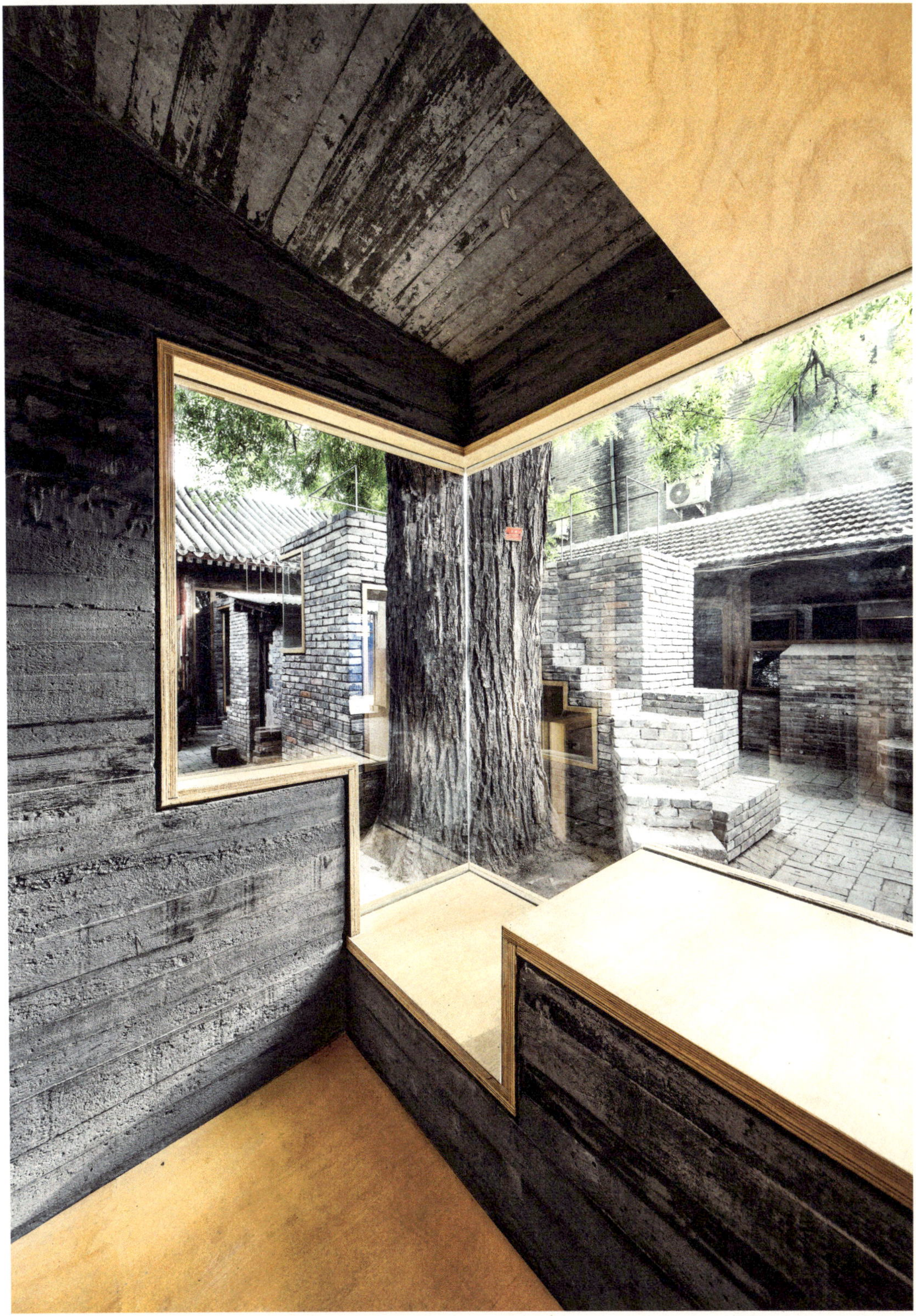

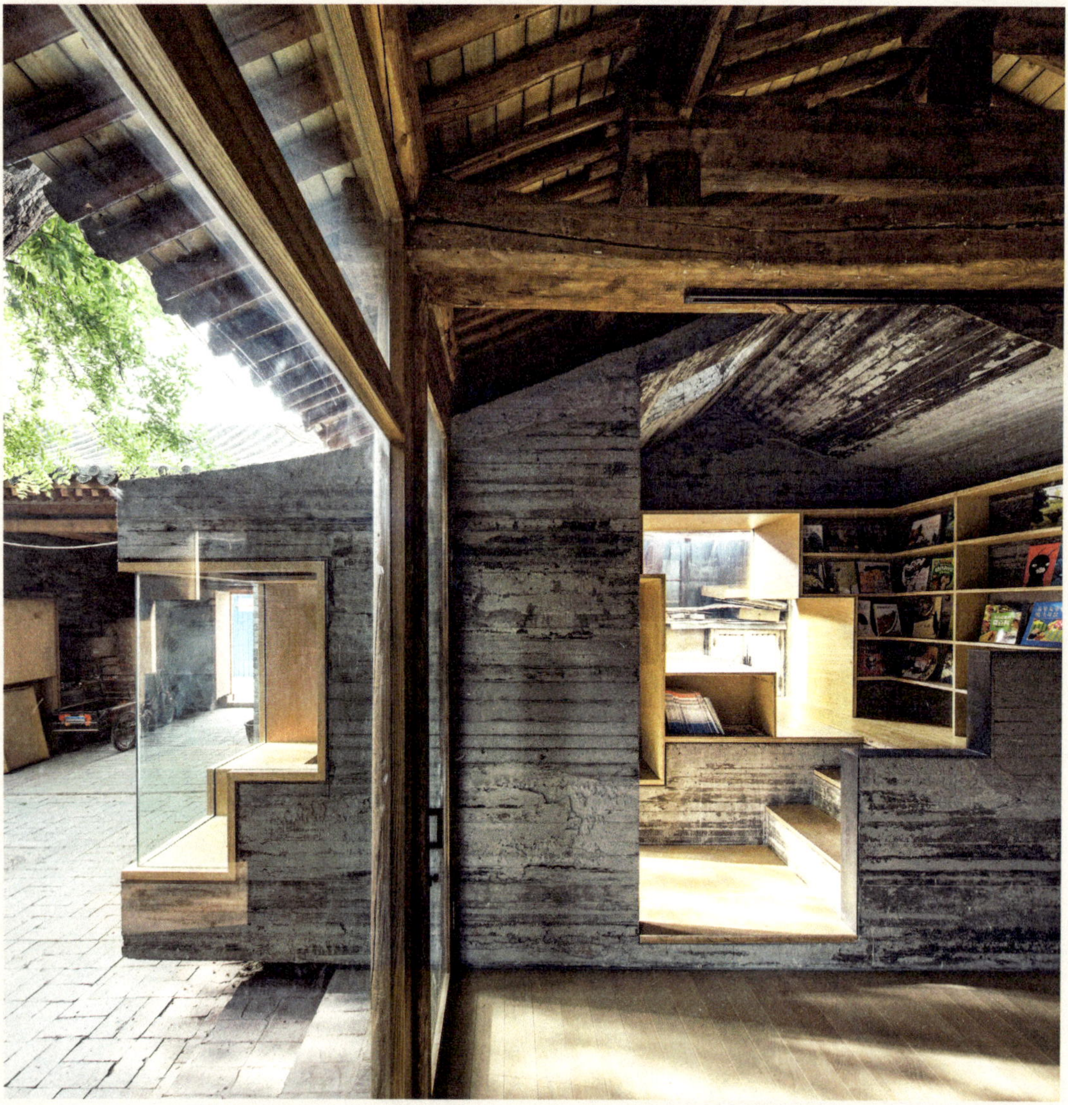

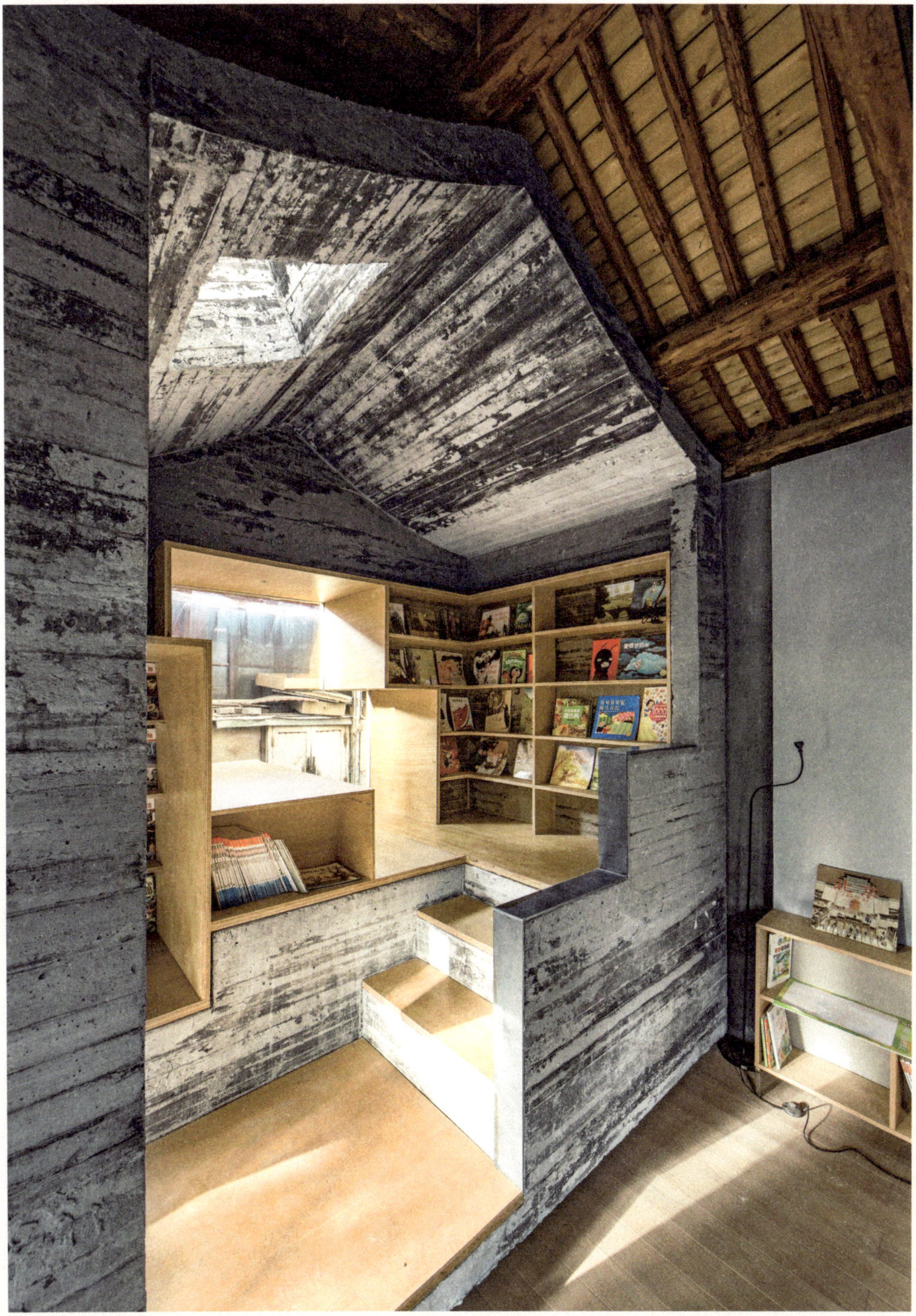

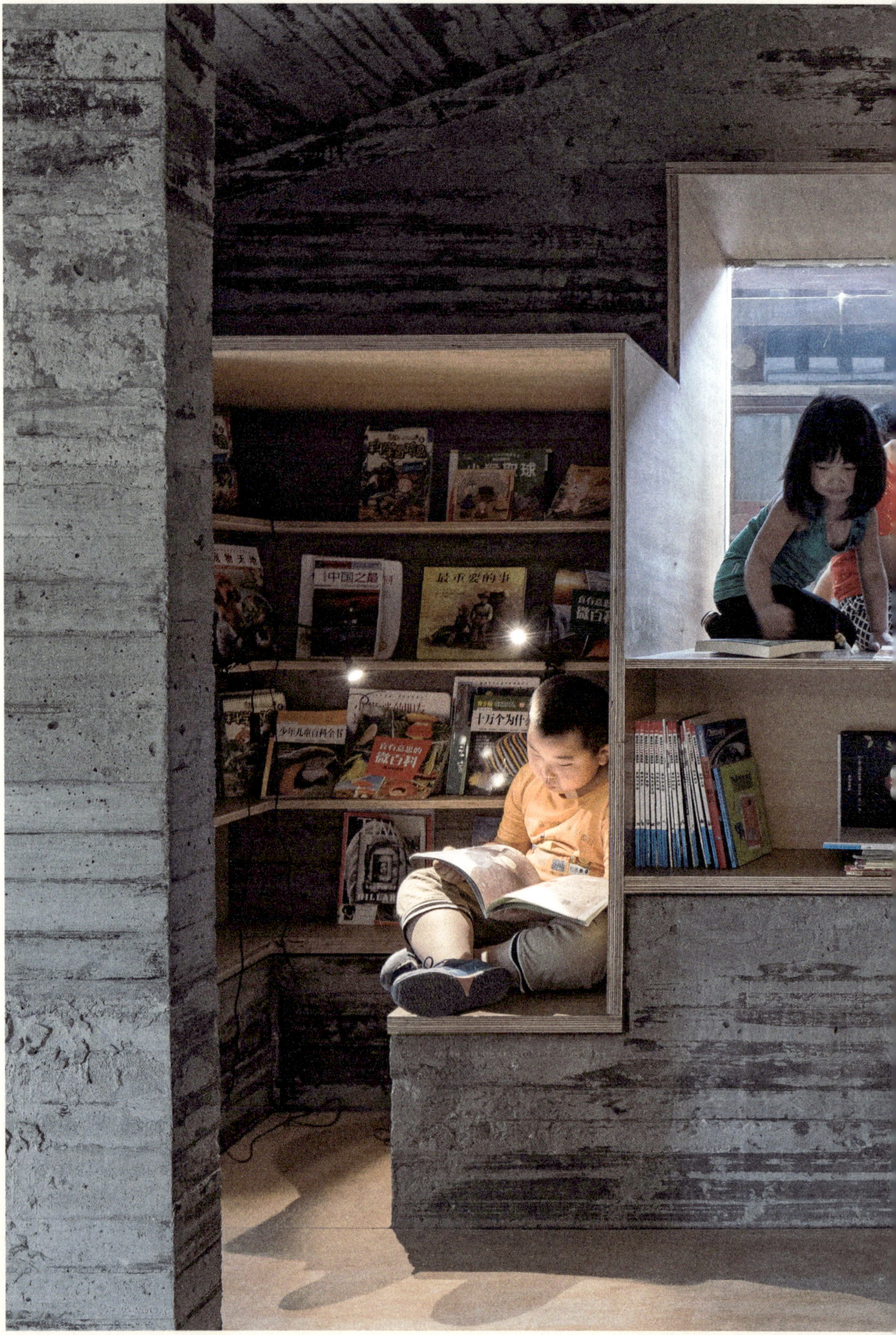

最重要的事
少年儿童百科全书
微百科

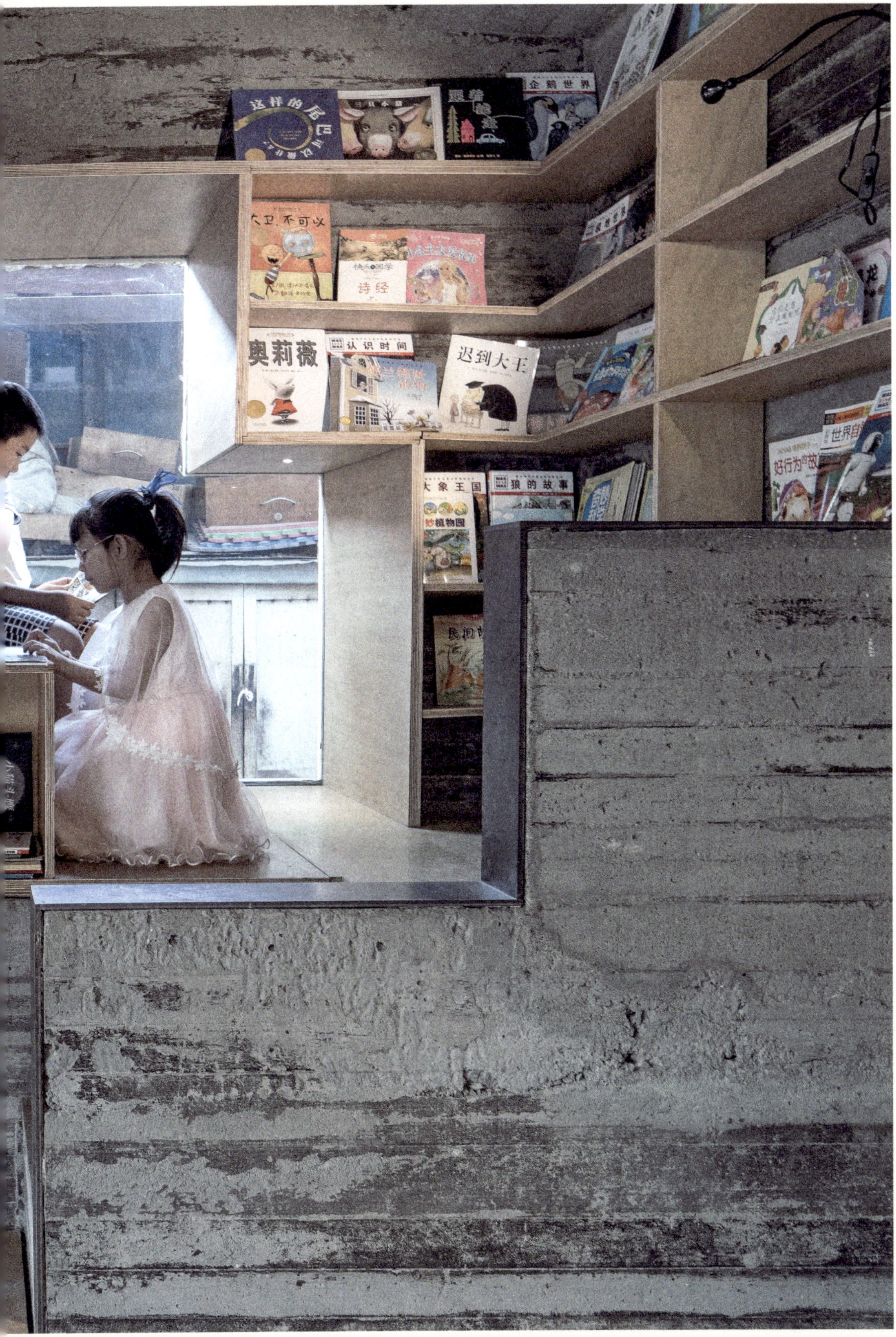
这样的尾巴
企鹅世界
大卫，不可以
诗经
奥莉薇
认识时间
迟到大王
大象王国
狼的故事

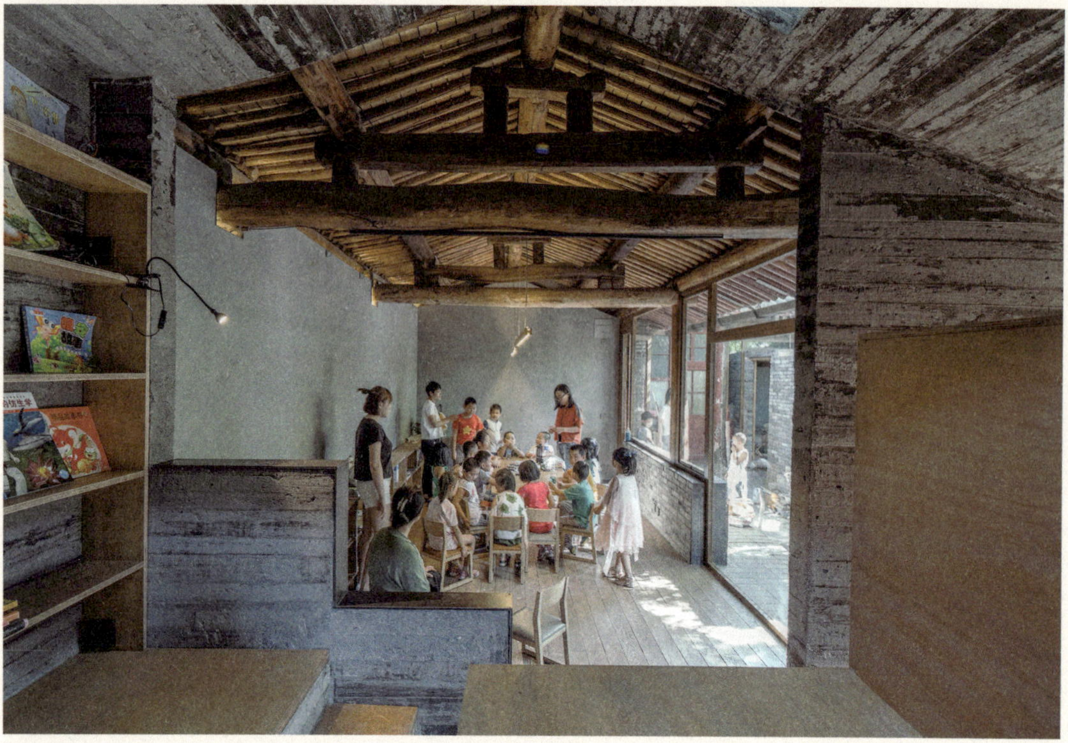

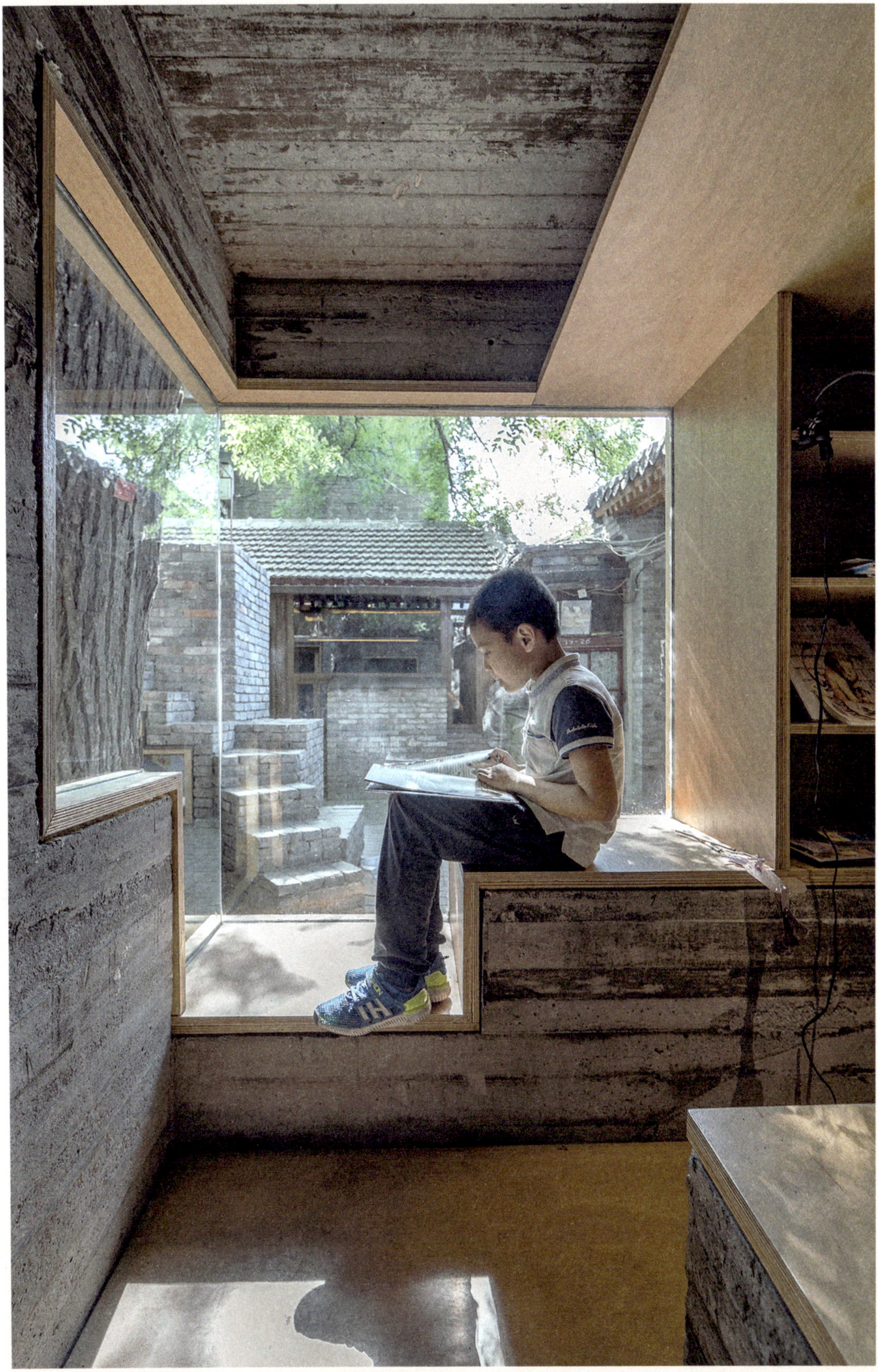

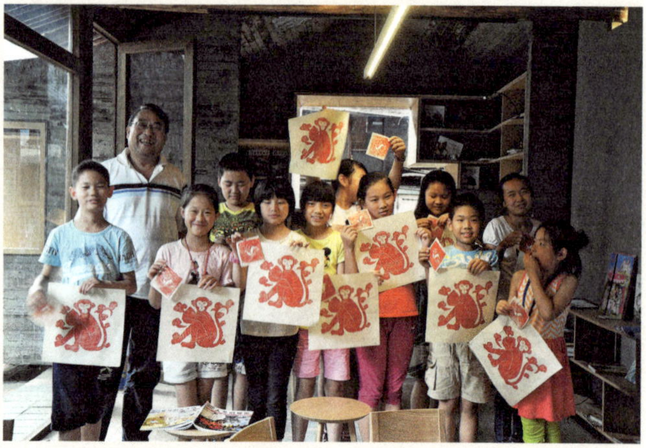

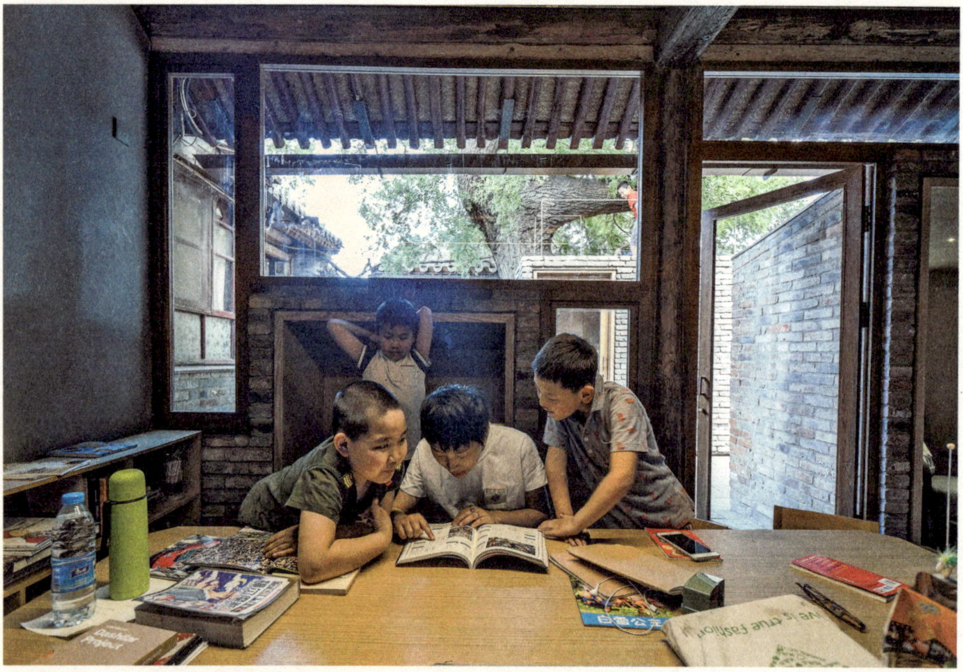

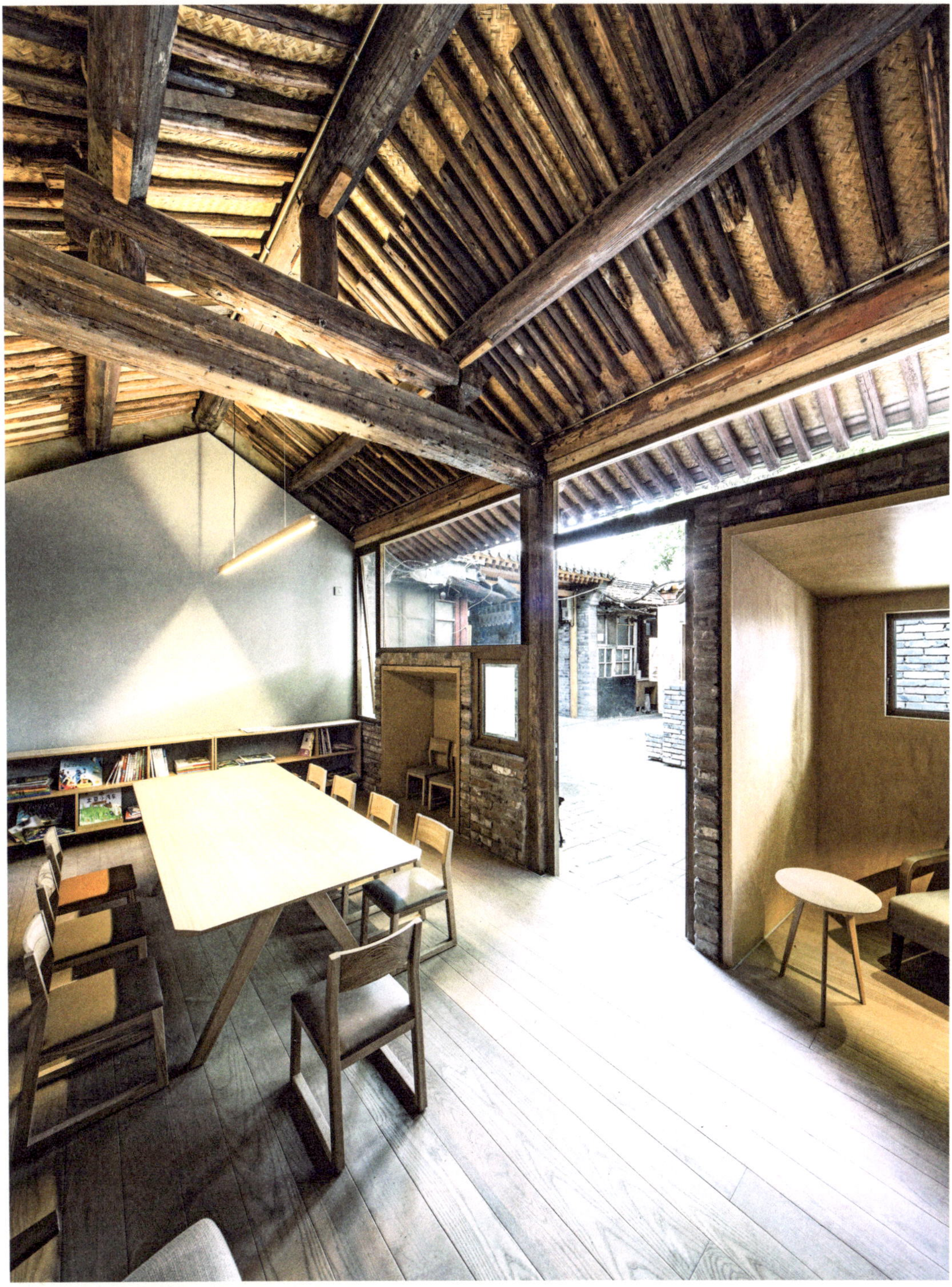

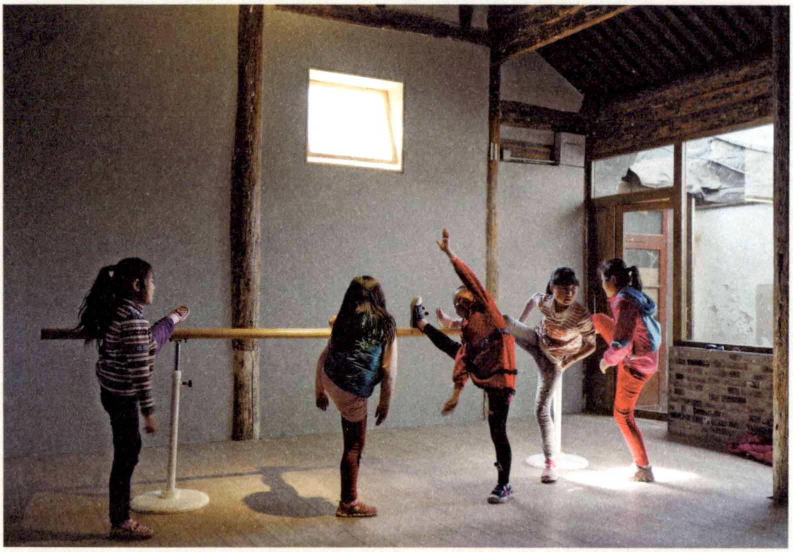

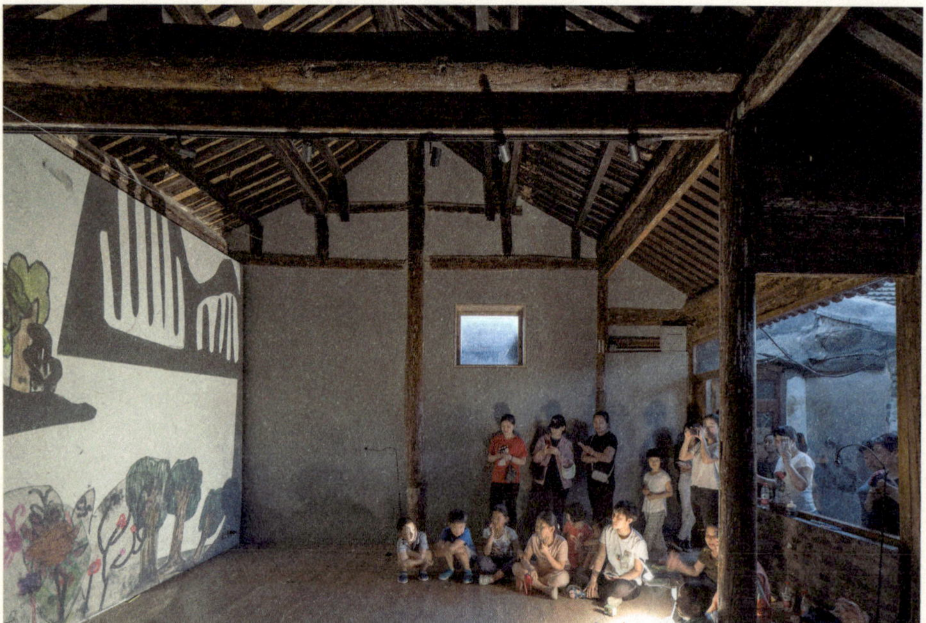

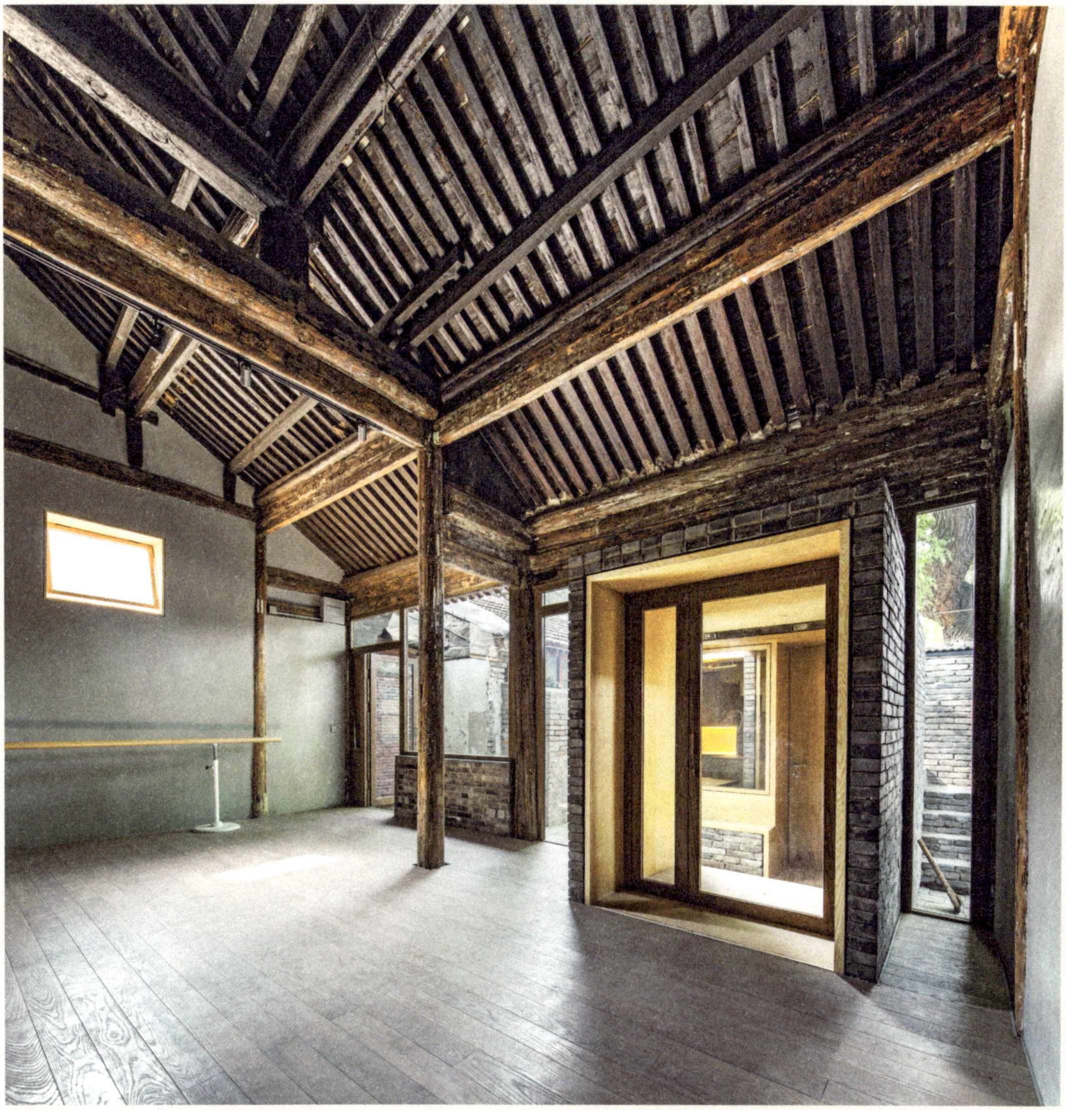

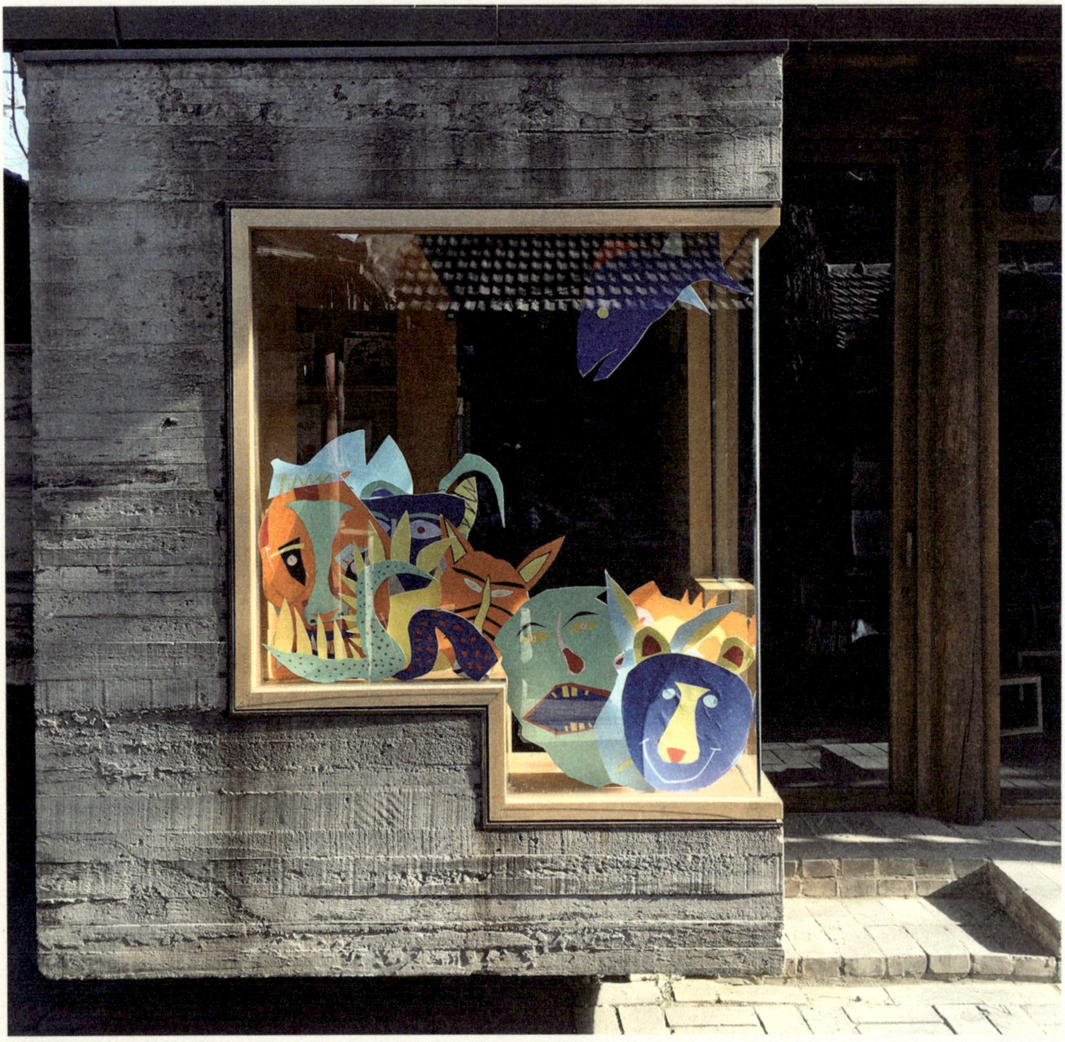

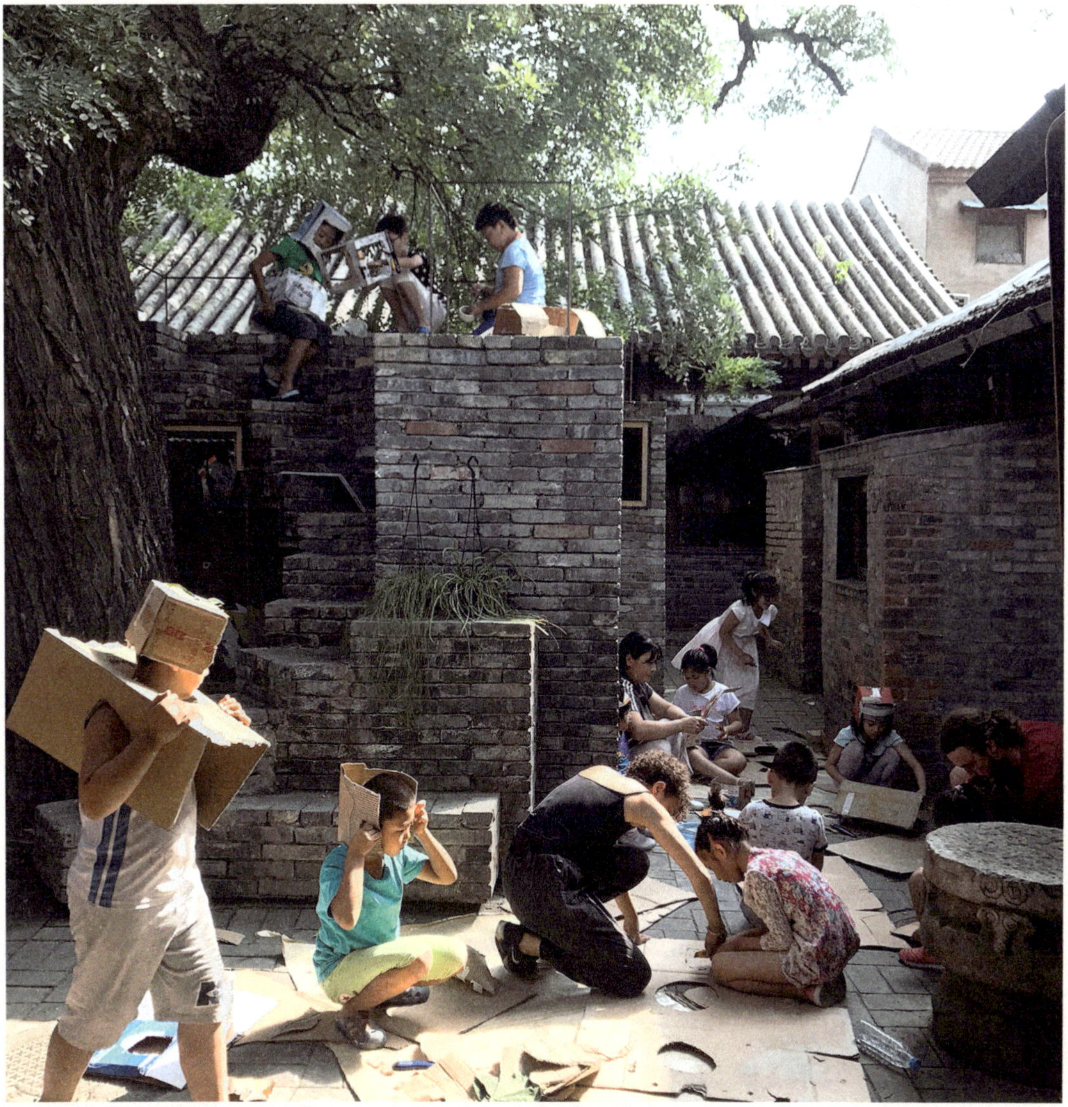

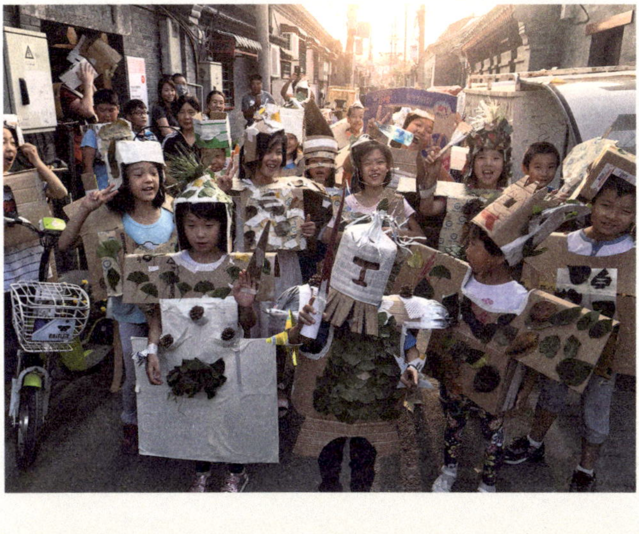

Models of the Micro Yuan'er Children's Library and Art Centre, exhibited at the Venice Biennale in 2016

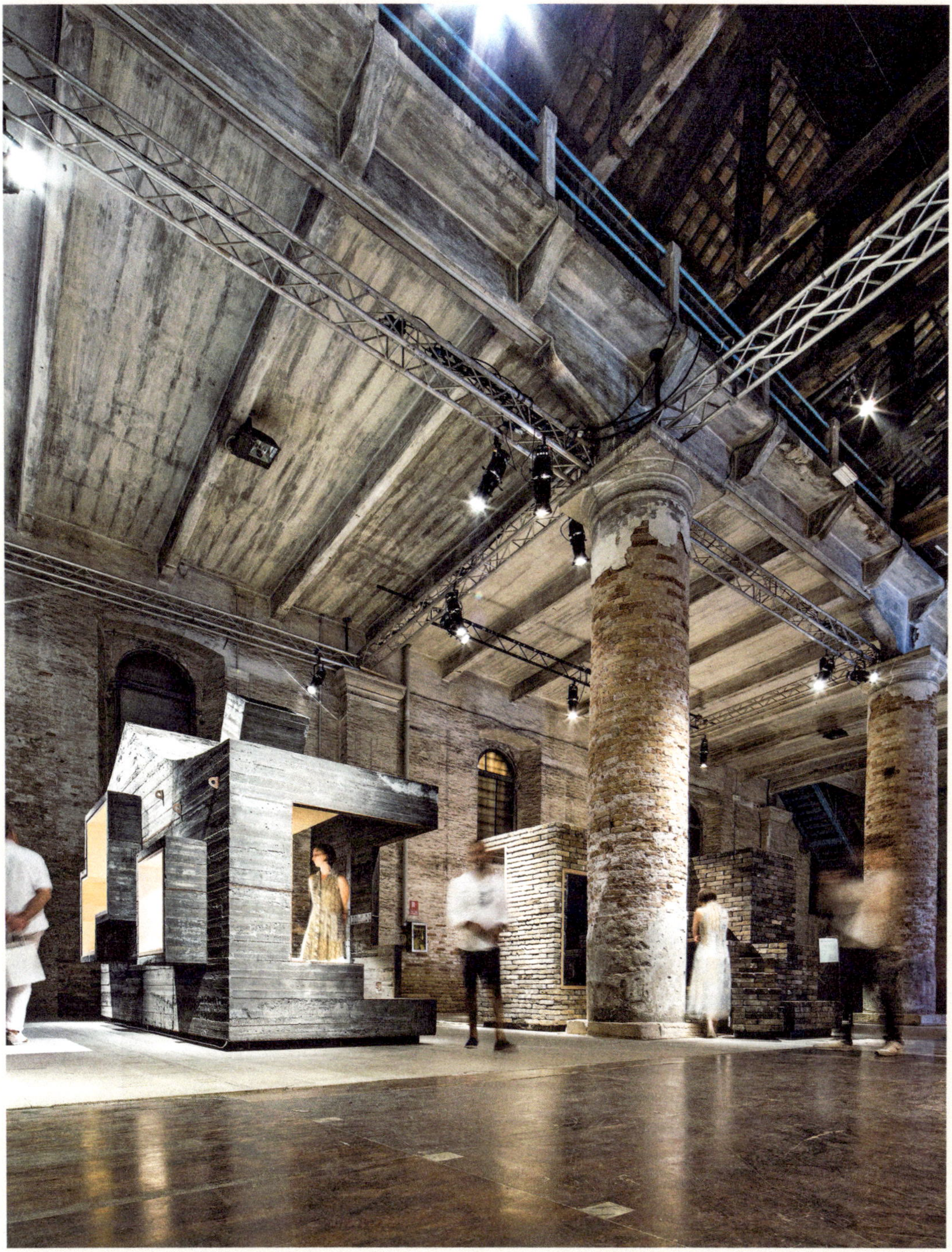

Changing Character: China and the Idea of Contemporary Architecture
Mohsen Mostafavi

Contemporary architecture in China is in a state of transition, with design practice being represented by several competing and evolving positions. There is of course nothing unusual about this situation. What is distinct, though, is the relative speed with which changes in forms of design practice have affected architectural production at every level, from concept to implementation. Then there is the added complexity of a nationally organised and planned design delivery system which impacts nearly all aspects of the country's design, approval and building process.

In China, the preparation of the documents necessary for construction is invariably either produced or aided by one of the country's "design institutes" – essentially offices for enablement – which came into existence in the 1950s under Mao Zedong's regime. There are now some two thousand design institutes across the country. The original mandate for these generally large, state-owned offices was to facilitate the technical knowledge necessary for the rapid rebuilding of the nation and its transformation from an agrarian to an industrial or urban society. The formation of design institutes was also a means for the state to enforce the centralisation and control of every step of the building process.

The design institutes have undergone some changes over the years. Some are now affiliated with major universities, such as Tsinghua in Beijing, or Tongji in Shanghai. Others are led by well-regarded architects, who have used the immense opportunities offered through the state sector to help improve the quality of the design outcome for a diverse range of projects. As quasi-governmental entities, the institutes possess different capabilities depending on their circumstances, expertise and location. In general, however, facilitating design delivery on such a large scale, and through centralised and often speedy procedures, has led to homogenisation. It is hard, after all, to avoid the allure of repeating the same "established" methods when there is so much emphasis on reducing the time available for either design or construction. Too often, the pressure to complete buildings quickly leads to a seamless alliance between the institutes and the construction industry that reduces the likelihood of experimentation or the emergence of new or unexpected ideas.

At the same time, when architects have embarked on ambitious projects in collaboration with design institutes, the results have been uneven in terms of both construction details and their execution by contractors. Under the immense pressures of the marketplace, many contractors resort to using relatively unskilled labour, with further deleterious consequences in terms of the outcome. The combination of power structures and potential financial rewards has made it

The Shanghai Center designed by John Portman Architects, 1990

hard for the younger generation of architects to make the commitment necessary to establish and develop practices resistant to the temptations of the status quo. There are those, however, who still try.

China opened its doors to international architects soon after the end of the Cultural Revolution, with architects such as John Portman, among others, establishing themselves within the country in the early 1980s. Soon the list of international practices expanded in response to the demand, especially for large-scale, corporate-style buildings. But most contemporary Chinese architects did not start their own private practices until the 1990s or later, especially after the housing reform of 1998, which led to market-based housing. Increased demand for cultural buildings further encouraged these private practices. What is important to bear in mind, therefore, is that most of the international and local architectural projects in China are less than thirty years old. Furthermore, despite the sheer scale of production, it is a relatively small group of practices that have been responsible for the creation of many of the significant and bespoke works of the recent past.

To put this in a wider historical context, those considered to be modern China's first generation of architects - figures such as Yang Tingbao and Liang Sicheng - were all born around the year 1900, or soon thereafter. These architects - some of them among the first Chinese architects to study abroad - helped pioneer the development of systematic studies on the history of Chinese architecture, cities and gardens. Tong Jun, one of the group's main figures, wrote the pioneering *Glimpses of Gardens in Eastern China*. Liang Sicheng, who together with his wife, Lin Huiyin, studied at the University of Pennsylvania (in his case with the French-born Beaux Arts architect Paul Philippe Cret), was instrumental in the formation of both Northeastern University's department of architecture in Shenyang and, later on, the department of architecture at Tsinghua University. Liang's and Lin's careers suffered numerous upheavals due to political circumstances. The Maoist revolutionaries did not appreciate Liang's research on traditional timber construction, considering such efforts to be against the ethos of the regime. Lin, who had long suffered from ill health, died in 1955 at the age of fifty-one, while her husband survived and was eventually rehabilitated, and even celebrated by the authorities.

Liang Sicheng approached the young architect and scholar Wu Liangyong (born 1922), who had previously served as his assistant, for help when Liang first began his plans to set up the

Cover of the book *Glimpses of Gardens in Eastern China* by Tong Jun

Lin Huiyin and Liang Sicheng in the Temple of Heaven

An early building by Yang Tingbao: the Da Hua Cinema in Nanjing, 1934

A contemporary response based on the courtyard typology of traditional hutongs: Ju'er Hutong by Wu Liangyong, 1989

A traditional hutong, not yet restored and in poor condition

department of architecture at Tsinghua University in 1946. The collaboration between the two men, as well as other colleagues, led to the founding of one of China's pre-eminent schools of architecture. Wu went on to teach at the university for more than fifty years. Now aged ninety-nine, he remains the nation's most celebrated living architect and planner.

Like the generation before him, Wu Liangyong's career is enmeshed with the task of studying and understanding the relationship between the past and the present in a country with a paradoxical relationship to its own cultural longevity. Part of this conflictual condition has at times been evident in the neglect of the material heritage of the past, despite a deep intellectual connection or appreciation of its cultural traditions. The sinologist Simon Leys has touched on what he calls "the parallel phenomenon of spiritual preservation and material destruction that can be observed in the history of Chinese culture".[1]

Preserved hutongs contribute to the value and importance of the historic parts of the city

The presence of the past is constantly felt in China. Sometimes it is found in the most unexpected places, where it hits the visitor with added intensity: movie theatre posters, advertisements for washing machines, television, or toothpaste displayed along the streets are expressed in a written language that has remained practically unchanged for the last two thousand years . . . Yet, at the same time, the paradox is that the very past which seems to penetrate everything, and to manifest itself with such surprising vigour, is also strangely evading our *physical* grasp. This same China which is loaded with so much history and so many memories is also oddly deprived of ancient monuments.[2]

According to Leys, the disappearance of monuments and other physical manifestations of the past cannot be attributed solely to the Cultural Revolution (1966–76). Although it clearly bore some responsibility for the destruction of historic artifacts, the Cultural Revolution was itself only the latest incarnation of a broader, more enduring attitude. Leys refers to the poet, archaeologist, and sinologist, Victor Segalen, whose studies of Chinese buildings one hundred years ago suggested that they were built from "fragile" and "perishable" materials that created a form of "in-built obsolescence". "The transient nature of the construction is like an offering to the voracity of time; for the price of such sacrifices, the constructors ensure the everlastingness of their spiritual designs".[3]

Consistent with Leys' arguments, the development and modernisation of Beijing and most other Chinese cities took little notice of the historic fabric and the physical manifestations of the past – a process of modernisation that has led to the "Westernisation", at least in terms of appearance, and consequent homogenisation of many cities. The value and importance of the historic parts of the city, as well as its vernacular architecture, is one of the subjects of study for Wu Liangyong and some of his colleagues. Wu's Ju'er Hutong, in a northern neighbourhood of Beijing, is a contemporary response based on the courtyard typology of traditional hutongs.

The work undertaken by Professor Wu has in some sense oscillated between the preservation of the old hutongs – which had become, with their many additions and often haphazard transformations, unhygienic and unsustainable places to live – and the use of the courtyard typology to build dense residential quarters that followed the historic pattern and morphology of the city. In the end, Ju'er Hutong is more a project of rebuilding, using the past as precedent, than of conservation or adaptive reuse. Professor Wu's interest in the traditional Chinese courtyard typology is also linked to a broader concern with what has been called the science of human settlements, or ekistics. Developed by the Greek architect C.A. Doxiadis and his collaborators, this concept focuses on achieving harmony between a human settlement and its physical, social and cultural environment. Wu's elaboration and articulation of the concept of human settlement has influenced the education and thinking of a generation of Chinese architects.

Over the years, the realities of the Chinese real-estate market, perhaps in tandem with the efforts of the elite, have significantly increased the value and appreciation of hutongs and other traditional structures as more people realise – despite resistance at multiple levels – the need to preserve them. However, the work carried out by Professor Wu and others raises questions about the nature and methods of conservation and the necessary distinctions between restoration, conservation and appropriation of traditional styles of architecture within the context of a modernist rationale. It should also be said that in many cases the condition of the hutongs is too poor for significant portions of their structures to be saved. Equally important is the debate regarding the use of historical models as precedents for contemporary architecture. For example, to what degree should the Chinese courtyard be visually and spatially dependent on the use of a specific style or material form? This is a debate that has been ongoing since the Republican Era with the idea of a style that would promote "modern content in a Chinese form". The question is whether it would be possible to consider such topics without their nationalistic agendas and with precedents being understood more in terms of their spatial qualities and characteristics than mere appearance alone.

Peace Hotel by Yang Tingbao, 1954

Fragrant Hill Hotel, the first project in China by I.M. Pei, 1982

Contemporary Chinese architects who began their studies and careers during or soon after the end of the purges of the Cultural Revolution were attuned to the impact of its consequences on architecture. The opportunities offered to private design practices since then have been significant compared to many other parts of the globe, yet modest in relation to the scale of development in China. While there is an increasing number of commissions from the private sector, most still come from the state or quasi-governmental agencies. As a consequence, certain formal and stylistic preferences have at times been promoted over others.

The Beaux-Arts, or rather a combination of Beaux-Arts ideas and Chinese elements, was often the preferred style for major buildings until recently. There were exceptions to this rule, in the form of projects such as the Peace Hotel in Beijing (1952) by Yang Tingbao, who is considered as one of the four original modern architectural "masters", together with Liang Sicheng, Tong Jun and Liu Dunzhen (Liu-Tun Tseng). Yang, like many of his contemporaries, was a graduate of the University of Pennsylvania.[4] With its modernist, planar facade and repetitive window treatment, the building remained a rare example of functionalist aesthetics. Much more common was a symbolic architecture that often included a large Chinese-style roof as the culmination of the building – or what Liang Sicheng dismissively called "wearing the Western suit with a Manchurian Hat". Such combinatory juxtapositions flourished during the postmodern period and to some degree persist today.[5] It is interesting, for example, to compare the architecture of the Peace Hotel with the first Chinese project of I.M. Pei, the Fragrant Hill Hotel, completed outside Beijing in 1982. Having left his home in 1935 to study and then practice in the US, Pei was keen to develop an architecture at the intersection of modernity and Chinese vernacular architecture. At the time, however, the outcome proved to be as challenging for both his American and Chinese critics to accept. The hotel also demonstrates the complications and the difficulty of achieving architectural unity based on the juxtaposition of stylistic motifs.

The arrival of additional international architects in recent decades, combined with a more ambitious, "liberal" and pragmatic project of modernisation, has exacerbated and prolonged the prevalence not only of corporate modernism but of postmodernism as well. In many cases what these styles share is the need for the architecture to impress. The most common method of achieving this goal has been the use of the technique of *aggrandisement* – literally making the buildings bigger or using elements such as large columns or pediments to create a sense of awe in the onlooker. The idea of aggrandisement is, however, more than mere bigness: it refers to the inflating of the object and its elements with the purpose of making it seem more powerful and important than it actually is.

Under such conditions, even international modernist architects have perhaps tended to give buildings stronger iconic and expressive identities than would be done in other contexts. Examples include OMA's CCTV; Herzog & de Meuron's Beijing National Stadium, often referred to as the Bird's Nest; and Zaha Hadid Architects's Galaxy and Leeza buildings for the office development company SOHO China. But the unexpected formal and spatial explorations of these projects, whether reductive or exuberant, have also resulted in architectural and engineering innovations – a claim that cannot be made for most modernist corporate buildings in the country.

In light of Simon Leys's observation about the tenuous nature of physical artifacts from the past, it is strange to witness such dedication to the production of contemporary monuments. Images of the CCTV building are often used as an emblem of modern Beijing. But already there are signs that China is considering other architectural directions, away from what President Xi Jinping has termed "weird" or unusual architecture. How long will these artifacts – all of them designed by foreign architects – last? Will they be appreciated and maintained? What role will they play in the consideration of tangible and intangible heritage in the years to come?

In some ways, contemporary Chinese architecture is still in a state of infancy, with new and changing ideas and directions. Some Chinese architects have not been in practice for as long as

CCTV Headquarters by OMA, 2012

Galaxy SOHO by Zaha Hadid Architects, 2012

many of the international firms established in China. Yet at least three generations of Chinese architects have emerged in the years since the country opened up to the West. The first generation, with founders in their fifties and sixties, includes Atelier FCJZ-Feichang Jianzhu (Yung Ho Chang and Lijia Lu), who began their practice in 1993, and MADA s.p.a.m. (Qingyun Ma), established in Beijing in 1996 and then in Shanghai in the early 2000s. Amateur Architecture Studio (Wang Shu and Lu Wenyu) was founded in 1998, Jiakun Architects (Liu Jiakun) in 1999, URBANUS (Xiaodu Liu, Yan Meng and Hui Wang) in 1999, while Studio Zhu-Pei, Li Xiaodong Atelier and Neri&Hu Design and Research Office were all established in the early 2000s.

These architects had to build their practices and their careers in the aftermath of the Cultural Revolution. In addition to the intellectually complex and conflictual conditions of architectural production, many directly experienced the suffering inflicted by Mao's regime – one example being Yung Ho Chang. Chang's father had been a respected architect and hoped to study abroad. It was Yung Ho and his brother, however, whose studies in China were interrupted by the Cultural Revolution, and who in the end were able to travel to the US to complete their education. Yung Ho Chang traveled first to Muncie, Indiana, to study at Ball State University, before moving to the University of California, Berkeley. At Ball State, he was taught by the South African architect and artist Rodney Place, who incidentally had been a classmate and my close friend at the Architectural Association School of Architecture in London. At Berkeley, Chang was influenced by Lars Lerup, the Swedish architect, writer, and theorist, and by Stanley Saitowitz, another South African and the designer of a series of beautifully crafted houses. Between Muncie and Berkeley, Chang experienced many diverse and complex sensibilities encompassing the AA, Sweden, South Africa, the connections between art and architecture, and the role and importance of drawing. These influences, plus his own upbringing and cultural heritage, including the work of his own father, were at play when he and his partner, Lijia Lu, returned to China from Houston, where Chang had been teaching at Rice University, to set up their practice, FCJZ. During those early years – 1998 to be precise – I was fortunate to be able to invite Yung Ho Chang together with two other Chinese architects, Kay Ngee Tan from Singapore and Ti-Nan Chi from Taiwan, to participate in a collaborative exhibition called "possibly big, possibly small". Part of the motivation for the invitation, apart from the fact that they all seemed to be doing interesting work, was to find out if the architects shared certain sensibilities despite their geographic distance.

Like Chang, many of this first group, including Qingyun Ma, Zhu Pei, Li Xiaodong and Neri&Hu, had spent part or all of their academic and professional training abroad – Ma, Zhu, and Neri&Hu in the US and Li in the Netherlands. What difference, if any, did those foreign encounters make in

Different types and colours of brickwork: Xiangshan Campus, China Academy of Art in Hangzhou by Amateur Architecture Studio, 2007

shaping contemporary Chinese architecture? How have these architects positioned themselves and their work in relation to such concepts and complexities as modernity, tradition, "Westernisation", vernacular, and local, material, and geographic specificities and identities? Is there a noticeable difference in the work of those who left and came back and those who stayed? (Wang Shu is among those who completed all of their education in China.) Is there a difference between urban and rural projects? What influence, if any, does the location of the practice have on the nature and character of its work?

It is not so much that the works of these architects provide all the answers to these and other questions about contemporary Chinese architecture, but rather that these architects began their careers tackling at least a number of these issues. One of the common sources of interest and influence among these architects is the role of local materials and traditions of building construction. For example, this combination of modern architectural forms and the use of traditional materials is found in the work of Amateur Architecture Studio. Equally important is the freedom gained from the practice of establishing multiple buildings in proximity to each other, as Wang Shu and Lu Wenyu have done with their buildings at the China Academy of Art in Hangzhou, where their practice is also based. The familiarity and ease with which these architects use their palette of materials can only be attained through deep knowledge, experimentation and trial and error on site. At times, they juxtapose or "compose" the material elements of a wall

Tsingpu Yangzhou Retreat by Neri&Hu Design and Research Office, 2017

by using different types and colours of brickwork. These types of insertions into the wall, akin to the use of spolia, result in an appearance that can be described as geological in character. The material colours and tonalities of the buildings undermine any specific stylistic consistency that could otherwise be assumed by the architecture.

Wang Shu, like many architects before him, is deeply interested in traditional Chinese culture and the arts. At his Kenzo Tange lecture at Harvard in 2011, "Geometry and Narrative of Form", I recall that he spent most of his time discussing Chinese landscape paintings, as if he wanted the audience to know that to understand his work one had to understand the material and gestural sensibilities of a landscape painter toward nature, terrain, mountain, water and atmosphere.

This ethos is in some ways necessary for the understanding of the most productive and provocative versions of contemporary architecture and design more broadly, for painting, according to

Shou County Culture and Art Center by Studio Zhu-Pei, 2019

the Chinese-French writer and scholar François Cheng, occupies the supreme position among the arts. "Compared with poetry, the other pinnacle of Chinese culture", Cheng says, "painting, through the original space that it embodies and through the vital breaths that it arouses, seems far more apt to go beyond description of the spectacles of creation and to enter into the very gestures of creation".[6] In part, this is why Chinese painting has also been called "philosophy in action". A central element of this worldview, Cheng claims, is the concept of emptiness (*hsü*),[7] which in painting is best exemplified by the areas left unpainted between water and mountains in landscape paintings. The gap created by the empty space helps to overcome the rigid opposition between certain elements and to introduce relations between them, enabling water to reach high into the mountains, for example, or vice versa. According to Cheng, "Emptiness introduces discontinuity and reversibility into a given system and thus permits the elements composing the system to transcend rigid opposition and one-sided development. At the same time, emptiness offers human beings the possibility of approaching the universe at the level of totality".[8]

The use of emptiness as a form of discontinuity or disruption persists in the other arts, such as silence in music, or *parallelism* in poetry, by suppressing certain words as purely grammatical insertions. These manifestations of emptiness are seen as prerequisites for the wholeness, or fullness, of a specific artistic enterprise. Perhaps in the same vein, Amateur Architecture often deploy interruptions, spacings, cuts, or gaps in their buildings and their surfaces. The visual appearance of these buildings is as contingent on cultural and philosophical principles as it is on architectural or disciplinary discourses and debates.

The idea of emptiness, as found in the unpainted areas between two scenes in landscape painting, also bears a resemblance to the Japanese notion of *Ma*, best articulated by the architect Arata Isozaki as a form of in-betweenness or liminality. The exploration of this theme is evident in the work of other practices as well, for example in the Tsingpu Yangzhou Retreat completed by Neri&Hu in Jiangsu Province (2017), or in Studio Zhu Pei's Shou-County Culture and Art Center in Anhui Province (2019), where courtyards, cuts in the ground, and perforated passageways can be seen as explorations of the idea of "in-betweenness" and of reconciliation between different spatial conditions. The combination of materials, textures, tonalities and craft, together with references to ideas such as emptiness or liminality, has enabled a generation of Chinese architects to explore an architecture that is at once contemporary but also in tune with the past.

The specific qualities of this architecture, while generally still under-described, are nevertheless increasingly acknowledged not only in China but also in the West, where many members of this generation and the subsequent generation of Chinese architects have been recognised through teaching appointments, exhibitions and awards. For example, both Yung Ho Chang (2002) and Wang Shu (2011) taught as visiting Kenzo Tange Professors at the Harvard Graduate School of Design. Chang was subsequently appointed as the Head of the Architecture Department at MIT, while Qingyun Ma, a graduate of the University of Pennsylvania, was appointed Dean of the University of Southern California School of Architecture in 2007. These posts were to be followed by many other visiting appointments and lectures in recent years – at Harvard, for example, Yan Meng (URBANUS), Liu Yichun (Atelier Deshaus), Zhu Pei, Zhang Ke and Neri&Hu have all either taught studios or given lectures. Zhang Ke of ZAO/standardarchitecture conducted a series of design studios, some under the aegis of the Aga Khan Programme, when the theme of Hutong Metabolism first emerged. International recognition has been followed at home, with many contemporary architects receiving appointments at institutions such as Tsinghua and Tongji Universities.[9]

In terms of awards, beyond Wang Shu receiving the Pritzker Architecture Prize in 2012, it has been the Aga Khan Award for Architecture that has made the most deliberate and concerted efforts toward acknowledging the contribution of Chinese architects, within the context of promoting a broadly defined pluralistic society. The series of shortlisted and awarded projects include the Bridge School by Li Xiaodong Atelier, in Xiashi, south of Hangzhou; the Tulou

The Aga Khan seated with Yang Tingbao at the Aga Khan Award's seminar in China, 1981

Collective Housing scheme by URBANUS (Xiaodu Liu and Yan Meng); Museum of Handcraft Paper, in Gaoligong, Yunnan Province, by Trace Architecture Office; Micro Yuan'er Children's Library and Art Centre, in Beijing by ZAO/standardarchitecture (Zhang Ke); and, most recently, the Courtyard House Plugin by People's Architecture Office (PAO).

These projects, in addition to their architectural merit, demonstrate a social commitment to their specific contexts and geographies. The Bridge School accommodates the everyday functions of a small school while also linking and supporting two small communities in need of revitalisation. The school's proximity to a rural tulou structure in need of maintenance further reinforces the role and value of contemporary architecture in relation to its community. Similarly, the Micro Yuan'er Children's Library demonstrates the importance of a carefully crafted addition or insertion within the context of a historic building. The juxtaposition of old and new, which is also the theme of the Courtyard House Plugin, is made possible through the careful understanding and manipulation of every part of the hutong's interior, including all the physical and natural elements of its traditional courtyard. The design approach is part architecture, part site-specific installation, part cabinetry and craftsmanship. The project's focus on modification and adaptive reuse

Tulou Collective Housing in Nanhai by URBANUS Architecture & Design Inc., 2008

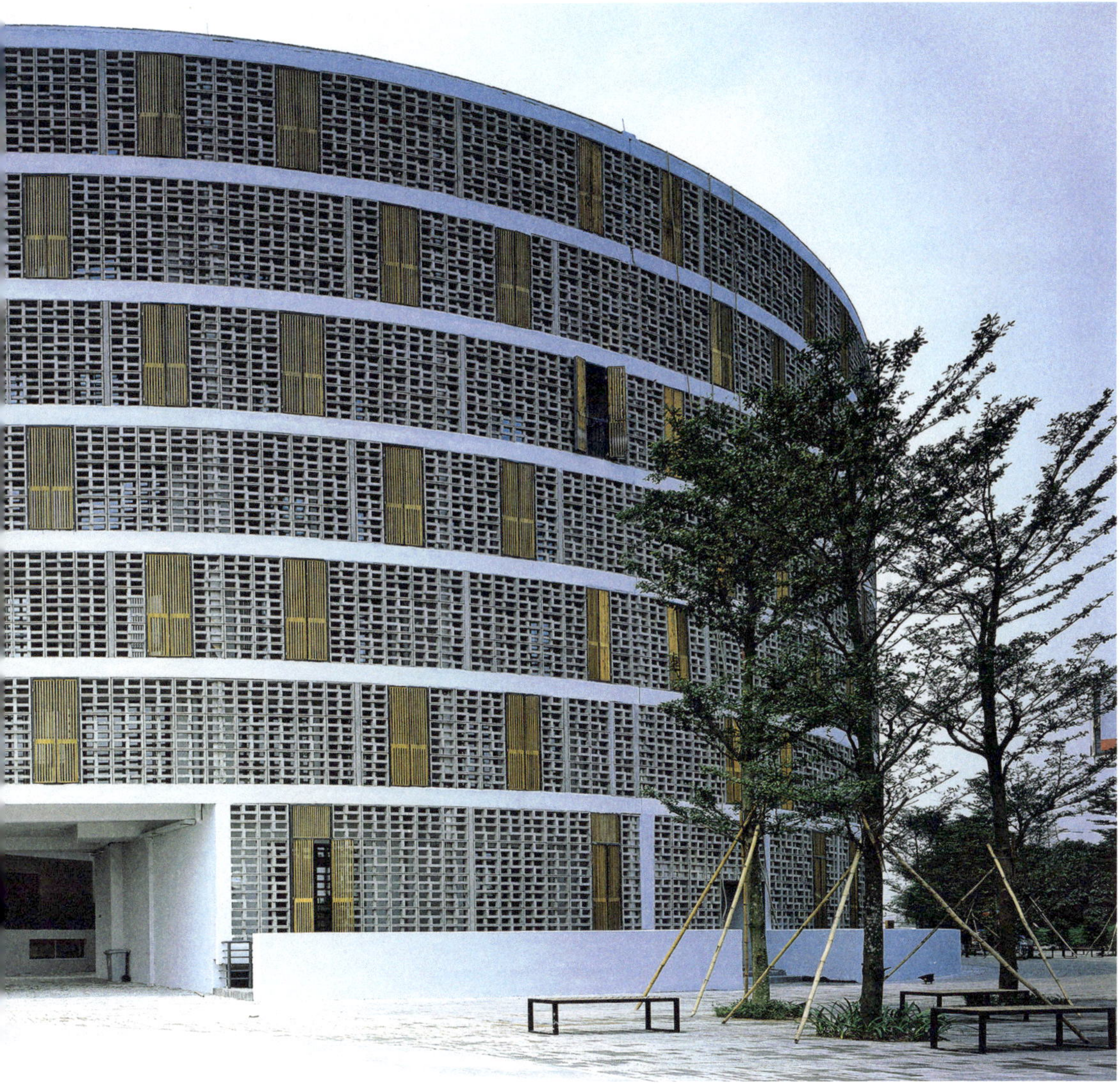

Bridge School in Xiashi by Li Xiaodong Atelier, 2008

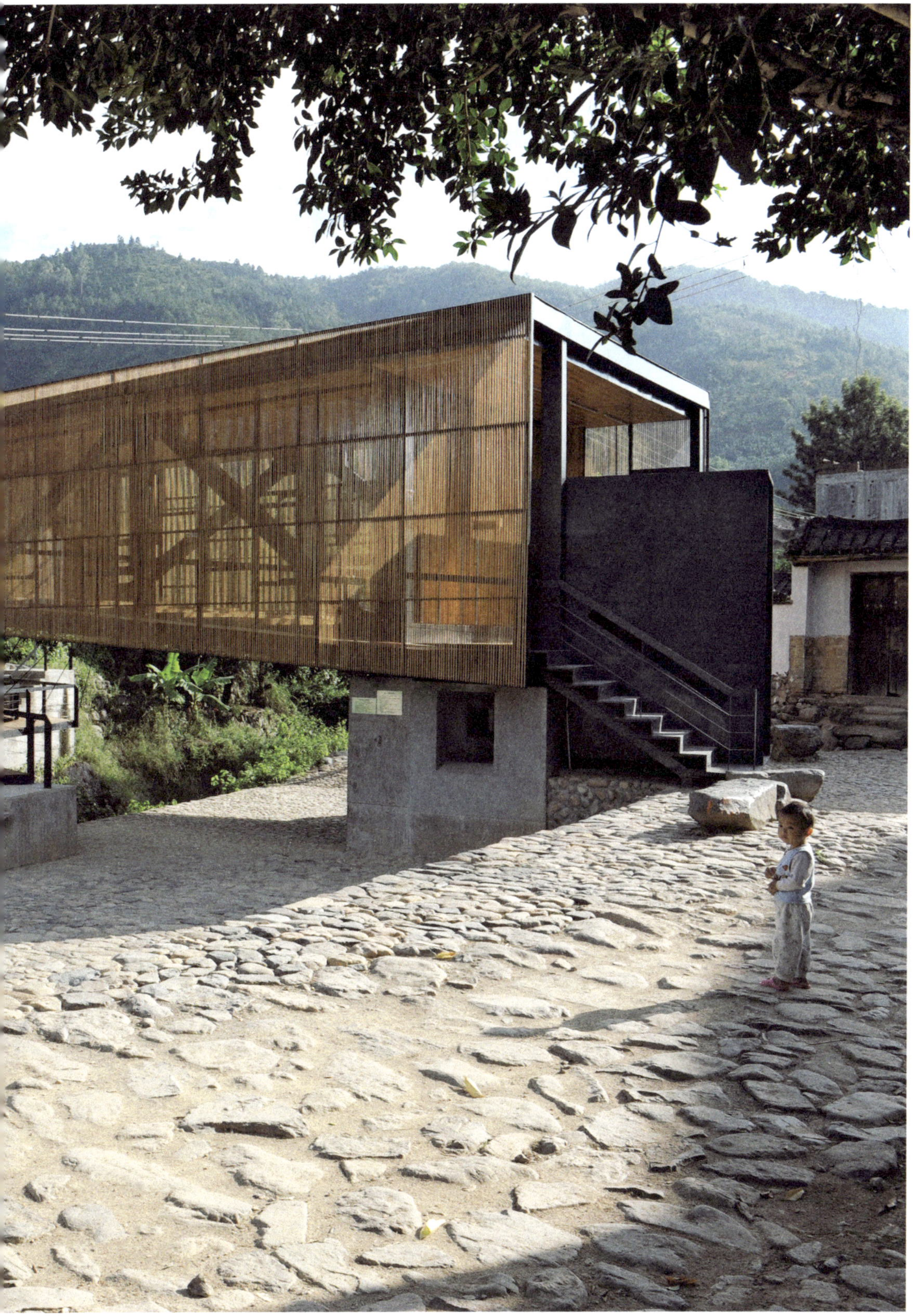

Gaoligong Museum of Handcraft Paper by Trace Architecture Office, 2010

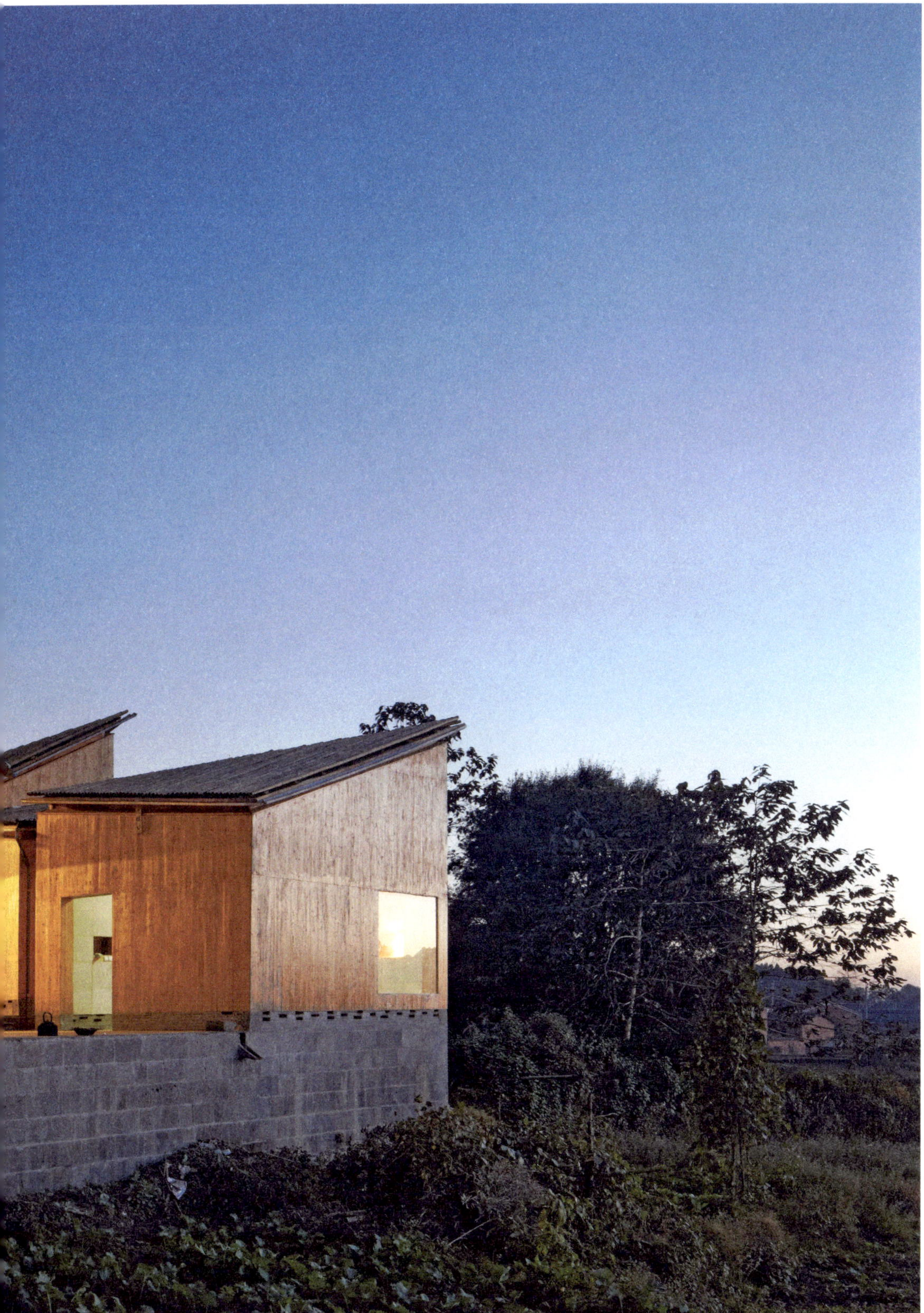

Courtyard House Plugin by People's Architecture Office, 2014

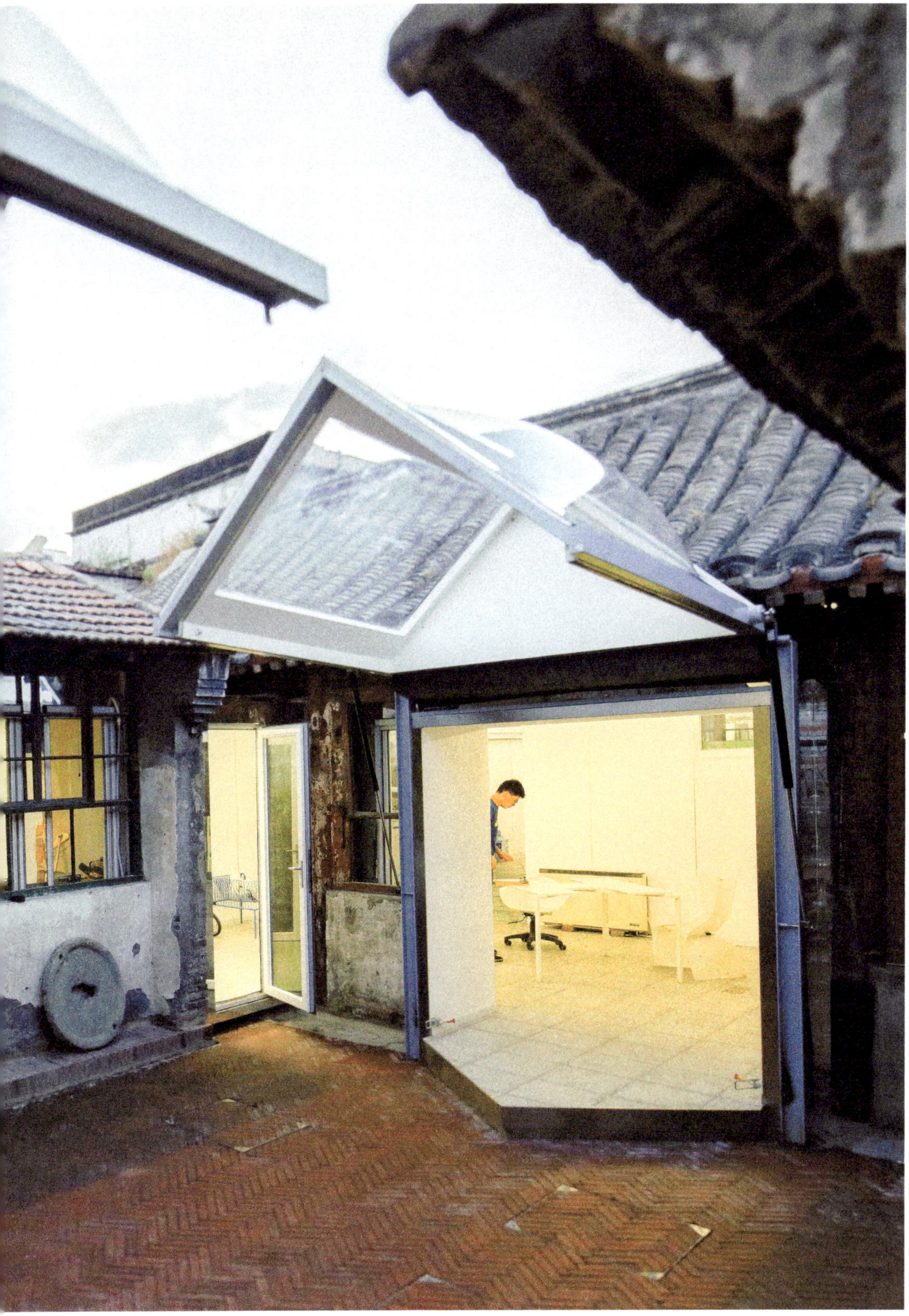

Courtyard of the Micro Yuan'er Children's Library and Art Centre by Zhang Ke, 2014

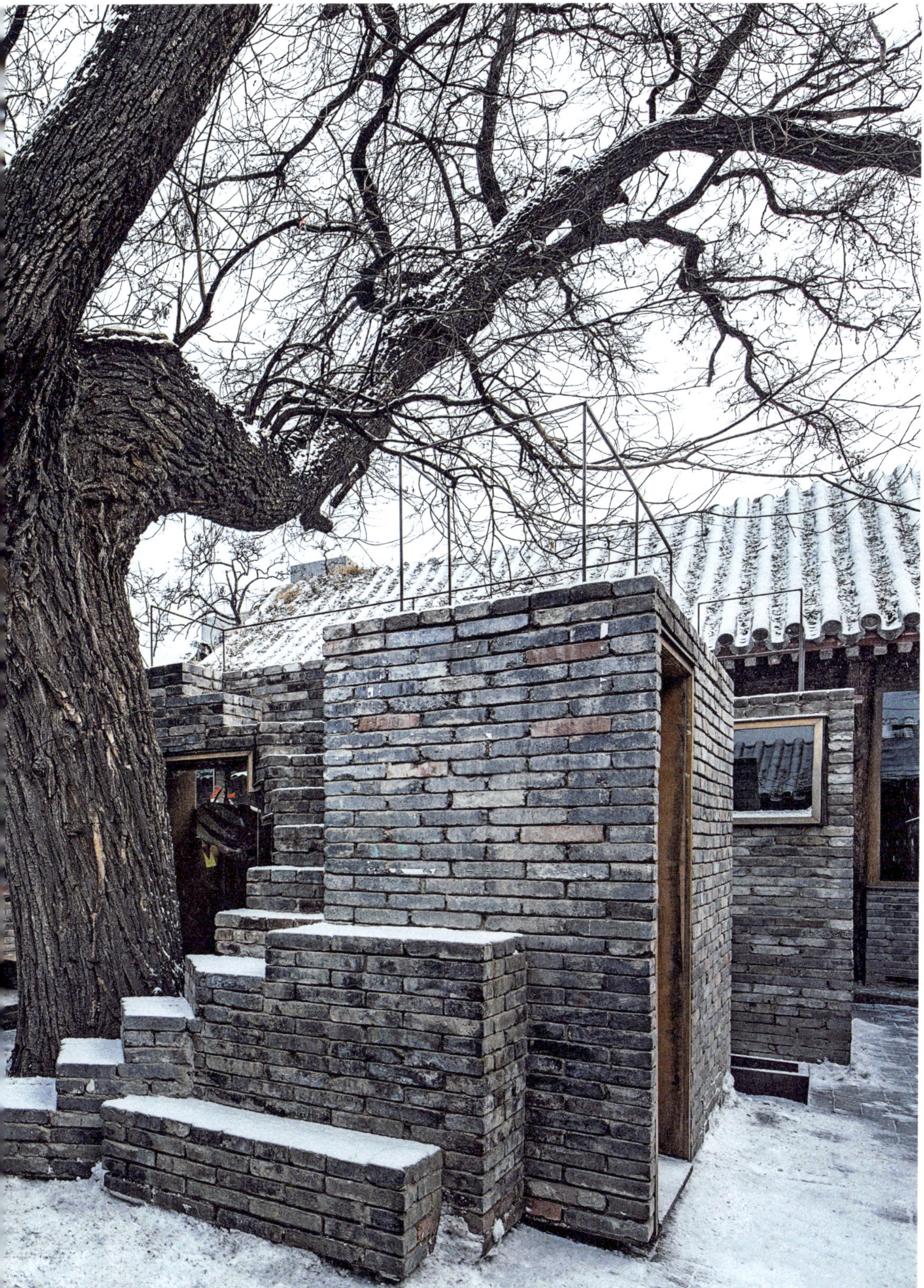

of a historic structure allows it to sensitively, and organically, respond to the contemporary needs of society. This dynamic and responsive strategy is not solely applicable to the courtyard house but to its surrounding area as well.

The iterative and small-scale characteristics of the project's interventions insinuate a form of micro-urbanism that provides an alternative to the demolition and the reconstruction strategies that have been in place for hutongs during the recent past. Such strategies have broader potential in relation to the demolition of old neighbourhoods, which are often replaced by an anonymous fabric that mimics certain characteristics of traditional Chinese architecture. The programmatic diversity of the Hutong Metabolism combines functions that help bring multiple constituencies together. The project used the idea of play to create a magical environment for children as well as bring them into social contact with the hutong's elderly inhabitants – a mutually beneficial situation. Such opportunities for programming variation and juxtaposition are more difficult to identify in the context of the functional separation and zoning of new neighbourhoods.

While such projects can be of significant value in relation to existing neighbourhoods, it has been harder for contemporary architects to intervene in a significant manner in the more challenging task of the increasing privatisation of housing in China. The *xiaoqu* – large-scale and often gated communities constructed by private developers – has its origins in the Soviet and post-Soviet microdistricts, high-rise neighbourhoods built to house a large number of residents. The anonymity of this "modernist" and "utopian" vision of housing, with its accompanying public and retail spaces and institutions, is a far cry from the sense of neighbourly proximity and interaction which was typical of traditional hutong or courtyard neighbourhoods in Beijing or the *lilong* or *longtang* linear residential communities, and the 19th century *shikumen* (stone gate) districts which combined Western and Chinese styles, in Shanghai.

If the first generation of contemporary Chinese architects was mainly responsible for the task of articulating an alternative and locally specific architecture, some members of the new generations of Chinese architects feel partly relieved of this responsibility. Firms such as MAD Architects (Ma Yansong) have already demonstrated their preference for the parametric architecture that shares more with practices such as Zaha Hadid Architects and others in Europe and North America than it does with their Chinese counterparts. Rather than being focused on the local, they seem to aspire more to international success. Firms like MAD are now being joined by an increasing number of both foreign and Chinese-trained architects with access to an ever-greater array of both theoretical and technical tools and modes of defining architecture.

Children's class at the Micro Yuan'er Children's Library and Art Centre

The xiaoqu housing projects, first built in the 1980s, are large-scale and often gated communities constructed by private developers

Nevertheless, architecture's relations to the wider territory, urban and rural, remains one of the most pressing issues facing Chinese architects, landscape architects and urbanists today. In this context, the interest in rural and agrarian communities is potentially as fecund as those investigations that consider new forms of urban living. Alongside academies both in China and abroad, younger practices such as DnA Architects (Xu Tiantian), among others, are increasingly interested in the possibilities of architecture within a rural context. The landscape architect Kongjian Yu and his practice Turenscape, which interestingly employs significantly more staff than any of the contemporary architectural firms, have played an important role in promoting an ecological approach in the planning and shaping of both urban and rural project sites across

Tofu Factory, built from wood in the traditional mountain village Caizhai, by DnA_Design and Architecture, 2018

China. A deeper understanding of environmental issues, including urban degradation, rising sea levels, climate change, resource management and sustainability will need to form an indispensable part of the future of architectural pedagogy and practice. The incorporation of this knowledge and the specificity of its geographic diversity could also contribute to a greater clarity and distinctness among Chinese cities, counteracting their increasing homogeneity.

This homogeneity is in many respects a product of the boom in the market economy, with its pressure on the speed of development, combined with the relatively small number of architectural firms. The private housing sector has come to be dominated by ever-larger projects by real-estate companies such as Country Garden, Evergrande Group and Vanke. Many real-estate developers have internal architecture and design divisions, with deep design and lifestyle knowledge of their various markets. Some Chinese real-estate companies have now expanded to other parts of the world, including Europe and the United States, even though the Chinese real-estate market remains the largest in the world.

On the urban front, many of the big developers, including those from Hong Kong, have hired foreign design firms, mainly those from the US, for their expertise in large-scale commercial and retail projects. These developments, many of them high-rises on individual parcels of land, have transformed, and "privatised", the urban core of many of the "second-tier" cities, such as Nanjing, Wuhan, Tianjin, Chongqing and Chengdu, which serve as the main regional centres of their respective provinces.

These two aspects of the current realities of real-estate development in China – on the one hand the large-scale privatisation of the housing market, and on the other the dominance of corporate towers in major cities – have limited the possibilities and range of projects for contemporary Chinese architects. Despite this, many have benefited from the boom of public sector projects, such as libraries and theatres. This is also why it is so valuable that research projects like Hutong Metabolism produce the experimental as well as the experiential context for alternative models of architecture and urban development. The task facing the current generation of contemporary Chinese architects, however, had already been established by one of the so-called first generation "masters" of architecture: according to Wu Liangyong, the concept of "physical environment construction" was introduced to China by Liang Sicheng in 1947 upon his return from lecturing in the US. The concept refers to the harmonious development and relationship between all the elements of the physical environment, from furniture to houses, from cities to regions. Furthermore, such an approach calls for the integration of the various disciplines – not just architecture, city planning, and landscape architecture, but science and technology as well.[10] Only when this is achieved will architecture truly be able to enhance its contribution to the everyday lives of the people in China. The number of talented Chinese architects, whether trained at home or abroad, is rapidly increasing. What's more, these architects seem eager to take on the responsibility of using architecture to transform the physical environment for the better. They only need to be given the opportunities to do so.

1   Simon Leys, "The Chinese Attitude Towards the Past", in *The Hall of Uselessness: Collected Essays* (New York: New York Review Books, 2013), p. 285. Simon Leys was the pen name of the Belgian sinologist and author Pierre Ryckmans.

2   Ibid., p. 286.

3   Ibid., pp. 288–89.

4   The work of twenty Chinese architects who studied at the University of Pennsylvania between 1918 and 1935 was the subject of an exhibition, *Accomplishment*, at Tsinghua University in 2019. It was curated by a group that included Tong Ming, a professor at Tongji and the son of the architect Tong Jun.

5   For a discussion on the background of the current situation in Chinese architecture, see Jianfei Zhu, "Beyond Revolution: Notes on Contemporary Chinese Architecture", *AA Files*, 35 (Spring 1998), pp. 3–14.

6   François Cheng, *Empty and Full: The Language of Chinese Painting* (Colorado: Shambhala, 1994), p. 1.

7   The idea of emptiness can be described by the words *wu* and *hsü*, which were later complemented by the Buddhist term *k'ung*. During the Sung period, the expression *t'ai-hsü* (supreme emptiness) was coined by the philosopher Chang Tsai. Cheng, *Empty and Full*, p. 43.

8   Ibid., p. 36.

9   In recognition of the emerging importance and contribution of contemporary Chinese architects, the Harvard University Graduate School of Design showcased the work of some sixty practices with the exhibition *Towards Critical Pragmatism*, curated by Professor Li Xiangning of Tongji University in 2016.

10 Wu Liangyong, *The Science of Human Settlements in China* (New Jersey: Homa & Sekey Books, 2015), p. 62.

Micro Hutong

Location: **Beijing, China**
Client: **Beijing Dashilar Investment Ltd.**
Design period: **2013-16**
Construction period: **June 2015-October 2016**
Site area: **35 m²**
Building area: **35 m²**
Total floor area: **30 m²**
Architect: **ZAO/standardarchitecture**
Project architect: **Zhang Ke**
Design team: **Zhang Mingming, Huang Tanyu, Ao Ikegami, Dai Haifei**
Collaborating design institution: **Tongji Architectural Design & Research Institute**

The goal of this project, a 35 square metre house, is to find ways of creating ultra-small-scale social housing within the limitations of the super-tight traditional hutong spaces of Beijing.
The result is an architectural operation that brings back the courtyard as a generator of the programme, for it activates the building by establishing a direct relationship with its urban context. Apart from enhancing the flow of air and light, the courtyard fosters a direct connection between the living space contained in the dynamic volumes and an urban vestibule in the front part of the building. The flexible urban living room acts as a transition zone from the private rooms to the street, while serving as a semi-public space to be used by both the inhabitants of the house and the neighbours in the community.
The main body of the project was cast on site using concrete mixed with Chinese ink, including mini living spaces with a shared courtyard, which is a public area with two trees faced by five inwardly staggered rooms. As part of the design to improve quality of life in the hutong, the main building is supported by the central air-conditioning system, with radiant floors in each room to provide a comfortable interior situation against the severely cold winter weather in Beijing, when a dramatic view is framed by the entirely transparent facade of every room. Besides the three openable skylights on the roof, all of the rooms allow for natural ventilation so that the fresh air can circulate through the whole building.

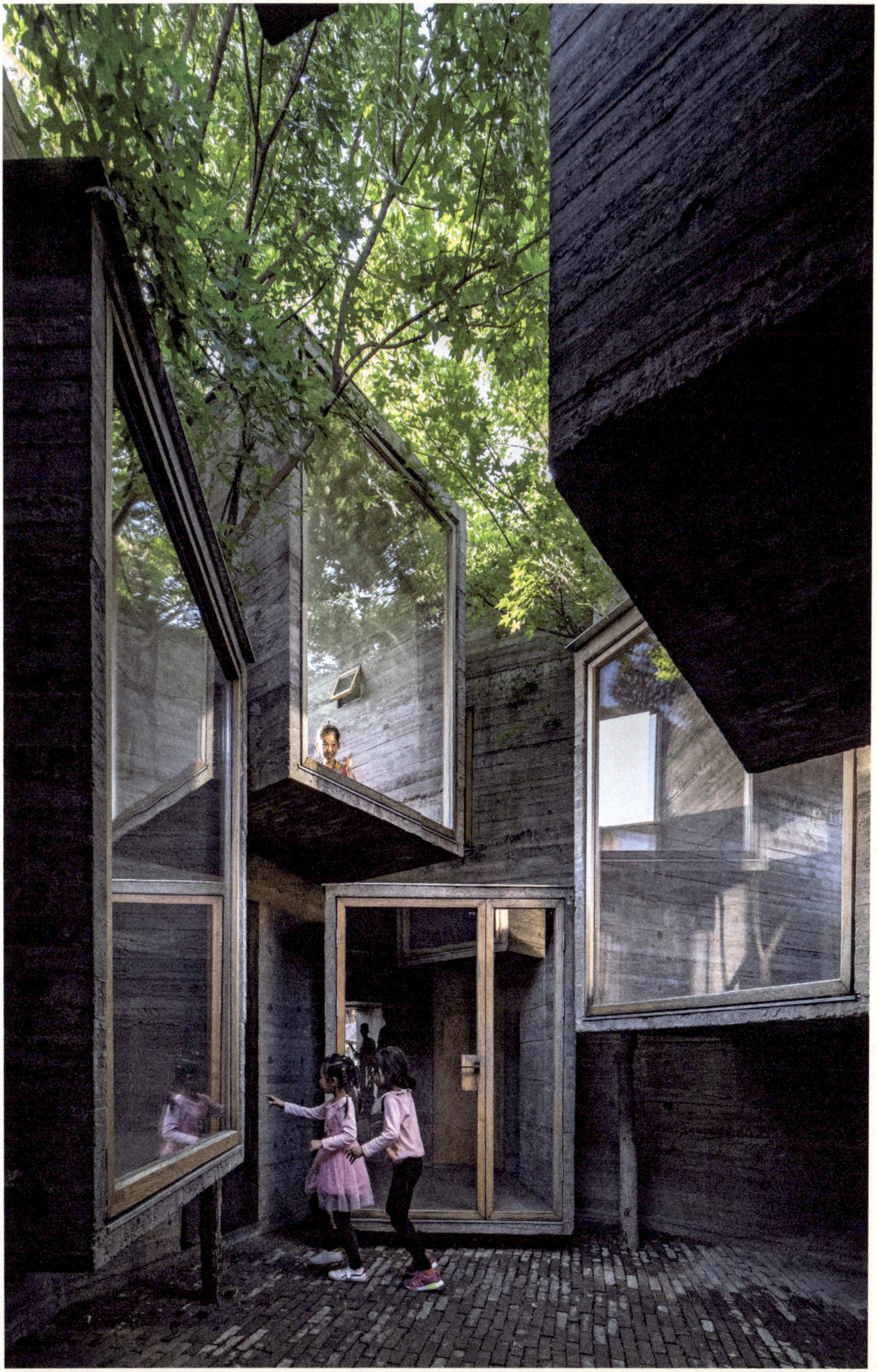

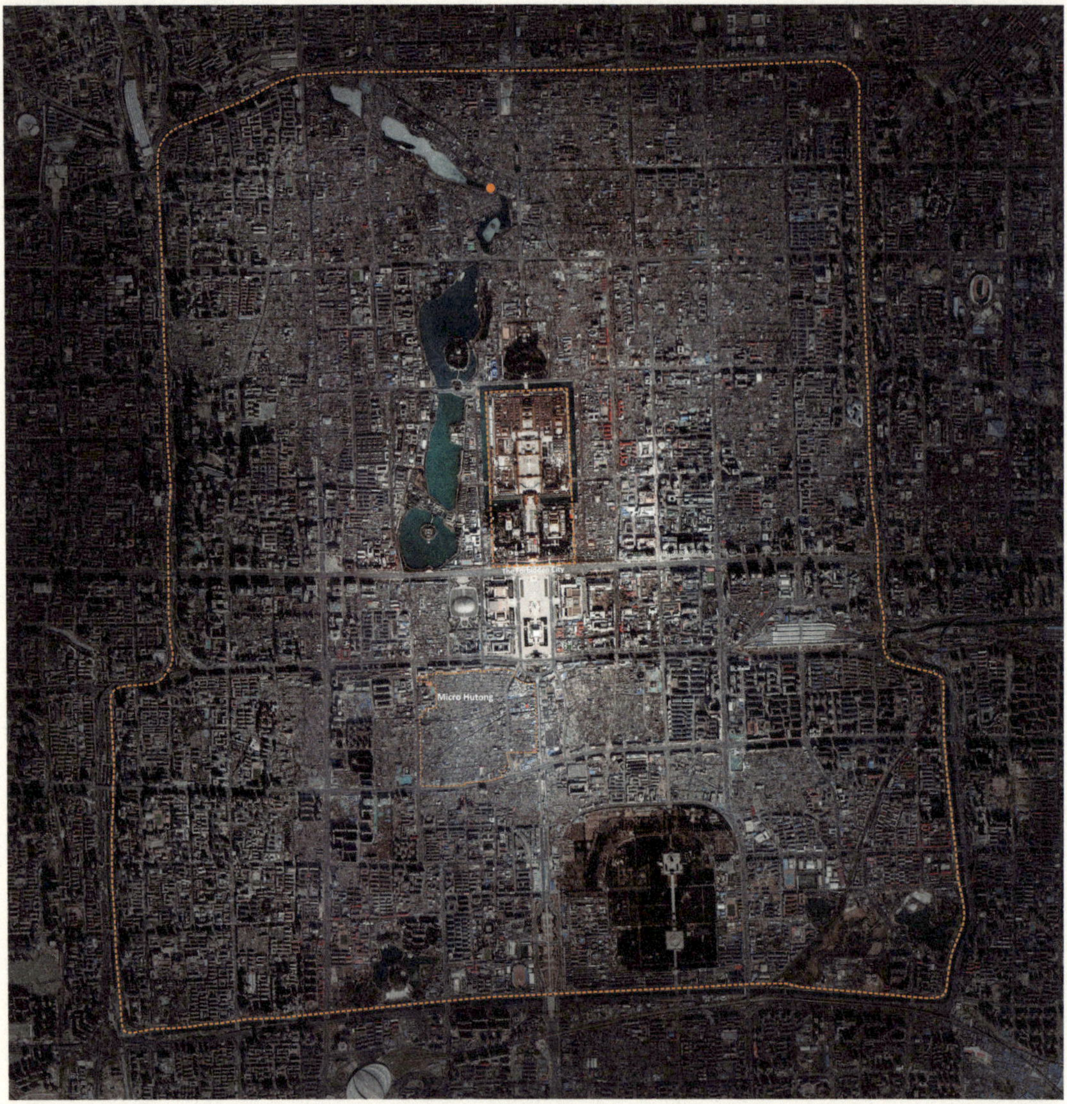

Micro Hutong

箁帚胡同　　Tiaozhou Hutong

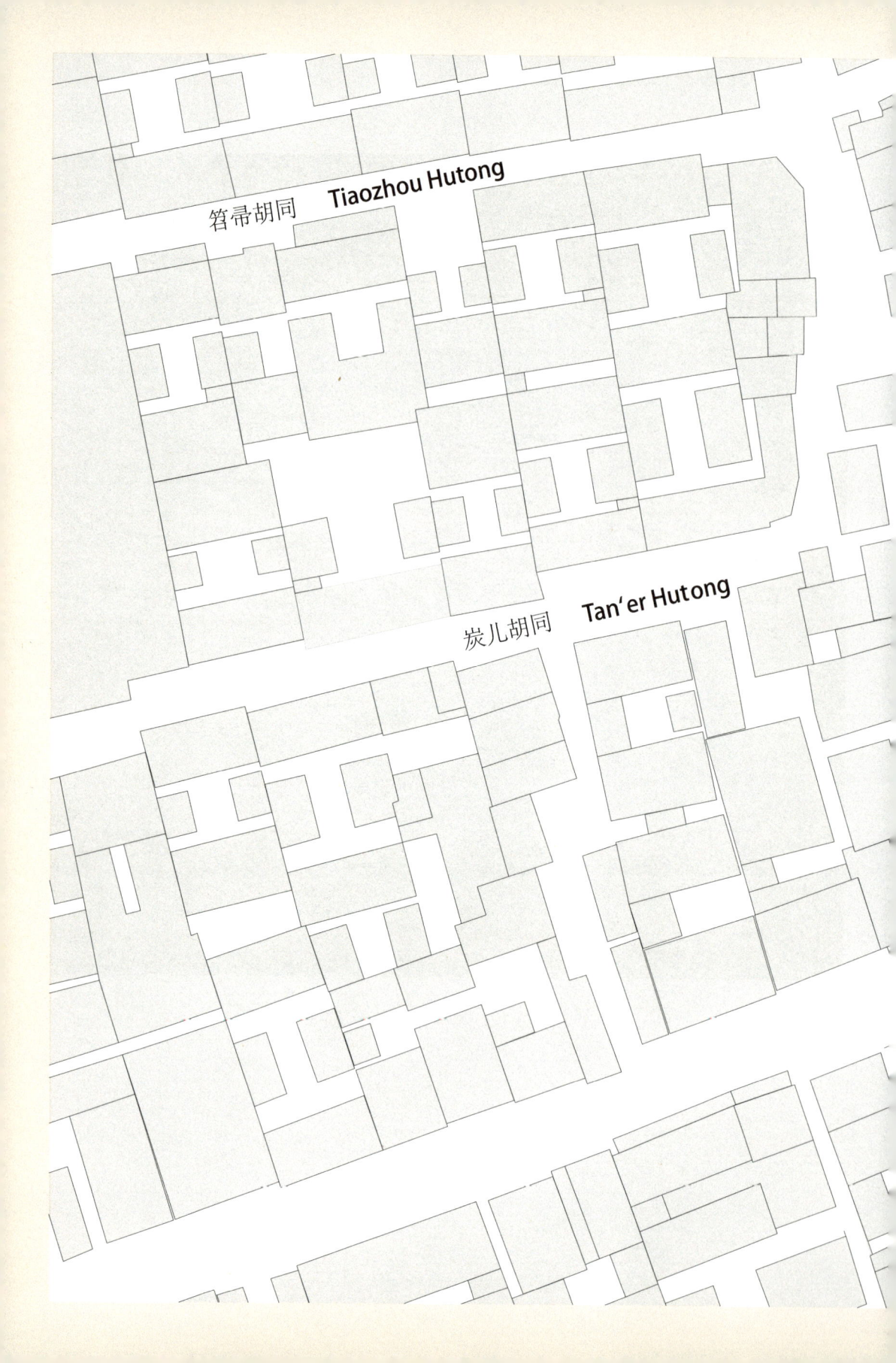

炭儿胡同　　Tan'er Hutong

杨梅竹斜街　**Yangmeizhu**

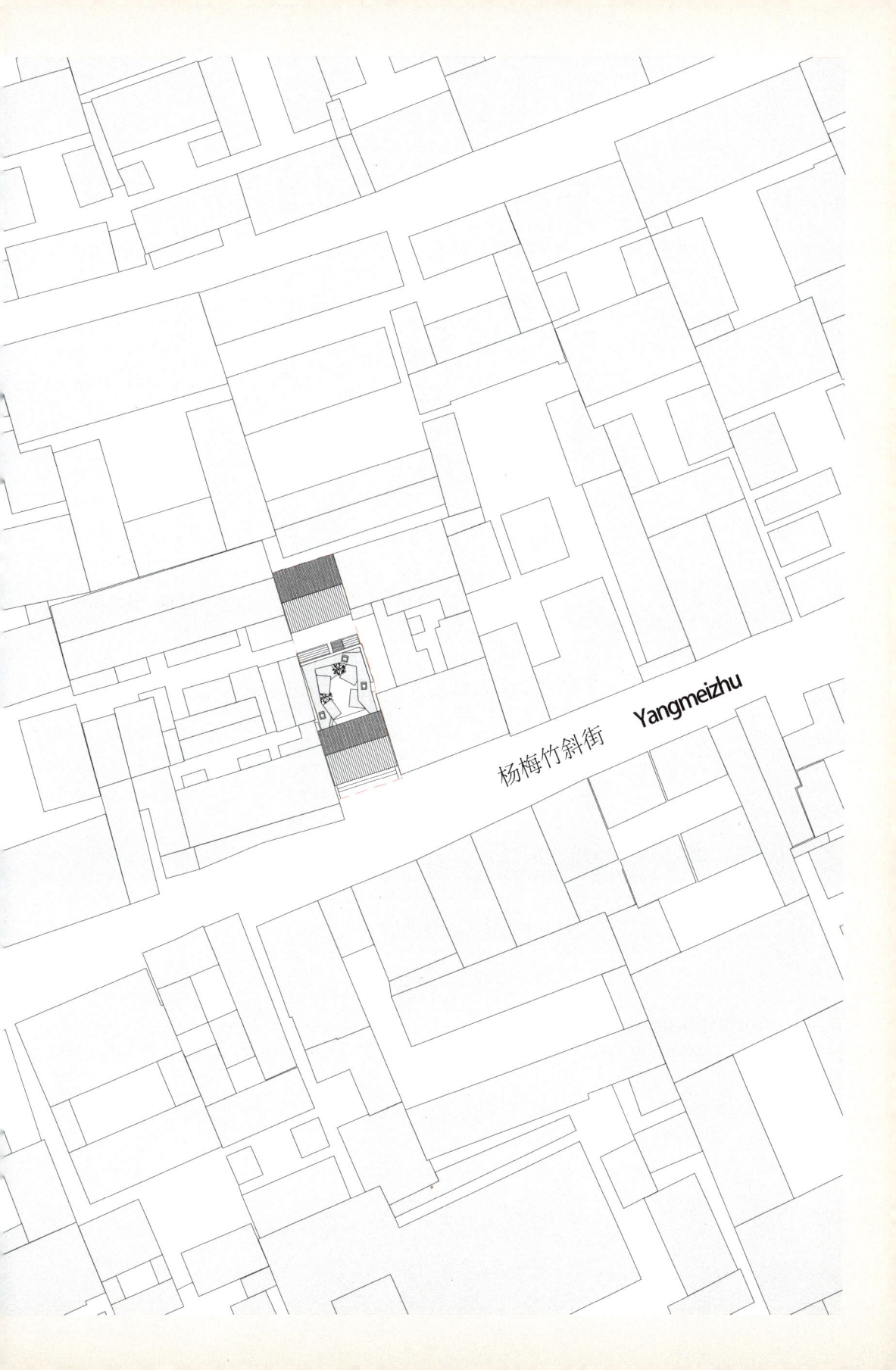

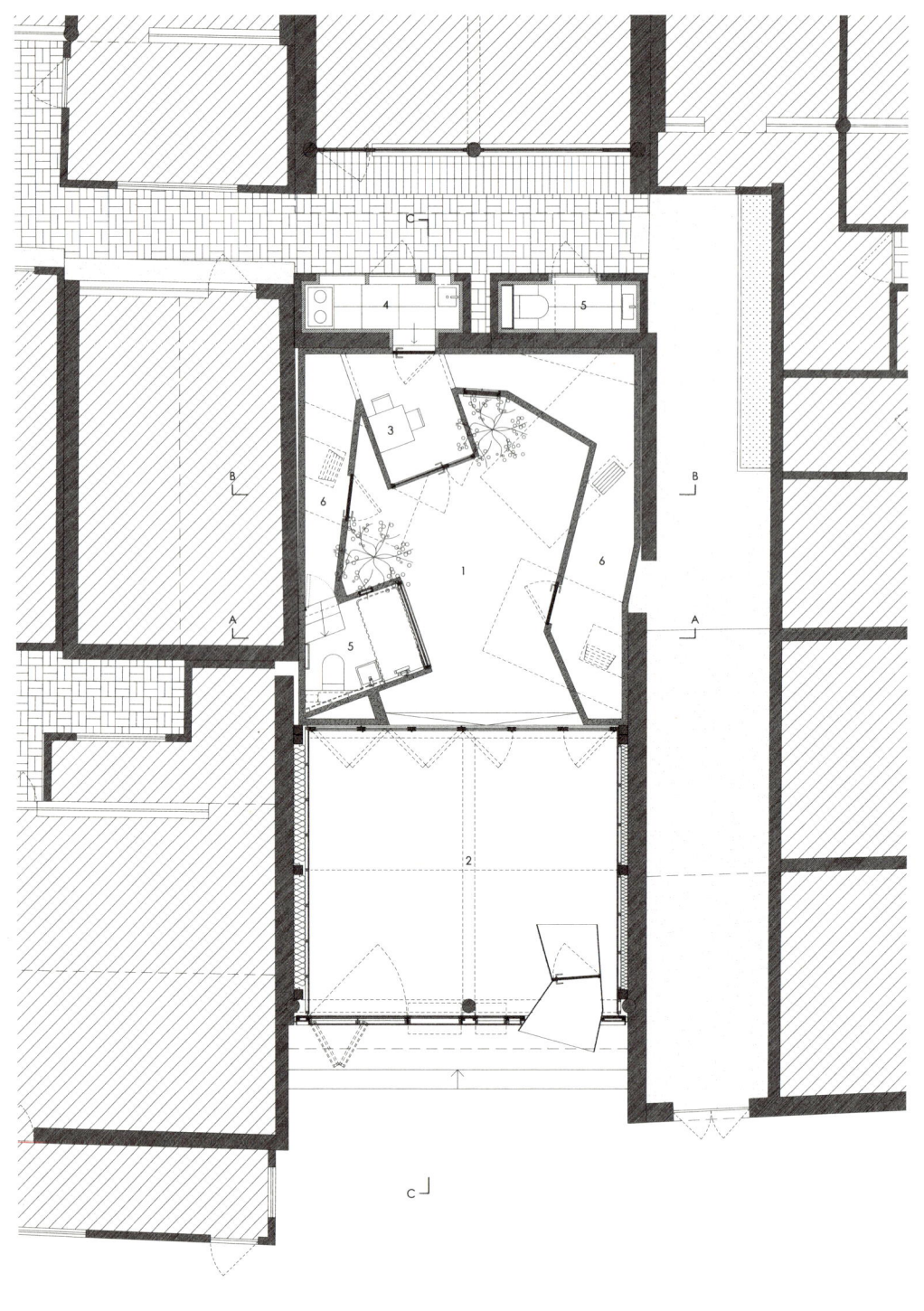

GROUND FLOOR PLAN
1. Courtyard 2. Exhibition room 3. Dining room 4. Kitchen 5. Toilet 6. Corridor

SECOND FLOOR PLAN
1. Courtyard 7. Bedroom 8. Study Room 9. Teahouse 10. Terrace

ROOF PLAN   0   1m

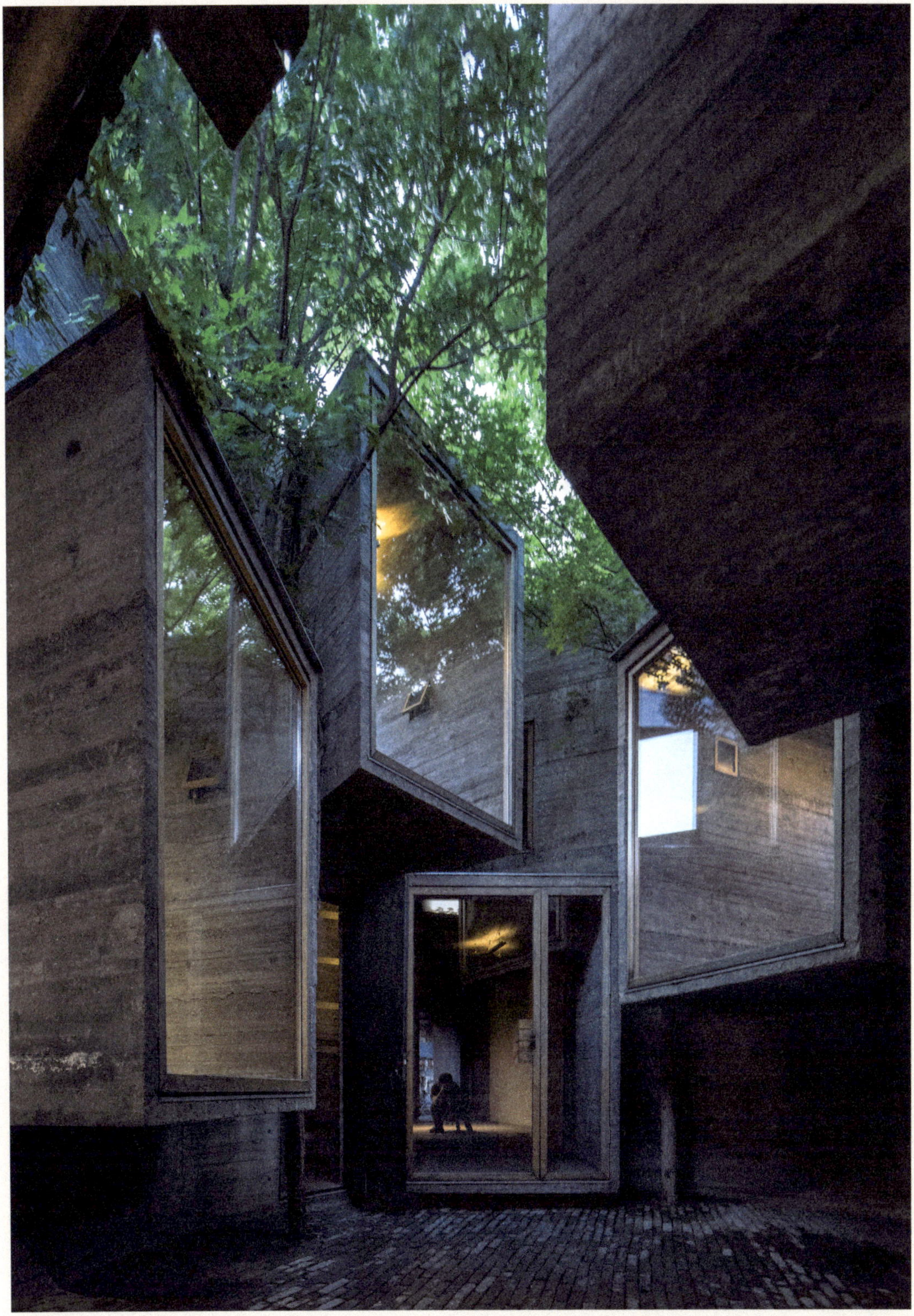

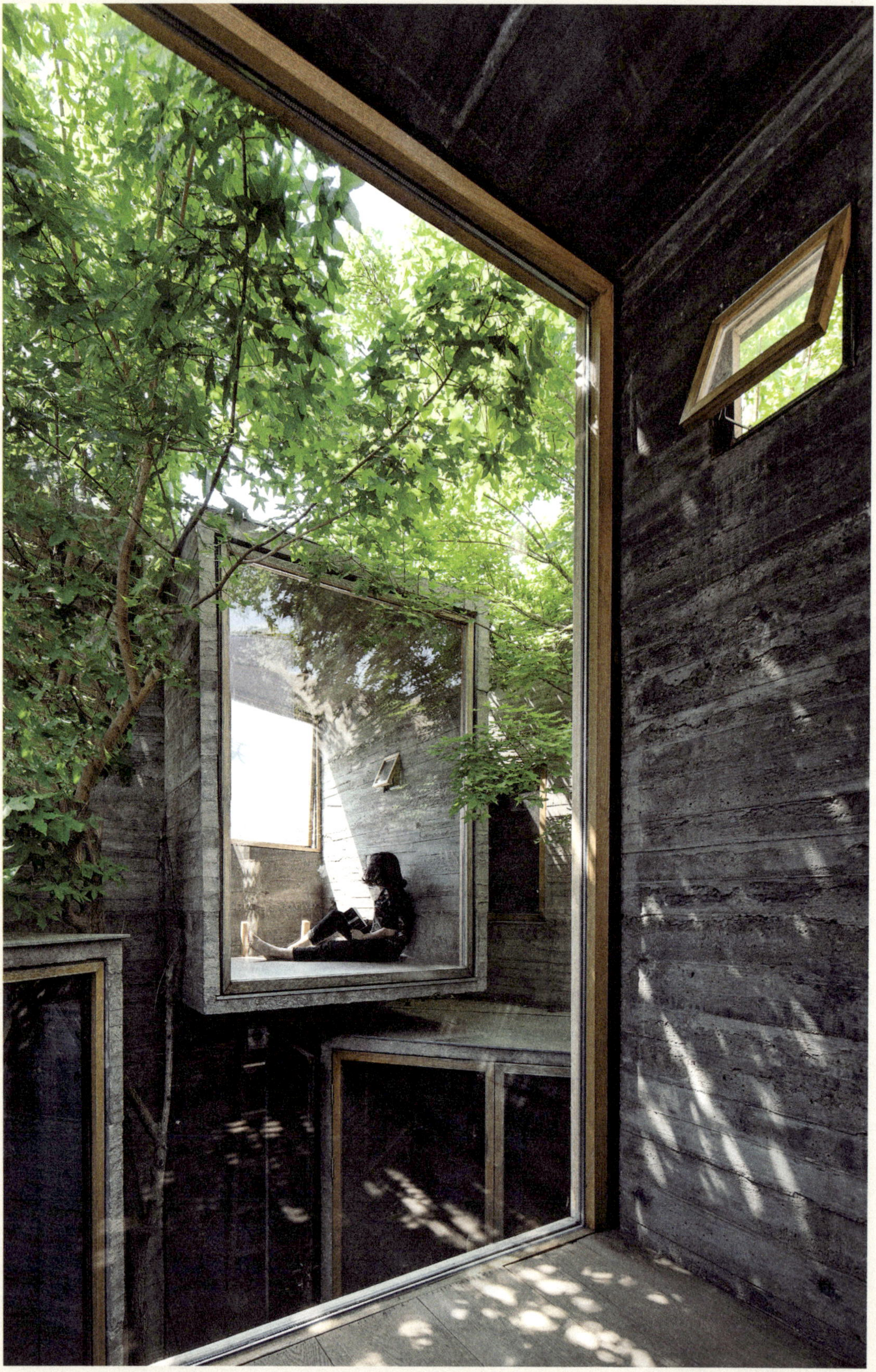

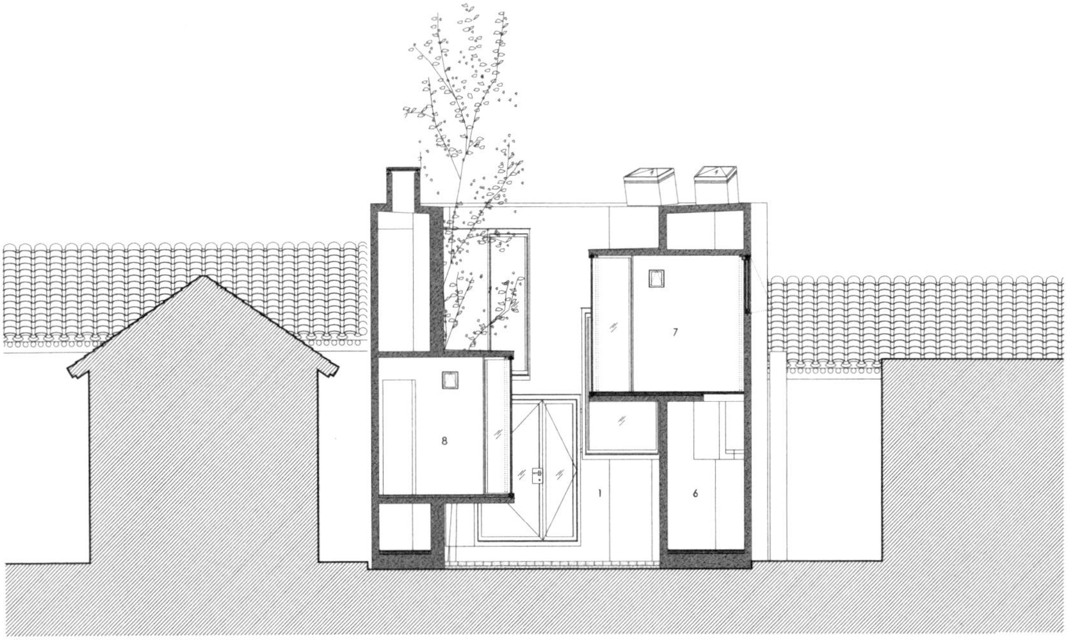

7
8
1
6

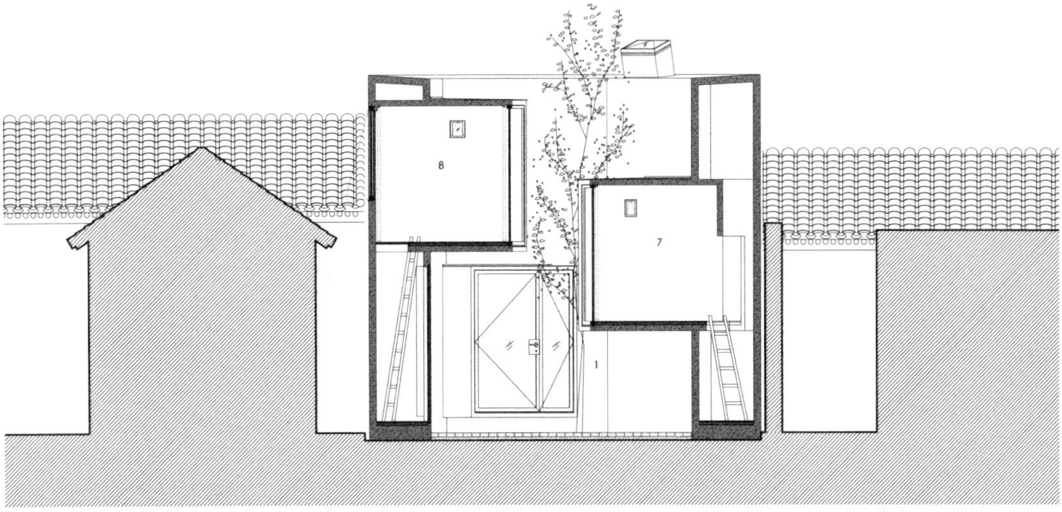

8
7
1

this segment to remove. walls and small buildings to stay.

window

shifting tiles wall inside

2013/09/10.
after demolition started on site, revisions have to be made because of new restrictions. the small kitchens are not removable because neighbores request them to stay. well, maybe this can generate even better result!

to make the new
grow out of the
old. to have a surprising
at the same time humble
co-existance in the hutong
to open-up new passage ways
to make the old-hutong + DaZaYan
大杂院 a bit more public.

"We-hutong"
30m², 5 rooms
aned a courtyard!
+ steel
wood structure

2013/09/09

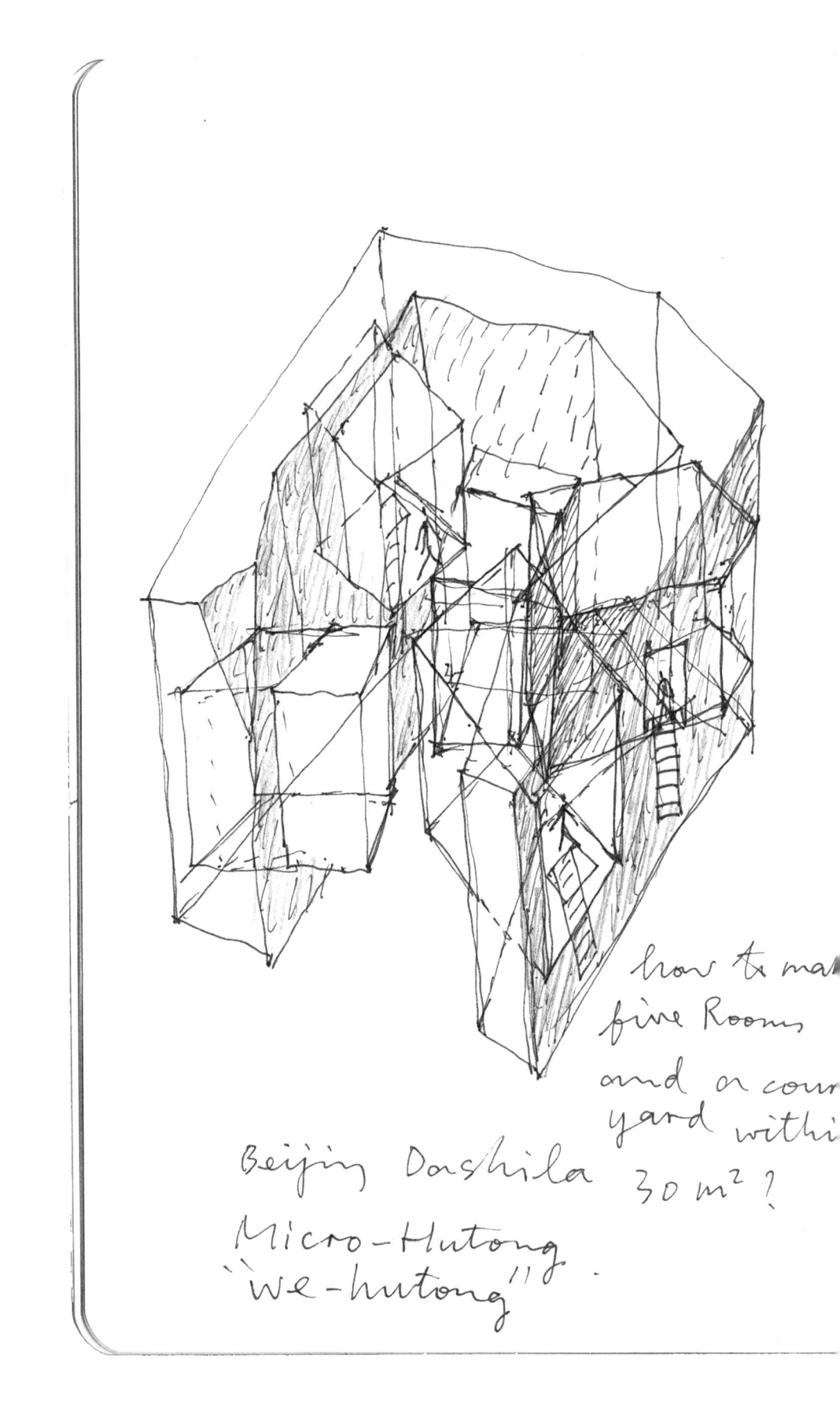

how to ma[ke]
five Rooms
and a cour[t]
yard withi[n]
Beijing Dashila 30 m²?
Micro-Hutong
"We-hutong"

inward space. To design the void vs. to design the mass. the void inward space as the substance of making Architecture

陰陽

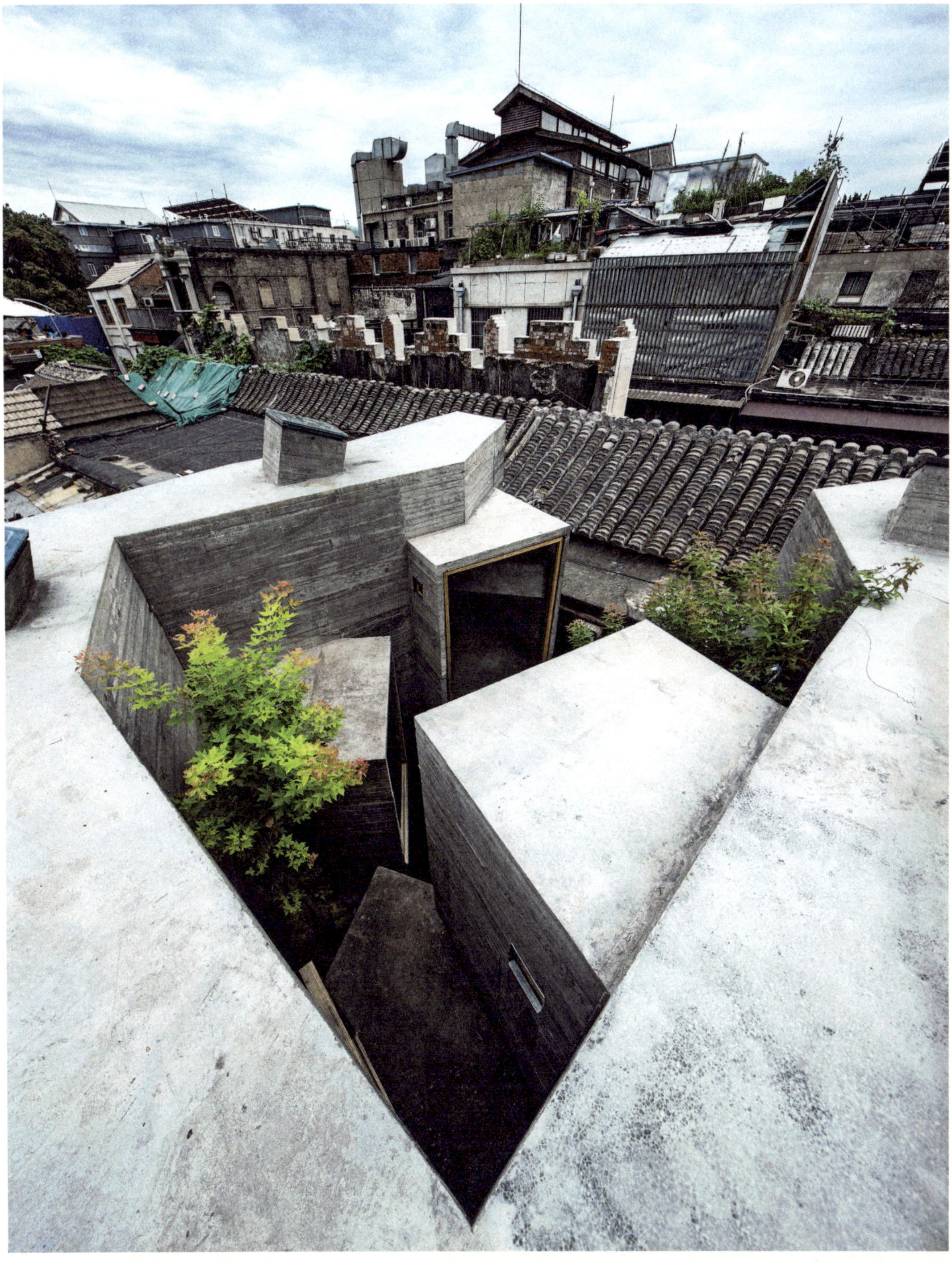

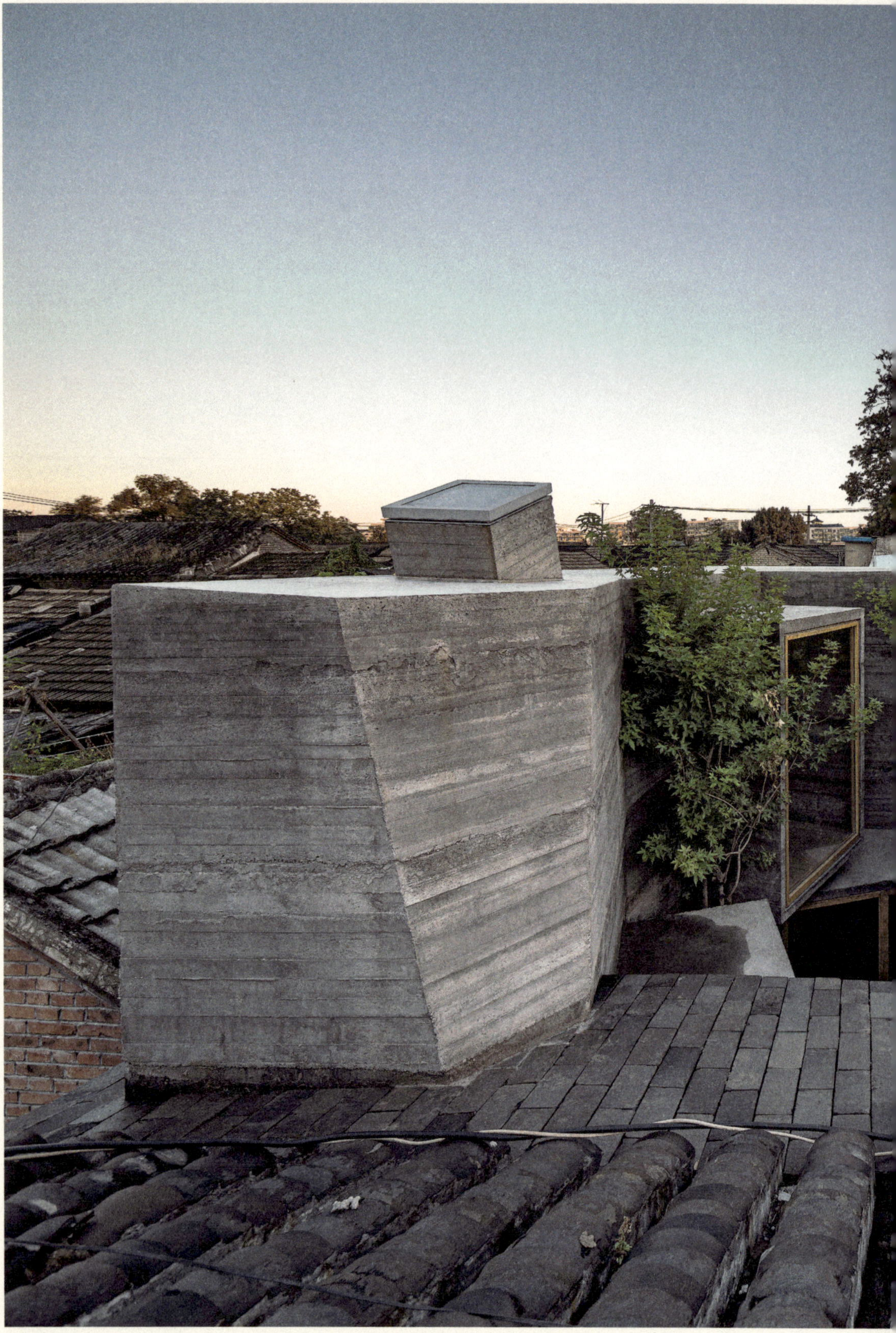

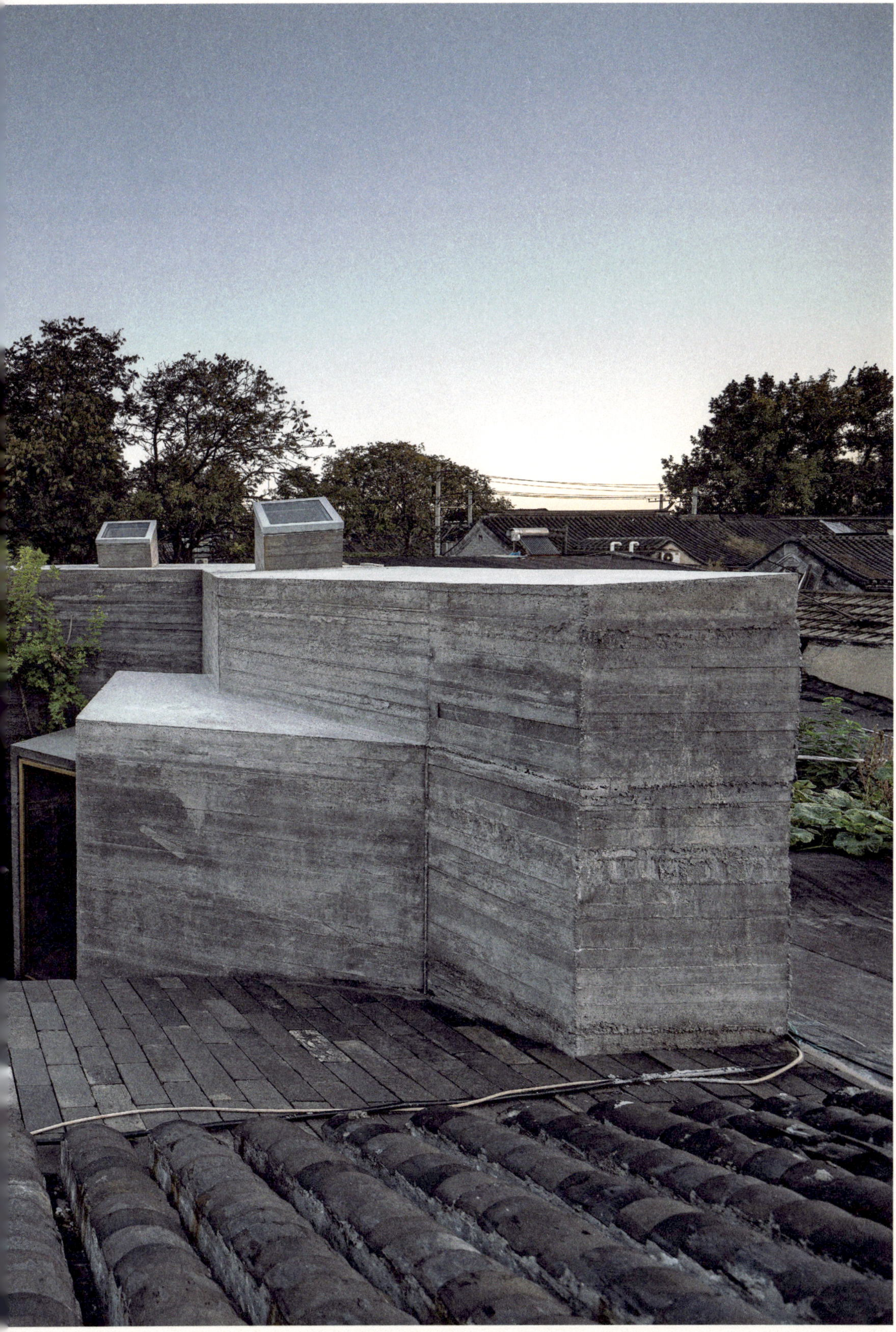

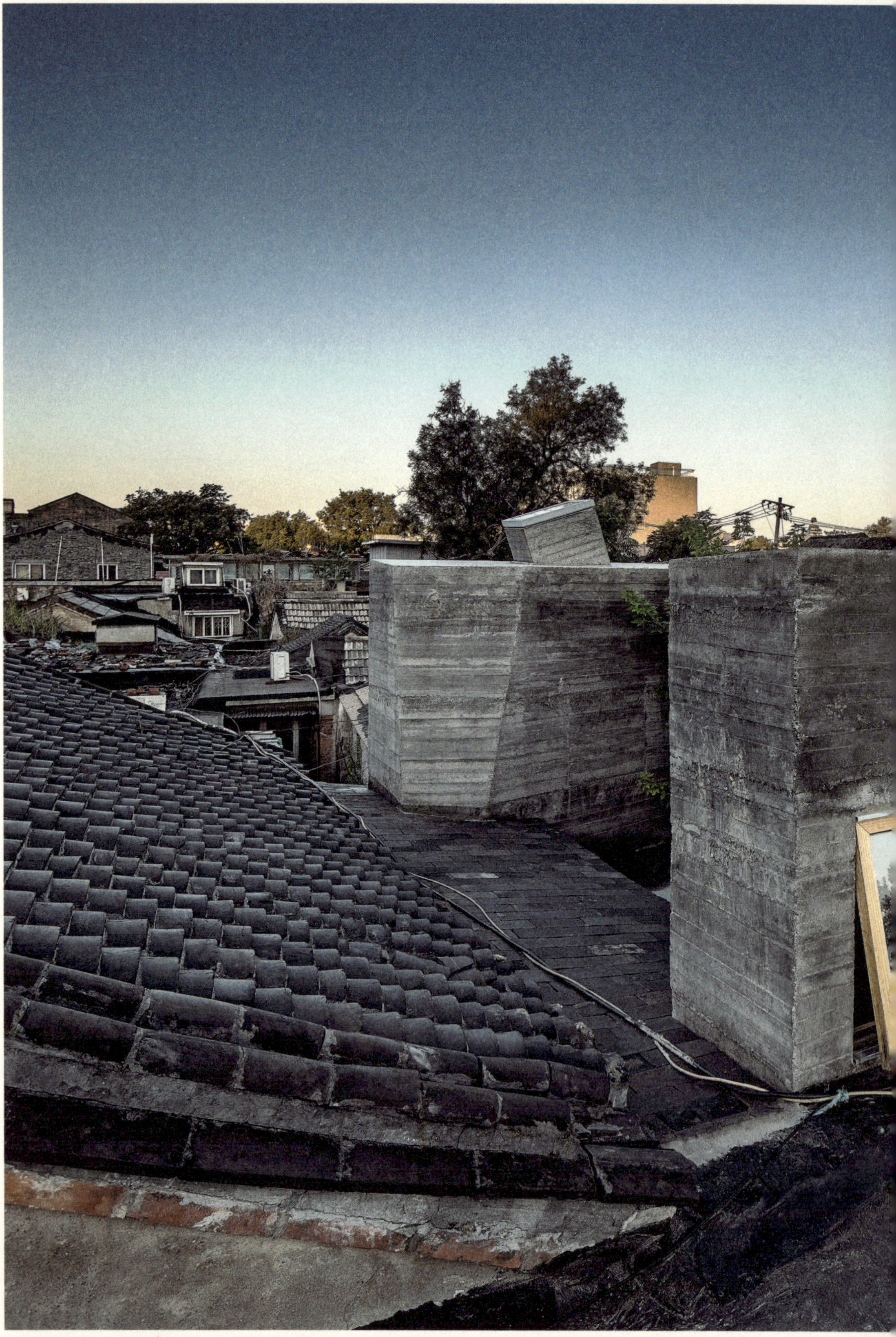

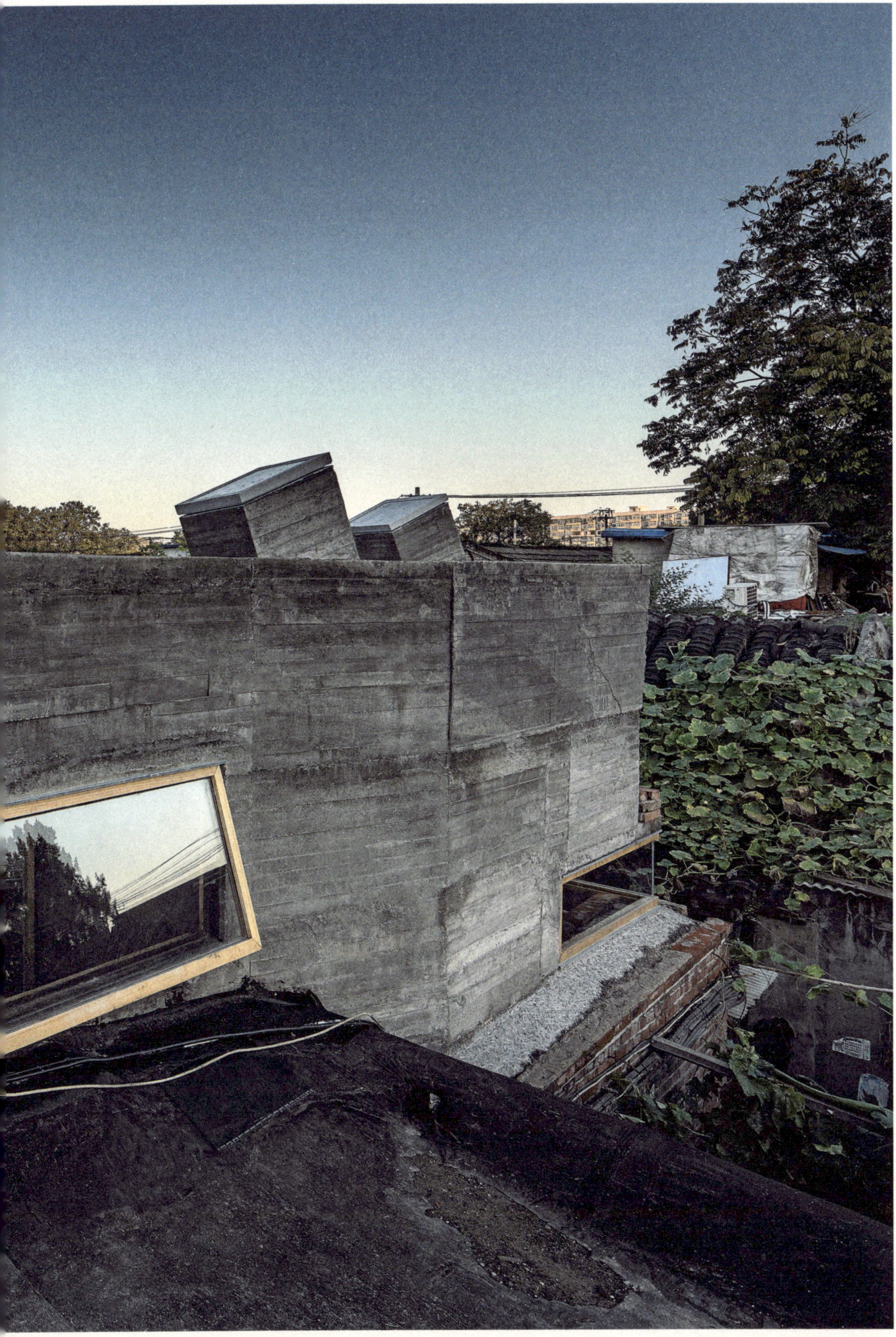

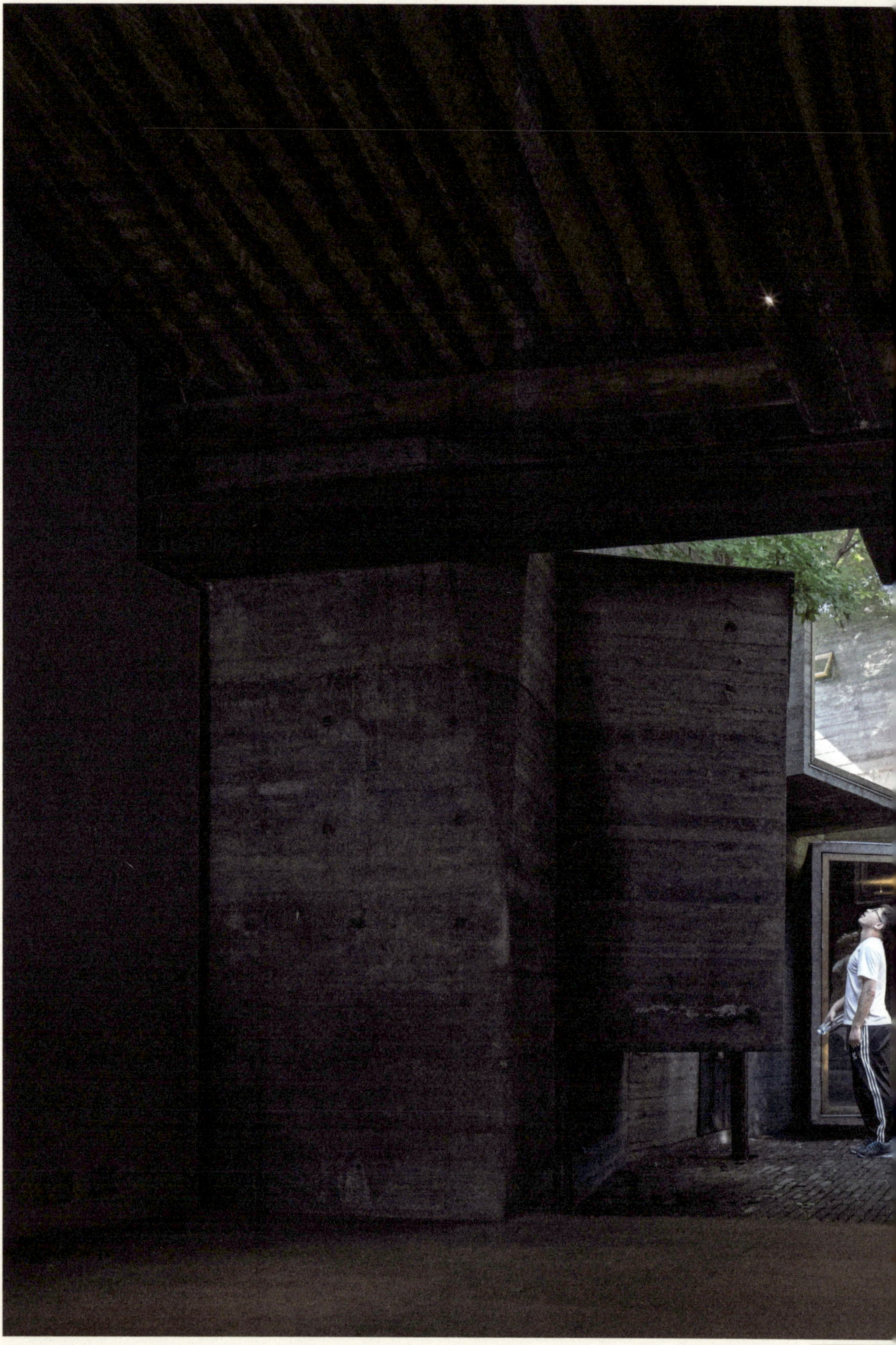

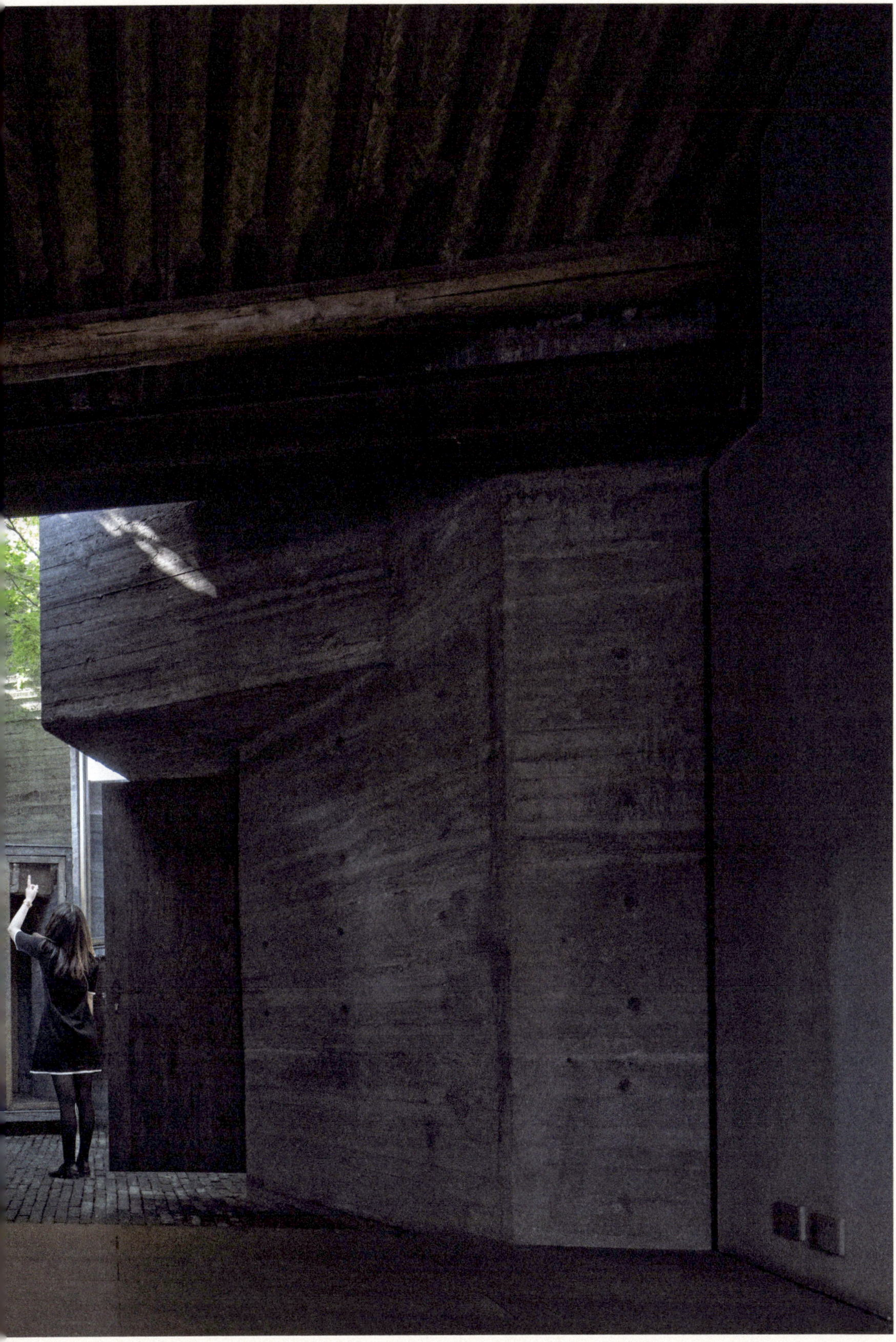

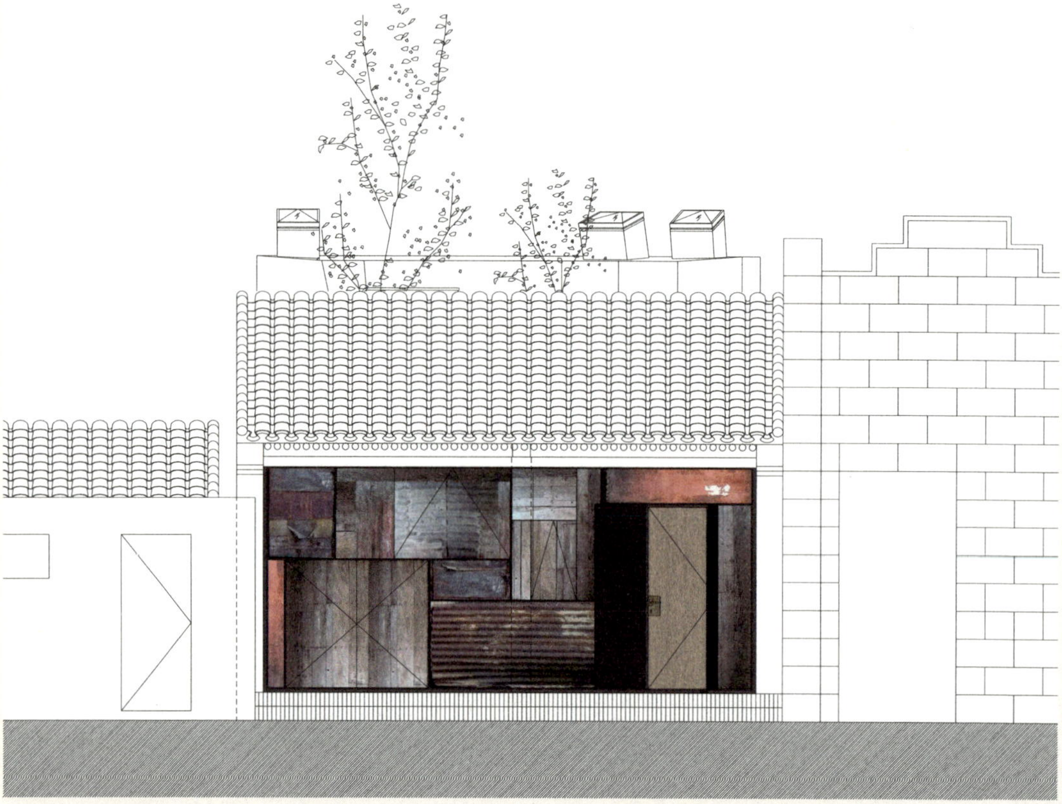

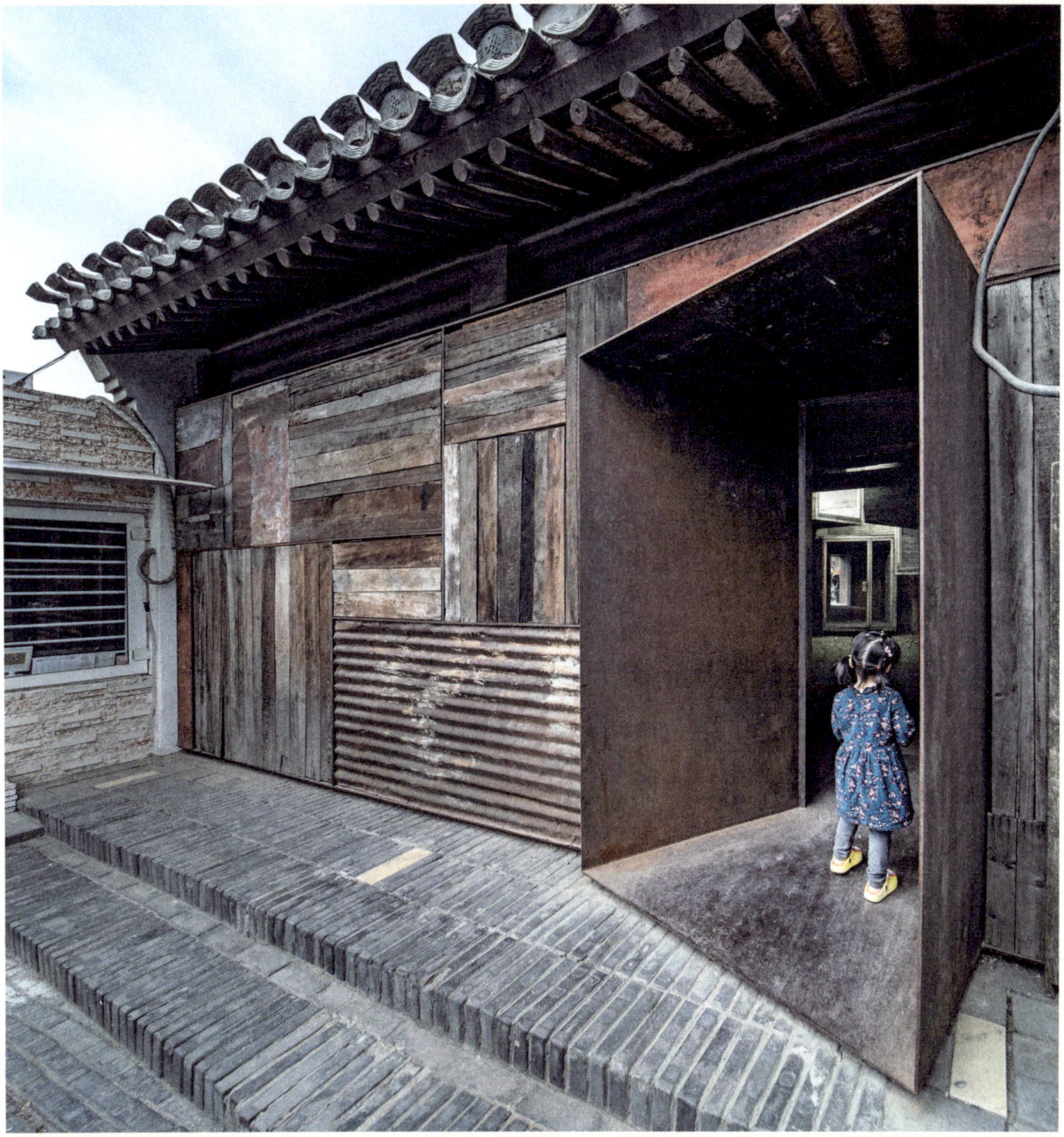

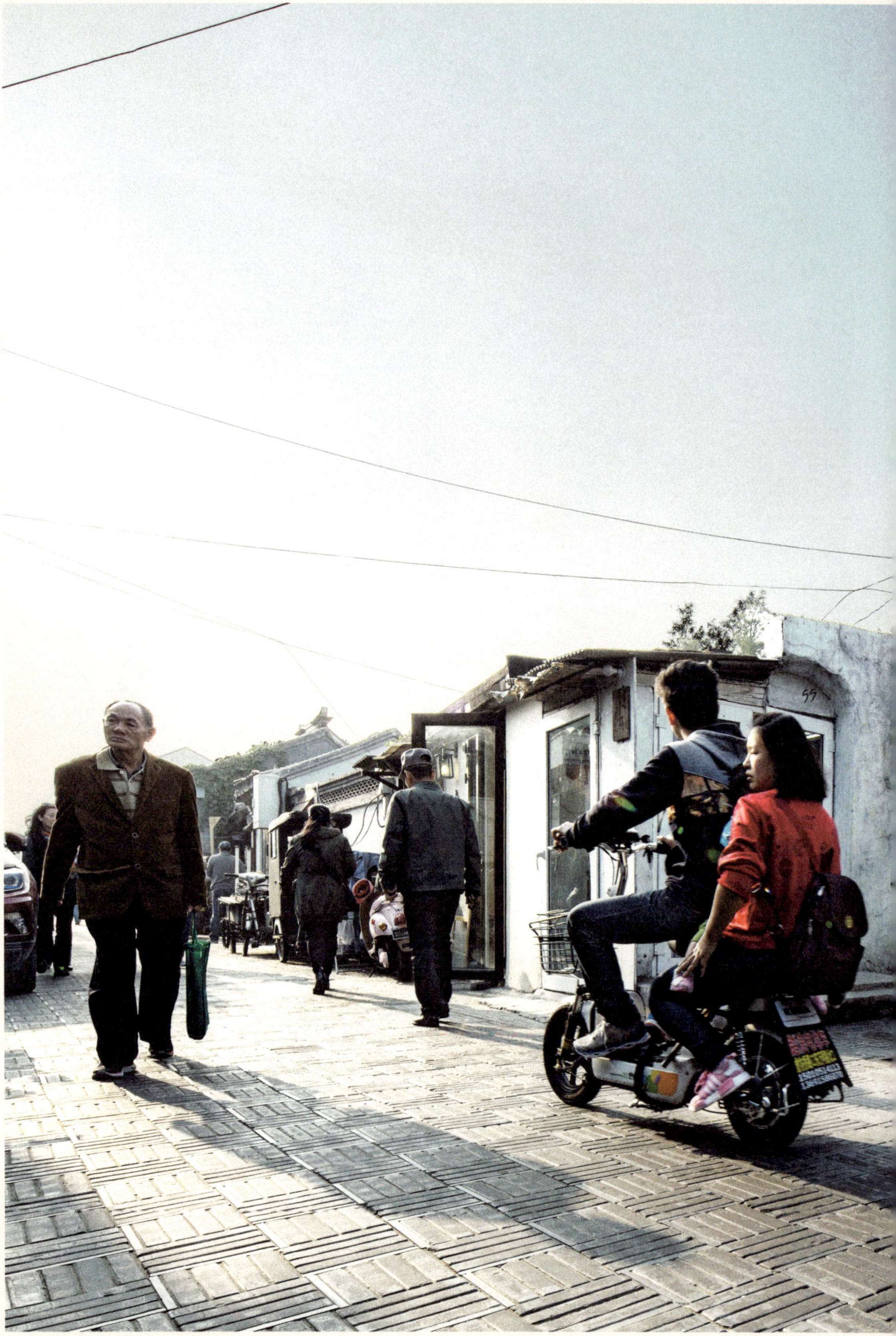

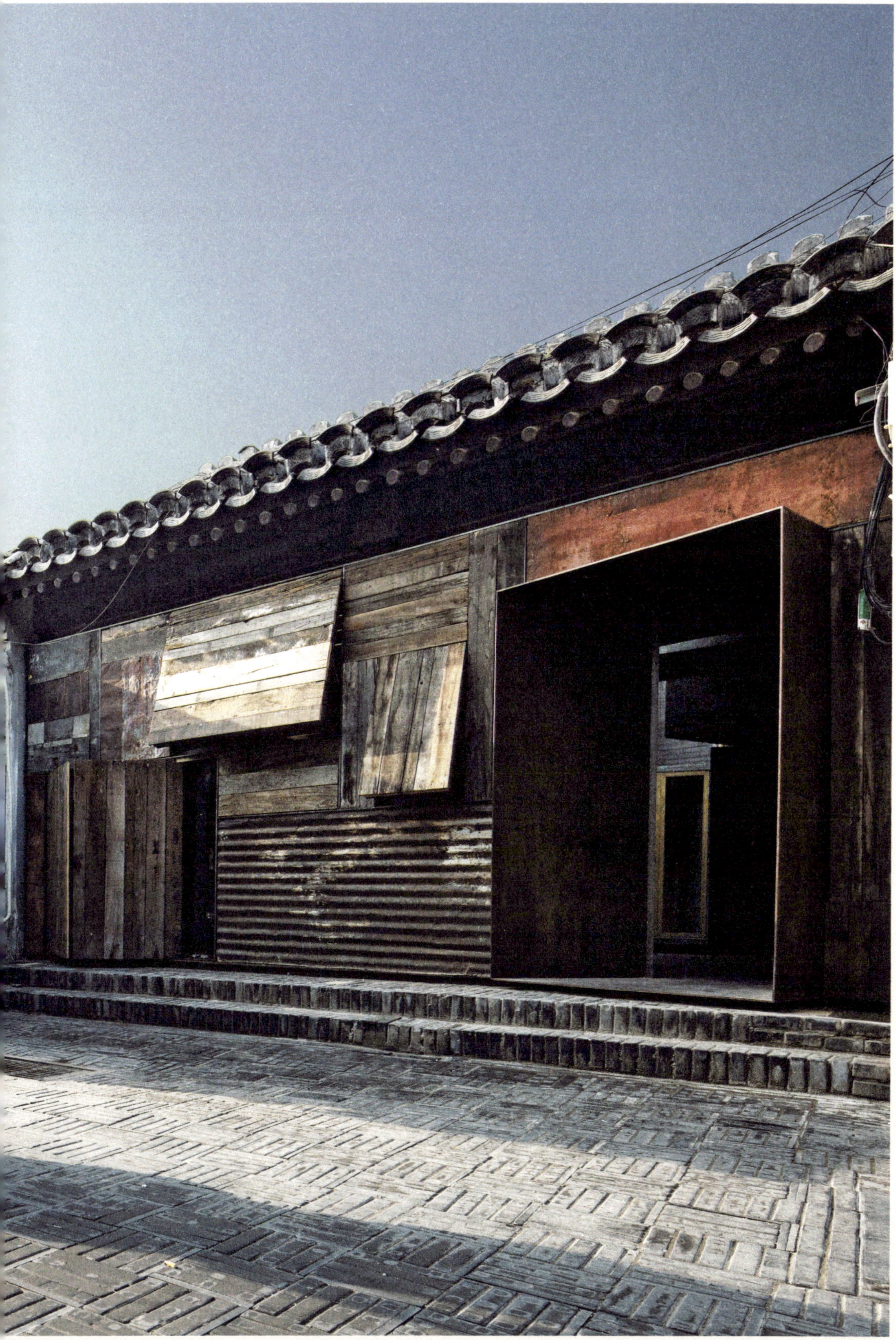

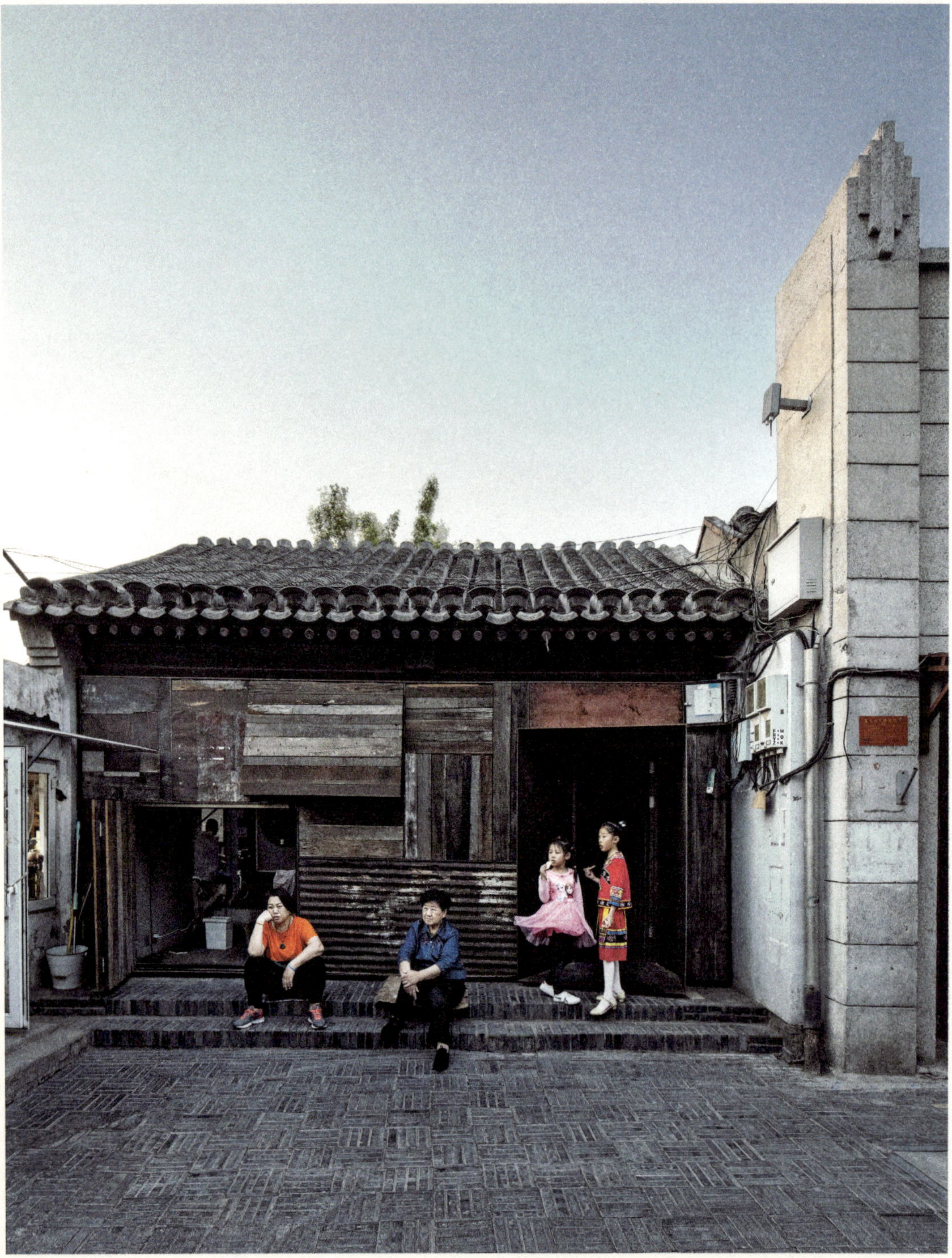

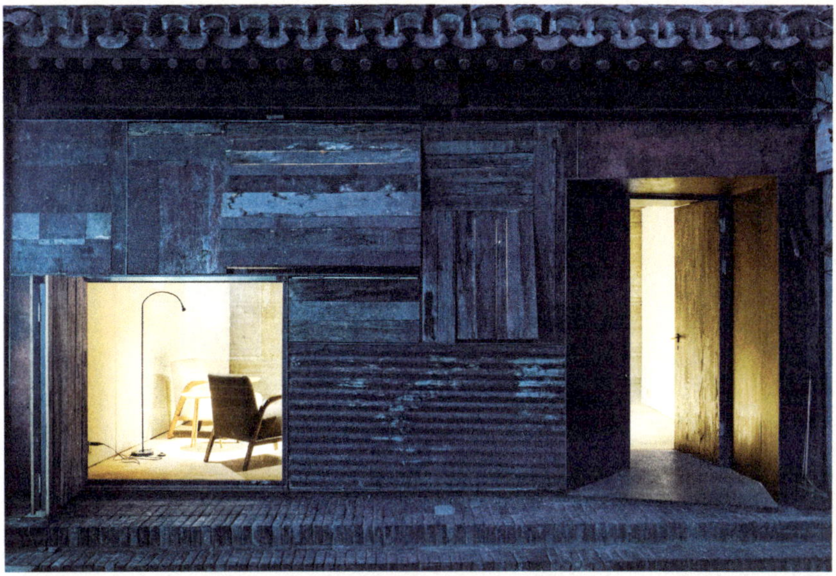

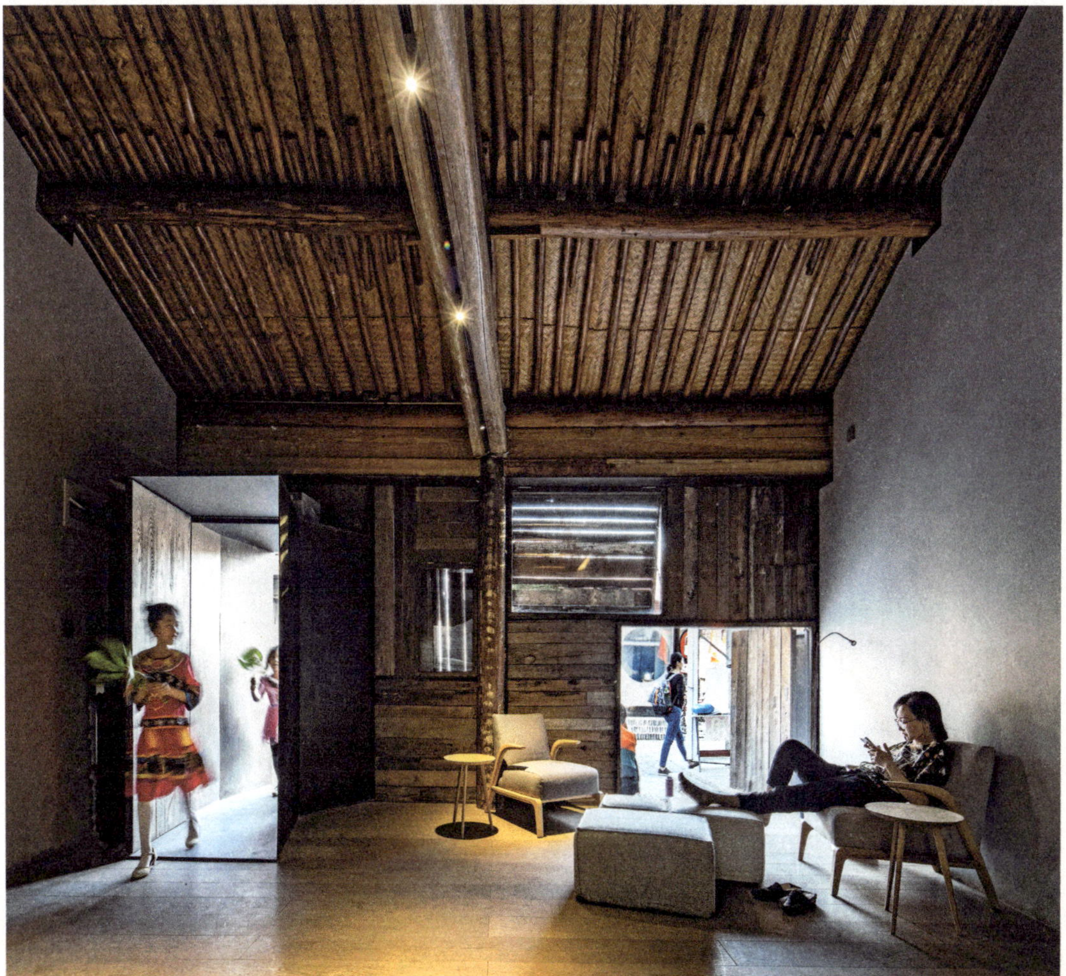

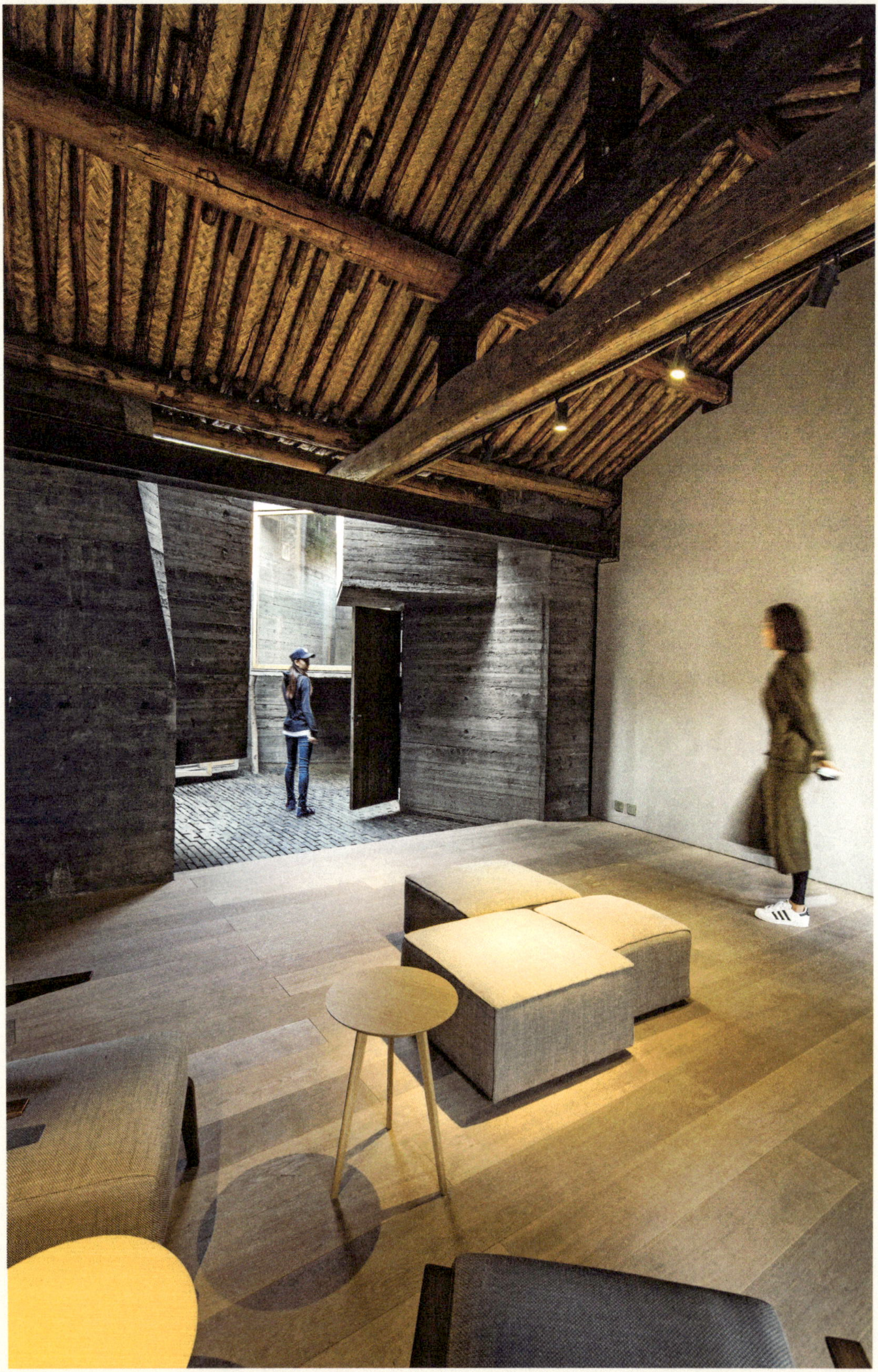

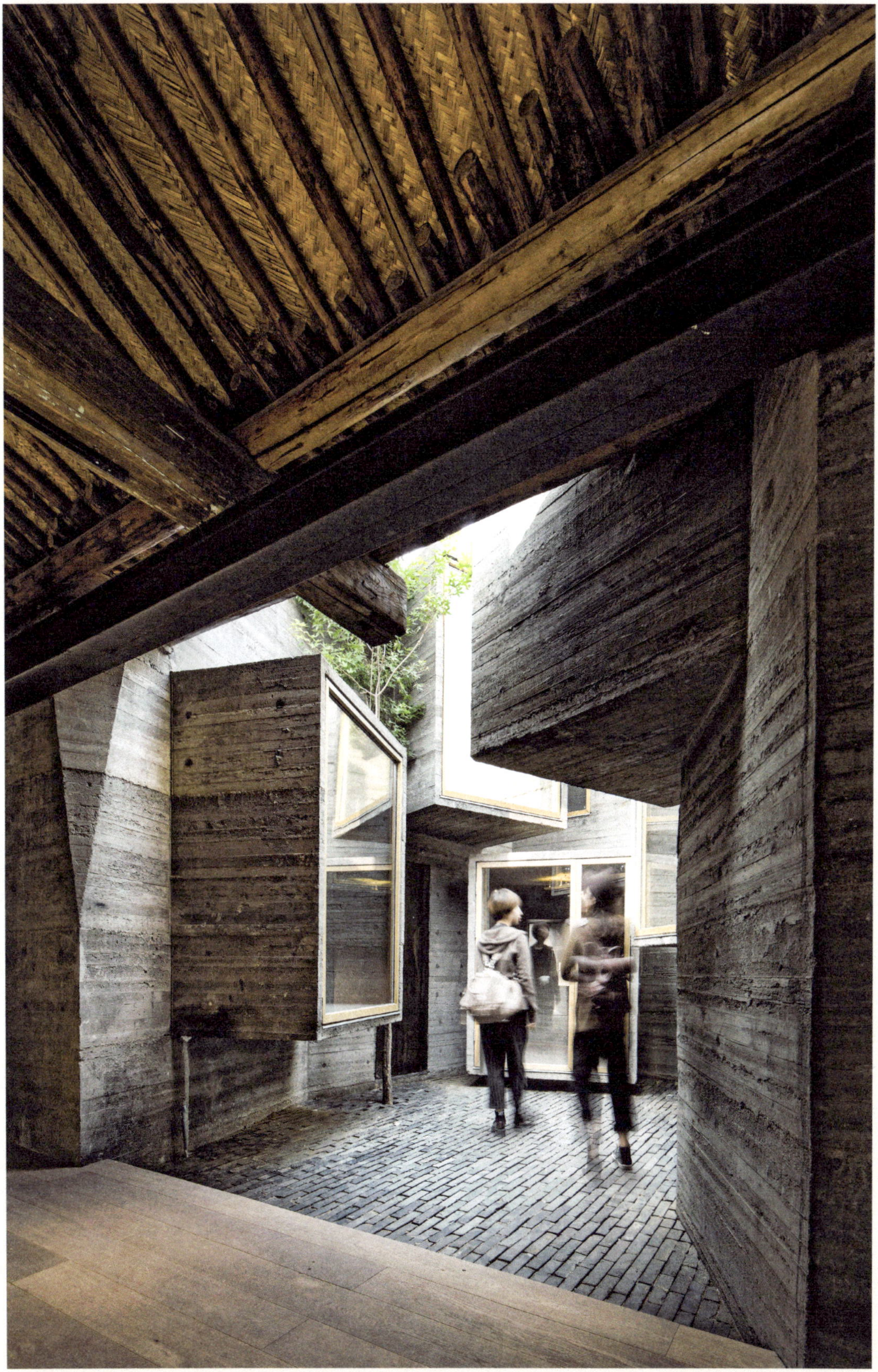

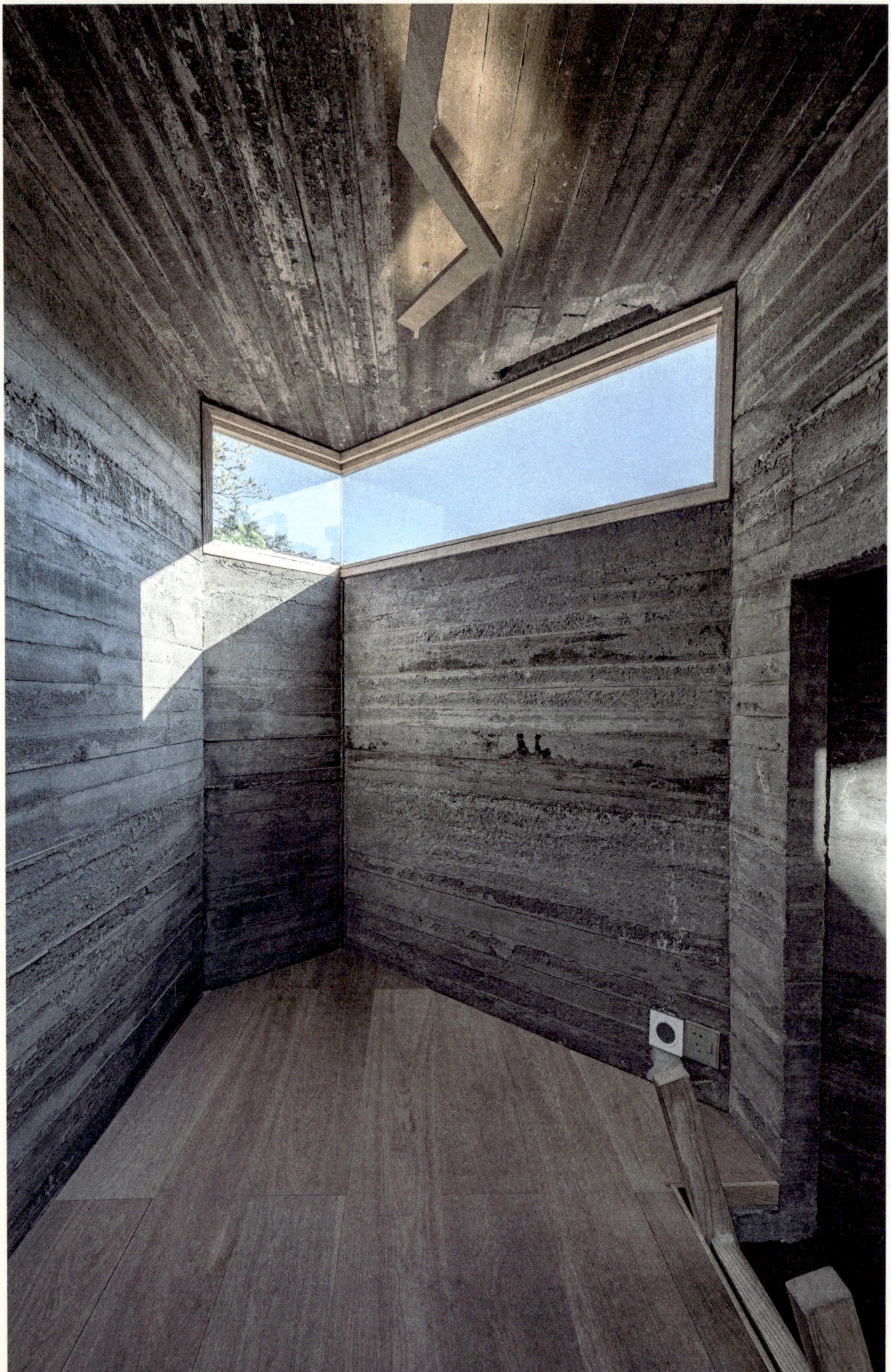

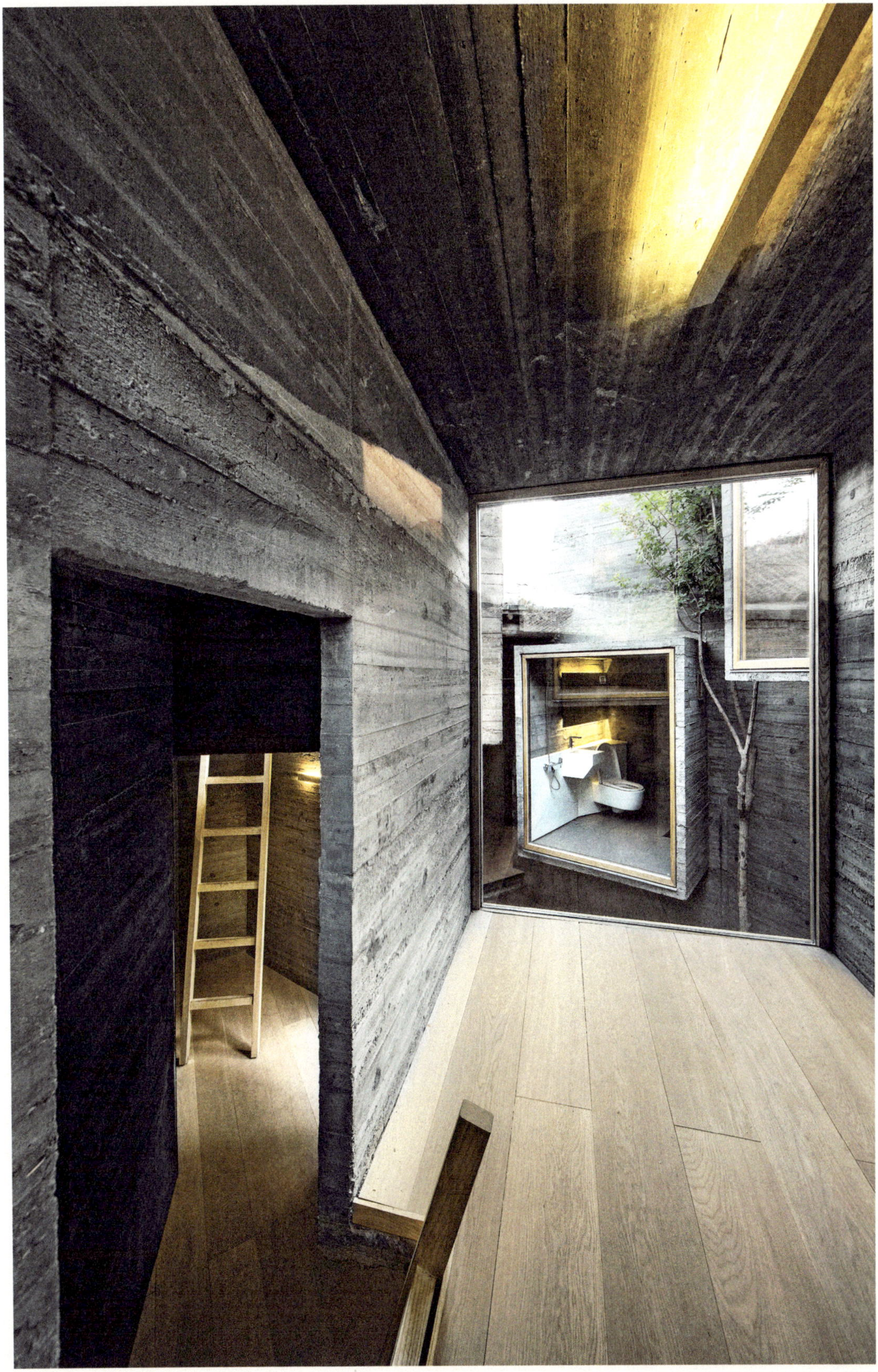

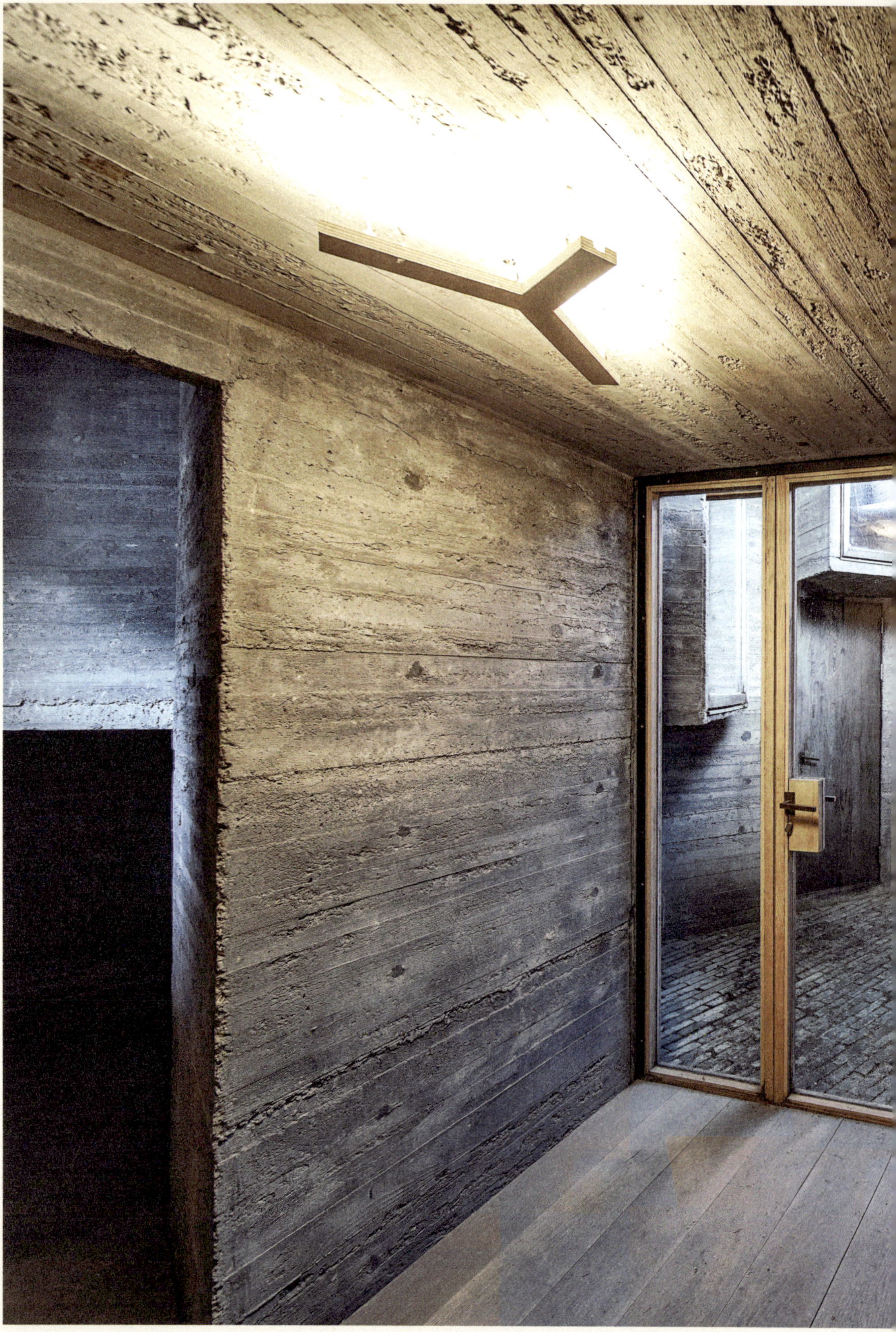

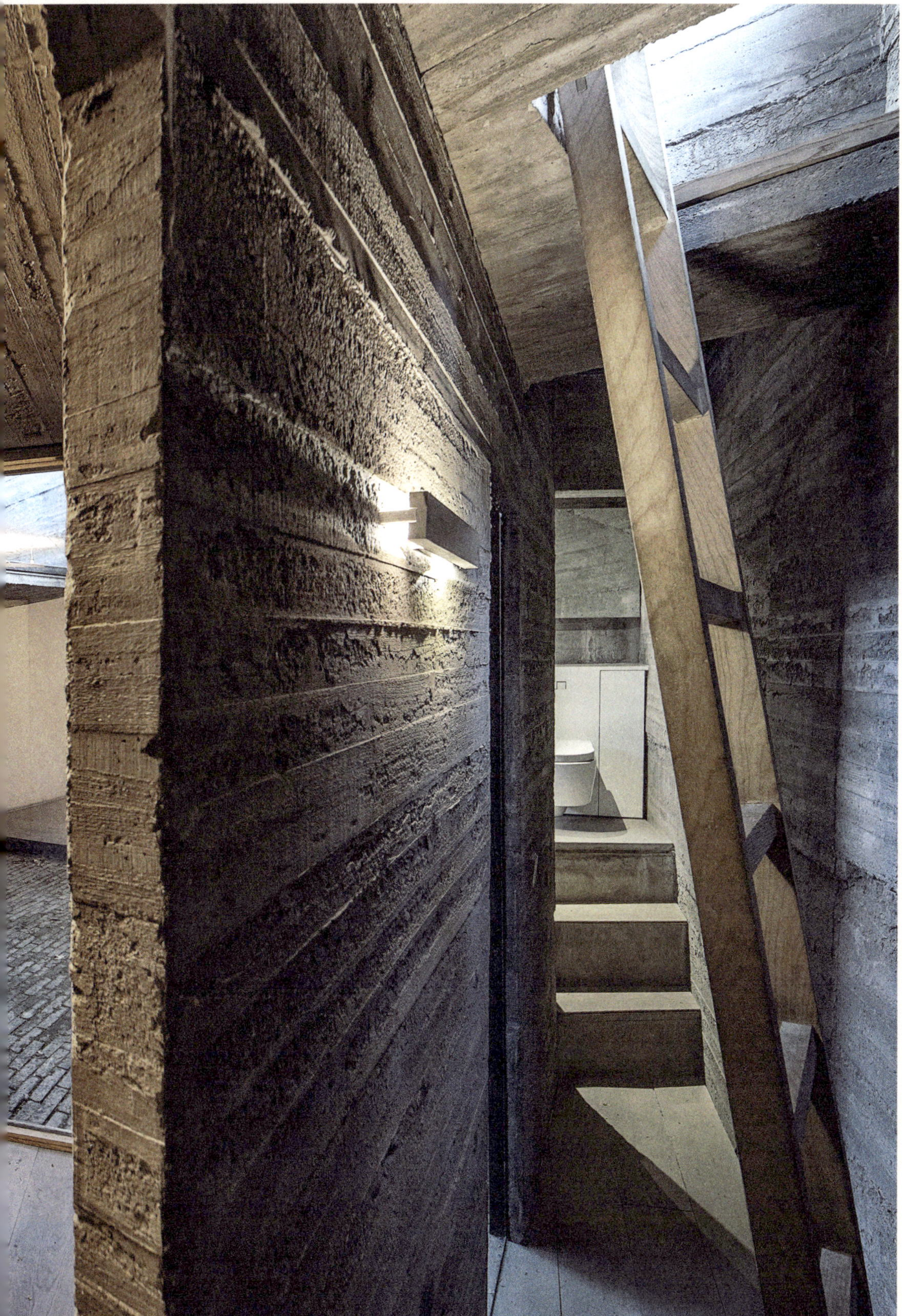

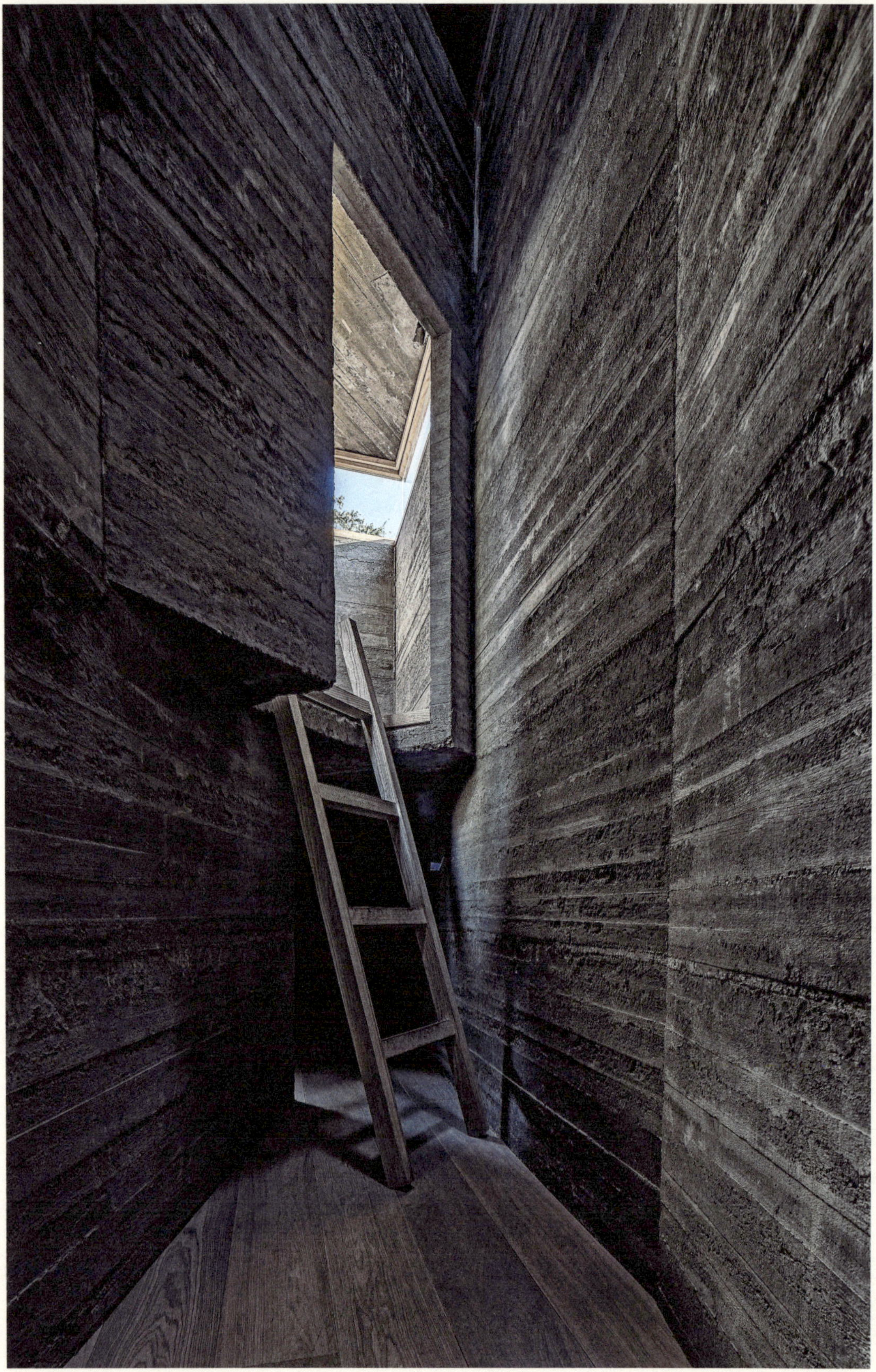

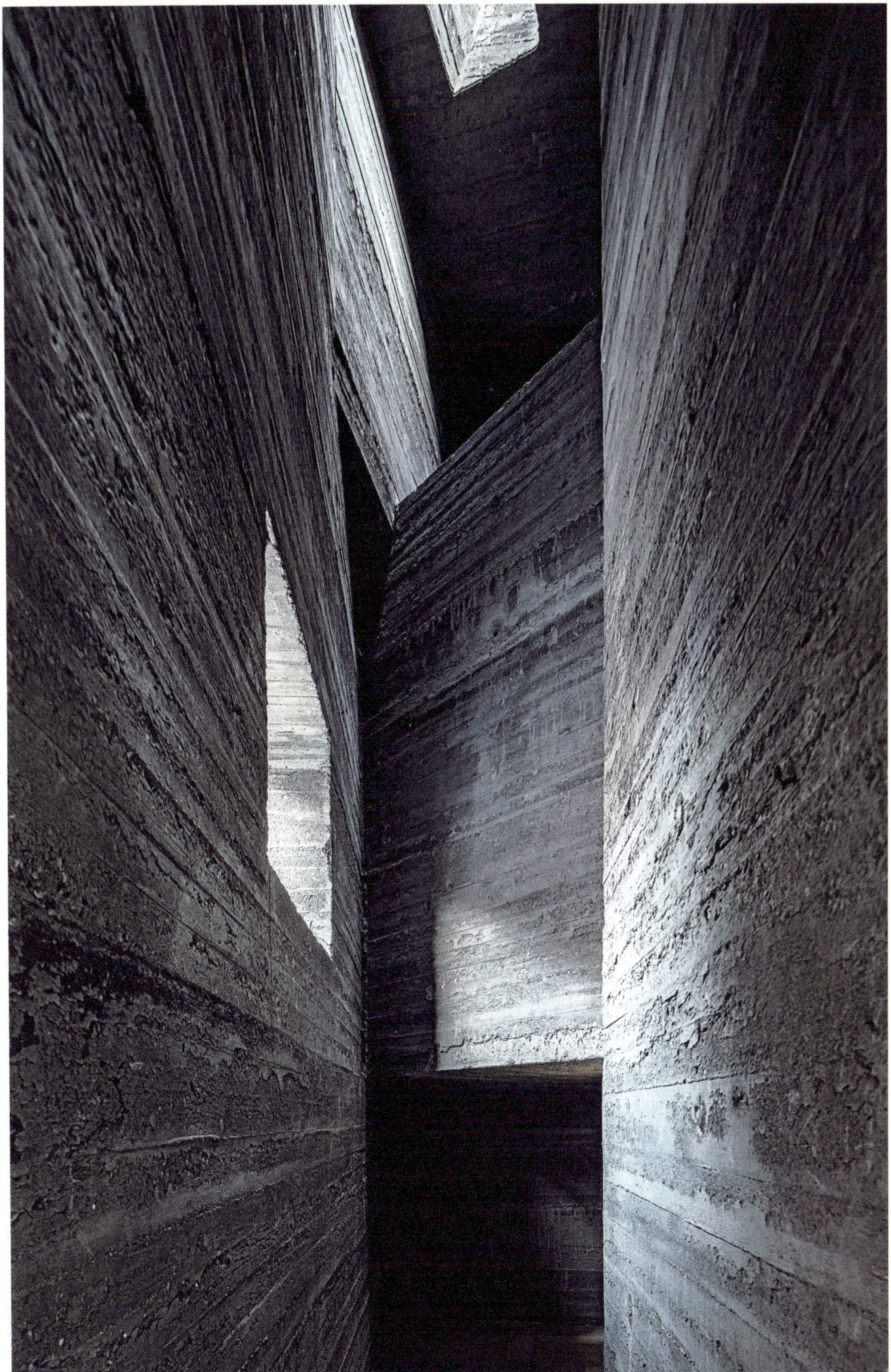

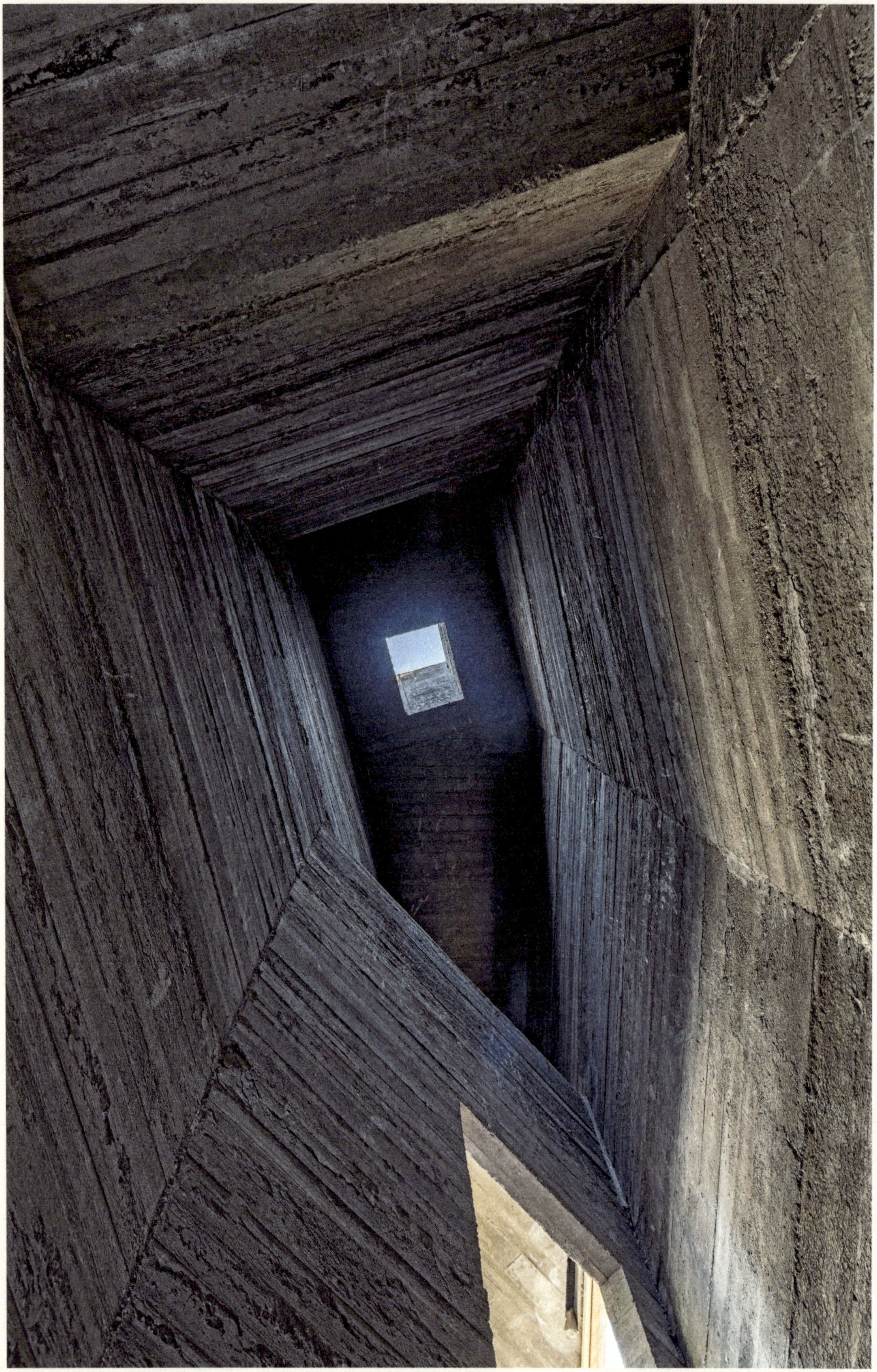

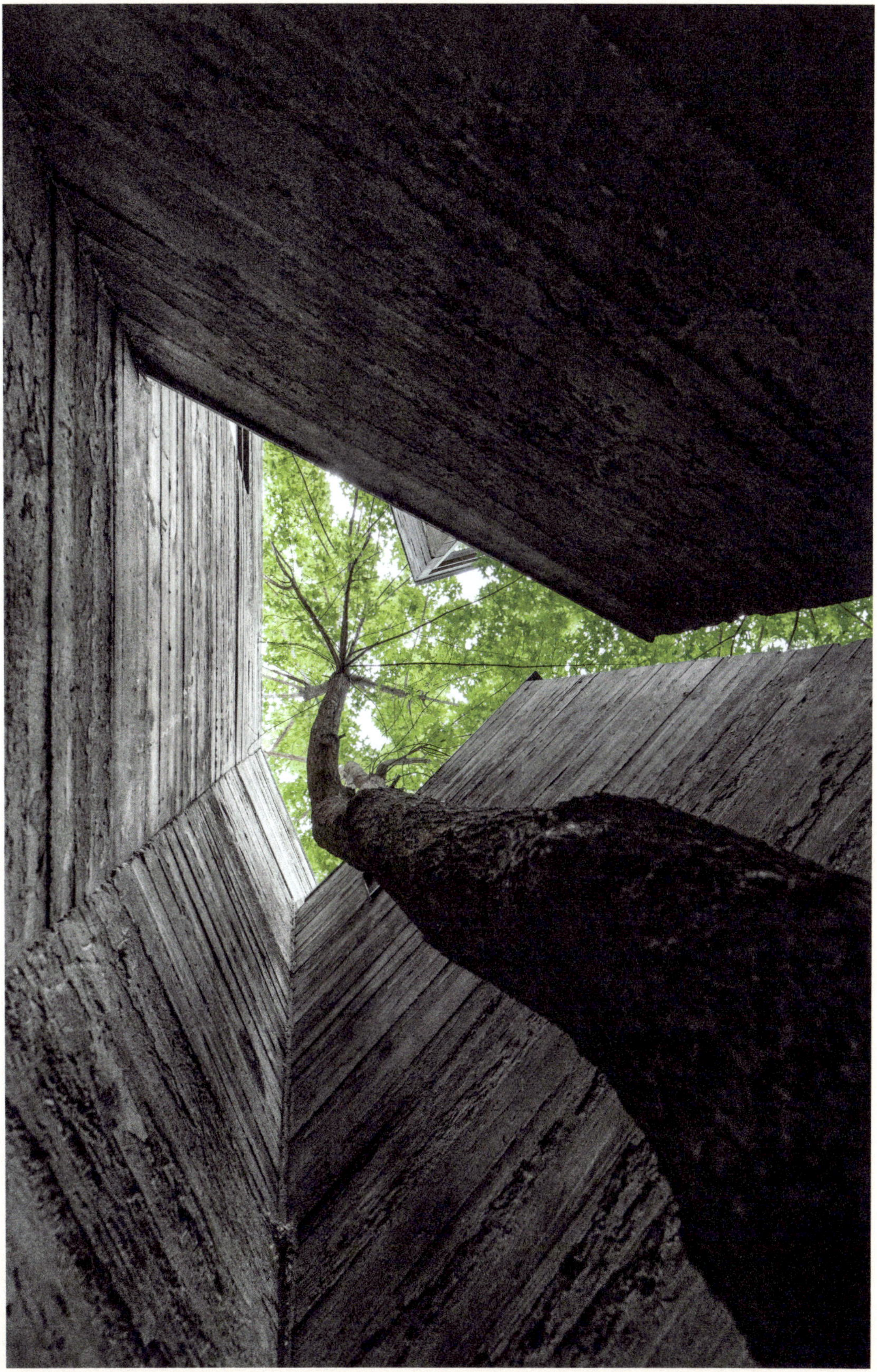

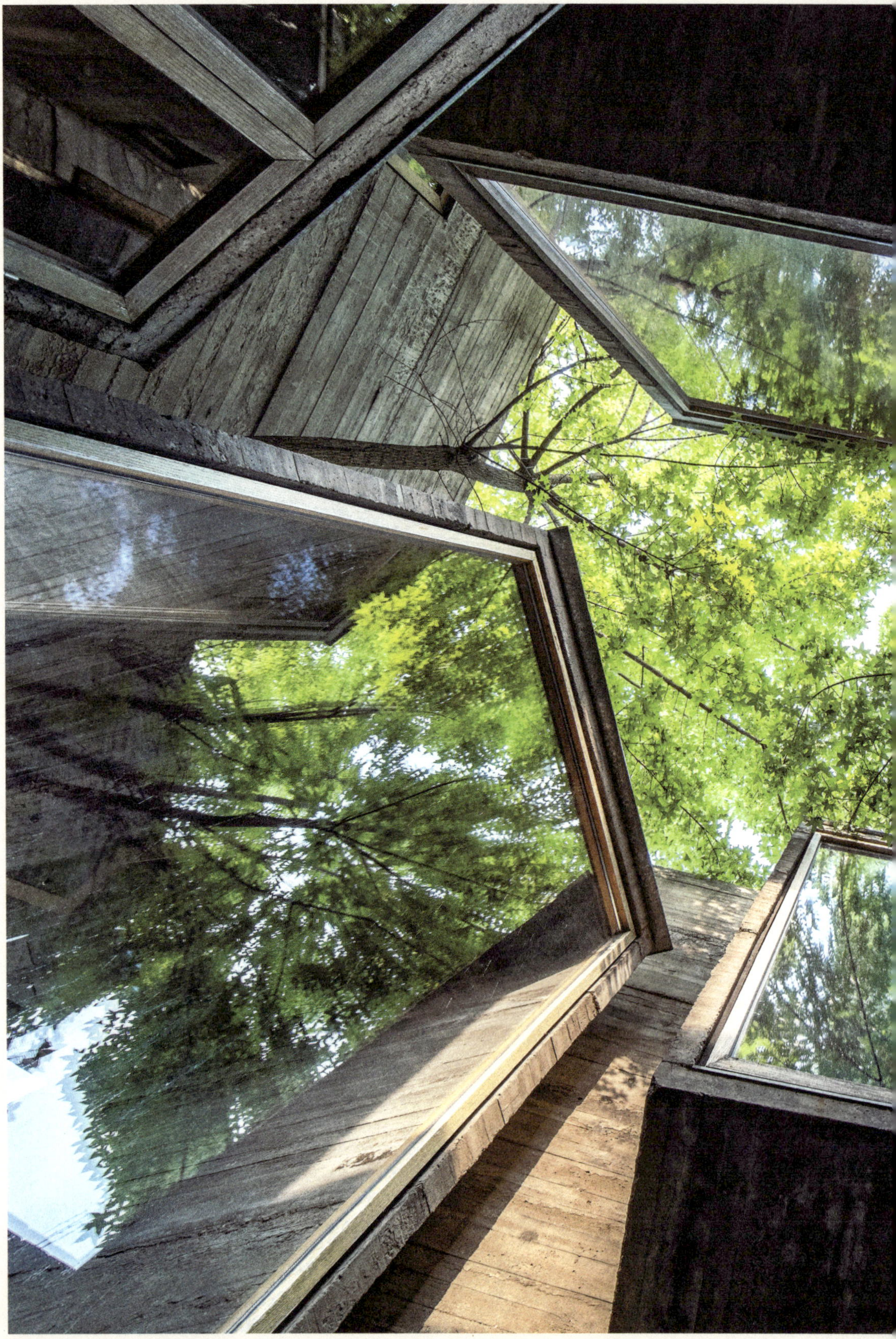

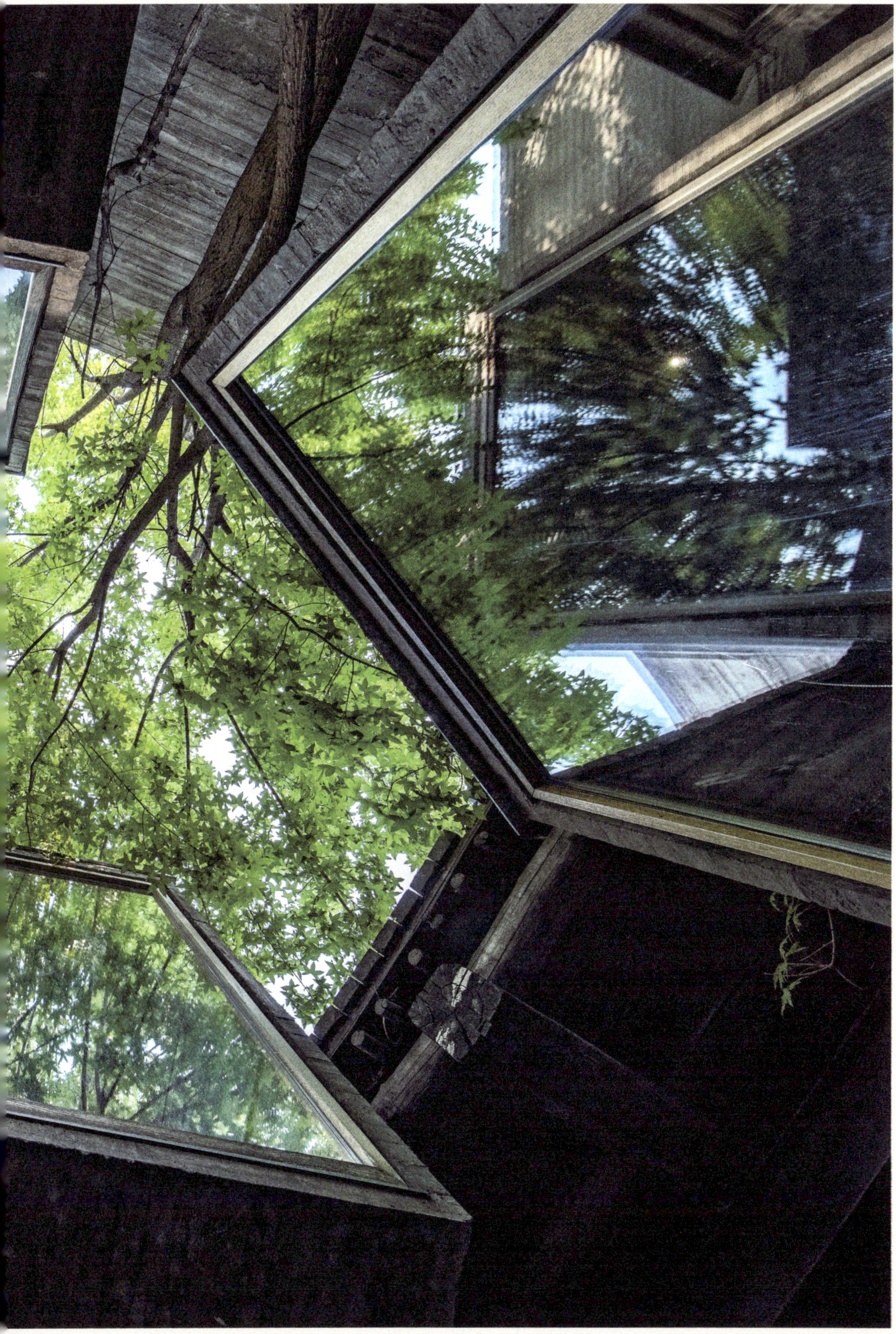

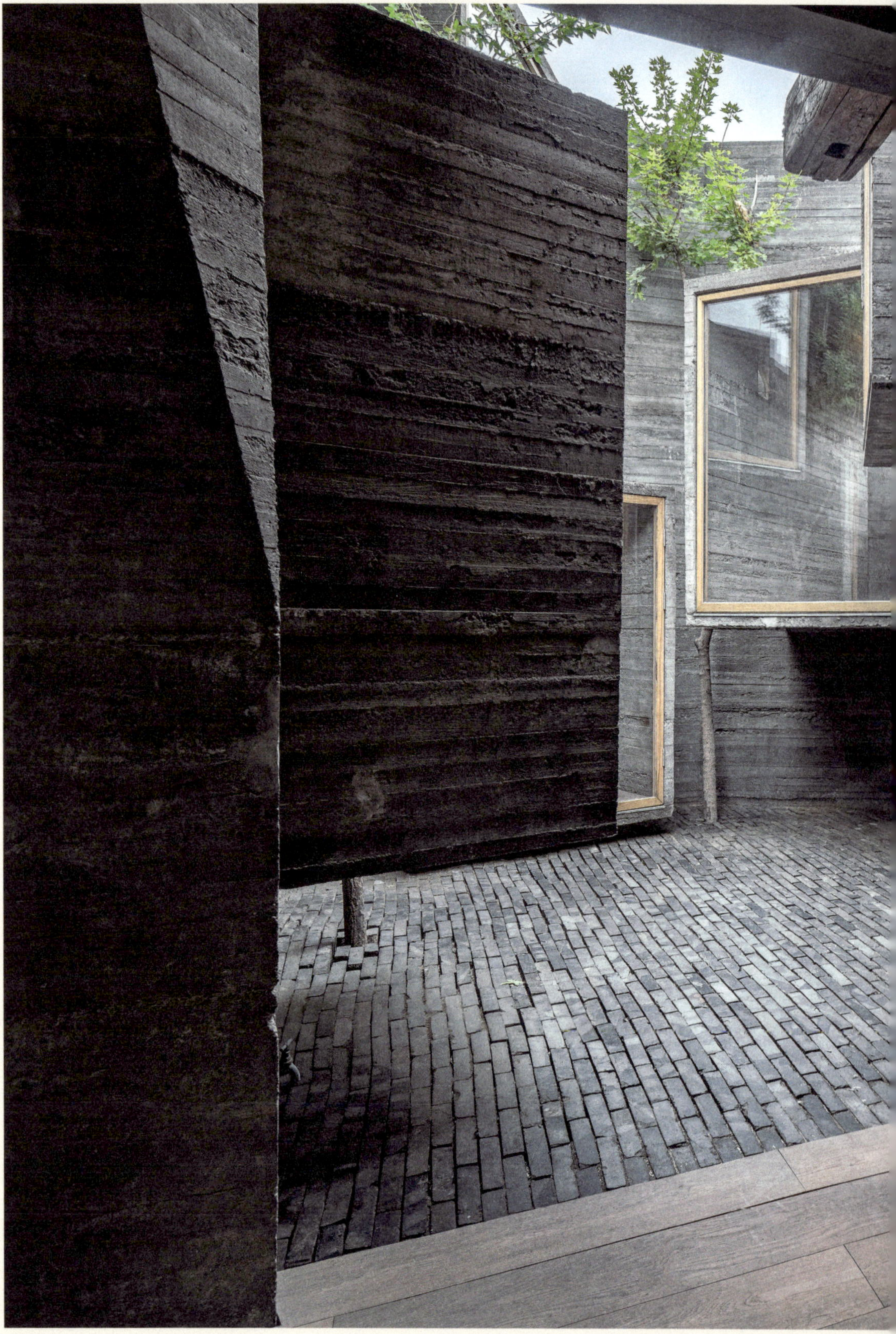

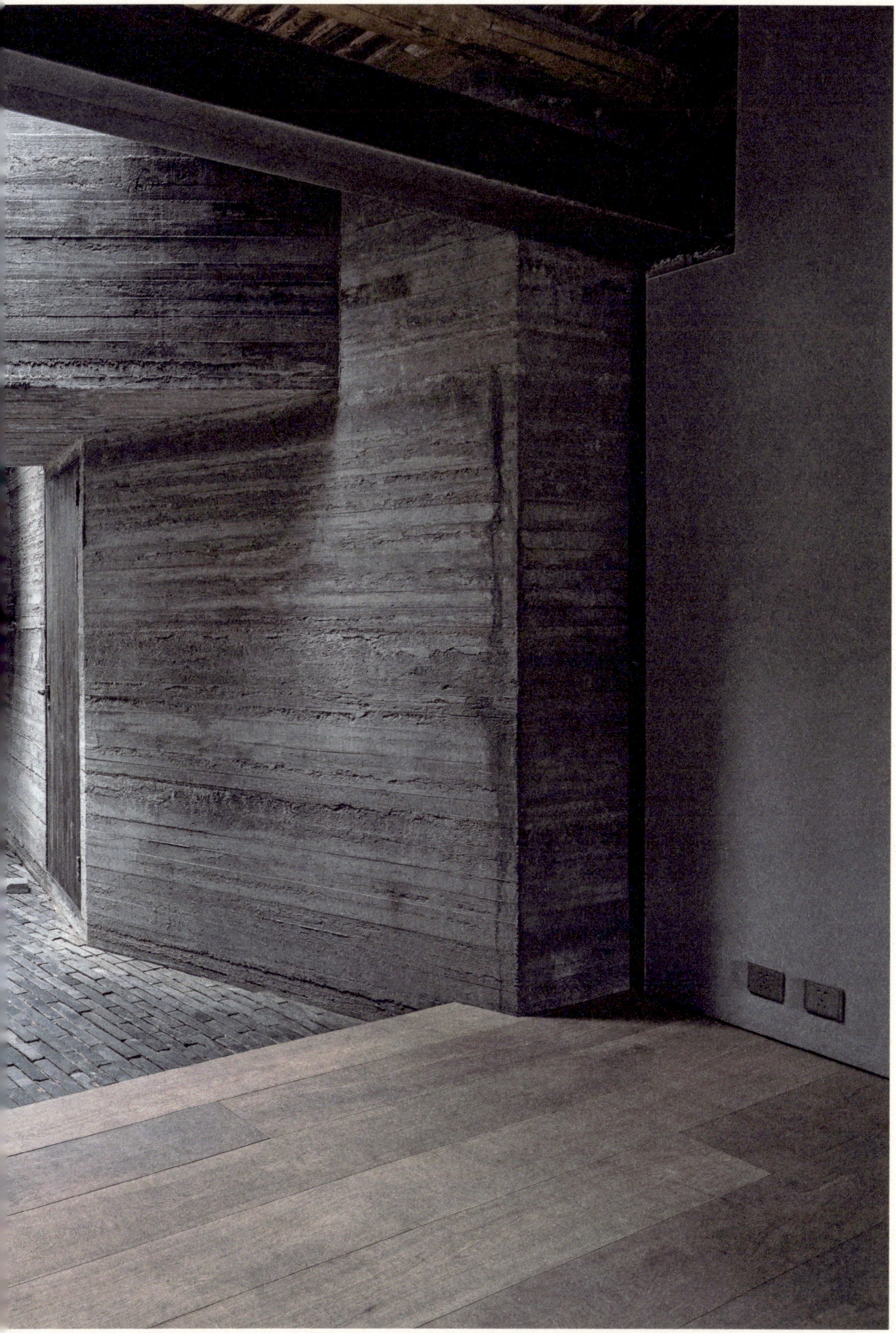

Hutong Metabolism: Silence Is the Power of Architecture
Martino Stierli

China's unparalleled economic and societal transformation of the past three decades has been accompanied by an unprecedented building boom that made the country the largest construction site in human history. After years of privileging urban megaprojects and spectacular objects by international architectural offices, a remarkable shift has started to take hold of architectural discourse in China in the more recent past. Critical of the detached formalism of many of these megaprojects, and likely encouraged by the government's desire to realign contemporary cultural production with the country's ancient traditions and values, a younger generation of talented local architects, all of whom are working independently of the still dominant state-run design institutes, is rethinking architecture toward social and environmental sustainability. The diverse practices of this generation are marked by a general skepticism of the tabula rasa approach to urbanisation, its disregard for existing structures and social contexts in many instances having led to a sense of cultural and social alienation. Pursuing an alternative strategy of converting, renewing, and recycling the existing structures, materials and craft traditions, these architects are invested instead in relatively small-scale interventions that seek to meaningfully engage with the pre-existing cultural and natural environment.

The increased attention that the work of this younger generation is garnering internationally is evidenced not only in a number of related exhibitions in major centres of architectural conversation in Europe and North America, in a growing number of publications and monographs by leading architectural publishers and, perhaps most consequentially, in the inclusion of examples of their work in the official selection of the Chinese Pavilion at the 16th International Architecture Exhibition of the Venice Biennale in 2018, which focused specifically on a selection of projects in China's vast yet rapidly depopulating rural hinterland.[1] This inclusion signaled a remarkable shift in perception of the work of this generation, placing it in the limelight of international architectural discourse. The exhibition *Renew, Reuse, Recycle: Recent Architecture from China*, which is being presented at The Museum of Modern Art in New York in the fall of 2021, will likewise provide an international stage to some of the exponents of this promising generation, albeit with a somewhat different thematic emphasis. The projects assembled in this exhibition serve not only as a survey of recent work, but also as a blueprint for a fundamental rethinking of architectural practice at large toward a less extractive and more resource-conscious future.

The Beijing-based architect Zhang Ke and his office ZAO/standardarchitecture are among the leading representatives of this generation. Born in 1970 and trained at the renowned Tsinghua University in Beijing and at Harvard University, Zhang Ke has made a name for himself primarily with his subtle interventions in the traditional hutong residential districts of his home city. All

Spectacular objects are part of the unprecedented building boom that made China the largest construction site in human history: Herzog & de Meuron's Beijing National Stadium, 2008

four of these interventions are characterised by a respect for the existing social and spatial structures of these districts, combined with an unwavering commitment to a contemporary architectural language. This has allowed the architect to breathe new life into these traditional neighbourhoods, and thus to save them from the threat of demolition. Consequently, and deservedly so, Zhang Ke was awarded the Aga Khan Award for Architecture for his Micro Yuan'er Children's Library and Art Centre in 2016 and the Alvar Aalto Medal of the Museum of Finnish Architecture and the Finnish Association of Architects (SAFA) in 2017. Since then, he has impressively proven his skills as a designer with a series of other buildings and thus expanded his repertoire to include various typologies and scales, but without losing sight of his sensitivity to the location and the material presence of history.

The hutongs in the Chinese capital originally go back to the Yuan dynasty. They are densely built-up, one-storey residential districts that are accessed via a system of narrow alleyways, which are in turn bordered by traditional courtyard houses (so-called *siheyuan*).[2] While the interior courtyards were initially part of the layout of stately residences, today they frequently form semi-open spaces for the numerous inhabitants of the small dwellings around them and are used for a range of different purposes, including, for instance, open kitchens or sanitary facilities. The hutongs are thus a unique meshwork of public, semi-public and private spaces, as becomes particularly

The entrance to the Micro Yuan'er Children's Library and Art Centre, 2021

apparent in aerial views. From the 1990s onward, and as a consequence of the pressures of the real-estate market, many of these districts fell into disfavour as unhygienic and unproductive and thus faced demolition. It was first in connection with the 2008 Beijing Olympic Games that a rethinking began, and the authorities recognised the touristic marketing value of these historic neighbourhoods. This, however, further accelerated the displacement of the long-term residents to newly erected neighbourhoods at the outskirts of the city. It was (and is) not uncommon for historically inhabited structures to be authorised for demolition in the dead of night without the consent of the generally underprivileged residents, to then be replaced with pseudo-historicising new buildings of dubious architectural and cultural merit, mainly reserved for touristic offerings.

Zhang Ke's interventions in Dashilar Hutong, located in the centre of the city of Beijing, only a few minutes by foot away from the Forbidden City and Tiananmen Square, provide an alternative model. His projects – which have become tourist destinations themselves due to their success

A Beijing hutong area from above

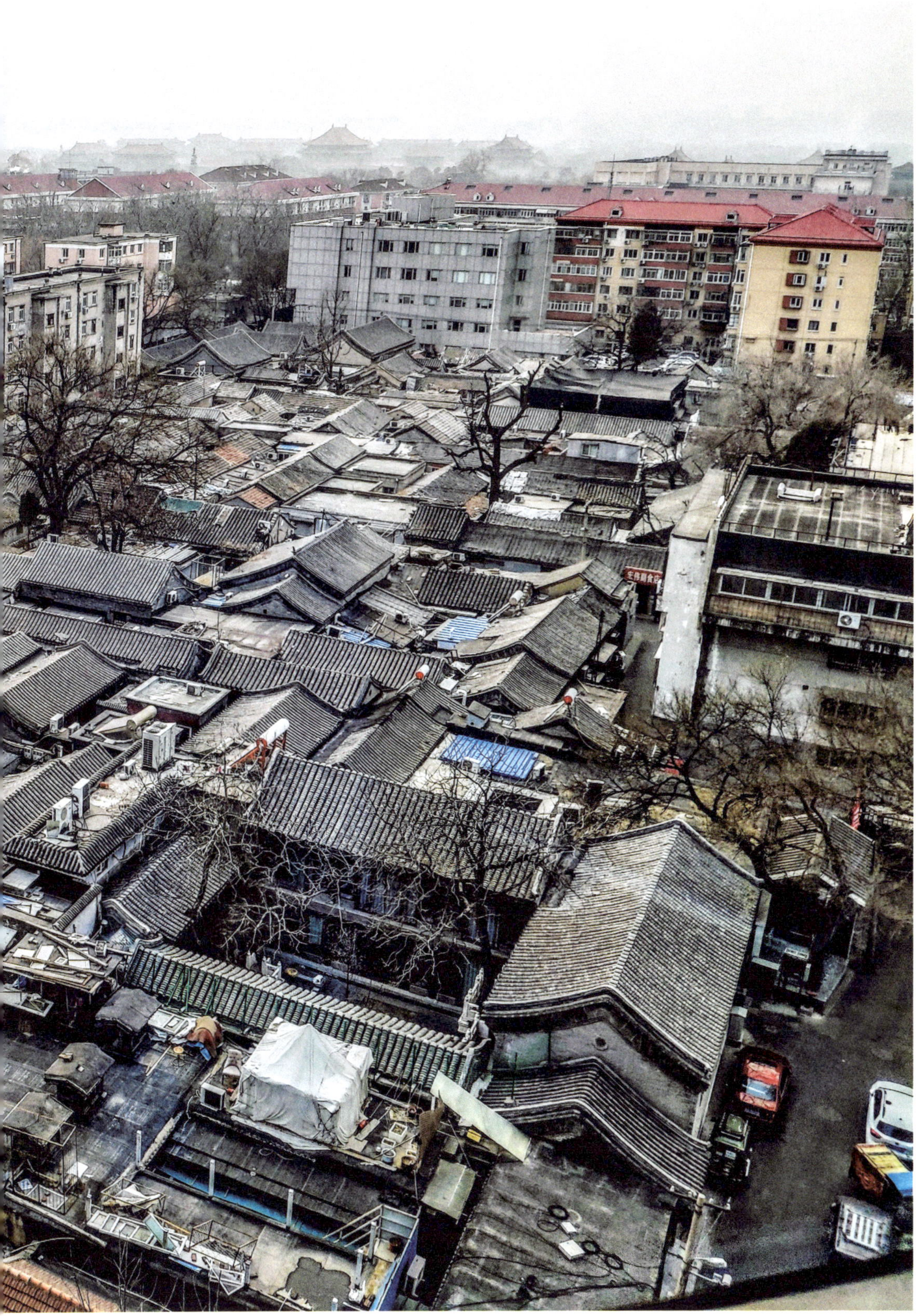

Street in the Dashilar Hutong area before the interventions by Zhang Ke

and presence in the media – are a balancing act between (undesired) gentrification and a strengthening and updating of the neighbourhood's social infrastructure. With the Micro Yuan'er Children's Library in Beijing, the architect and his team succeeded in creating a sense of place in an existing suite of two linked interior courtyards that has been accepted as a meeting place for the district's residents across all generations. This insistence on place-making is reminiscent of phenomenological conceptions of architecture from the 1970s and 1980s and is exemplified by the work of figures such as Christian Norberg-Schulz, Juhani Pallasmaa and others. It is also reaffirmed in Zhang Ke's statement that "architecture, is, after all, a very local discipline".

The Micro Yuan'er Children's Library left many of the informal elements untouched, such as the outdoor cooking places of the semi-private courtyard, so as not to interfere with the daily routines and rituals of the long-term residents. It simultaneously added a public dimension with a series of modest but nevertheless striking new buildings that benefit the entire neighbourhood. These small-scale, newly created spaces are reserved for cultural and recreational uses, such as a library, a tea room, or a scenic overlook. Zhang Ke's architecture thus enters into a respectful

One of the hutong interventions by Zhang Ke: Micro Hutong Hostel at Yang Mei Zhu, 2013

dialogue with the anonymous built testimonies of the past, and the way they have been inhabited by the current residents, preserving the homes of five of the originally ten families. His interventions are executed with recycled grey bricks and laminated wood as well as concrete. By adding Chinese ink to the latter, the architect provides a uniform aesthetic appearance that resonates with the neighbourhood's traditional grey brick architecture. Through his careful interventions, Zhang Ke has not only succeeded in keeping the district attractive for residents, but also in defending it against the economic interests of developers. Moreover, the many informal structures built by the inhabitants, never formally approved by the government, were retroactively validated through the architect's approach, thus ensuring not only their preservation, but also their continued usability.

This approach is indicative of Zhang Ke's deep respect for the users and inhabitants of these buildings, whose interests he deems equally important as those of the clients. Even though the architect is firmly committed to modern building materials and a contemporary design vocabulary, and hence rejects any overt reference to traditional form, his interventions are organic additions to the existing context. His approach is an original contribution to a progressive understanding of

The Yuan'er Hutong before the intervention by Zhang Ke

Art classroom, Micro Yuan'er Children's Library and Art Centre. A subtle renovation of the different historical layers of the existing hutong structure.

historic preservation that expands beyond the preservation of individual buildings and focuses instead on larger structural contexts – a proposition that promises to serve as a precedent for the future, not only in Beijing, but beyond. It is a design philosophy that does not seek the immediate bold effect, but is instead subtle and quietly surprising. It perfectly aligns with Zhang Ke's notion that "Architects in China have tried to be very loud, but most of the time silence is the power of architecture".[3]

In 2018, MoMA acquired a model, together with a series of digital prints, of Zhang Ke's Micro Hutong from 2016, another of the architect's projects in Beijing's Dashilar Hutong and in close vicinity to the Micro Yuan'er Children's Library. The model in black concrete and plaster had first been presented to great acclaim at the 2017 Chicago Architecture Biennial under the rubric "Make New Hutong Metabolism", together with the other two related interventions.[4] The word choice of the metabolism first introduced here not only points to the notion of the city as a living organism; it also explicitly references the Metabolist movement of postwar Japanese architecture, which likewise conceptualised urban growth according to a biological model (even though it was less concerned with respecting existing urban structures). The Micro Hutong was built on the site of an old house without a courtyard and made use of the same concrete with added Chinese ink as the Micro Yuan'er Children's Library. Zhang Ke's experimental insertion is a series of guest rooms grouped around a central courtyard on an ultra-small scale. Hardly noticeable from the street in front, the projecting cubes with large window fronts create a dramatic and

The Micro Hutong concrete model by Zhang Ke acquired to the permanent collection of MoMA in New York, 2017 (72.4 × 73 × 61.6 cm)

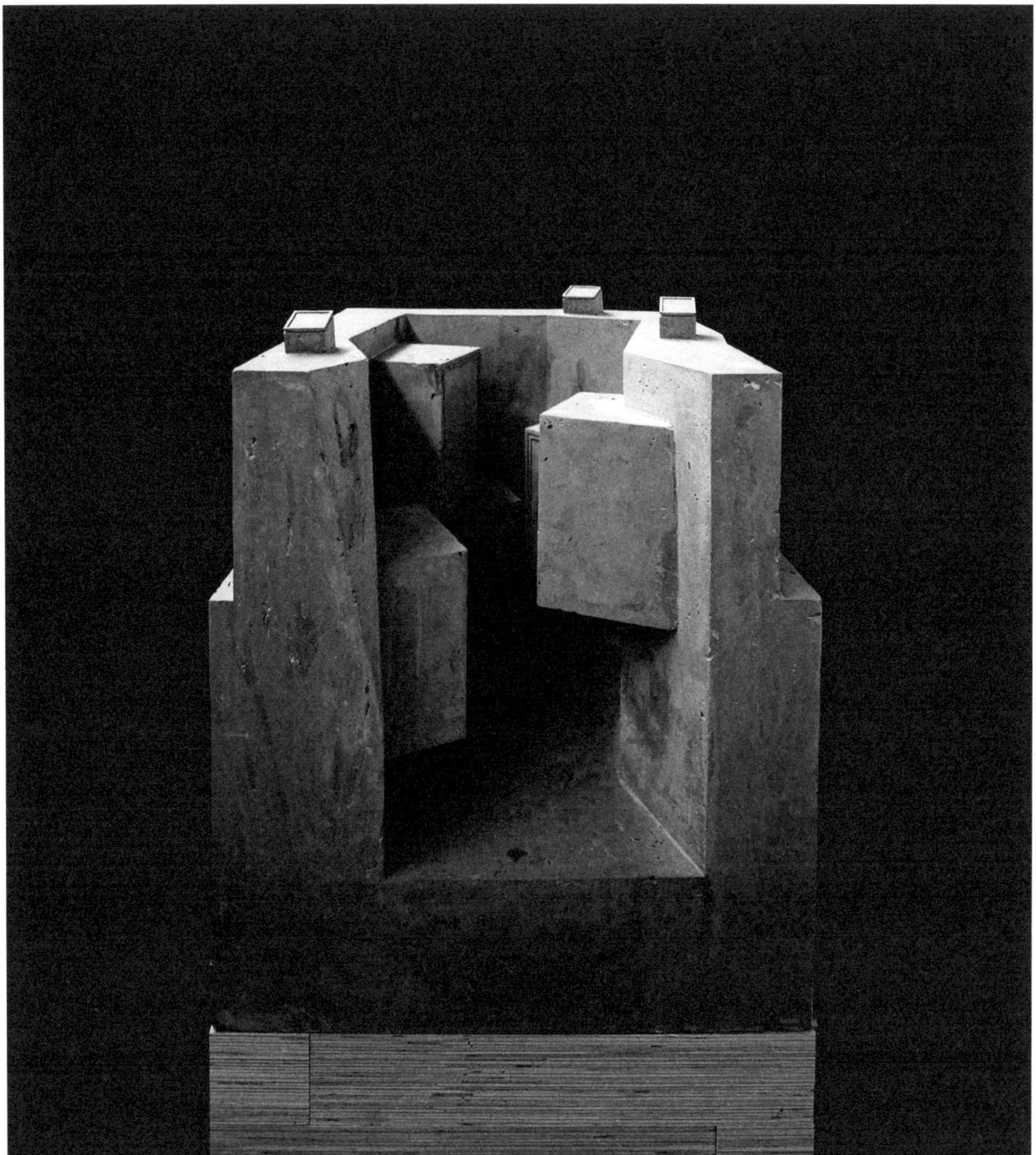

The first architectural drawing to enter MoMA's collection in 1947, by Theo van Doesburg, 1923

unexpected spatial experience, which the concrete model seeks to emulate. The project is intended not so much as a place for an actual family to live, but as an experimental contribution to how the traditional neighbourhood could potentially be reimagined through new typologies of publicly accessible spaces.

MoMA's exhibition and collection strategies have frequently been described as primarily or even uniquely centred on aesthetic criteria, and conversely as disregarding architecture's manifold intersections with socio-political concerns. The famous 1932 *Modern Architecture: International Exhibition*, which inaugurated the Department of Architecture at the museum and spread the gospel of the so-called International Style, has often been seen as translating the radical socio-political agenda of the European architectural avant-gardes into a "style"; in other words, into a matter of formal and aesthetic principles, as opposed to utopian politics. However, it is often forgotten that this inaugural exhibition included an entire section on housing, which, curated by Lewis Mumford, explicitly called out the "shoddy and sordid" state of mass housing in America's big cities.[5] Exhibitions with a similarly activist stance followed in the ensuing years, and into the postwar period.[6] The "Issues in Contemporary Architecture" series, inaugurated in 2010 as a loose sequence of research projects and exhibitions that present commissioned works by contemporary practitioners on a given urgent topic, can be seen as a continuation of those early endeavors.[7] However, many of these socio-politically minded exhibitions did not result in acquisitions into the museum's collection; and in fact the first piece of architecture was only admitted into the collection in 1947, taking the form of a (aesthetically stunning) drawing by Theo van Doesburg – indicative of the fact that early architectural acquisitions were made primarily or exclusively based on aesthetic considerations.[8]

While this bias continued for much of the 20th century, there are notable exceptions to be called out, in particular the acquisition in 2000 of the Gilman Collection of utopian architectural drawings from the 1960s and 1970s.[9] While it is in the very nature of utopian drawings to refuse to

Clorindo Testa's large-scale multipart mural *Habitar, Circular, Trabajar, Recrearse*, 1952/1974, acquired by MoMA in 2016

engage with the conditions of reality, their bold assertion of the possibility of a different reality is perhaps the most poignant form of critique and socio-political engagement possible. In more recent years, curatorial attention has decidedly shifted toward a more sustained engagement with such questions. Prominent examples would include a large suite of drawings of Álvaro Siza's SAAL Bouça Social Housing in Porto, Portugal, from the mid-1970s, brought into MoMA's collection in 2012 and first presented in the exhibition *9+1 Ways of Being Political: 50 Years of Political Stances in Architecture and Urban Design* of the same year;[10] the Argentine architect Clorindo Testa's large-scale multipart mural *Habitar, Circular, Trabajar, Recrearse* (Inhabiting, Circulating, Working, Recreating) from 1974 and acquired in 2016; or the substantial bodies of works that were brought into the collection as a result of the large research and exhibition projects *Latin America in Construction: Architecture 1955–1980* (2015) and *Toward a Concrete Utopia: Architecture in Yugoslavia, 1948–1980* (2018), both of which explicitly addressed the societal transformations in these respective regions from an architectural perspective.[11] The inclusion of Zhang Ke's Micro Hutong project in MoMA's collection is further evidence of this ongoing shift in curatorial thinking.

Editor's note: This essay is a revised and expanded version of thoughts first articulated in "Hutong: Adding Organically to the Built Context", in Kristin Feireiss and Hans-Jürgen Commerell (eds.), *YING-ZAO: HUTONG METABOLISM+*, exh. cat. Aedes Architecture Forum (forthcoming).

1 See Li Xiangning (ed.), *Building a Future Countryside*, Pavilion of China, 16th International Architecture Exhibition, La Biennale di Venezia (New York: The Images Publishing Group, 2018).

2 See Nancy Shatzman Steinhardt, *Chinese Architecture: A History* (Princeton: Princeton University Press, 2019), pp. 307–8.

3 Zhang Ke's Guest Lecture series in 2019 for the Røros Seminar in Norway.

4 See http://2017.chicagoarchitecturebiennial.org/participants/zao-standardarchitecture/ (all URLs accessed in July 2021).

5 Lewis Mumford, "Housing", in *Modern Architecture: International Exhibition* (New York: The Museum of Modern Art, 1932), p. 181.

6 See MoMA's exhibition history at https://www.moma.org/calendar/exhibitions/history/.

7 See "Issues in Contemporary Architecture", https://www.moma.org/calendar/groups/37.

8 See Matilda McQuaid, "Acquiring Architecture: Building a Modern Collection", in *Envisioning Architecture: Drawings from The Museum of Modern Art* (New York: The Museum of Modern Art, 2002), pp. 18–37; Martino Stierli, "Curating Architecture at MoMA: Collections, Archives and Display", in Marina Gorreri and Francesca Zanella (eds.), *#Grand Tourists: Immersion in the Collections, Accumulations and Obsessions of the Museums and Archives of Parma* (Parma: Monte Università Parma Editore, 2018), pp. 118–27.

9 See *The Changing of the Avant-Garde: Visionary Architectural Drawings from the Howard Gilman Collection* (New York: The Museum of Modern Art, 2002).

10 See https://www.moma.org/calendar/exhibitions/1289.

11 See Barry Bergdoll, Carlos Eduardo Comas, Jorge Francisco Liernur and Patricio del Real (eds.), *Latin America in Construction: Architecture 1955–1980* (New York: The Museum of Modern Art, 2015), and Martino Stierli and Vladimir Kulić (eds.), *Toward a Concrete Utopia: Architecture in Yugoslavia, 1948–1980* (New York: The Museum of Modern Art, 2018).

Fused Traditions: The Making of an International Contemporary Signature

Hans-Jürgen Commerell and Kristin Feireiss

As early as 2001, when Zhang Ke was only just founding his office in Beijing, Aedes in Berlin was instigating a conversation about China's contemporary architecture scene. This transcontinental exchange has continued into the present day. Back then, just past the turn of the century, the still young architecture avant-garde in China – practicing independently of large, state-controlled architecture and planning offices – was introduced for the first time in the Western cultural scene through the exhibition *TU MU Young Architecture from China* at the Aedes Architecture Forum.

By no small coincidence, Zhang Ke, who belongs to the generation below the main protagonists of the *TU MU* exhibition, had founded his architectural practice ZAO/standardarchitecture in the same year, exactly two decades before the link between Beijing and Berlin was to come full circle through his own exhibition in Berlin. The Chinese character for *zào* means making, building, producing, or inventing. The word "standard" raises the expectation of something programmatic in the practice's architectural approach.

And yet, when it comes to his out-of-the-ordinary designs and buildings, Zhang Ke sets his very own standards. Overall, their expression is a manifestation of a congenial merger of Eastern and Western approaches to architecture and the city. While reflecting, for example, his intensive engagement with the oeuvre of the Indian architect Charles Correa, whose modern designs are deeply rooted in their local cultural context, Zhang Ke's work does not lose sight of the influences gained during his studies in Boston, including Western icons such as Rafael Moneo, Peter Zumthor and Álvaro Siza.

Zhang Ke's buildings and landscape designs are situated firmly in their respective historical and cultural contexts. In the pursuit of intellectual expansion, he often finds himself thinking even beyond this positionality. In his playfully experimental way, Zhang Ke continuously renews and transforms his building methods based on historical Chinese customs, thereby imbuing structures with his unique signature. His investigations of hutongs, which are the traditional residential courtyards in Beijing, have resulted in exemplary materialisations of this approach. Only a few of these structures, which were the prevailing residential building typology in the city until the 1990s, have been preserved to the present day, due to rapid modernisation in Beijing. This inspired Zhang Ke to investigate the situation through the project Micro Hutong Renewal, with the aim of highlighting the potential of these urban quarters and their uniqueness, as they are only found in the capital city. The goal of the investigation is to find out how to adapt the traditional courtyard houses and to avail the local communities of their resources, from playgrounds

The *TU MU* exhibition at Aedes Architecture Forum in Berlin, Germany, 2001

for children to coworking spaces. By thinking about the concept of metabolism and allowing it to pervade his work, Zhang Ke conveys ideas of life cycles with birth, growth and renewal in both the city and the buildings. By avoiding conventional, historicising methods of restoration, he rather explores hutongs as flexible, extendable spaces of possibility that can serve the community as catalysts for social exchange.

Zhang Ke's strategy is extremely sustainable, and it anticipates a further engagement and development of his projects after their completion. He is an extraordinary observer, attentive to the behaviour of individuals and groups of residents and users of his buildings, which he analyses to draw conclusions about the needs of the people he builds for. He has also accumulated extensive knowledge about historical and contemporary Western culture. These ingredients combine to make up his unique recipe for contemporary architecture that has an unmistakable, strong, yet unobtrusive presence in both cultures. The acknowledgement of this feat resulted, among other things, in him being contracted to build an office building at the Novartis Shanghai

Novartis Shanghai Campus Building by Zhang Ke, 2016

Campus, and being invited to participate in the competition for the Exile Museum in Berlin in 2019. His impressive design for the latter reflects the potent feelings of abandoning and abandonment, as well as the hopes, of people who flee into exile. The design shows glimpses of the principle of connectedness between interior and exterior spaces familiarised by his hutong investigations.

While Western investors and architects have continuously pervaded China with their "missions" since the mid-1990s, it has rarely occurred to protagonists in the West to invite Chinese architects to competitions in Europe or the United States. We are convinced, however, that this will change in the future – due not to China's dream of expansion, but rather to the independence, creative confidence, and intercultural sensitivity of contemporary Chinese architects, of whom Zhang Ke is a remarkable representative.

Design submitted by ZAO/standardarchitecture to the 2019 competition for the Exile Museum in Berlin, Germany

Co-Living Courtyard

Location: **Beijing, China**
Client: **Beijing Huarong Jinying Investment & Development Co. Ltd.**
Design period: **2015-16**
Construction period: **2015-17**
Site area: **150 m²**
Building area: **90 m²**
Total floor area: **90 m²**
Architect: **ZAO/standardarchitecture**
Project architect: **Zhang Ke**
Design team: **Fang Shujun, He Kuang, Ao Ikegami, Stefano Di Daniel, Hou Xinjue, Li Yalun, Ilaria Positano, Farzad Lee**
Collaborating design institution: **China Academy of Building Research**

Co-Living Courtyard further explores a sustainable renewal strategy for the historical fabric of Beijing's old city, following two other building experiments, Micro Hutong and Micro Yuan'er. It aims to explore co-living possibilities between the public and private spheres in a traditional courtyard structure, and to challenge ways of infrastructure integration in limited space, so as to create decent new hutong life.

Located in the historical area of the Baitasi Pagoda from the 13th century, the 150 square metre messy courtyard is renovated into a coexisting space with three courtyards of various scales shared by two different properties. One is a minimum inserted living unit of eight square metres, occupying only one bay of the building structure, which includes all needed housing amenities for a single household or a couple. The other relatively big and continuous space is intended to be an exhibition open to the public.

Furthermore, ZAO/standardarchitecture designed a service core facility for this project that combines a kitchen, bathroom, laundry room and storage area, which is embedded in the public space. The architects developed this block to be also placed interdependently in other hutong areas, providing amenities largely lacking in the old city.

Once the minimum inserted living unit and the service core facility are propagated throughout the old city, they may solve urgent infrastructure problems and improve the quality of life among hutong residents.

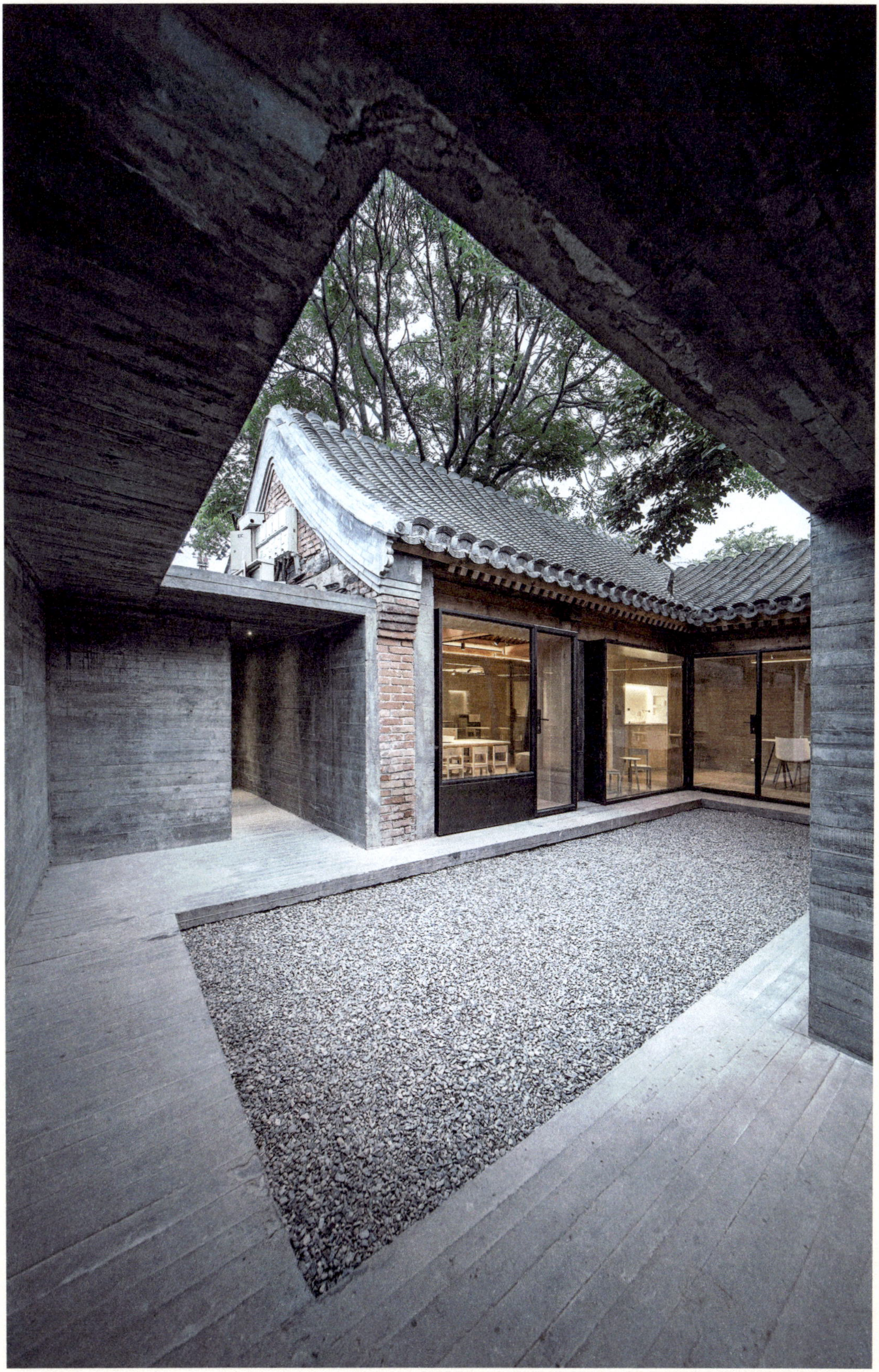

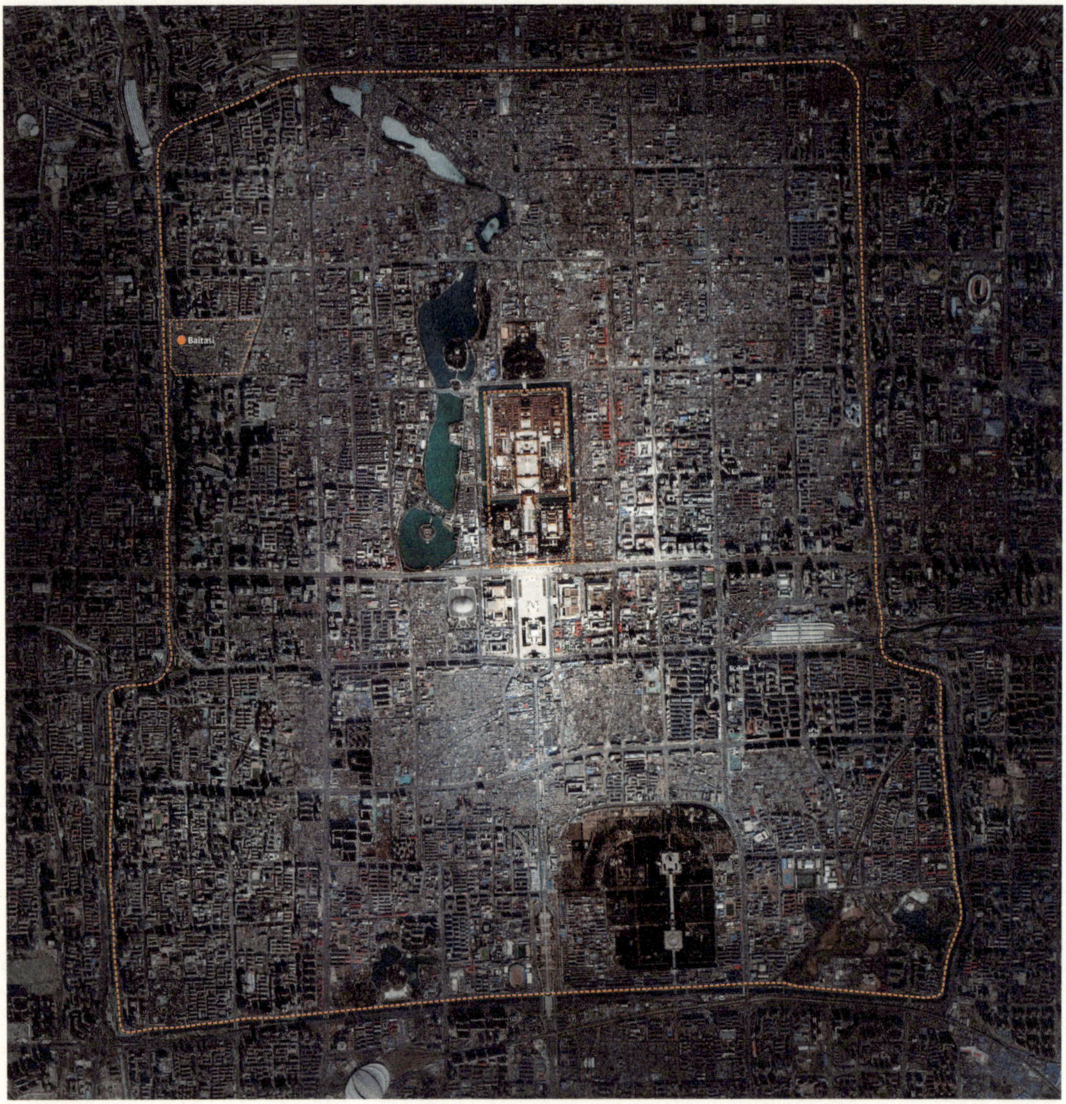

Baitasi

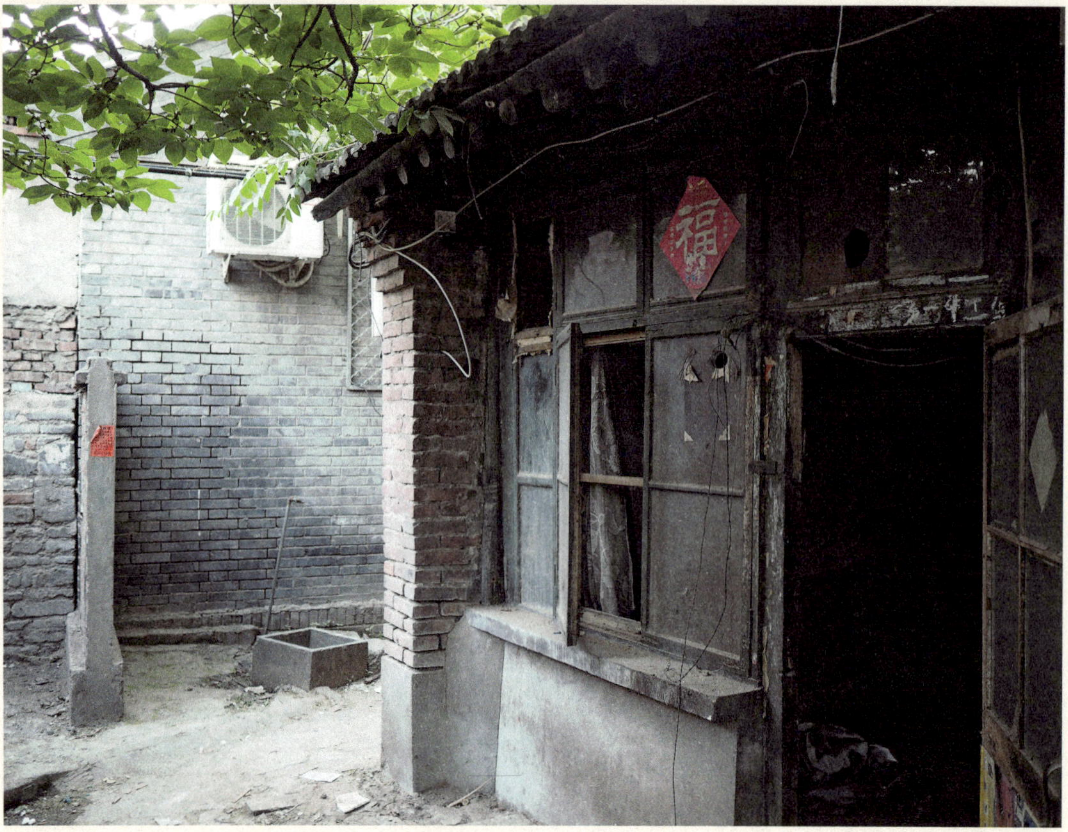
福

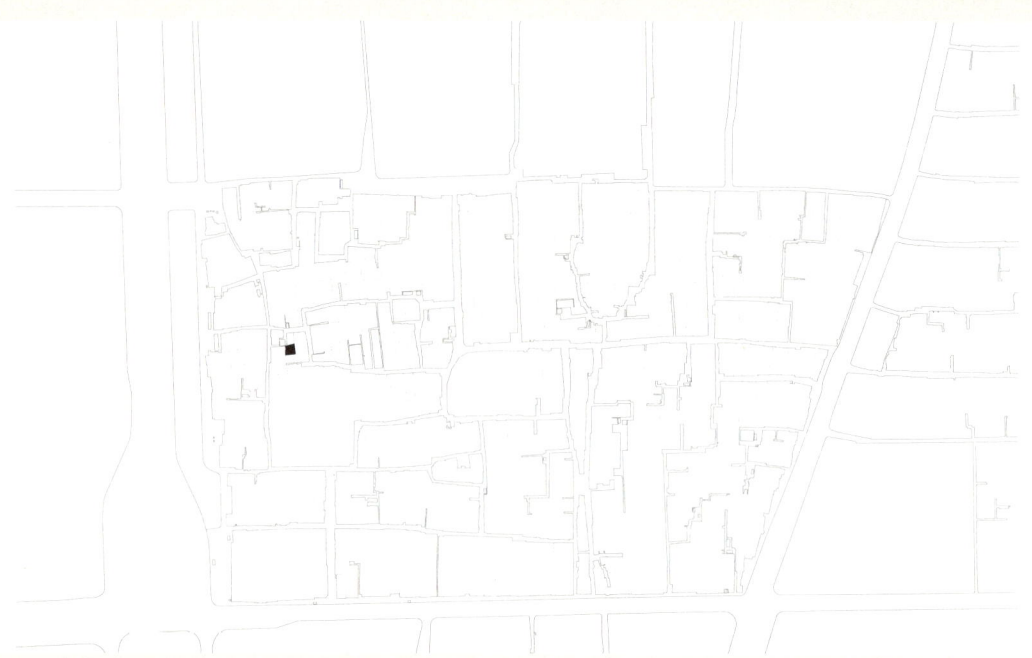

宫门口四条 Gongmenkou Sitiao

宫门口五条 Gongmenkou Wutiao

青塔胡同 Qingta Hutong

西皇 Xihuan

0 5 10m

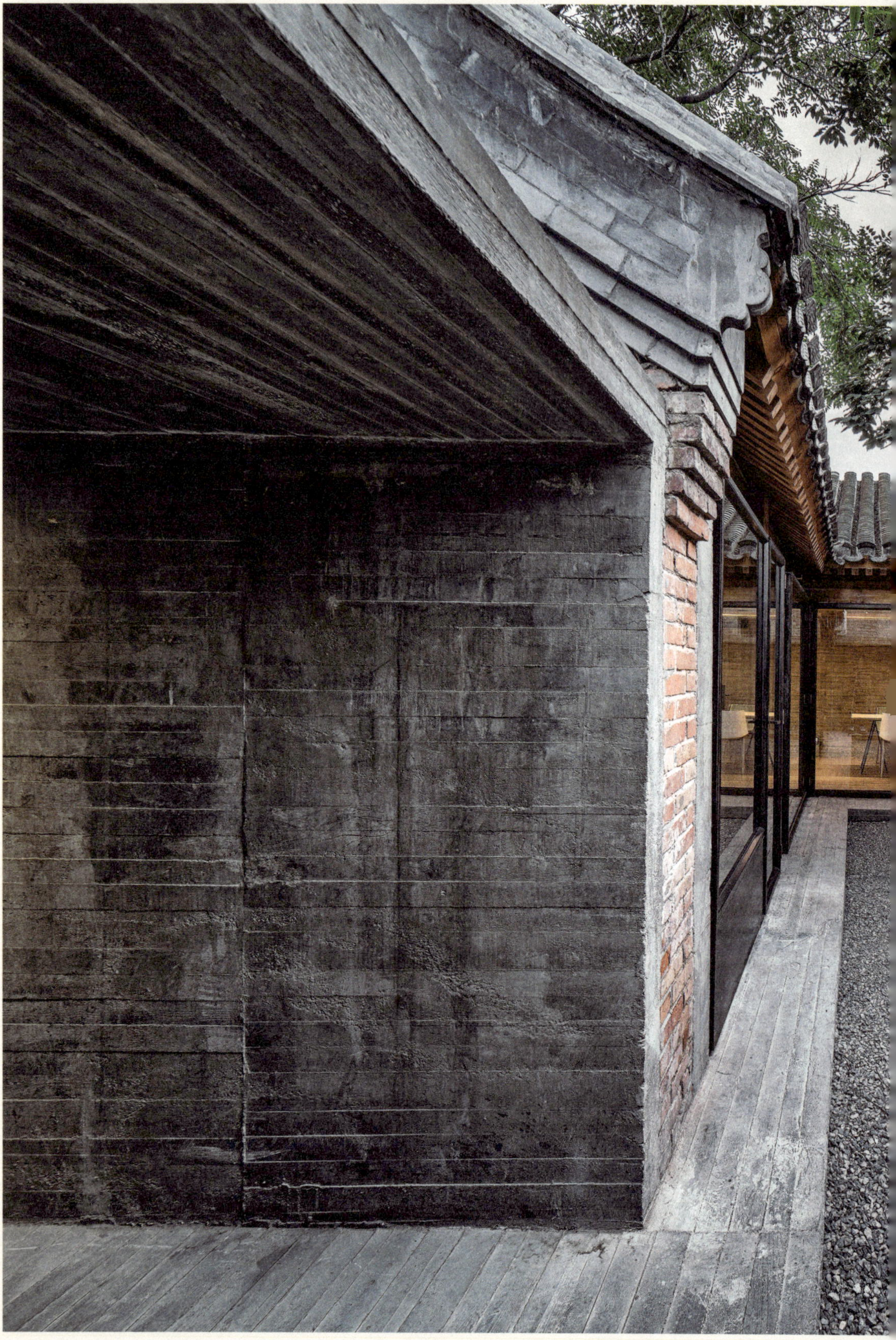

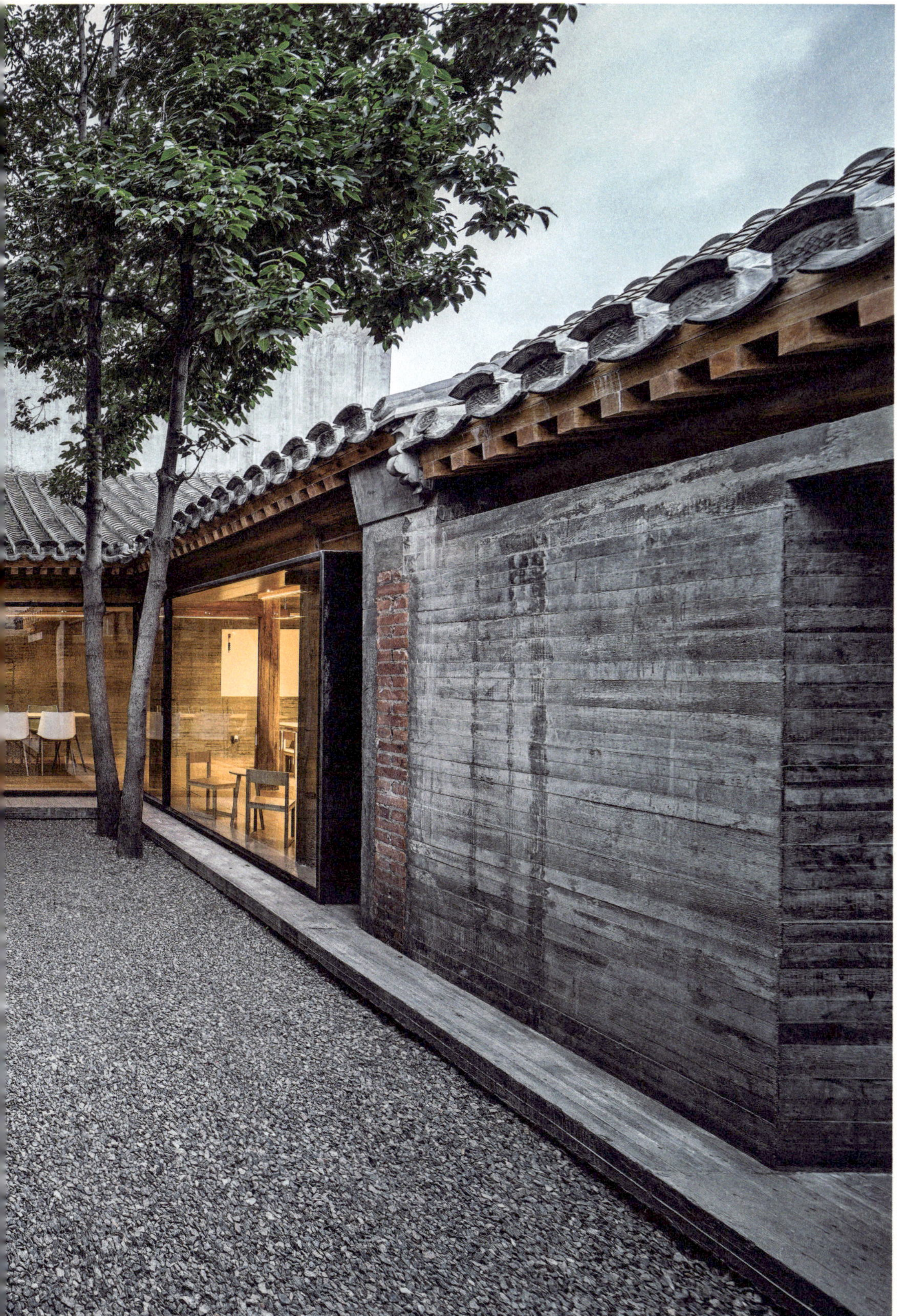

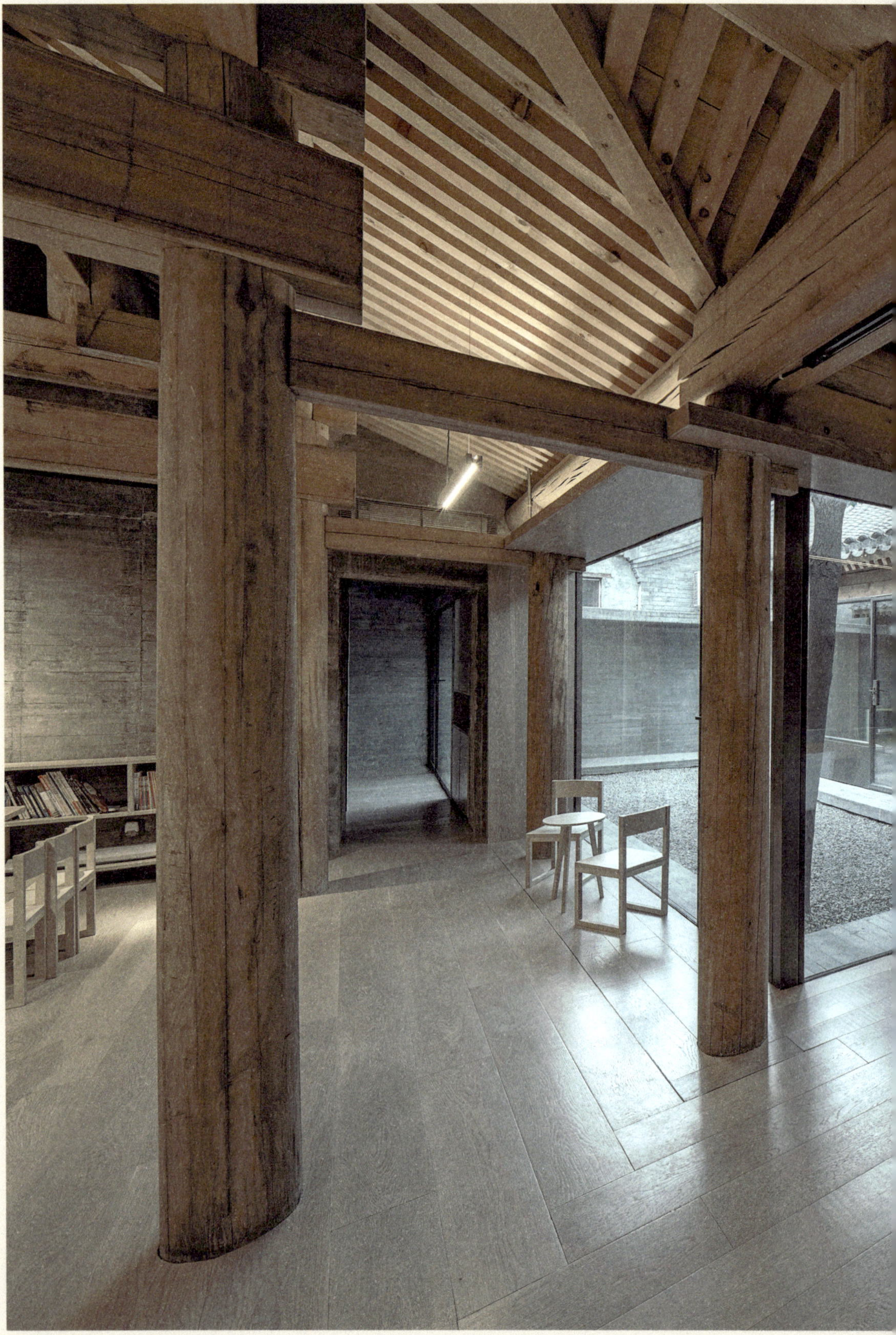

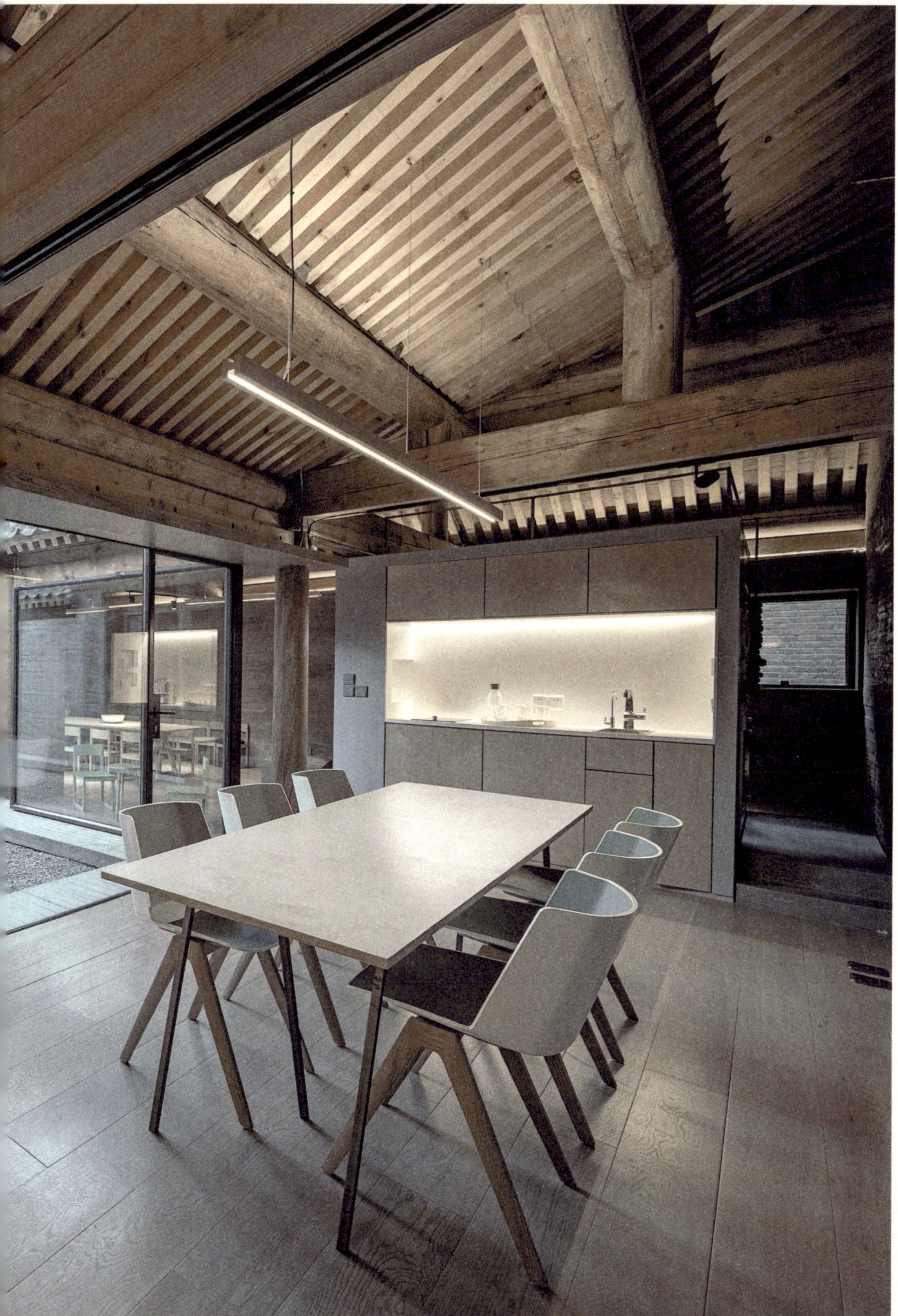

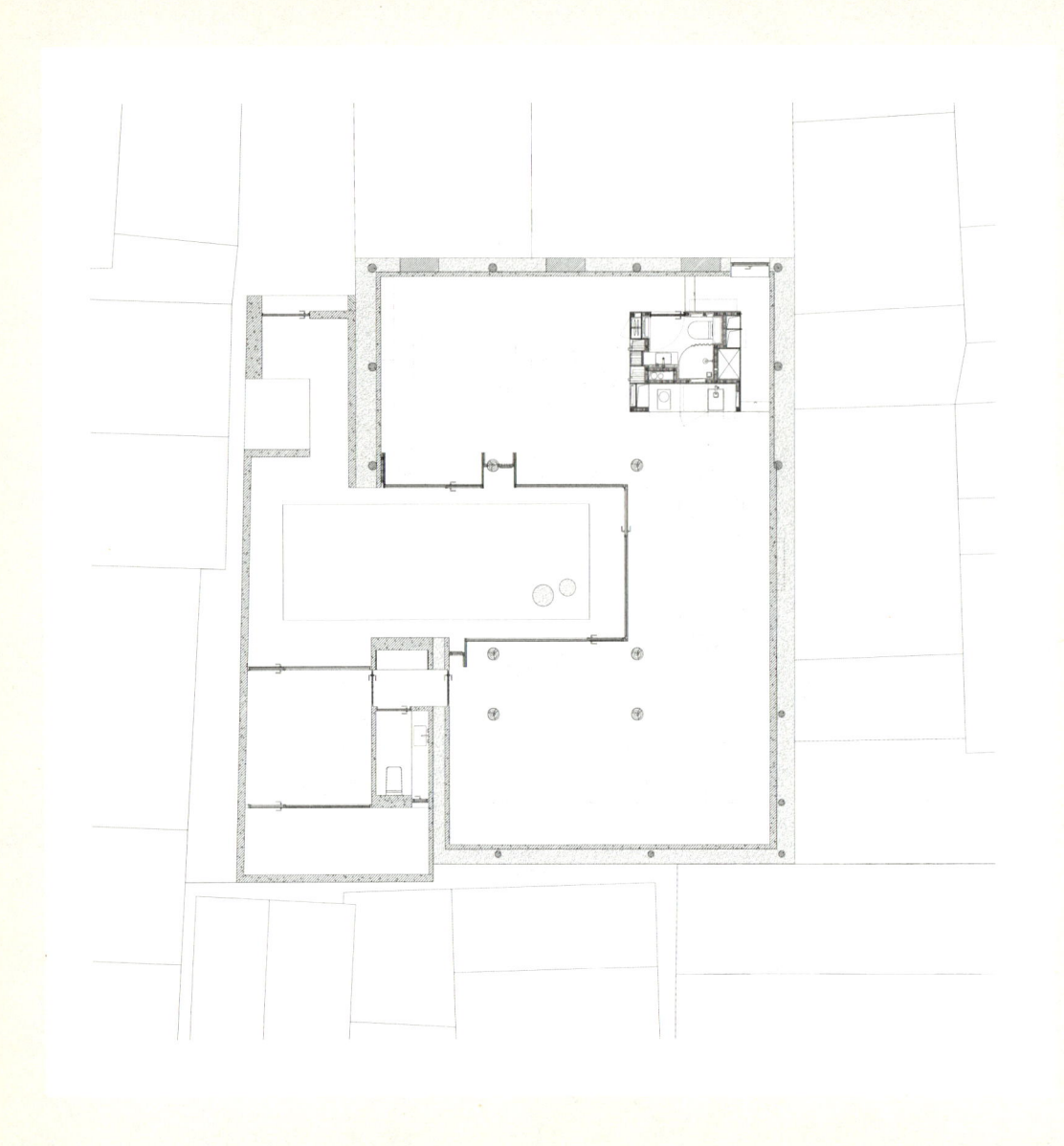

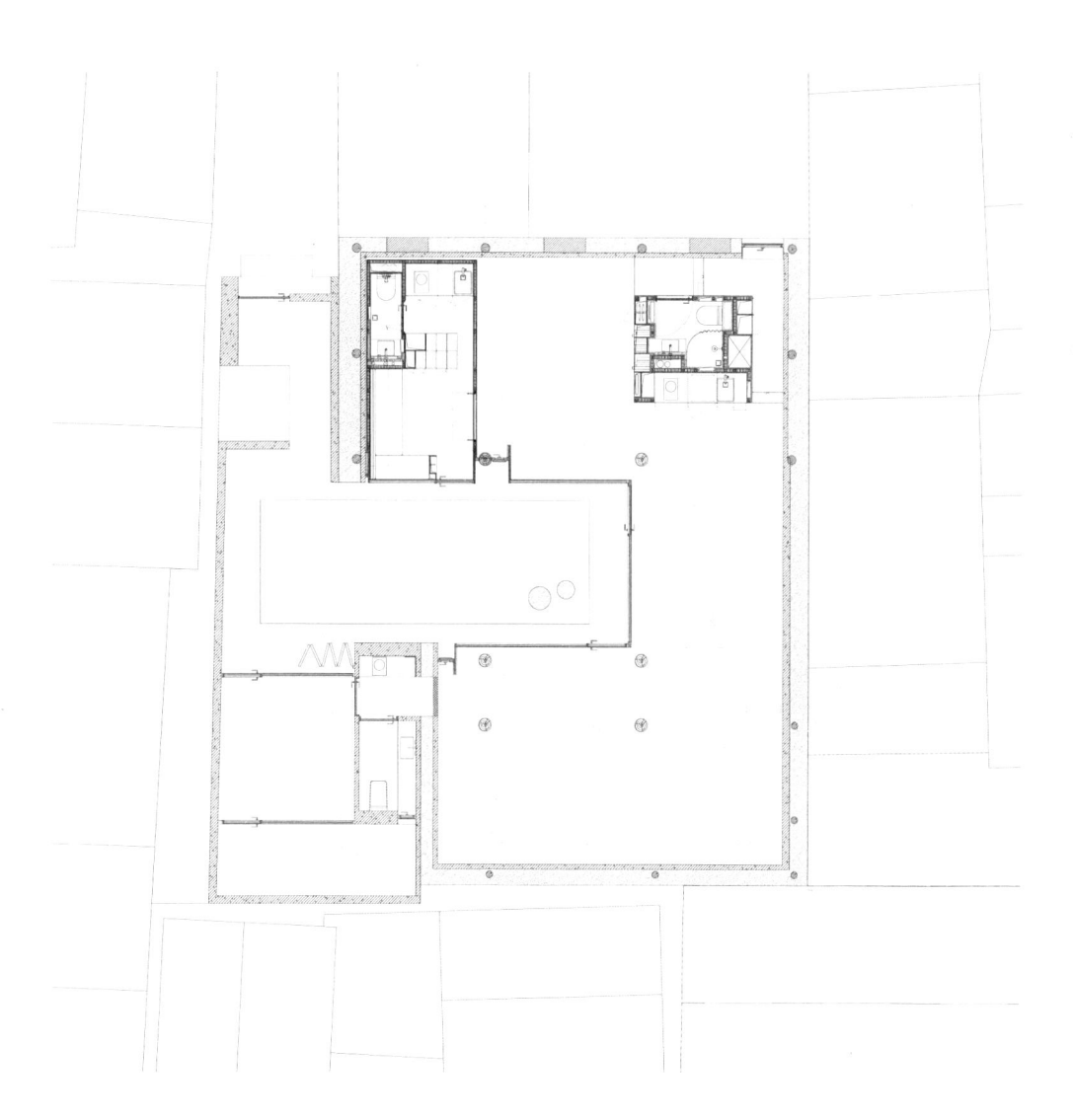

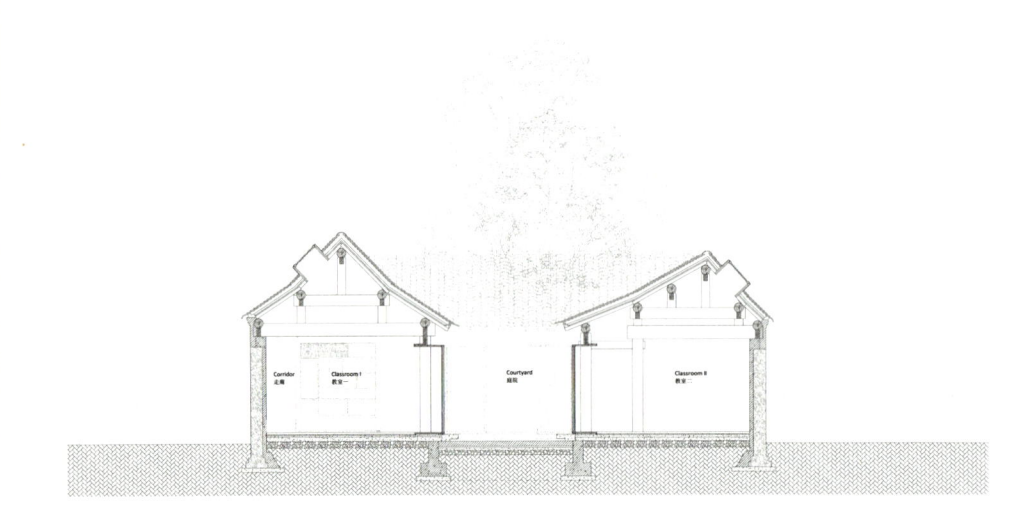

Section A-A
剖面 A-A

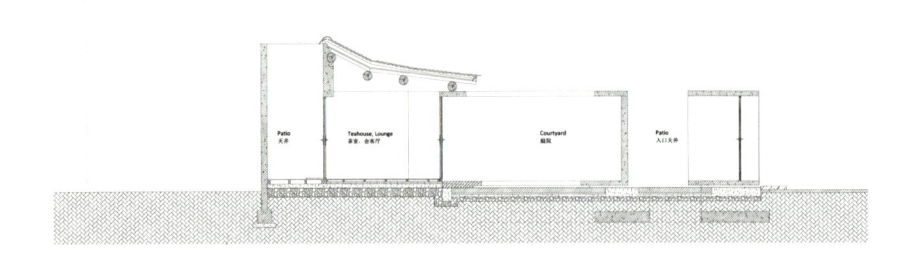

Section B-B
剖面 B-B

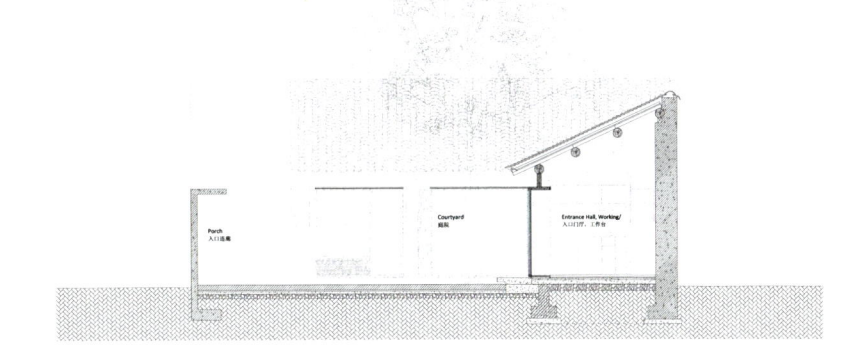

Section C-C
剖面 C-C

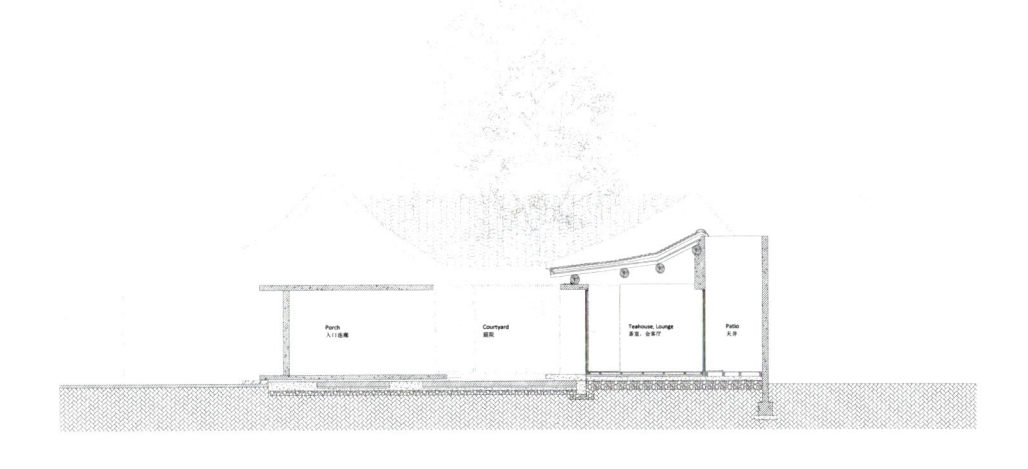

Porch 入口廊庵
Courtyard 庭院
Entrance Hall, Working / 入口门厅，工作台

Section E-E
剖面 E-E

Porch 入口廊庵
Courtyard 庭院
Teahouse, Lounge 茶室，会客厅
Patio 天井

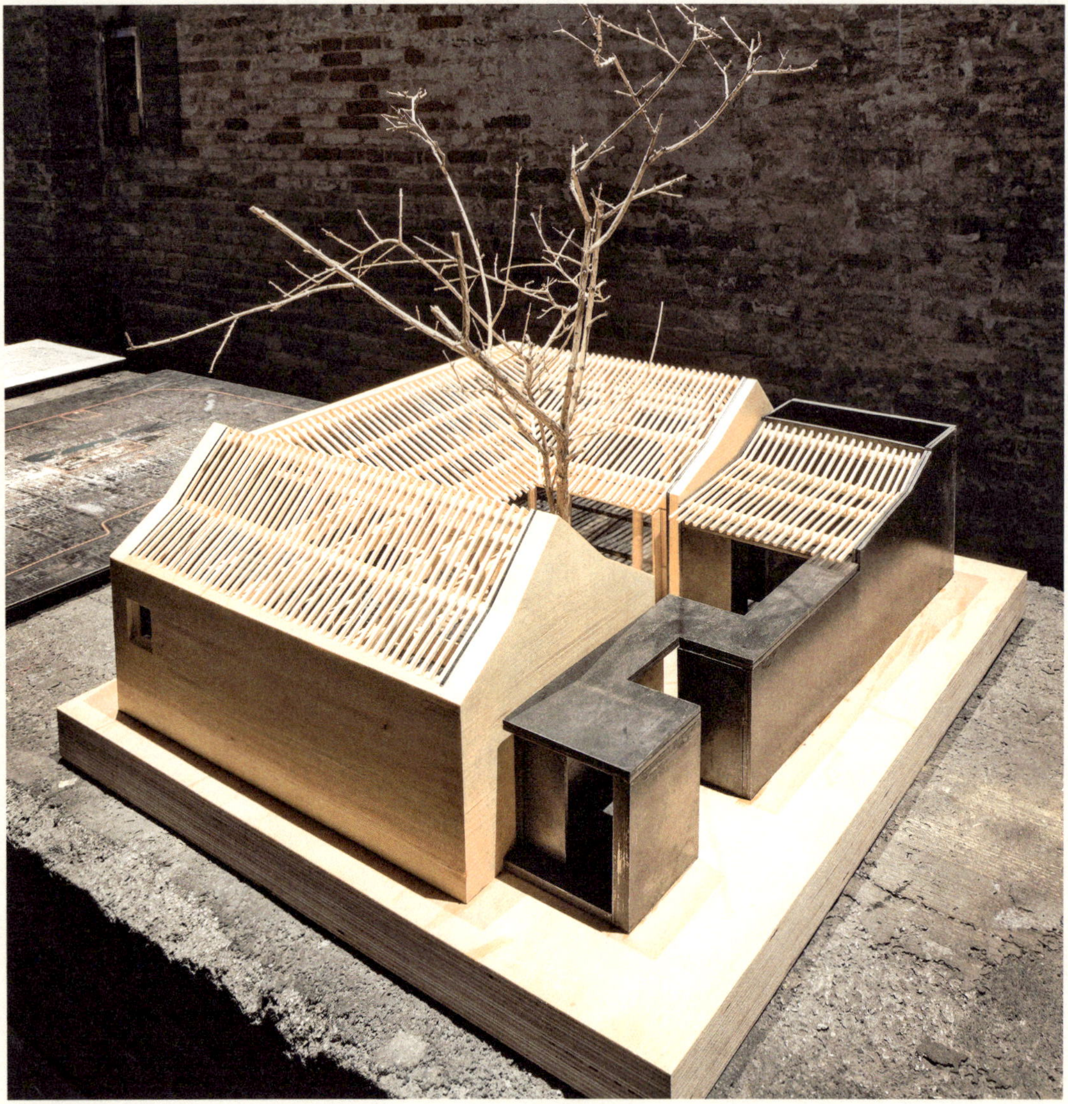

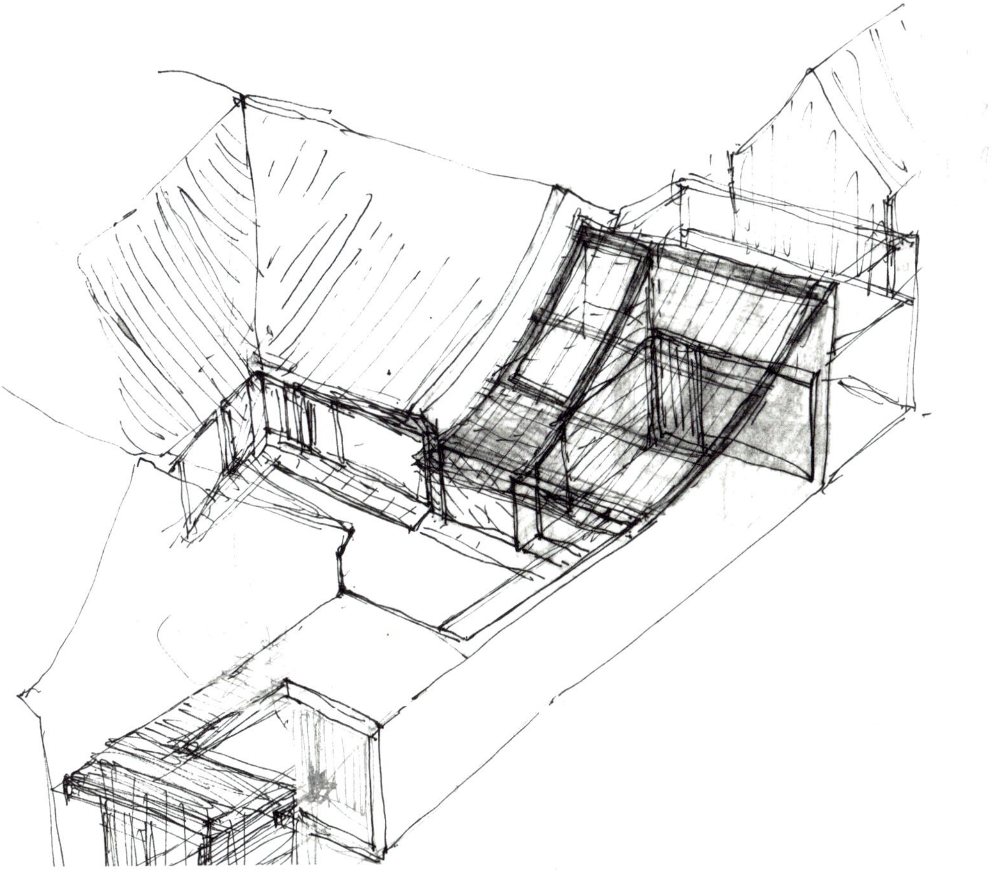

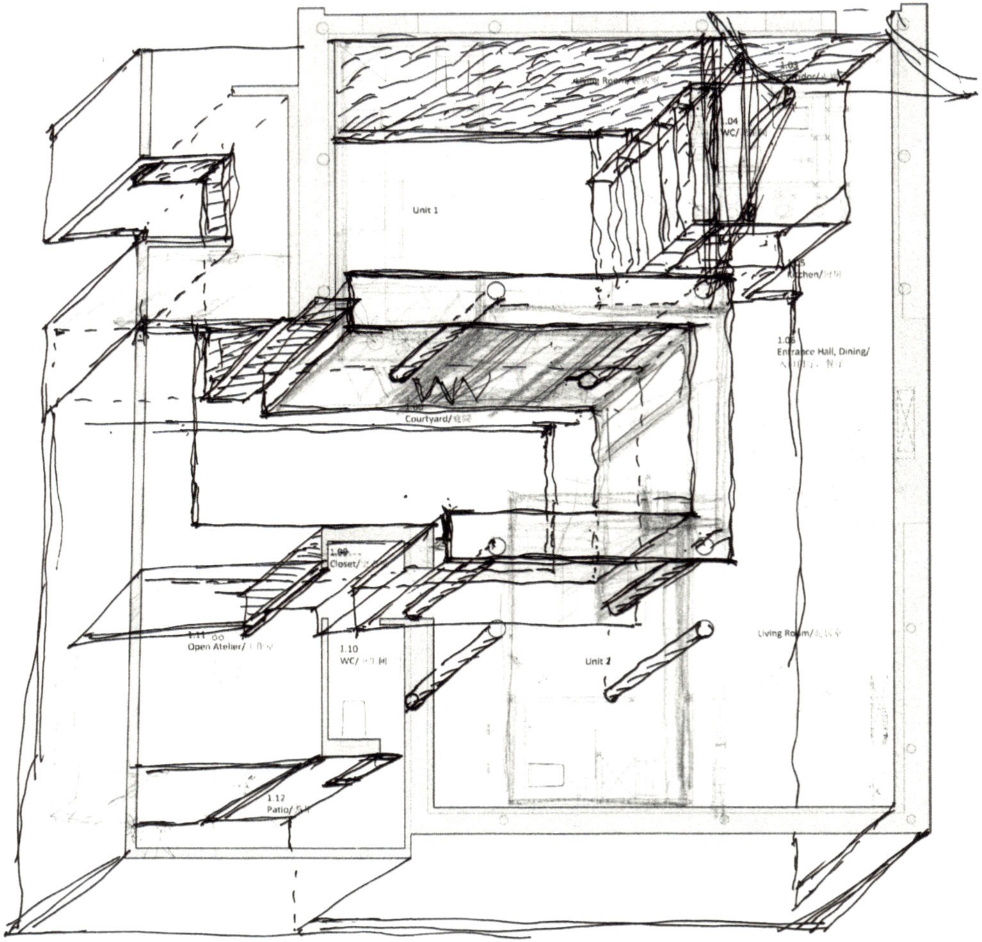
Unit 1
1.04
WC/
Kitchen/
1.06
Entrance Hall, Dining/
Courtyard/
1.09
Closet/
Living Room/
Unit 2
1.11
Open Atelier/
1.10
WC/
1.12
Patio/

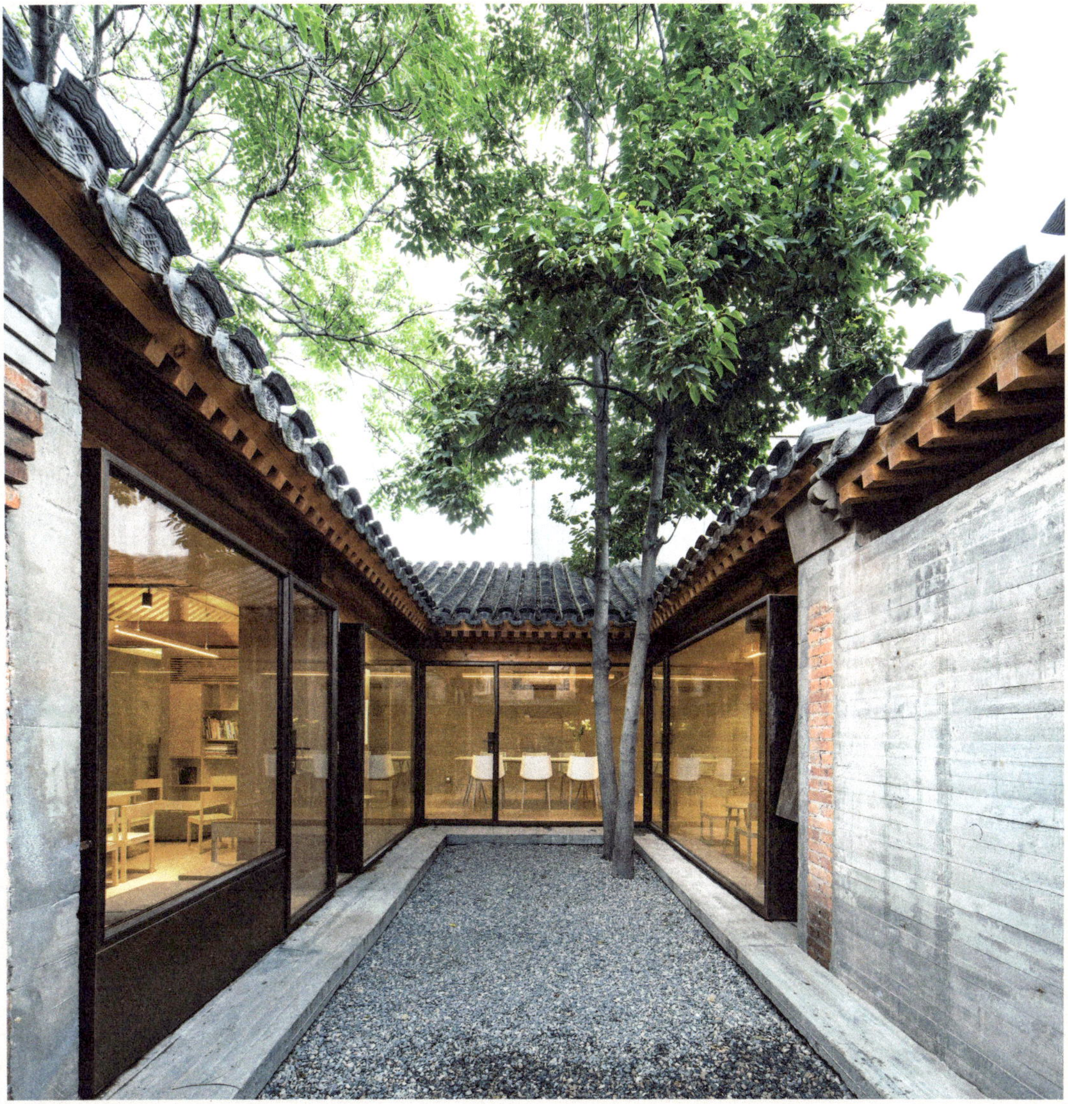

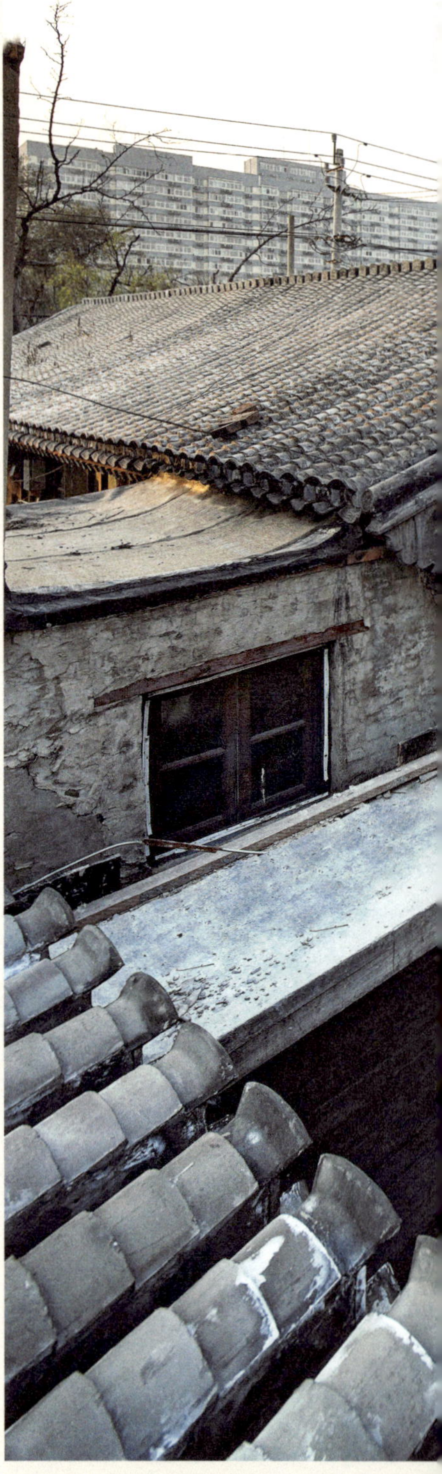

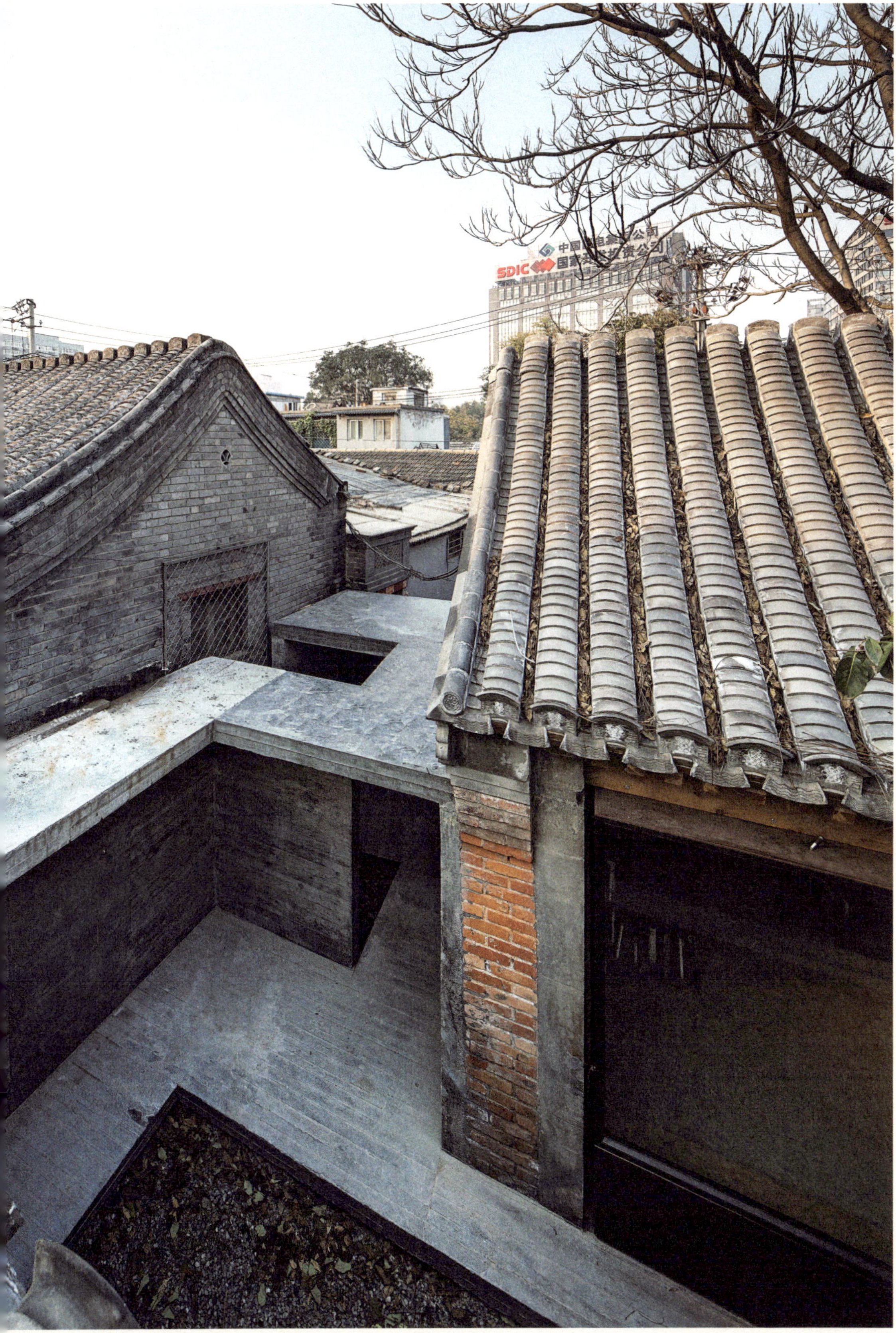
SDIC

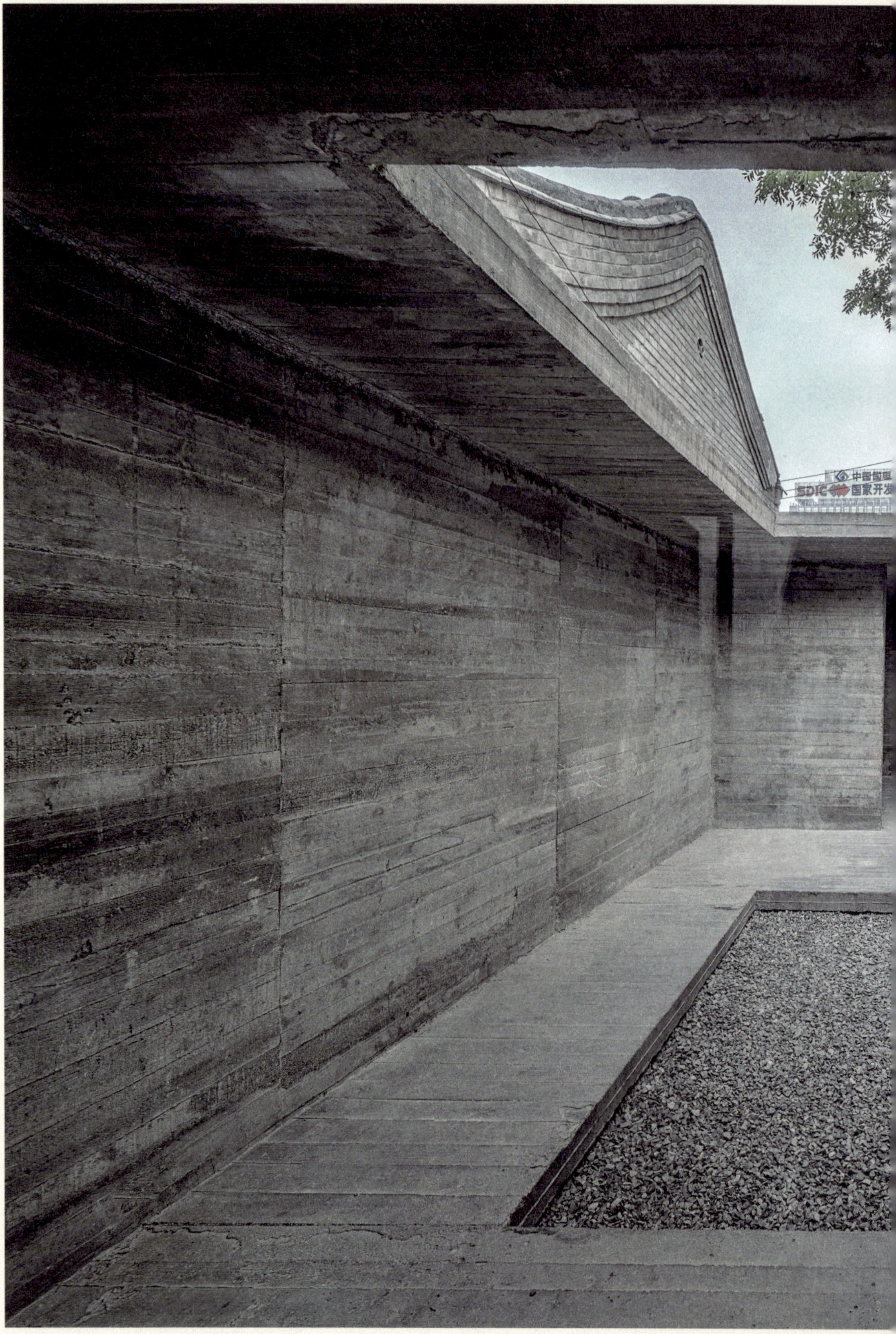
SDIC

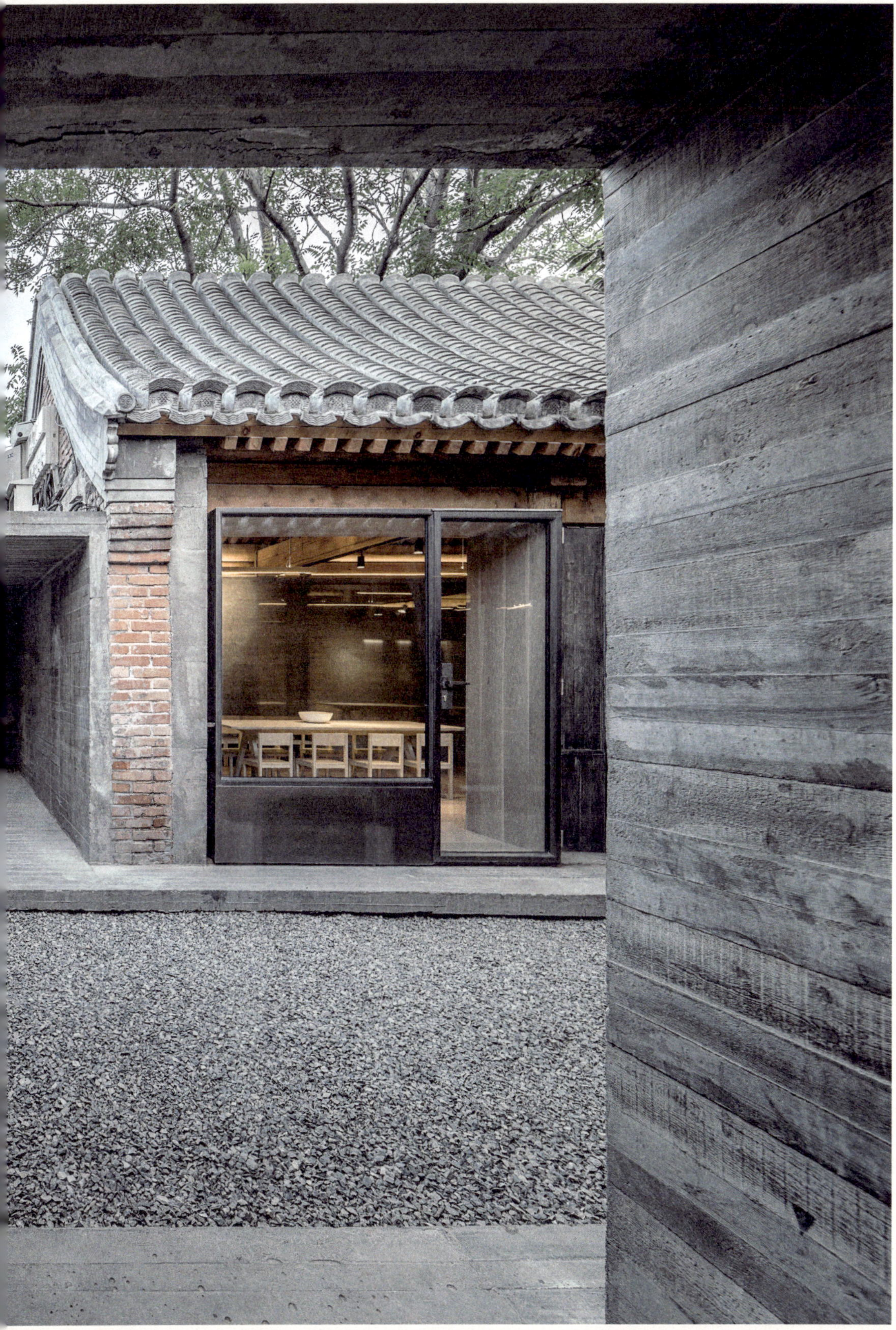

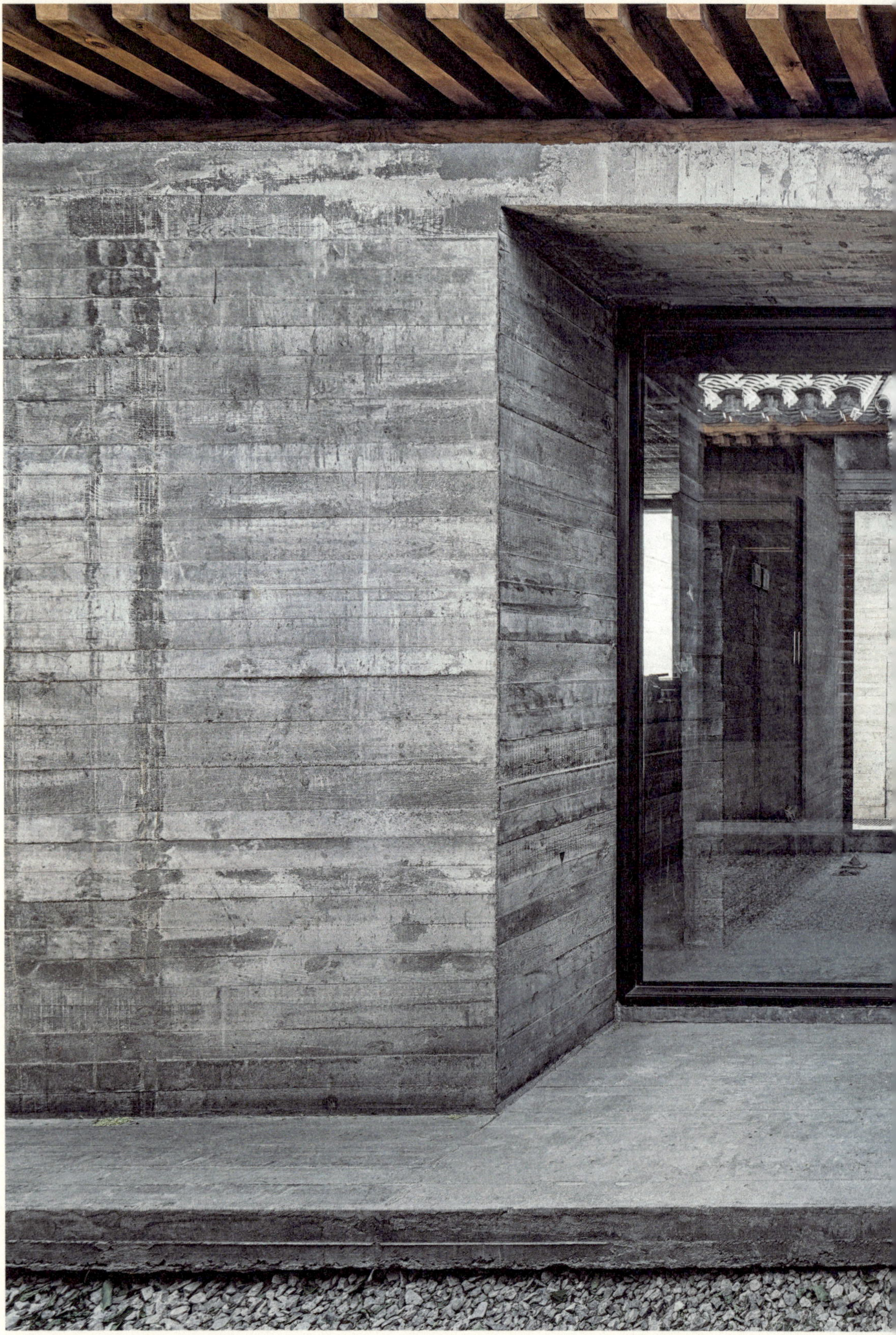

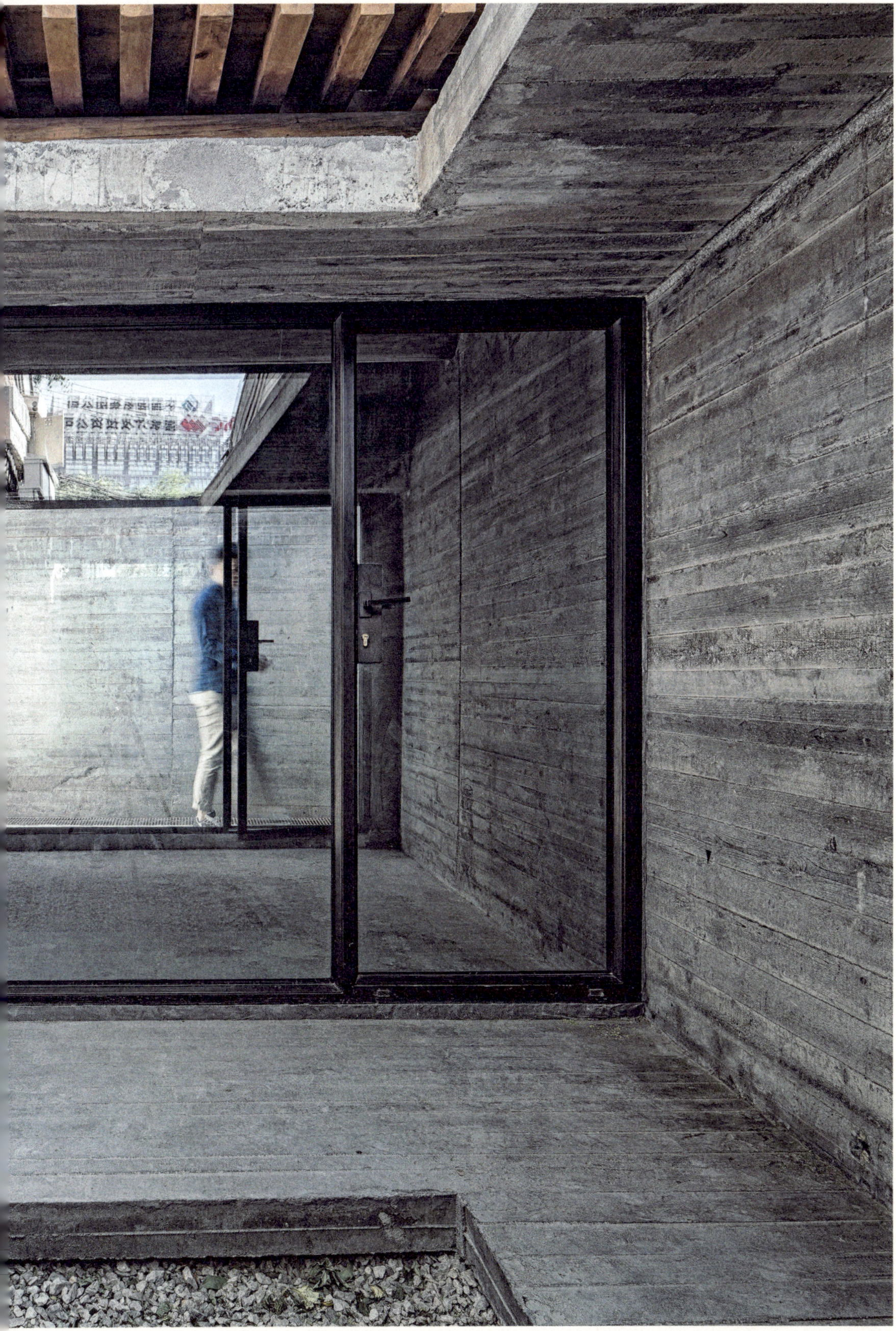

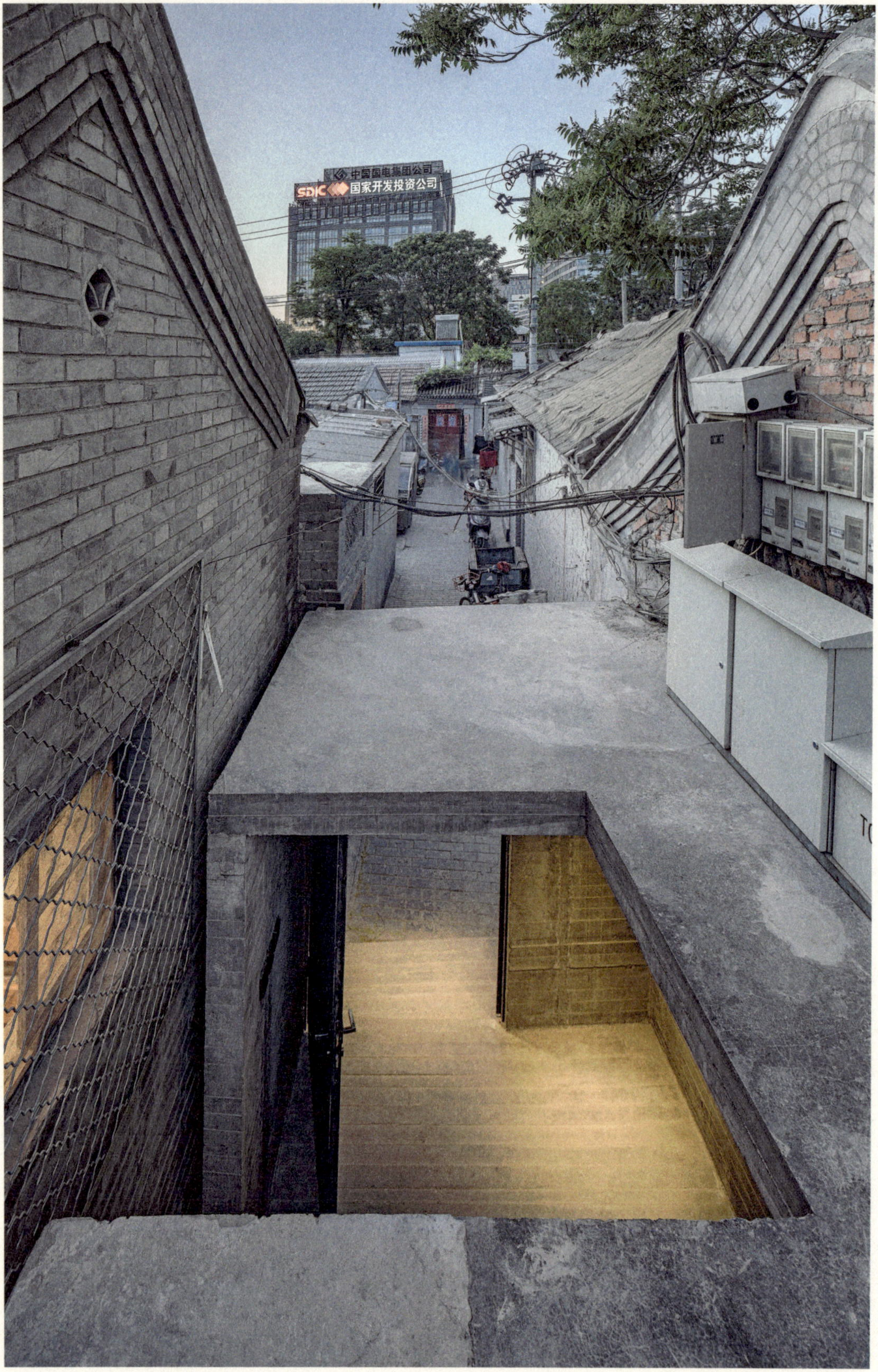
中国国电集团公司
SDIC 国家开发投资公司

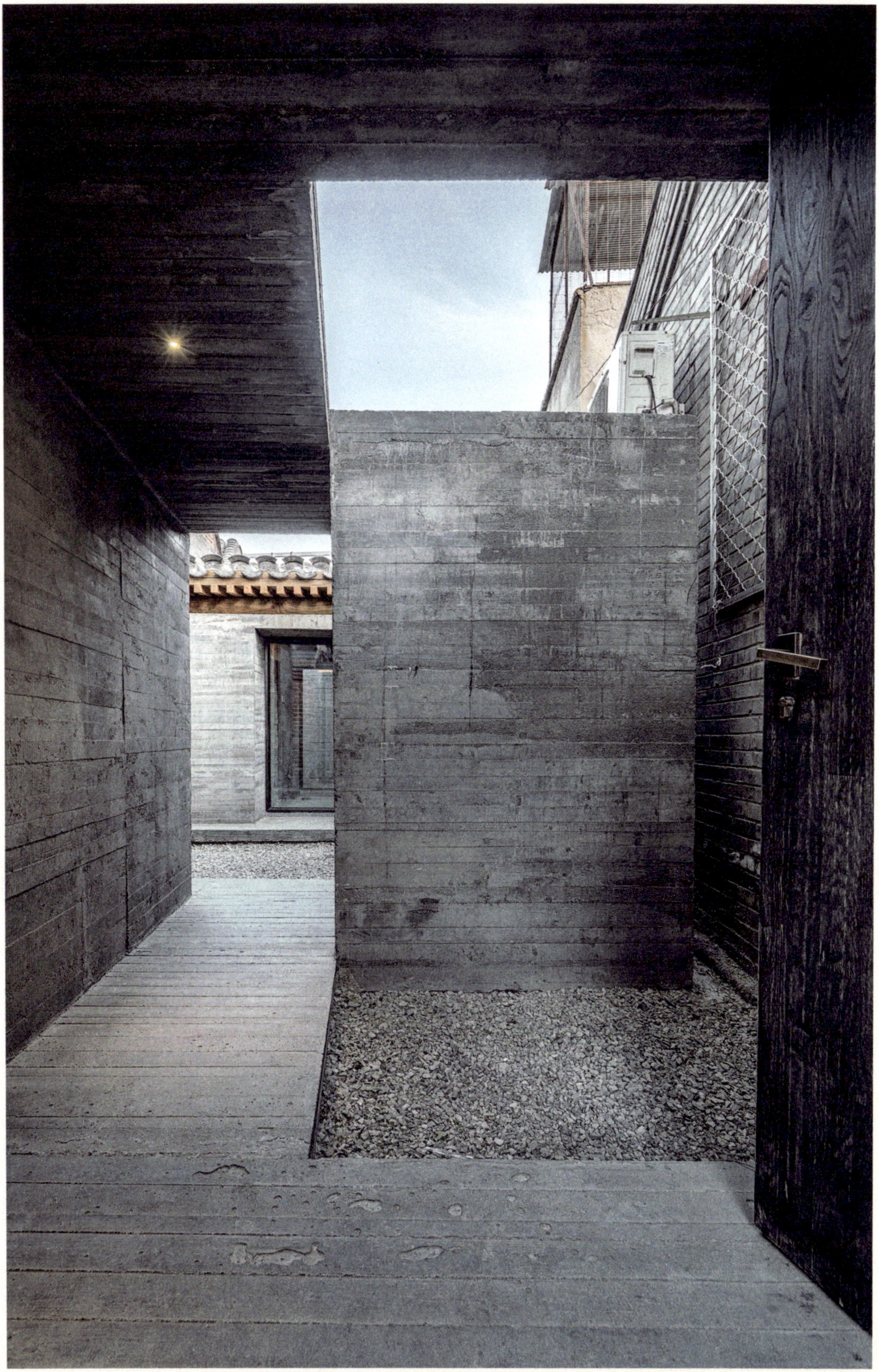

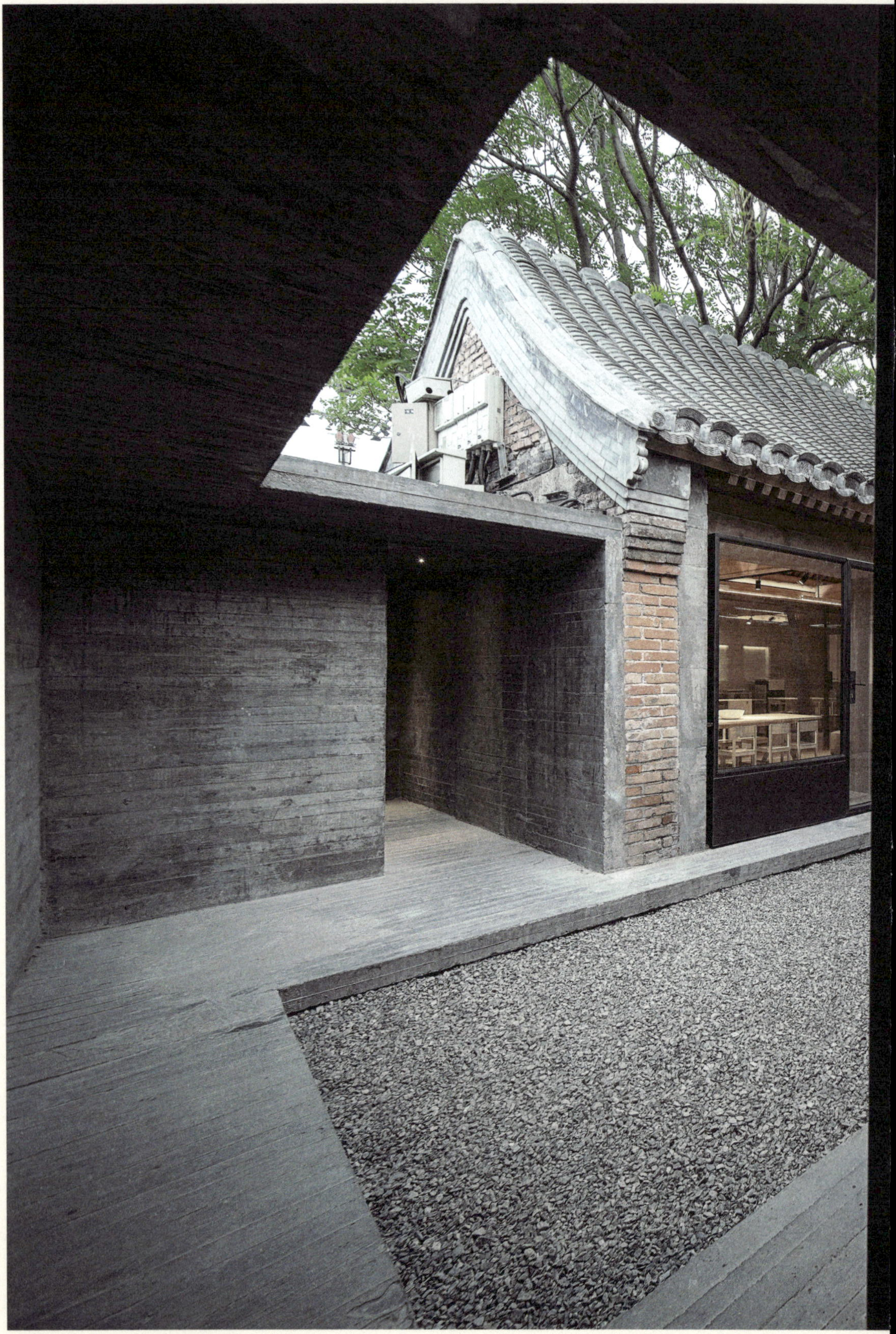

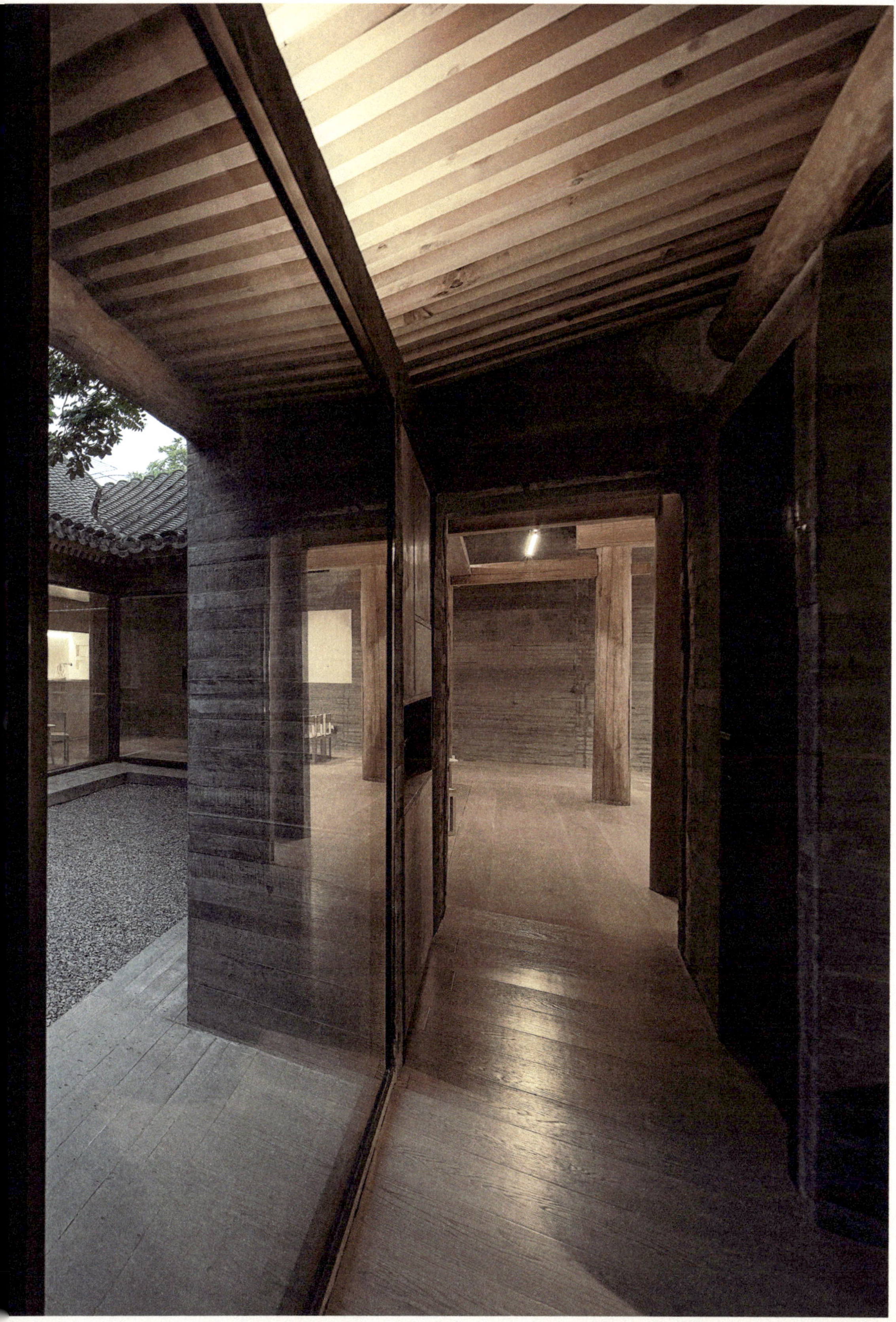

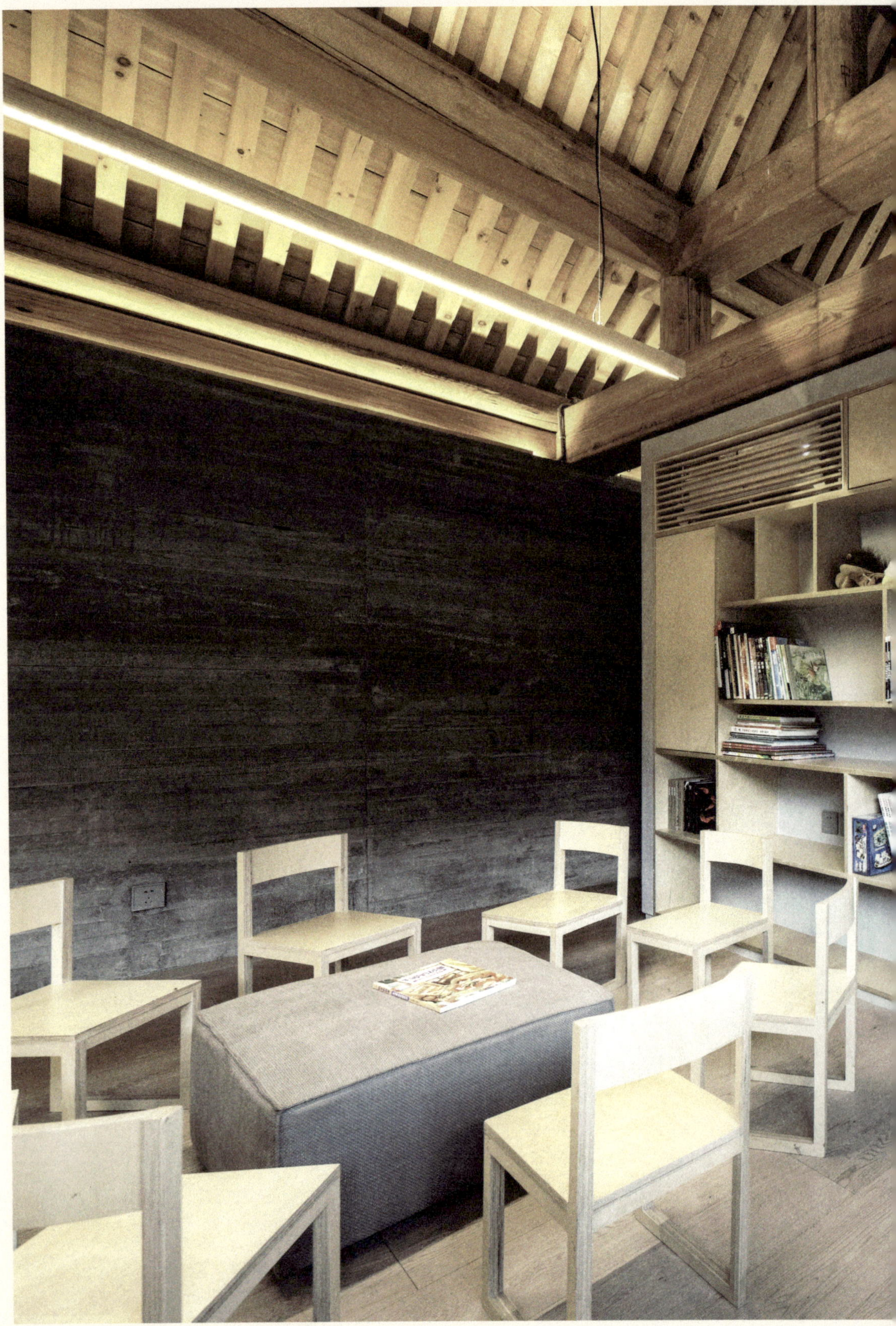

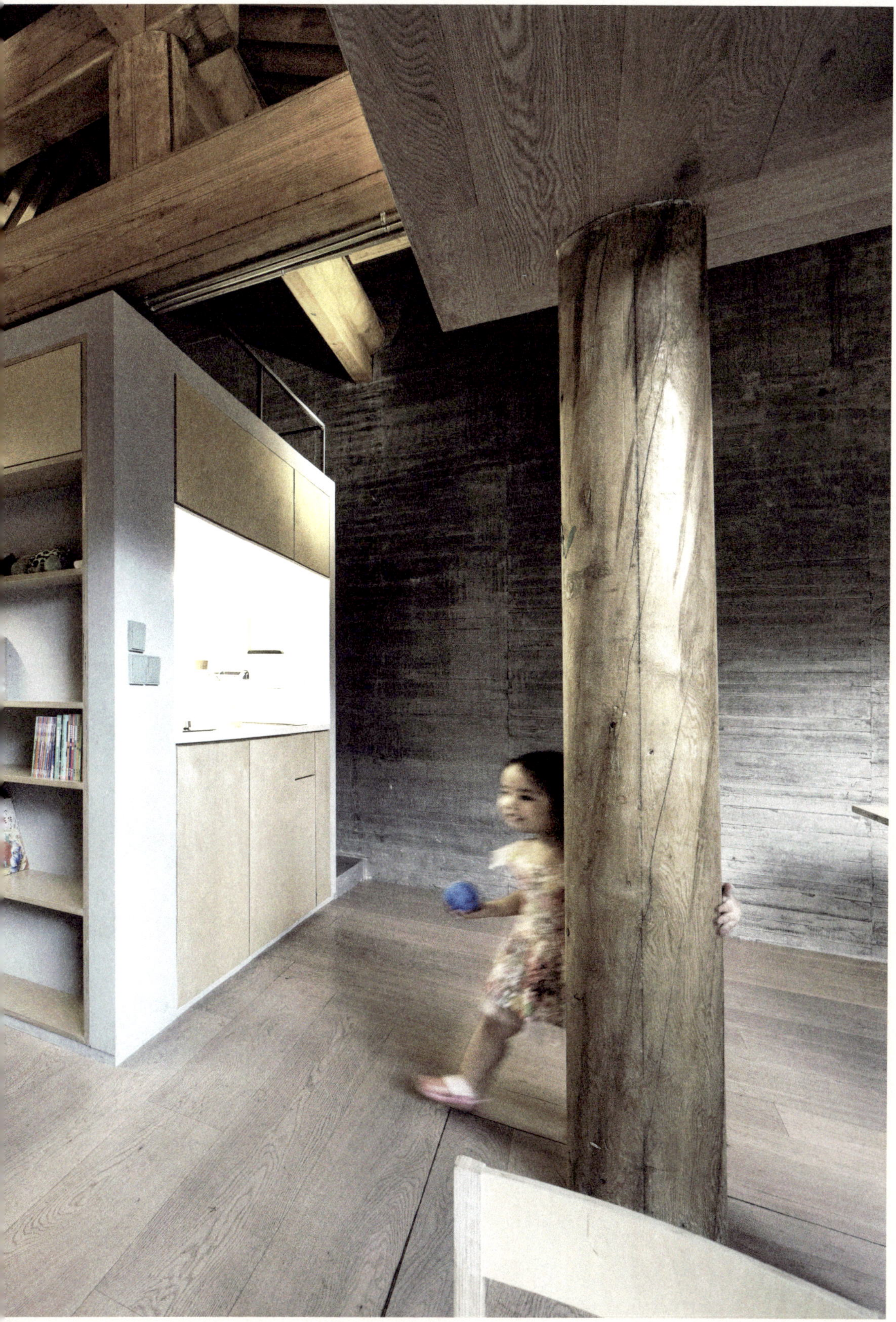

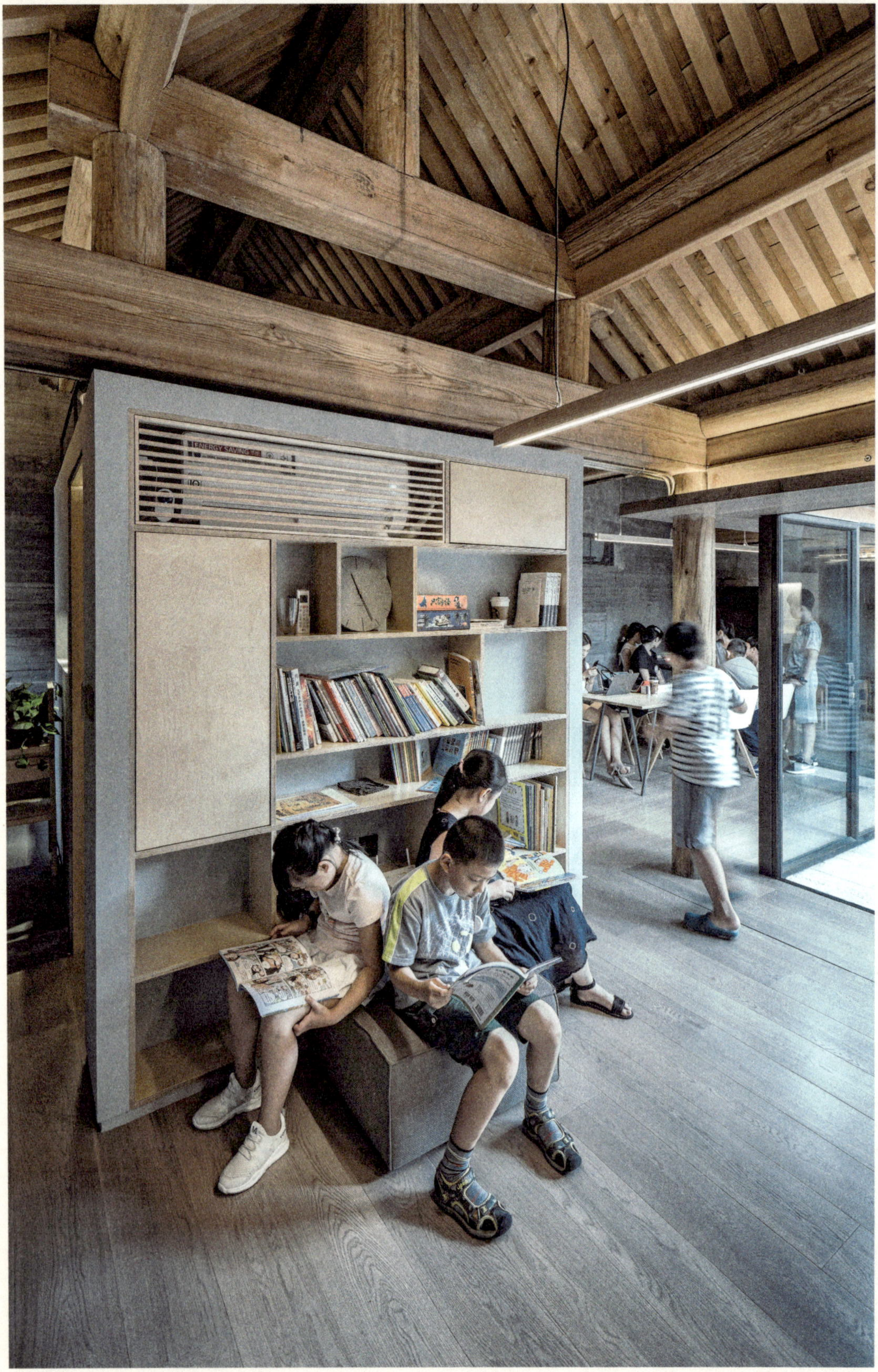
ENERGY SAVING

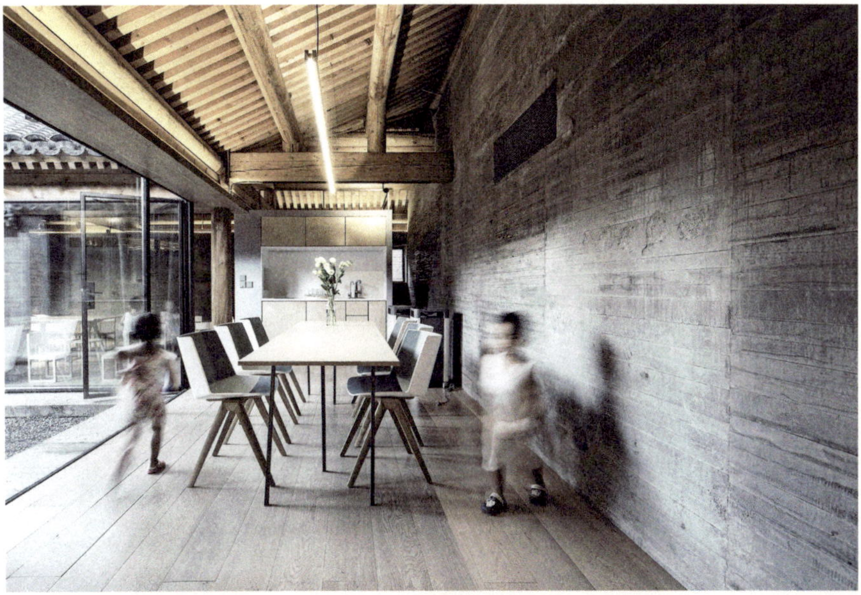

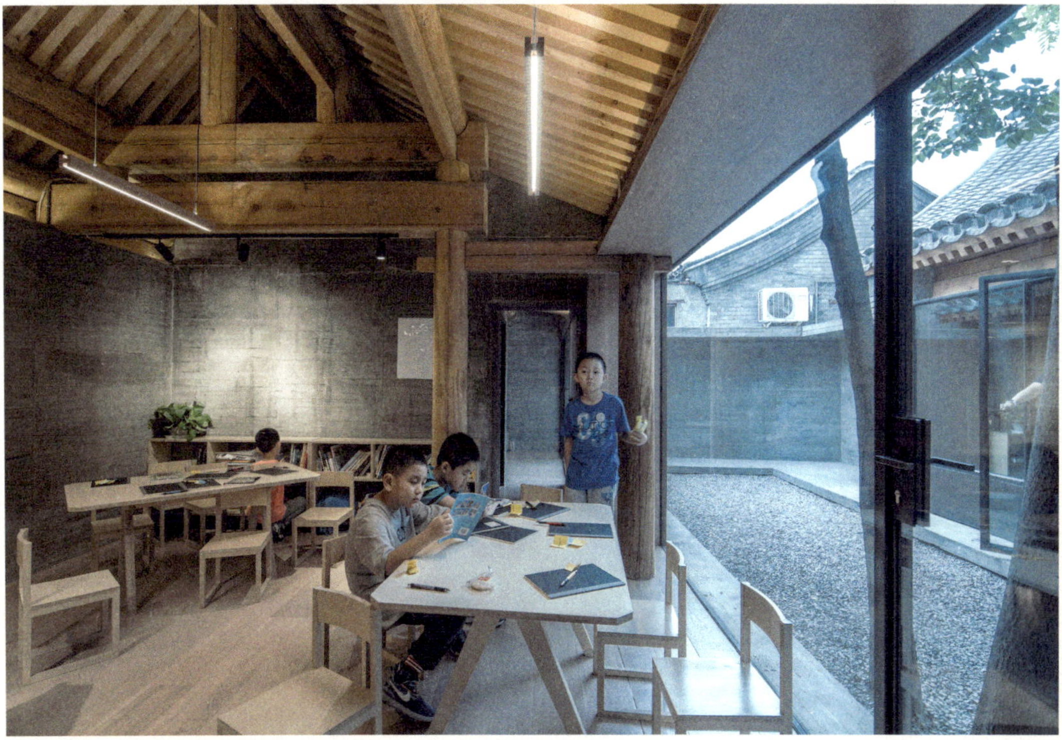

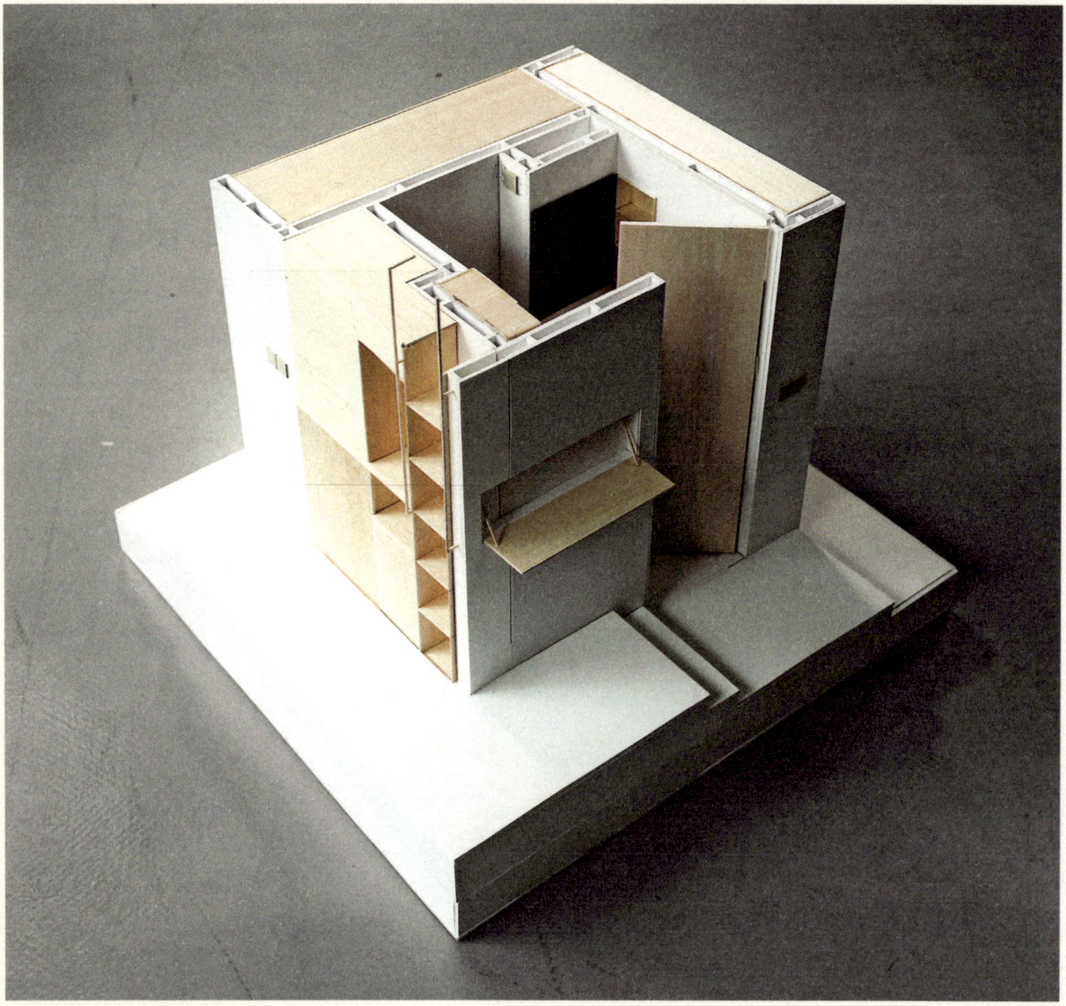

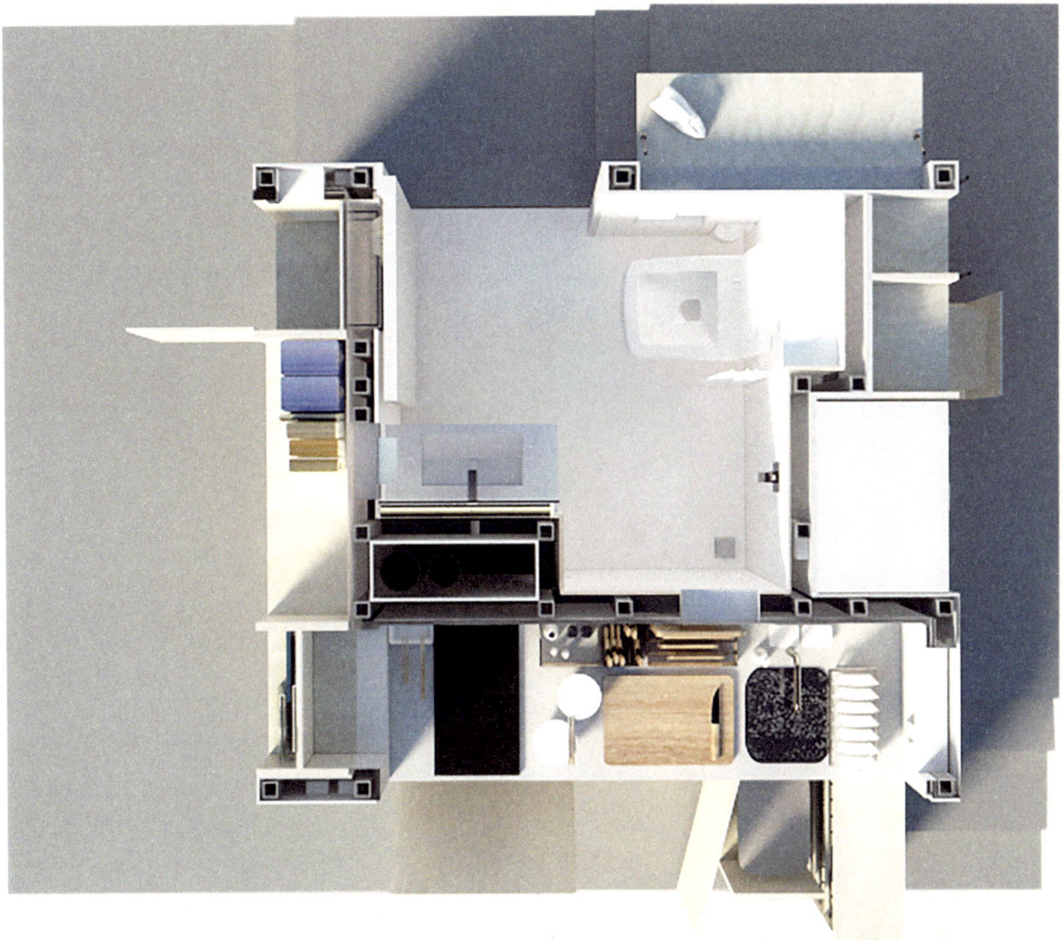

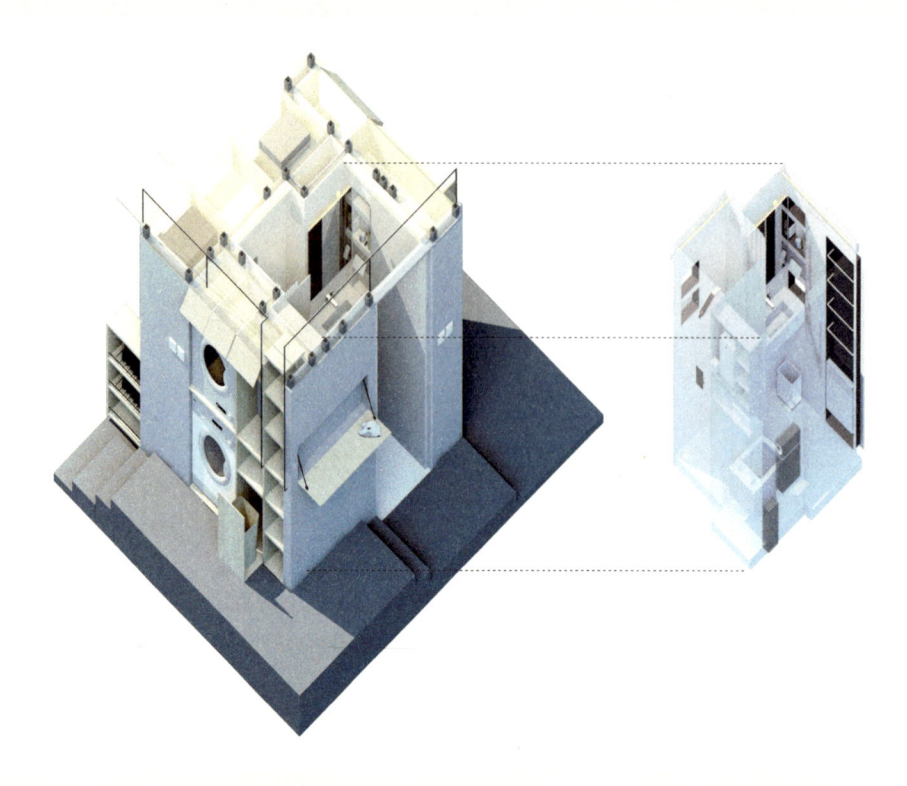

The service core facility is a 2 × 2.2 metre inserted unit, which took about a year and a half to develop. The aim was to design it as an industrialised product, which could be integrated into every household in the hutongs, providing amenities largely lacking in the old city of Beijing. In the long term, it could also be used in other rural and underdeveloped places in China and the rest of the world, raising living standards for more people globally.

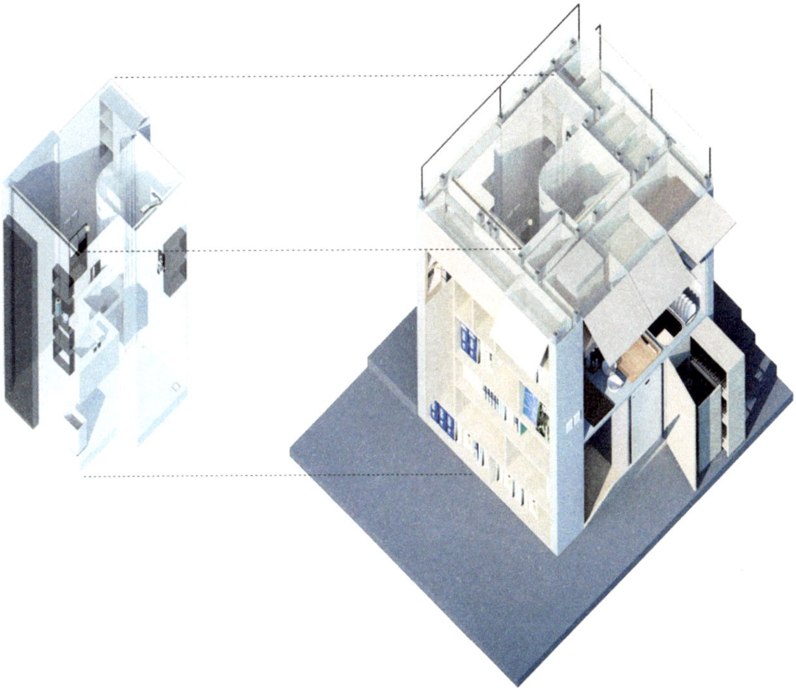

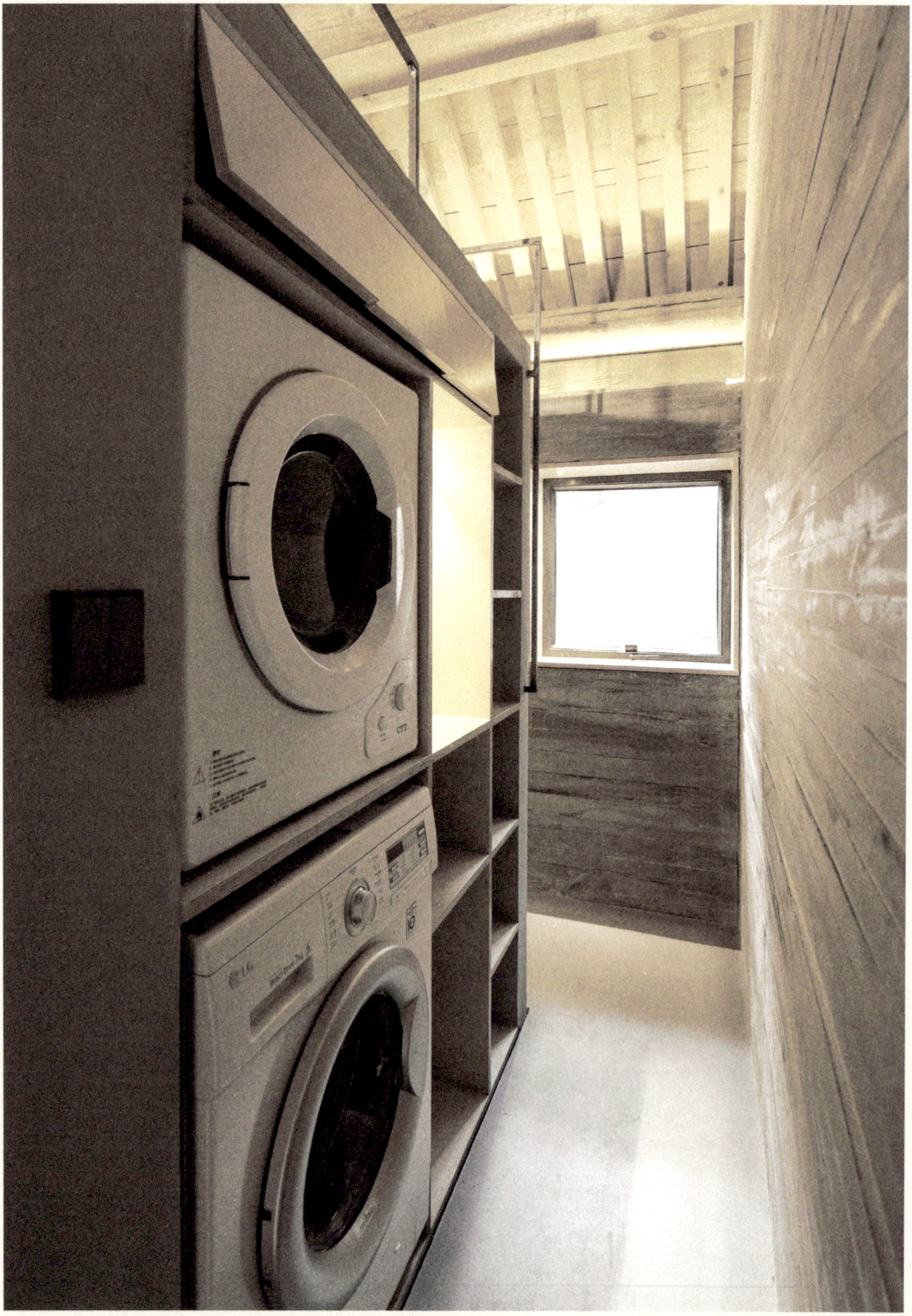

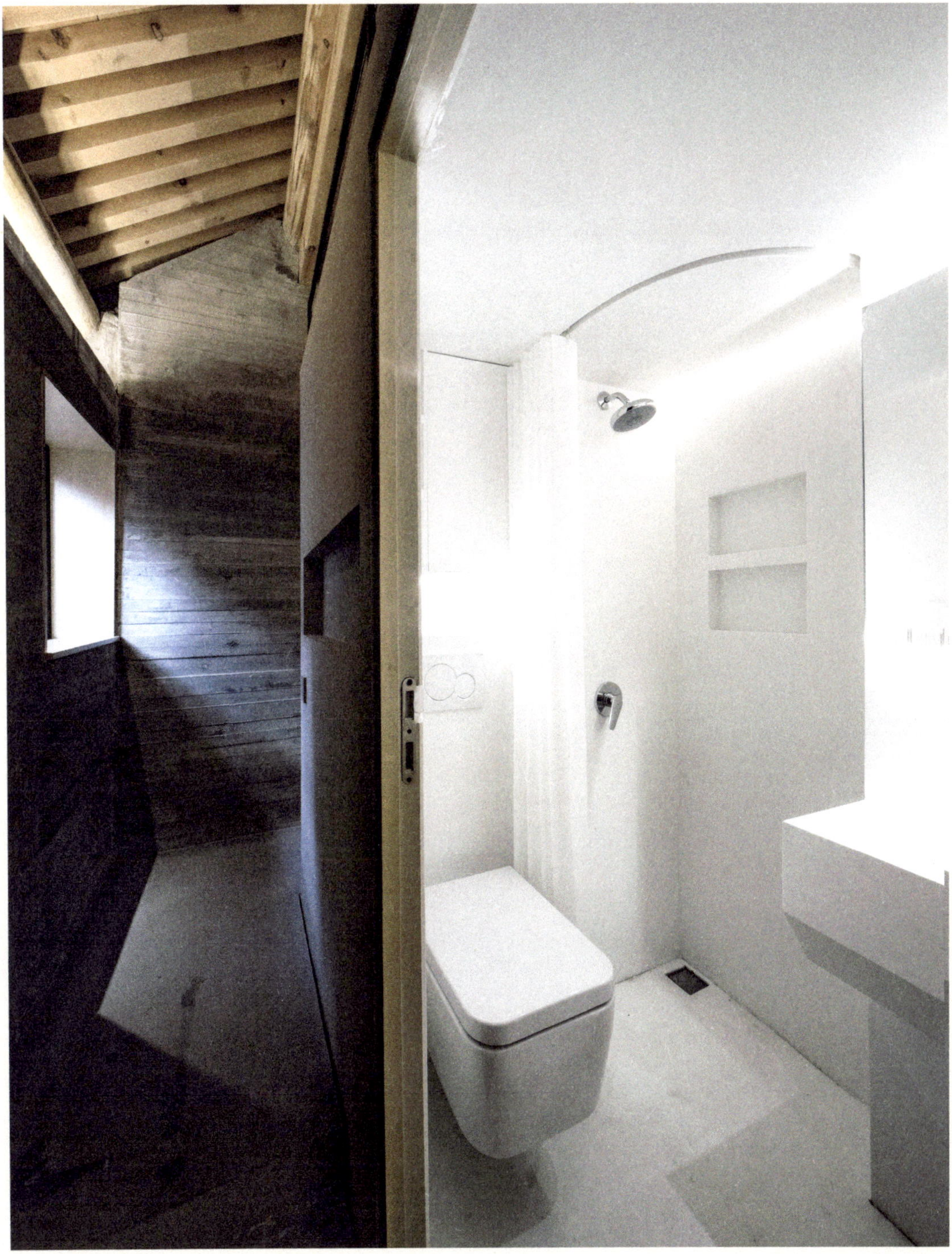

Hou Hai Courtyard
Hutong Home for the Elderly and the Children
Beijing Design Week 2016
Design year: 2016
Location: Shichahai, Beijing, China

This project for the Beijing Design Week in 2016 was built by
ZAO/standardarchitecture for testing the service core facility
before it was built in the Co-Living Courtyard.

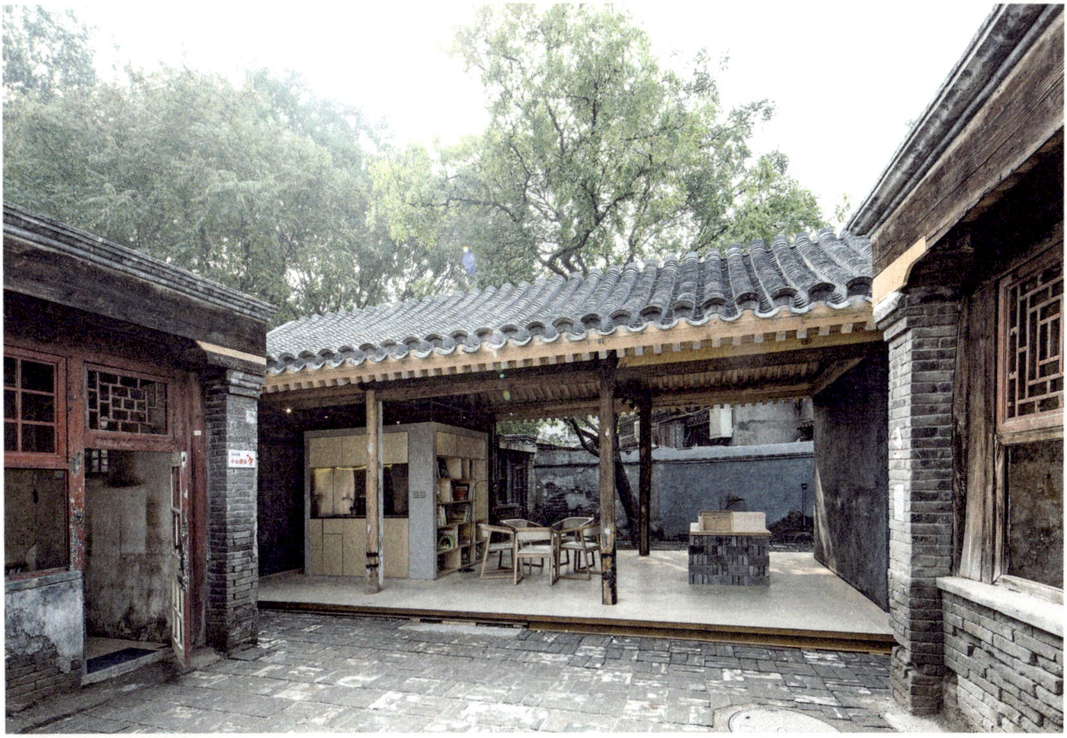

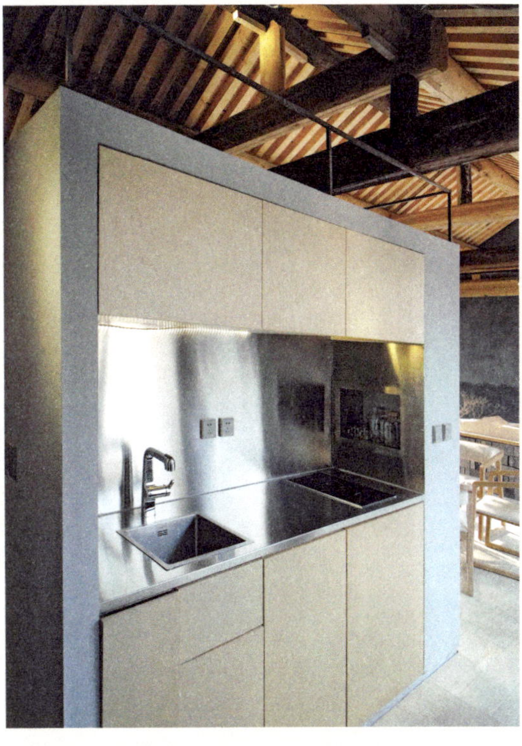

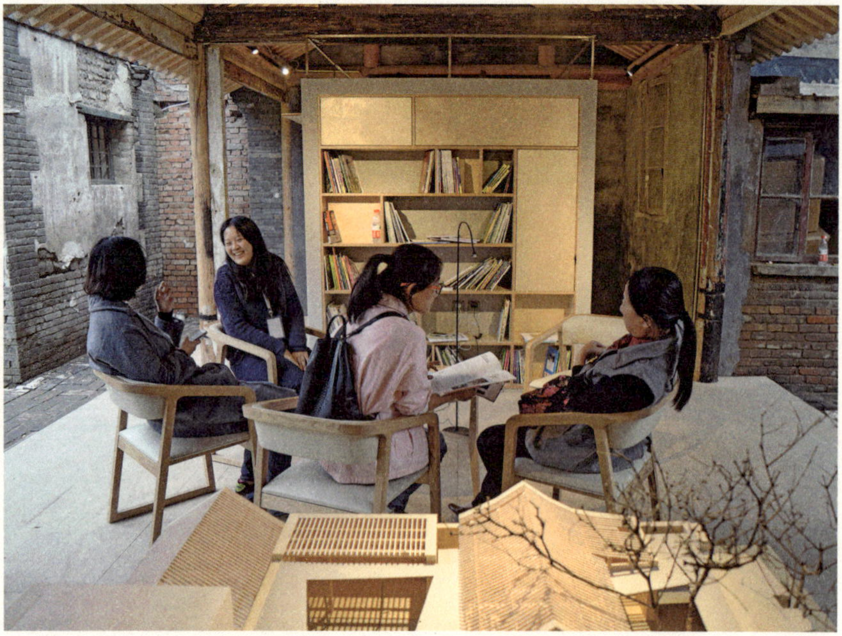

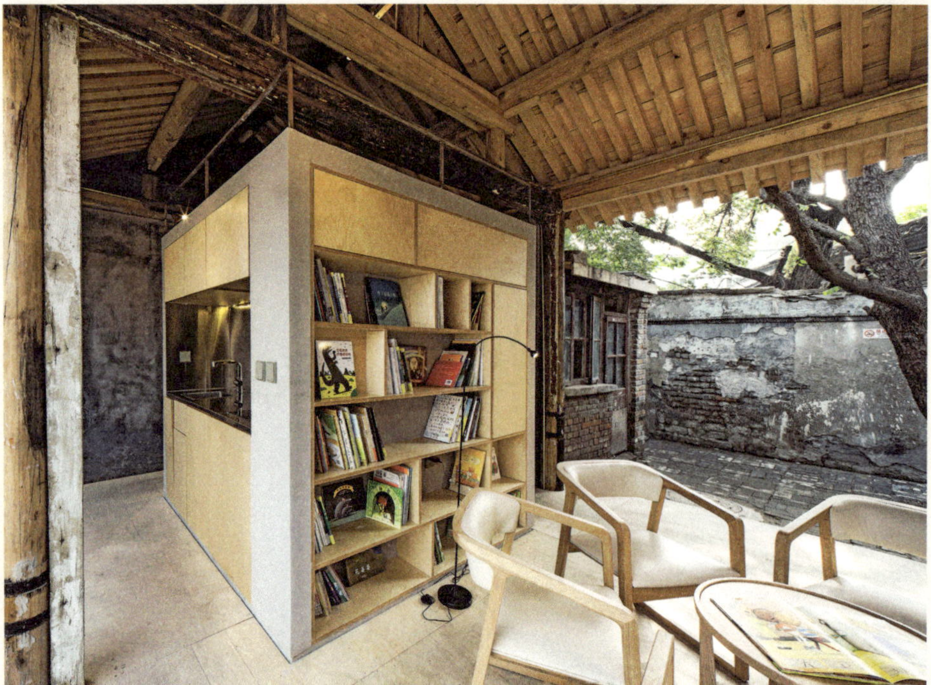

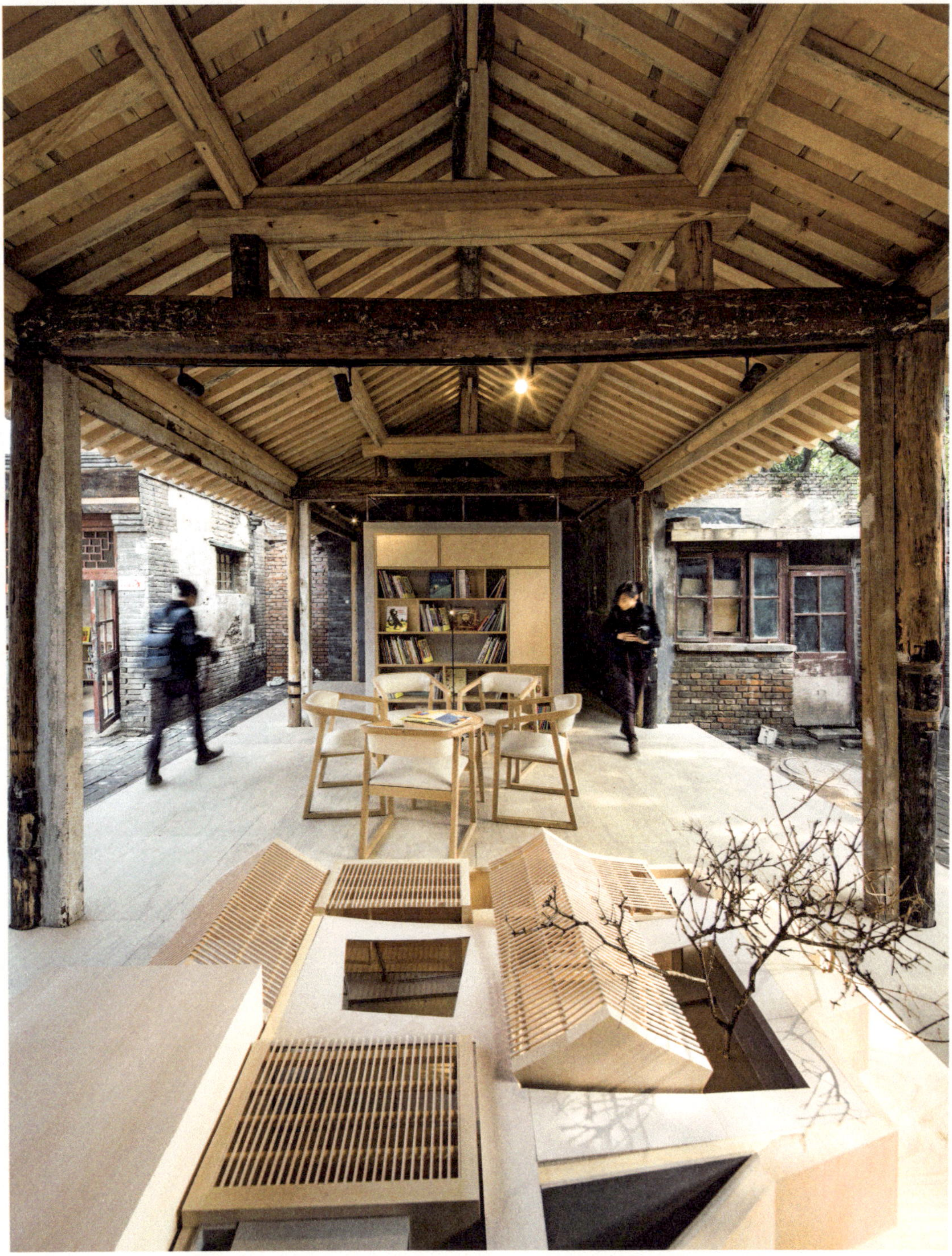

Hutong Living Conditions, Then and Now
Interview with Hai Daye, Wu A'yi and Wang Tong by Amanda Ju

Hai Daye (Uncle Hai) and Wu A'yi (Aunt Wu) are longtime residents of the Dashilar area. Both helped with the maintenance and activities that took place at Micro Yuan'er and Micro Hutong. Wang Tong is an architect at ZAO/standardarchitecture who worked closely with local residents during and after the hutong renovation projects. This interview took place on 6 July 2021, inside the Micro Yuan'er Children's Library. Hai Daye and Wu A'yi introduced to us the transformations of hutong living in the past decade, how they experienced the ups and downs of urban renewal, the degree of evacuation and relocation of the historical hutongs, and the activities that took place in Micro Yuan'er and Micro Hutong. Our conversation also covers the histories of Micro Yuan'er, how it transformed from a Buddhist temple built in the Ming dynasty (1368–1644) to a big messy courtyard after the Cultural Revolution (1966–76).

Hutong Living Conditions, Then and Now

Amanda Ju: How many years have you been living in this area? What are the major changes to these hutongs?

Hai Daye: I've been living in this hutong for sixty years. I moved here when I was sixteen, and I'm seventy-six now. Other than a couple years spent around the Hufangqiao area, I've observed every single change in the Dashilar region. All areas of life transformed. The facilities are much better now, more convenient.

Amanda Ju: What was the most inconvenient aspect of living back then? Bathrooms?

Hai Daye: Yes. Bathrooms. Although the locations of public bathrooms are still the same, it's much cleaner now.

Wu A'yi: Even a decade ago, public bathrooms were not cleaned regularly. Now there are designated sanitors cleaning multiple times a day. There's also air conditioning in the bathrooms now.

Amanda Ju: Hai Daye has been living here for sixty years. How long have you been here Wu A'yi?

Wu A'yi: Not as long, for about thirty years. My husband's family lived here, and when we got married, I moved in. That's how I got to know Hai Daye and other neighbours. I retired early from work in 2004, and since then, I've mostly stayed inside this hutong, helping to organise activities and events.

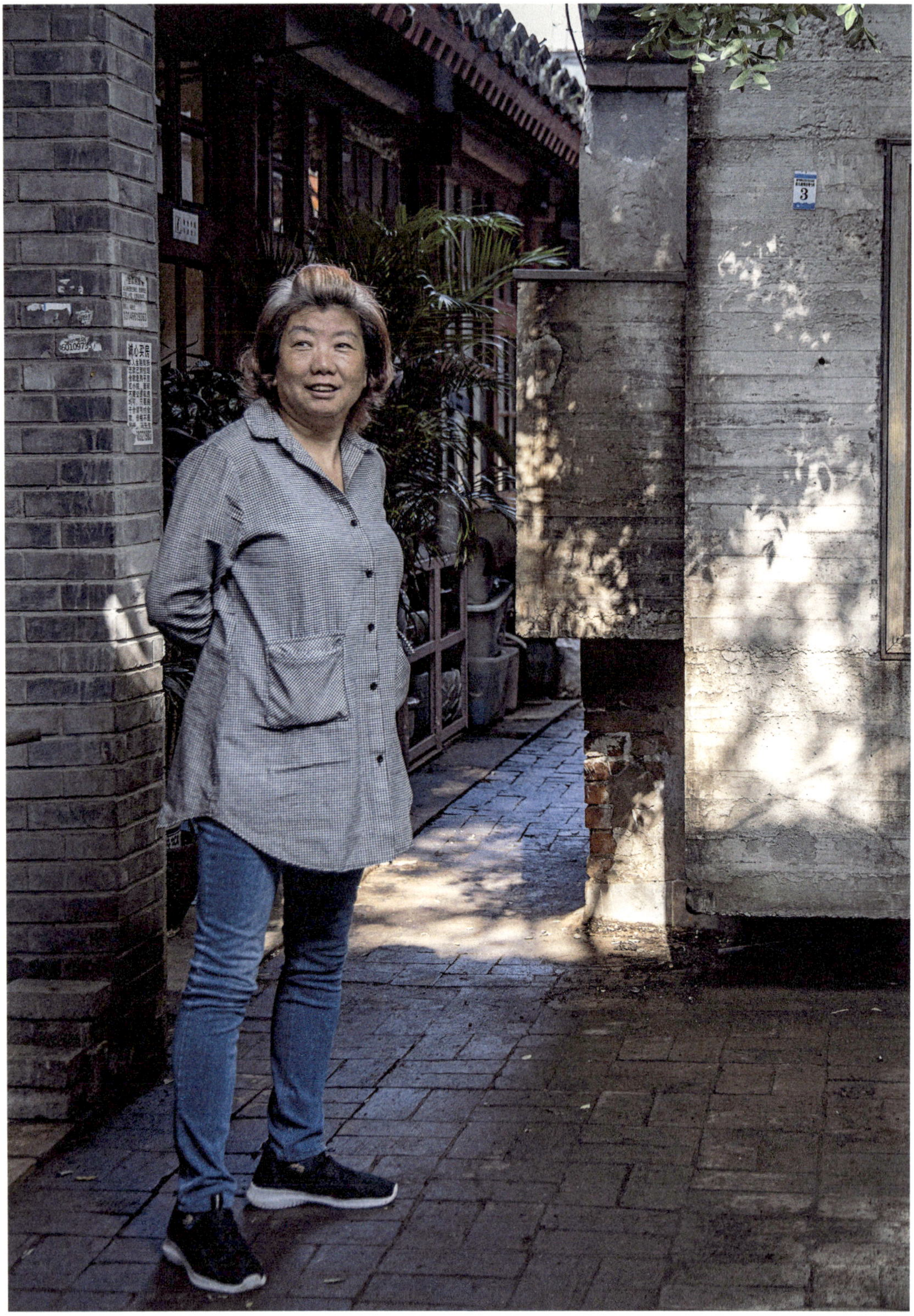
3

Hai Daye: Sanitation services have improved significantly in the past decade. I don't know if you've seen the television series *The Story of Zheng Yang Men*. It shows these large green trash cans that used to be on the side of the hutong lanes. No one wanted it near their door, so that was always trouble.

Wu A'yi: I remember those. Where to place them always caused conflict between neighbours. Now it's much better. Sanitors in this area take out the trash every day. The streets are lined with small bonsais and pots of plants.

Amanda Ju: The number of families living in Cha'er Hutong is much lower now, right?

Wu A'yi: Yes. Many original residents moved away during the *tengtui* (evacuation and relocation) process. There are also fewer renters now. You can't rent out public housing rooms anymore.

Hai Daye: Just next door to this courtyard (Micro Yuan'er), there used to be a renter who sold fried chicken. It was hard to keep the area clean. There would always be flies everywhere.

Tengtui (Evacuation and Relocation)

Amanda Ju: What percentage of hutong residents moved during the relocation process?

Hai Daye: At least half of the people who used to live here moved. It started early on for this hutong, about a decade ago. The relocation package was better when it first started, but it's increasingly scanty and less beneficial for us, so people are less willing to move. Sometimes there is the opportunity to move into a renovated courtyard, but those can be too expensive for local residents. It's not affordable.

Wu A'yi: We have a WeChat group with Xiao Yang, the artist who used to organise programmes for Micro Yuan'er and Micro Hutong. When she needs help communicating with the families and children in our area, I help her with that. The kids I knew from those activities all moved away. Some of them returned to their home cities to go to middle school.

Amanda Ju: Are those children mostly from migrant workers' families?

Wu A'yi: Yes. Most of them are not from Beijing. Compared to the high-rise apartments, hutong houses are cheaper. Rent is about 3500 renminbi a month. If you are only renting a room, it could be as low as 1000 renminbi a month.

Amanda Ju: Are there both privately owned hutong houses and public housing in this area?

Hai Daye: Yes, but less than 10 percent of them are privately owned. Those are the ones that can still be rented out.

Wang Tong: Tighter renting control policy started about five years ago. There used to be small grocery stores and restaurants all over the hutong area, with barbecue tables out during summer nights. That was all gone.

Communal Activities at Micro Yuan'er and Micro Hutong

Amanda Ju: When did the programmed activities for children begin at Micro Yuan'er?

Hai Daye: Micro Yuan'er opened on 25 March 2015. I remember the day clearly, and I was here to see it. When the reconstruction was first completed, Zhang Ke and his firm organised art classes and events for the children. Eventually there was an artist who did consistent programming for about four years. All the activities were free, and the kids from Tan'er Hutong Elementary School came after class. Sometimes they would dance or draw, and other times they just ran around and played. In the summer, the kids love to climb up the pavilion and hide under the tree. My grandson was one of them, but he hadn't even started school back then. In a way, he grew up playing in this courtyard.

Wang Tong: The summer concerts here are also memorable. There are artists playing various kinds of musical instruments. It's always a mixture of artists, a lot of them foreigners, and the kids. They get along well.

Hai Daye: Yang Jialin was the artist in charge of programming. I like to just call her "artist". She went to school in the UK and is connected with all of these foreign artists in Beijing. The artists would come and organise all kinds of art events for the kids. There was also this architect from Zhang Ke's firm, what was his name again?

Wang Tong: Stefano.

Hai Daye: Right, Stefano. He was often here playing music with the kids. He was a violinist before he learned to design buildings.

Wang Tong: Later on, another young woman from Hong Kong joined Yang Jialin. She had majored in sociology. The classes they organised were quite fun: there were paper-cutting lessons and warrior-dance lessons. One year they also put on a play.

Amanda Ju: Do most of these activities take place in the art classroom?

Wang Tong: In the art classroom and in this room, the children's library. Sometimes when there are no classes, Hai Daye will still come open the doors so the kids can use this space to read. Wu A'yi is in charge of the activities at Micro Hutong. She lives closer to that building.

Amanda Ju: What kind of activities take place there?

Wu A'yi: That place serves as an entertainment room for the community, and the activities tend to be geared toward older people. There are events like opera singing or film screenings. Sometimes Dashilar Investment Limited will also use that place and organise activities. Right now, they are planning an event about indoor plants. Also, Micro Hutong is a popular site during the annual Beijing Design Week. That's when we get the greatest number of visits by tourists and foreigners.

Amanda Ju: Is there another activity room in this community, other than in Micro Hutong?

Wu A'yi: I don't think so.

A Prehistory of Micro Yuan'er

Hai Daye: Because of the old tree, this courtyard has nice shade even during midsummer. You can feel the breeze when you walk by the front door.

Amanda Ju: I read somewhere that this tree is 300 years old.

Hai Daye: It must be over 500 years old. Did you see that the frieze on the front door says Lingjiu Si (Lingjiu Temple)? This courtyard was a temple built in the Ming dynasty. And so was the mosque down the street, also built in the Ming dynasty. This tree was planted when the temple was built. It is not the type of tree that regular households would plant.

Amanda Ju: This is a pagoda tree, right? It is so lush.

Hai Daye: It grows so nicely, and that is because of the well in the courtyard. In the past, all water used in the temple came from that well.

Amanda Ju: Do you know what kind of Buddhist deity was worshipped in this temple?

Hai Daye: I used to be confused about it as well. There were mostly nuns who lived here, but for a temple that houses nuns, it should be called "An" not "Si". Then there was this old man from Fangshan who told me the history of this place. He said that Lingjiu Si was a school for nuns. They came here to learn, and when they "graduated", they would be assigned to the individual "Ans" in Beijing.

Amanda Ju: I see. That's fascinating. So Micro Yuan'er used to be a Buddhist school for nuns?

Hai Daye: Yes. See, that multifunctional room was the main hall of the temple. The room that we are in right now, the children's library, and the room on the west side both housed Buddhist altars. The backrooms were dormitories for the nuns.

Wang Tong: When did this courtyard become residential? After the liberation (1949)?

Hai Daye: No. It wasn't until the Cultural Revolution (1966) that rooms were all given out to ordinary citizens. Some of the Buddhist altars were smashed during the clearing out of the "Four Olds" (old ideas, old culture, old habits and old customs) during the Cultural Revolution, and others were buried in the ground.

Wang Tong: We did find an old object underground during the renovation process. It is that stool which is now placed near the front door. Do you know what that is?

Hai Daye: It looks like a base for incense burners. That must be hundreds of years old.

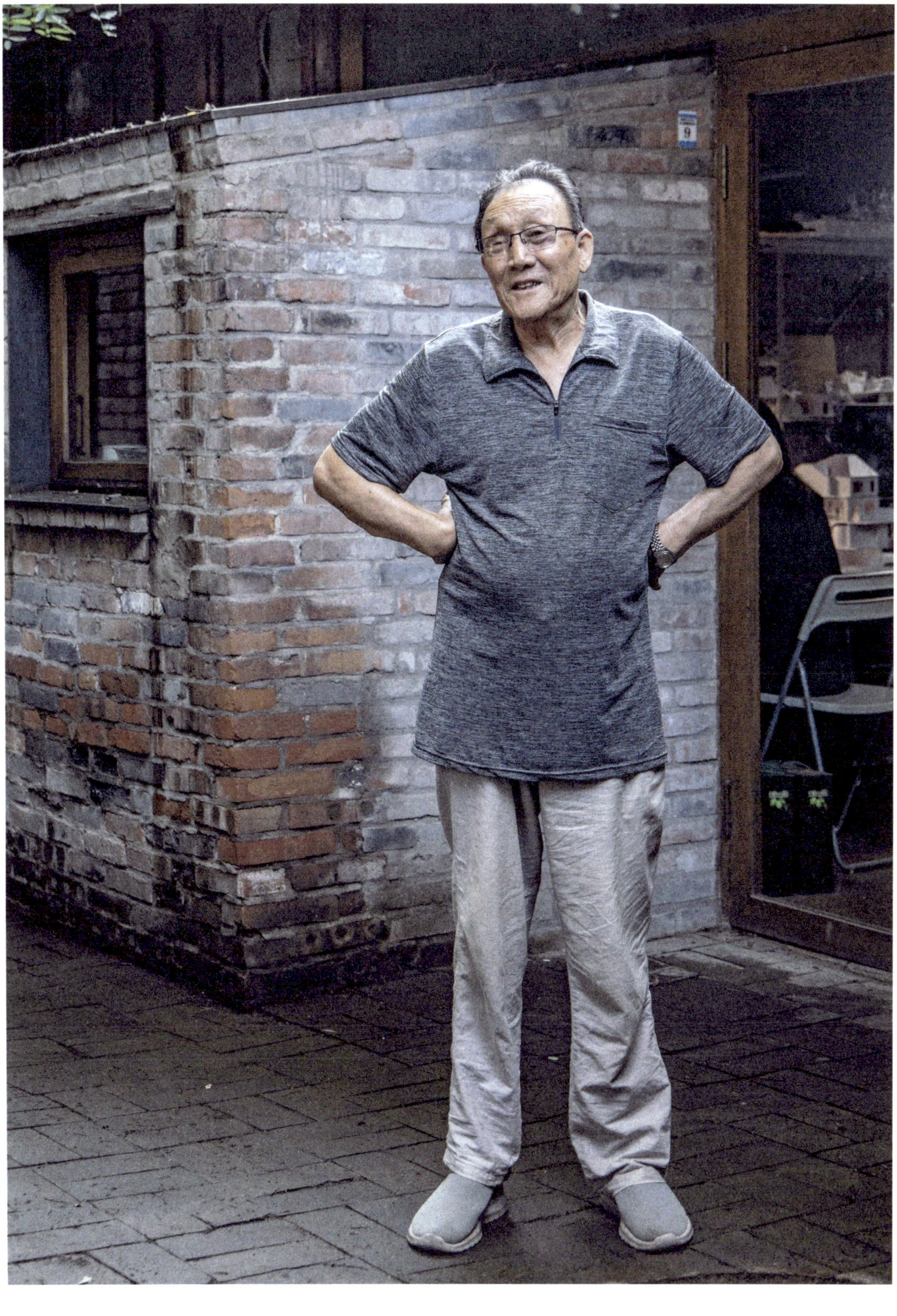

Amanda Ju: What about the mosque? You mentioned that it was also built during the Ming dynasty.

Hai Daye: The mosque was built by Chang Yuchun (1330–1369), the military general under the Ming Emperor Zhu Yuanzhang (1328–1398). The stories of Chang and how he built the mosque are documented on the stele inside the building.

Amanda Ju: When did people begin building those makeshift kitchen sheds in the hutong courtyards?

Hai Daye: Those began in 1976 during the Tangshan earthquake. They were initially homemade earthquake shelters. Back then, living conditions inside courtyards were so poor. People cooked inside their rooms during the winter, and in the summer, they used those sheds outdoors as cooking stands. Over time, the earthquake shelters became small kitchen sheds.

Wang Tong: This art pavilion that wraps around the pagoda tree was inspired by the structure of an original kitchen shed. Zhang Ke preserved the shape of that add-on structure.

Wu A'yi: It's in the same shape, except that now the floors are made of linoleum. You see those red bricks? Those were the original bricks, but the linoleum was from the reconstruction.

I heard that there are plans to transform one of the empty rooms in this courtyard into a bathroom.

Wang Tong: Yes. That is our plan.

Hai Daye: I've heard the same from Zhang Ke. He said: "Don't worry, the process is not over yet. We are planning to make a bathroom soon."

Intimacies in Scale
Interview with Brenda Fang, Kuang He and Naiji Tian by Amanda Ju

Brenda Fang and Kuang He are architects who worked at ZAO/standardarchitecture between 2014 and 2019. Naiji Tian is an architect currently working at ZAO. This interview took place on 6 July 2021, during the interviewer's visit to Micro Yuan'er, where Brenda and Kuang's own studio is now located. Our conversation began with the two architects' experiences working on hutong renovation projects at ZAO, the difficulties they experienced during that period, and the questions that the hutong renovation projects raised for them. We then moved on to talk about their return to the courtyard five years later as new residents, how they managed their relationships with the courtyard's original residents, and what they learned from the space's daily usage in terms of rethinking its initial design. Toward the end of the conversation, Brenda, Kuang and Naiji shared their understanding of Hutong Metabolism, and how this approach to "symbiotic renewal" differentiates from the more alienating trends of gentrification.

Amanda Ju: Let's begin by introducing ourselves. When did you join ZAO/standardarchitecture? And which hutong renovation projects did you participate in?

Brenda Fang: I joined in 2014, after graduating from architecture school in Switzerland. In late July, I joined the Micro Yuan'er project, which was my first project at ZAO. That summer, we built a plywood version of the children's library and the art pavilion as models of the renovation project shown during Beijing Design Week.

Amanda Ju: Are you still a member of ZAO?

Brenda Fang: Not anymore. I formed my own architecture studio in 2019. When it was first established, I needed a place to use as my office, so Zhang Ke allowed me borrow a room in Micro Yuan'er – the art classroom. It's a particular serendipity to be able to now work in the same space that I worked on as an architect.

Kuang He: I also joined ZAO in 2014, about two months later than Brenda. I had just graduated from college and moved back to China. During my first day of work, I came to visit the construction site at Micro Yuan'er. It was in an early stage of demolition. Brenda was there, adeptly looking after the process.

Amanda Ju: Is Micro Yuan'er also your first project at ZAO?

Kuang He: I didn't join this project. I worked on the design and construction of the Co-Living Courtyard in the historical Baitasi area, which included research for renovation plans of the entire area – an east-west fork located around Fuchengmen.

Amanda Ju: So ZAO designed a series of hutong renovation projects, and then there are other commercial projects?

Brenda Fang: Right. Zhang Ke was interested in exploring the different possibilities of hutong renewal. Micro Yuan'er was the first one of these renovation projects. Then there is Micro Hutong, not far from here, which is a study of the possibilities of creating social housing on a very small scale, and within the fabrics of a space like a hutong. After I worked on Micro Yuan'er, I also joined the renovation of the Co-Living Courtyard. That project began with research and planning of the entire area, then the implementation of reconstruction within a courtyard of 150 square metres. For interior design, we imagined a service core that would accommodate all essential facilities of a living space – kitchen, bathroom, laundry and storage – within 4.5 square metres. This project lasted about three years. More recently, ZAO has been working on a series of hutong renewals at Yu'er Hutong, which is a special conservation zone for Beijing's Dongcheng District.

Amanda Ju: What are some basic differences between these three renewal projects – Micro Yuan'er, Co-Living Courtyard, and the ones at Yu'er Hutong – both on the level of the design concept and in terms of their implementation?

Brenda Fang: First of all, their initial conditions were different. Micro Yuan'er had original residents, and a 500-year-old pagoda tree. There used to be a dozen families living in here, as you could tell from the number of electric metre boxes on the wall. It's a courtyard with a long history that is also layered: there is the history of this space as a temple, during the late imperial period. Then there is the history of it as a *dazayuan* (big messy courtyard) for the past fifty years or so. When the policy and practice of *tengtui* or "voluntary" evacuation came to be, some original residents moved away, but others were able to stay, adding yet another layer of temporality history.

When we were exploring redesigning concepts, we did not want to return this space to a past moment in time, but to articulate the multiple layers of temporalities that belie the linear sense of historical development. For example, the renovation did not wipe out some of the add-on structures built by the original residents – those makeshift kitchen stands – because they carry with them the particular history of housing scarcity in Beijing during the past couple of decades.

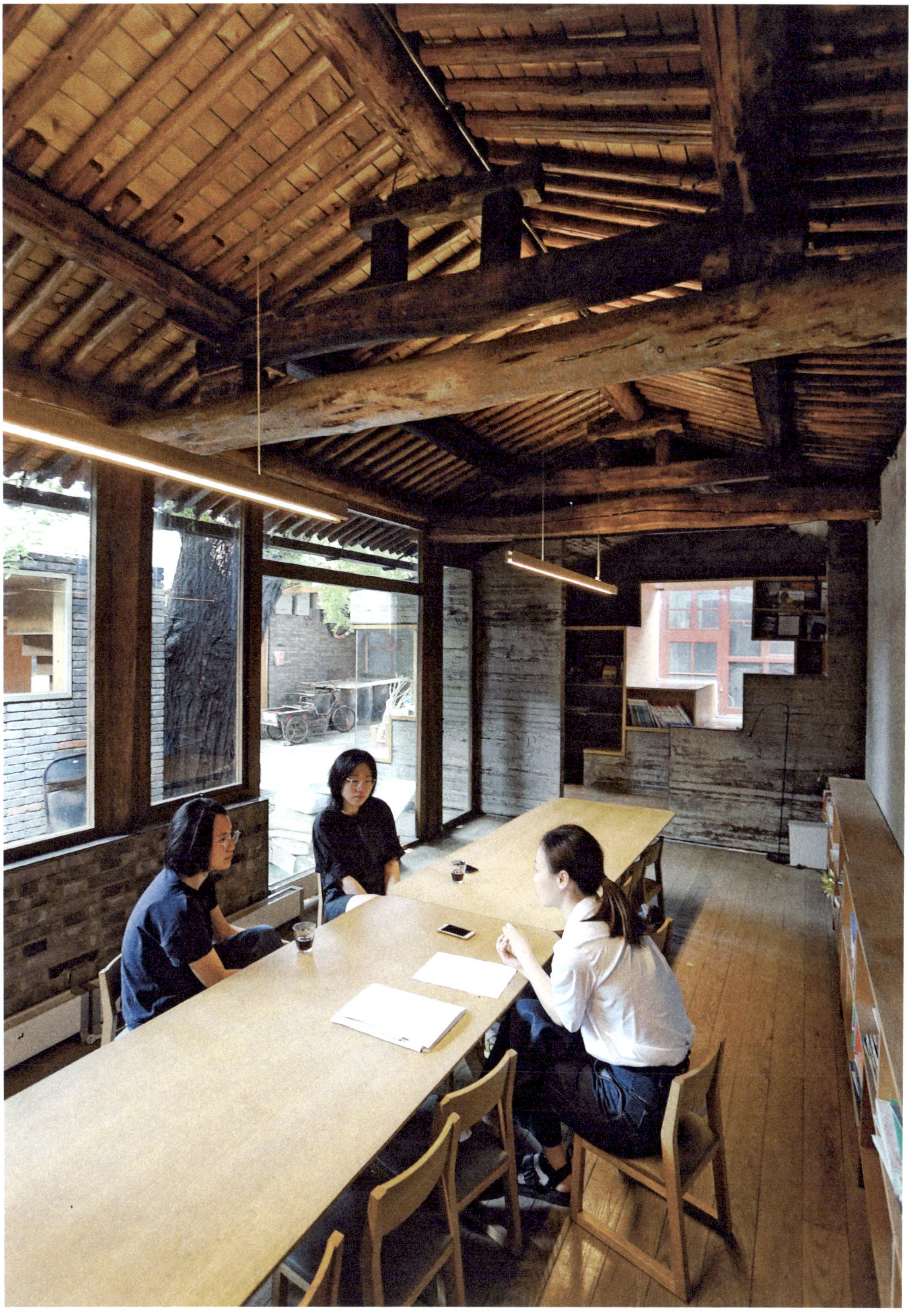

This more recent history of tension and scarcity is not of any less value than the one about religious diversity; they were pasts that are in symbiotic existence, and we wish to preserve that sense of tensegrity in our design.

Kuang He: The original residents of Micro Yuan'er built an add-on structure that wrapped around the pagoda tree, which became the inspiration for this pavilion with an external stairway going up around the tree.

Amanda Ju: I can sense that the texture of a lived space is preserved in this redesign. It echoes the spatial negotiations that go on constantly in a multifamily courtyard. I learned earlier today that these add-on structures were initially small earthquake shelters built by residents during the 1976 Tangshan earthquake. Those shelters eventually morphed into makeshift kitchen sheds.

Brenda Fang: Yes. They used to be homemade earthquake shelters. These transformations are interesting. You can see the two spatial protrusions that extend outside our studio wall. Those were initially spaces for storing coal. Now we use one of them as a printing corner and the other as a coffee stand. They have become interesting nooks in our office space.

Amanda Ju: During the research, design and renovation process of Micro Yuan'er or the other hutong renewal projects, were there any challenges that are particularly memorable?

Brenda Fang: To be frank, during the construction period, the biggest challenge was relations with the original residents. Not only relations with residents within the courtyard, but also other families living in the neighbourhood. A lot of the time, we had to understand how design concepts were reinterpreted by local residents, and communication with them was key to the progress of construction.

Amanda Ju: Many of these hutong areas are in the process of evacuation and relocation, and that in itself is a tension-filled state, requiring a lot of negotiations between parties of varying power.

Brenda Fang: Yes, for sure. There are a lot of hutong renovation projects in Beijing, and the question we posed to ourselves – both during the design process and during construction – was how we could attend to the communal and public nature of hutong living and avoid transforming the renovated courtyard into a private space. That foreclosure (to certain populations of original residents) is what we tried to avoid.

Amanda Ju: Are most hutong renovation projects in Beijing done on a small scale, like Micro Yuan'er and Co-Living Courtyard, both of which are implemented within the perimeters of one courtyard? Or are there more systematic reconstructions?

Kuang He: Hutong renovation in the Dashilar area is systematic, because there is a managerial entity – Dashilar Investment Limited (DIL) – that organises the implementation of evacuation, relocation and renewal. But in terms of actual design, individual projects have individual architecture firms. I don't think that having one architect, or one firm, in charge is a viable model; that would deplete the renewal process of possibilities.

Amanda Ju: Would the managerial entity, Dashilar Investment Limited, have their preference over design concepts? Or does the managing take place more on the organisational level?

Brenda Fang: DIL has more regulations pertaining to the houses and courtyards that face major streets, which would concern the historical area's general image after renovation.

Kuang He: They are more interested in controlling the retail format that would come into these renovated hutong lanes. For example, on Yangmeishuxiejie, where Micro Hutong is located, DIL would evaluate what kind of businesses can go into these newly renovated storefronts.

Amanda Ju: Did both of you leave ZAO at the same time?

Kuang He: No. I left in 2015 to prepare for a graduate degree in architecture. And you Brenda?

Brenda Fang: I worked at ZAO between 2014 to 2019, then left in 2019 to start my own studio. Kuang now works at my studio.

Amanda Ju: In your studio, Brenda, have you also worked on hutong renovation projects?

Brenda Fang: Yes. In 2019, we did a renovation project in the Dongdan area. Other than that, we are planning to rent a courtyard at the back of this hutong, in a similar way that ZAO rents this courtyard (Micro Yuan'er) on Cha'er Hutong. By doing so, we would have more freedom with design and usage, and really consider how our design could provide some livelihood to the local community.

Amanda Ju: Do you think that the hutong renovation projects you did at ZAO, at a relatively early point in your career, have influenced your work today?

Brenda Fang: Hmmm. What would count as "an early point in one's career"? Is Zhang Ke still in the early point of his career?

Kuang He: Maybe when we begin thinking as architects?

Amanda Ju: Let me pose the question differently. When I asked about your experiences as young architects, I was also thinking about some of my early writing projects. Intentionally or not, they have directed my curiosity to certain places. I wonder if working on hutong renovation did something similar for you? Did that experience spark particular curiosities? Did it raise questions in the long term?

Brenda Fang: What is interesting to me about the hutong projects is their sense of scale – not just the scale of the houses, but also of the streets, and of the environment. I would say that I became very sensitive to scale after these projects and have since then carried that sensitivity to other spaces.

Amanda Ju: Is it the scarcity of space, the narrowness and tension of inhabitance, that make a hutong a more pronounced articulator of scale?

Kuang He: A hutong presents a scale that is closer to the human body. It is filled with rich scenarios and moments of the built environment. Working on this scale has inculcated in me a cognitive sensitivity to these temporal instances. And I agree with Brenda, one does carry that sensitivity to other projects. Because even for buildings of a much grander scale, there are still small moments, experienced on a human scale.

Brenda Fang: Right, scale is crucial not just for small spaces, but also larger ones. And perhaps, especially for larger spaces, an architect has to be cognitively sharp about scale. It is a necessary skill. Otherwise, I would feel lost in a design.

Amanda Ju: I like how both of you are describing it. It's beautifully put. Your relationship to Micro Yuan'er is special because you've worked on it as architects during the renovation process, and now you are also residents. What is it like to work here? What kind of communal experience does this space currently allow?

Brenda Fang: It's something that we've asked ourselves. Frankly speaking, we don't have a lot of interaction with the original residents, but we try to establish a balanced relationship with them. The difficult part is that the original residents had their established sense of space. When we moved in, we brought a new set of relationships, as well as new functions, to this place. That newness presented challenges. Each courtyard must have its own dynamism. I've heard about stories of new residents who became like family for the original residents, but that is not the case here.

Amanda Ju: How many original residents still live here? I know that there is an elderly man living in the room by the corner, and then there is another man in the room near the entrance. Is there a third family residing here?

Kuang He: There used to be an elderly woman living in the room in the back, but she moved out last year.

Amanda Ju: Sometimes when we talk about hutongs, it carries a sense of nostalgia. It represents this lost fabric of life that brings people closer, that is more caring, and less alienating. But that closeness also comes with tension on multiple fronts: for example, the constant need to negotiate space, fighting for that extra metre in front of the door.

Kuang He: Yes. I think that because the living environment in a hutong is so compressed, constantly reduced by outside spaces and by the processes of gentrification, the residents here grow a stronger sense of spatial protection. They need to battle for that extra square metre of living space because it is ever more important. That is understandable; it is part of the symbiotic state.

Amanda Ju: Now looking back at the design and renovation concept of Micro Yuan'er, do you feel like its everyday usage matches the expectations of its design proposal? Are there any unexpected rewards or lessons to be learned?

Kuang He: The Micro Yuan'er design intended for this space to be open. There is a large population of children around this area, so we wanted to provide a space where kids can come and spend some time after school. That, I think, has been achieved. The kids living on this street often come and play during lunchtime or on the weekends. The redesign of this space is also about interactions with what is already here. For example, this stairway going up around the pagoda tree invites people to climb up and be closer to it. That is also a design feature that we experience every day. Brenda and I would go up and have coffee in the afternoon, and the kids love to play battle games up and down those stairs.

Amanda Ju: This is a perfect space for battle games! Both Micro Yuan'er and Micro Hutong are spaces that are very playful. I do get the sense that the bolder articulation of design at Micro Hutong can be confusing for some adult residents, in a way that it is not for children.

Brenda Fang: Yes. Kids interact with these spaces so naturally. But I think you are right; it could be confusing for adults.

Amanda Ju: When ZAO decided to renovate Micro Yuan'er into a space with a student library, an art centre and classrooms, was it because of the concentrated population of children around this area?

Brenda Fang: Yes, definitely. Just south of this hutong, there is an elementary school, the Tan'er Hutong School. This is an area of central Beijing where rent is still relatively low. When the renovation was first completed in 2014, and also in 2015 and 2016, there was a big population of children who were from migrant workers' families. They would come to take art classes, and read. That became rare after the rental control of public housing inside hutongs became tighter in the past few years.

Amanda Ju: The property rights of hutong housing are quite complicated.

Brenda Fang: Yes, they are. Most of the houses and courtyards collected by DIL are public housing, which means that the residents don't own the property rights to their home, but they do hold the right to use it. They are technically renters, but the monthly rent is very low.

The man who lives in that corner room of our courtyard once told me the story of how his grandmother first moved in here. This courtyard used to be a temple. When the number of worshippers dropped, the temple rented out rooms on the east–west wing to cover their finances. That's when his grandmother moved into that room. Eventually, after the 1960s, the whole courtyard became residential, and property rights became state-owned.

Amanda Ju: Are there hutong houses that are privately owned in this area?

Brenda Fang: Yes, but very few.

Amanda Ju: The title of this book project is *Hutong Metabolism*. Part of what this phrase invites us to consider is the relationship between a traditional "architecture project" and a kind of "symbiotic renewal" that is being proposed. In your experience as architects and residents of a hutong, what is your understanding of this difference? How would you explain a concept like Hutong Metabolism?

Brenda Fang: I think renovation designs can be created from a "God-like perspective", but once you begin to be in a symbiotic relationship with a living space and its sociality, you inevitably need to shift out of that aerial point of view. It becomes important to understand how the design is being interpreted – constantly and varyingly – on the ground level. And, of course, the communication and coordination with local residents is important work.

Before 2019, the studio room we are in was an art classroom. Now that space is used as an architecture studio, and maybe it will serve a different function in the future. That change in function is also a kind of symbiotic renewal. The design of space at Micro Yuan'er allows that flexibility.

Individual rooms are not strictly defined by function, nor do they intend to define how people of different age groups can interact with it. The design offers a framework, and that framework contains enough details for the space to be rich and open ended.

Kuang He: For me, it's important that the renewal process is not alienating. The English term "gentrification" describes a development process where the historical and cultural values of an area become packaged products for sale. Renovated buildings are no longer connected to the lives of the original residents. If hutong renewal is a tasked reality that architects must face today, then we need to ask ourselves what kind of spaces we are creating, and how we are positioned vis-à-vis this potentially alienating process.

Amanda Ju: Do you see hutong renewal projects like Micro Yuan'er as acts of resistance? Do projects like this make the developmentalist road of urban transformation more circuitous?

Brenda Fang: I think of it as a stance. The implementation may be on a small scale, but it is an expression of alternative possibility.

Naiji Tian: Design can be an accelerating factor of gentrification, and I think a lot of the eye-catching buildings designed by architecture firms in China participate in this acceleration. It flattens out an architect's ability to support spatial transformation as a commercial opportunity. I think that Hutong Metabolism as a concept resists that kind of capitalising tendency; it is less willing to spectacularise and entertain.

If we consider hutong as an organic body, then the people in it are also part of this metabolism. When Brenda and Kuang moved into Micro Yuan'er, they also brought new possibilities and functions to this space. Unexpected transformations of function can also be acrobatic, a part of this spatial metabolism.

Brenda Fang: Are we being too utopian? Or is it utopian from a certain perspective, on a granular scale?

Amanda Ju: I don't know, but if we think about the transformation of architectural function in the historical hutong areas, oftentimes the renovated courtyard becomes expensive single-family homes, or trendy coffee shops. Functional transformation seems to occlude certain kinds of spatial usage – like space as a site for creative work, for play, or for communal reading that is closer to life, and further from the acts of consumption.

Naiji Tian: What is legible and recognisable as Hutong Metabolism is a question worth posing. If a property owner builds an add-on structure at their house, then it is understood as a form of reconstruction and even redesign. But when hutong residents build add-on structures near their houses, they seem to be more problematic constructions. Maybe ZAO's approach to Micro Yuan'er is to make those forms of Hutong Metabolism more visible and recognisable.

In Conversation with Zhang Ke
Nondita Correa Mehrotra

Nondita Correa Mehrotra: Your beautiful hutong project, for which you received the Aga Khan Award for Architecture, is interesting as it is emblematic of the values that the award tries to bring to architecture. The award is really concerned with a series of issues, and although it is positioned as an Award for Architecture in the Islamic World, it clearly has a much larger resonance in the global debate on architecture – as a counter narrative to a Western-dominated construct. Having said that, what do you think are the issues in this project, for you personally, that resonate this broader message – one that goes across different geographies and societies, income groups, cultures? Is it to do with the formation of densities? Is it to do with the incremental nature of low-rise, high-density housing? Is it to do with how we can reclaim our historic environment, memory, cultural affinities, for contemporary purposes? And/or the culture of building, materiality, et cetera?

Zhang Ke: Yes, the hutong projects are indeed concerned with multiple issues at the same time. For me personally, they have to do with scale, memory, materiality, sustainability and a standpoint of resistance. The first issue is about scale. For the past few decades, the renewal of Beijing has been taking place on a large scale. This approach almost inevitably results in big buildings replacing the old fabric of courtyards and hutongs. At this larger scale, even conservation and so-called restoration means erasing and demolishing large compounds of courtyards, and rebuilding imitations of the old courtyards, which is in fact faking a nostalgic past. Therefore, scale is critical. If we focus on a smaller scale and inside-out renovation, with the renewal taking place from within, then we can avoid irreversible damage to the old urban fabric. At the same time, it provides a kind of freedom for us to do things that are contemporary and to meet the real needs of the residents who live there.

The second critical issue is about memory, in terms of what was created by the people who lived here in past centuries and also in recent decades. I think that recognising and revealing the more contemporary layers of history is important, instead of removing and wiping them out completely. Therefore, our approach to the so-called "un-registered" additions built by residents in the last six decades is not to remove them completely. Instead, we make them into useful spaces for the neighbourhood through reuse, renovation and redesign.

The third issue is materiality. Besides using recycled bricks and wood, we also use concrete mixed with black Chinese ink. The general intention is to create a quiet atmosphere, to create new buildings and additions in a historical context that do not shout loudly. We try to test the possibility of using materials that are not totally traditional but at the same time do not stand out too much. When you first see the space, the materials appear to be very coherent. When you look more carefully, the mix of new and old is clearly articulated, but without a sharp contrast. This was achieved through experiments of mixing concrete with Chinese ink to make a darker concrete that matched the grey bricks typical in the hutongs.

The fourth issue is sustainability, not only in terms of environmental sustainability but also cultural sustainability. By reusing, renovating and redesigning the courtyards and the spontaneous additions, we help to create a kind of continuity in the physical surroundings and materiality in the space. This allows children to grow up in an atmosphere their parents were used to. In the future, their own children would also be able to grow up in an environment that helps to preserve the culture and memory of their childhood.

In the end, it is about having a standpoint of resistance, about fighting against over-commercialisation and gentrification in the old city. It is easy to turn these courtyards into luxurious homes or expensive shops. I personally thought it was important to create a series of realised examples, simply to show the municipality that the idea of "micro renewal" is possible, and that it can be respectful to the urban history and the contemporary at the same time. It has nothing to do with faking old facades. Rather, the aim is really to improve living conditions from the inside out and to create more public programmes and spaces in service of the local community.

Nondita Correa Mehrotra: The very particular ecology and ensuing metabolism of the hutong I'm sure resonates with many parts of Asia, especially in Japan. How do you see these connections or influences?

Zhang Ke: Metabolism in Chinese is *Xin Chen Dai Xie* or 新陈代谢, which literally means letting the new replace the old at the micro-scale of a living organism. This concept fits the situation of our hutong renewal projects perfectly, as we consider the hutong and its residents together as a living organism. Hutong Metabolism is about the old city and renewals at a micro-scale, while the Metabolism movement in Japan in the 1960s was about the future city on a mega-scale. Nevertheless, there were certainly some influences from the masters of the movement, such as Kiyonori Kikutake, whose work I have long admired. From the other perspective, if we see the hutongs and courtyards as a mega system of the city created 800 years ago for a then futuristic Beijing, then our micro renewal of its most basic units and nucleus could be considered a continuation of its metabolism.

Nondita Correa Mehrotra: It is interesting that, at least from what I've understood from you, you were inspired by Charles Correa's work in your student days. It is very fascinating because the kind of theoretical framework that Charles came up with – including what he wrote in *The New Landscape*, his argument of "form follows climate" – actually involves arguments that resonate all across Asia. And his influence was deeply felt in the pan-Asian geography. The Global South, which is Africa and Asia, and parts of Latin America, was actually a counterpoint, or counter position, to the Global North. Not only do large populations reside here – and therefore architecture and planning cannot avoid the fact that people are central to their imagination – but the climatic constraints, the constraints of resources, also take us in particular directions. And therefore, the theoretical framework he was proposing addresses those issues. And this is what fundamentally ties China and India together, at least until about a decade or two ago when China embarked on another path of neoliberalism. So my question is: Do you think that those arguments that Charles framed are yet valid? Or are you arguing that the hutong project is the exception in today's China? How do you place your work, in the context of what is otherwise being built in China?

Zhang Ke: I think Charles's argument is certainly still valid in China. And I believe that "form follows climate" will continue to be valid throughout the world. In fact, it has become more valid now given the growing necessity and awareness of sustainability globally.

The hutong project at the time of its conception in the early 2010s was definitely rare for carrying out a small-scale, inside-out renewal approach and creating public space for the community in a contemporary way. By 2016, shortly after the Micro Yuan'er Children's Library was awarded the Aga Khan Award, the policy in China had also experienced a shift concerning renewal in the old city. Support shifted from large-scale redevelopment to putting more emphasis on conservation, and micro-scale renewal in the old city is now advocated throughout China.

Nondita Correa Mehrotra: I'm curious, as Charles Correa was someone who participated in the formative years of the Aga Khan Award, so his thinking about architecture, and vice versa – how the award influenced him – emanates in a project like yours, which gets the award. So, what were the specific influences, may I ask, that Charles's work has had on you? Could you be specific, down to the architectural scale?

Zhang Ke: I have great admiration for Charles Correa's work, and I certainly took inspiration from his writings and many of his projects. The influences from Correa for me are threefold. The first is about the ethics and responsibility of architects, especially in the developing world. In the last paragraph of his book *The New Landscape,* Charles raises the question of whether we as architects should "take action or simply stand by and watch" when confronting a difficult situation such as the renewal of the old city. In this case, I decided to take action. The first two realised projects, Micro Yuan'er and Micro Hutong, were initiated by ourselves. Funds were raised among my friends. I thought it was very important to realise some projects because this is probably the only way to show policymakers that micro renewal could be a different way of addressing problems and challenges in the old city.

The second aspect of influence is from Charles's interests in designing neighbourhood spaces – to, in his words, bring the micro-scale to the design of streets and neighbourhoods. In his design for the streets of Mumbai, he proposed a two-metre-wide arcade and platform, which could provide the migrants who come to work in the city a place to sleep at night. This design is very inspiring. A way to bring the human scale into the design of neighbourhood public space is also a key aspect of my hutong projects.

The third aspect of influence involves design. When it comes to design, a lot of Charles Correa's projects are inspiring, from the winding passageways of the early Handloom Pavilion to the rich levels and terraces of the Kanchanjunga Apartments and the use of steps in the later Surya Kund project. Years after I had first encountered them in Charles's work, these elements seem to have become a part of my own subconscious and intuition. These characteristics are also clearly evident in the design of the indoor and outdoor spaces of the Micro Yuan'er Children's Library.

Hutong Social Housing

Location: **Beijing, China**
Client: **Jingcheng Group**
Design period: **2018**
Construction period: **June 2019–November 2019**
Site area: **615 m², 1,489 m²**
Building area: **261 m², 470 m²** Total floor area: **261 m², 470 m²**
Architect: **ZAO/standardarchitecture**
Project architect: **Zhang Ke**
Design team: **Hua Yunsi, Epp Jerlei, Fang Shujun, Liu Yunan, Qin Yu, Du Boliang**
Collaborating design institution: **Beijing Institute of Architectural Design**

Yu'er Hutong Social Housing is a continuation of the Hutong Renewal series. The aim of this project is to further explore how to adaptably reuse and renovate living spaces for local residents after a series of hutong projects.
This courtyard also used to be a typical *dazayuan* or big messy courtyard. Addressing the improvement of living conditions, the strategy is to relocate the former residents back to the courtyard by creating a humane and cosy living environment with the inserted long-term rented living units. At the same time, it should attract new residents and encourage them to move in. The main concept is to create nine living units with three types of functional modules to provide a variety of living spaces. Each unit is equipped with essential amenities, such as a kitchen, bathroom and laundry room, which also meets the urgent needs of the infrastructure problem within the hutongs.
To preserve the character of the existing yard, the architects reused the original materials, such as recycled brick, stone, wood and metal, as much possible. Also, by removing messy and unnecessary material, original hutong materials were unveiled. Instead of fake traditional refurbishment, it subtly keeps and extends the old memories of the hutong. Yu'er Hutong Social Housing could be considered a new Hutong Renewal typology in contrast to both the "tabula rasa" approach to renovation and the common gentrification phenomenon.

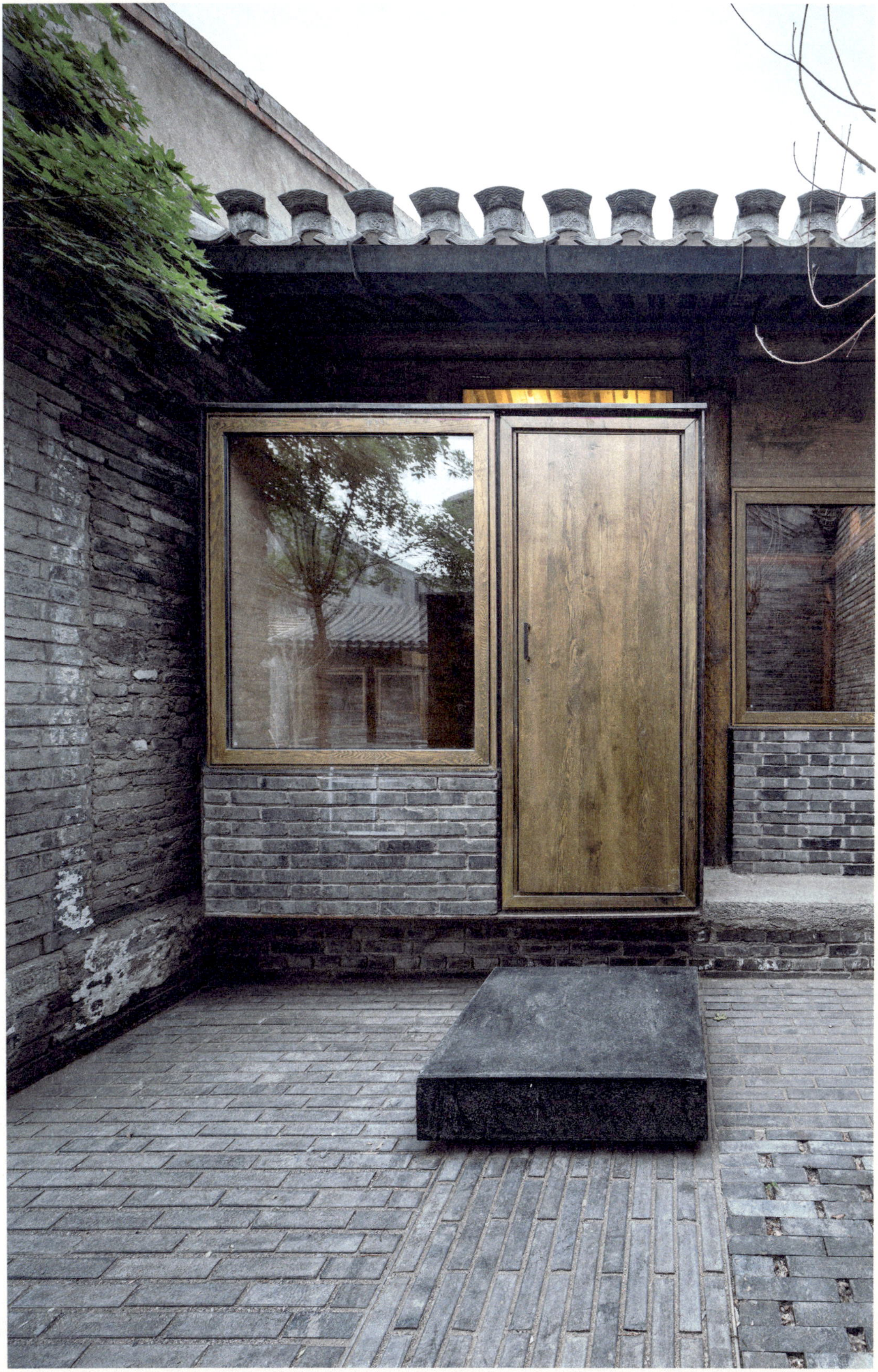

Yu Er Hutong Courtyard 10

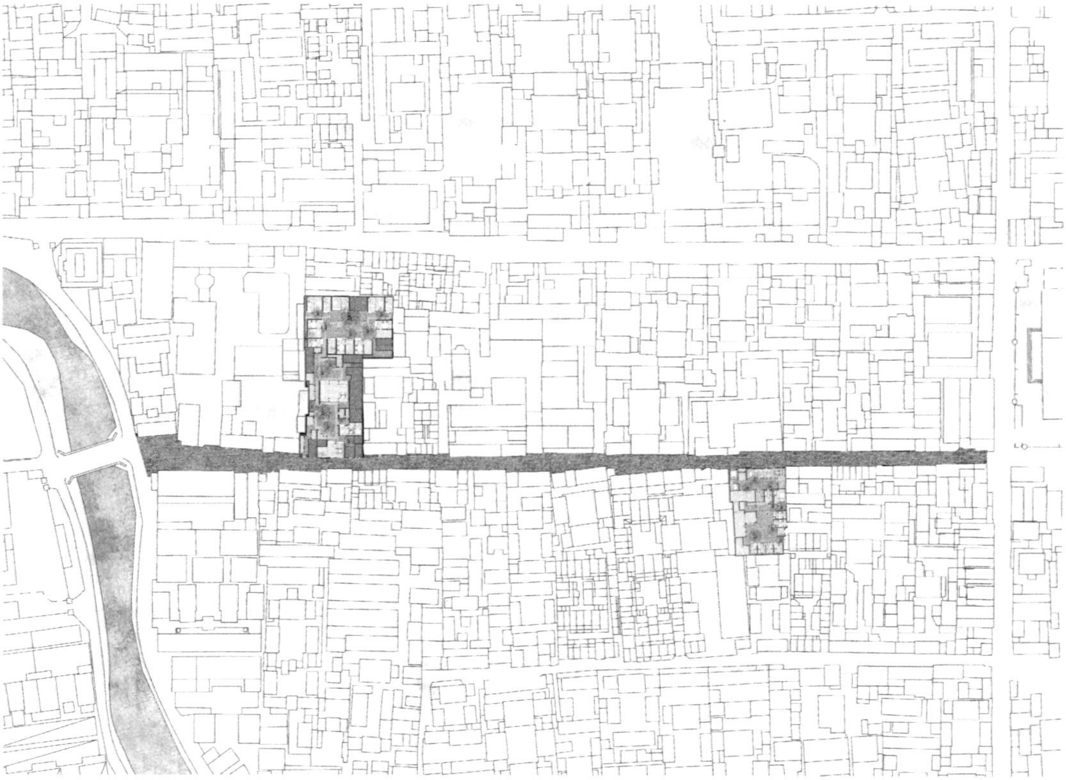

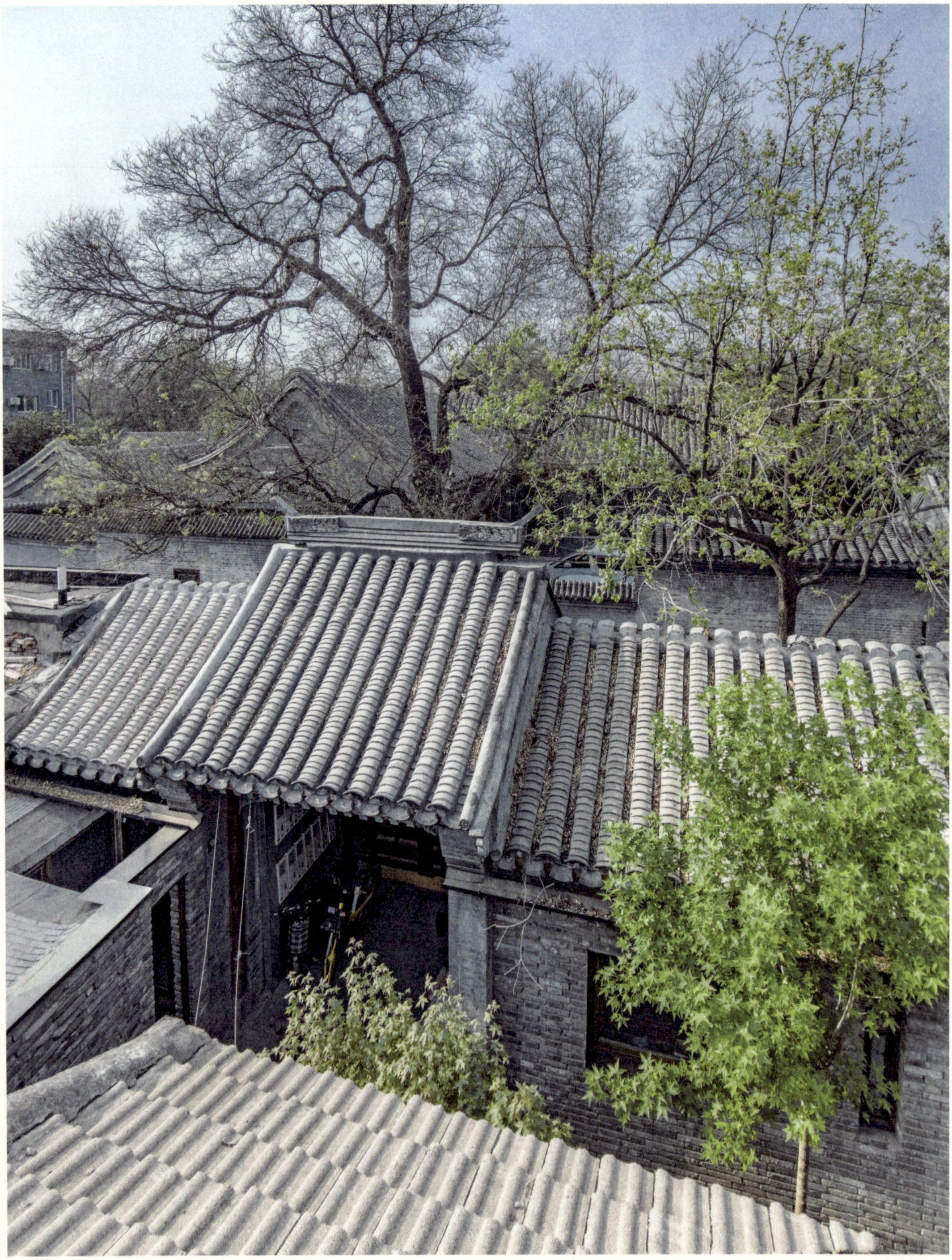

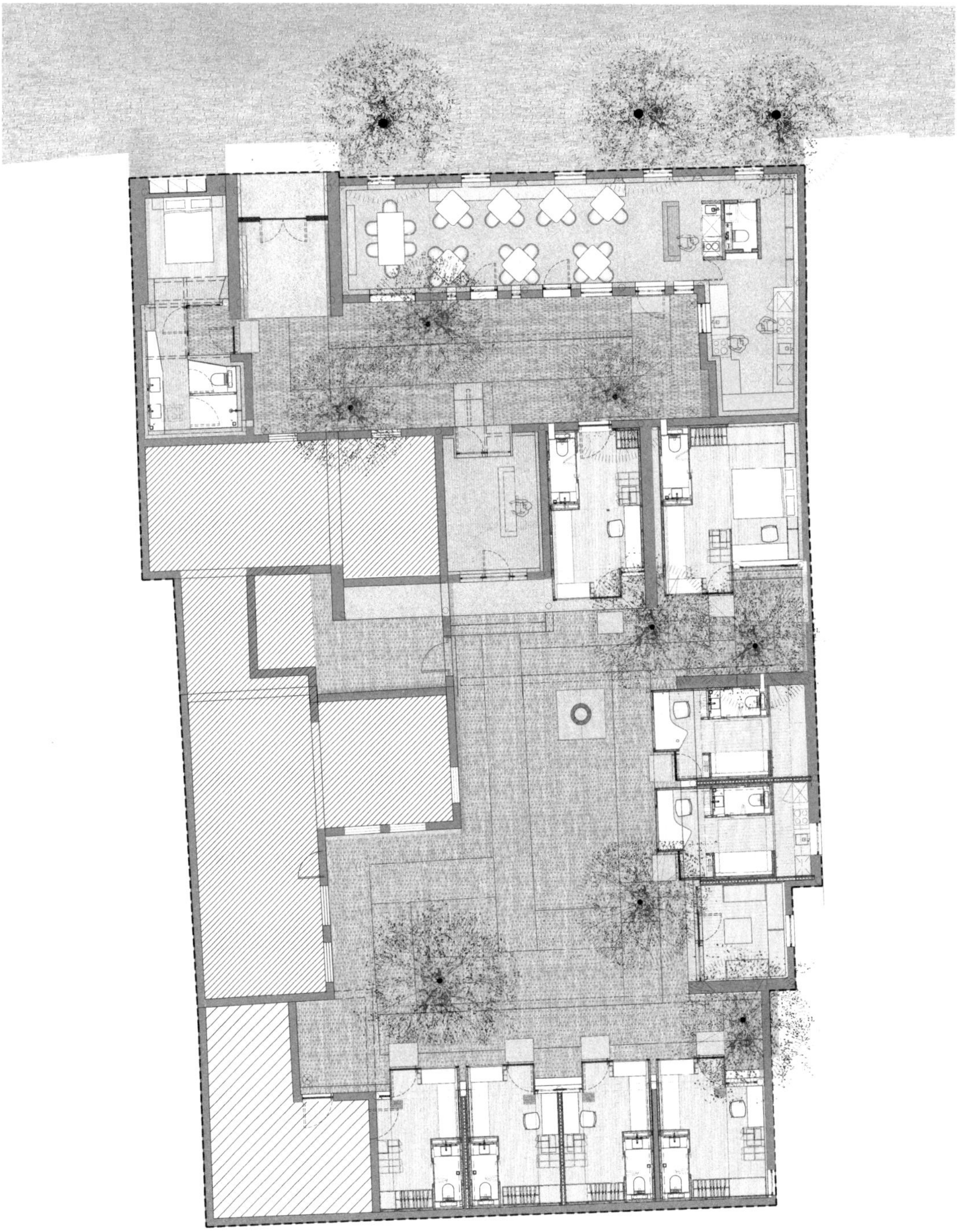

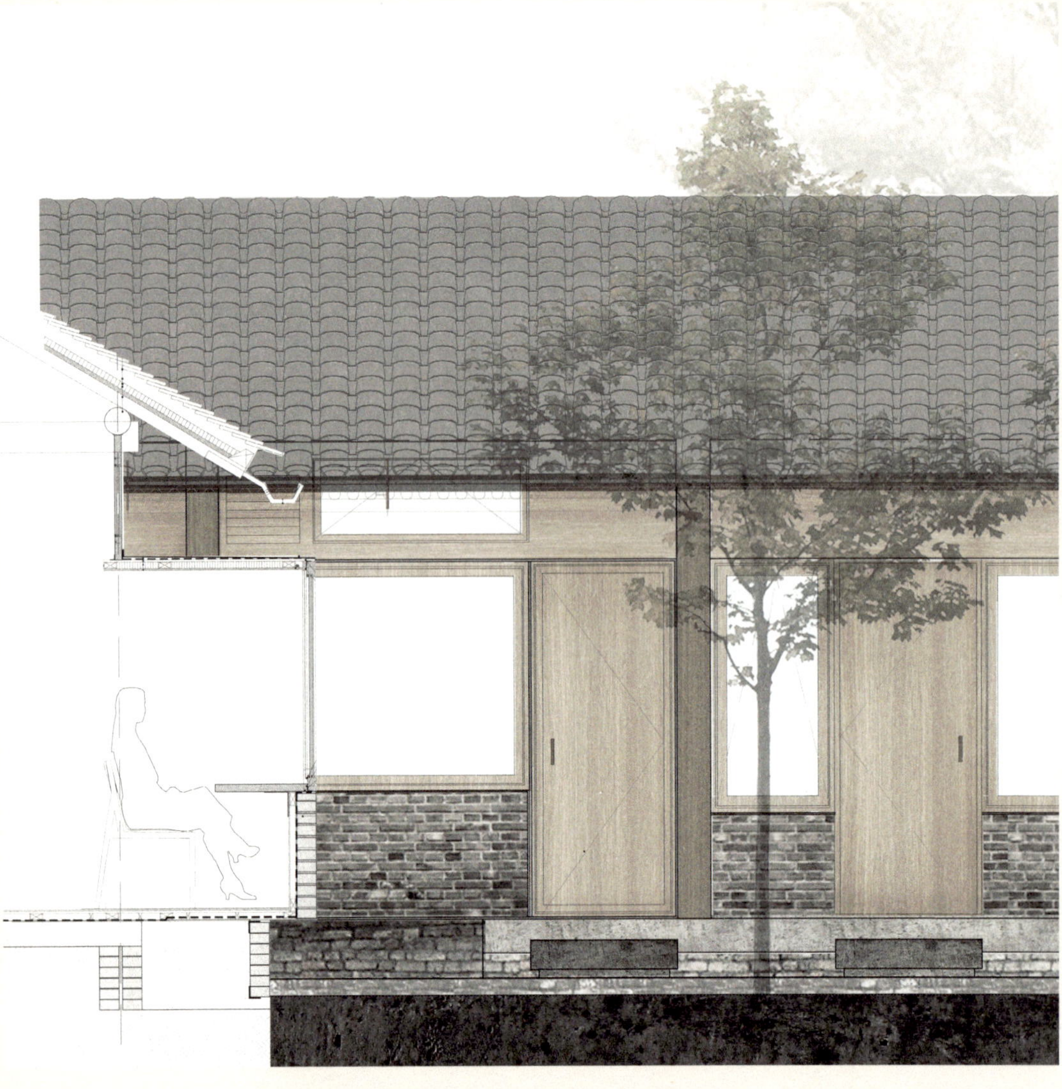

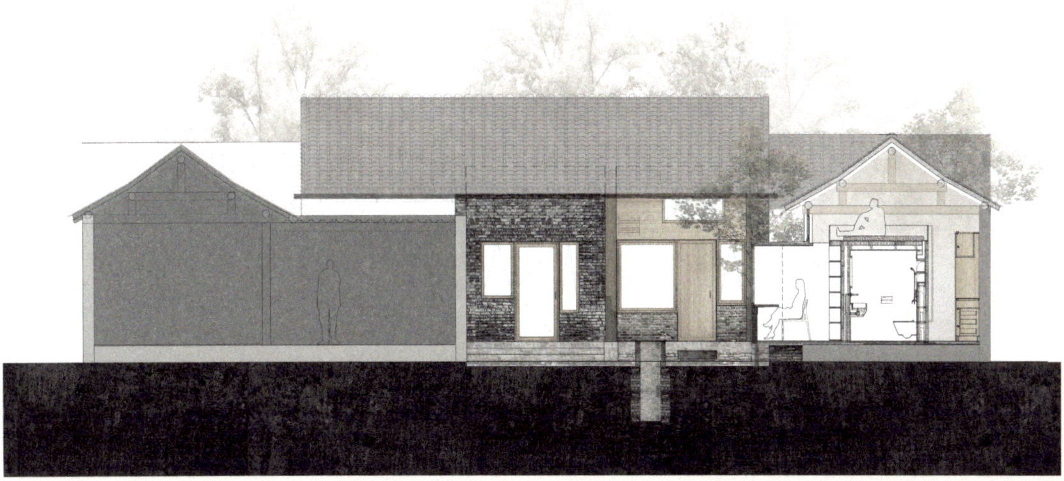

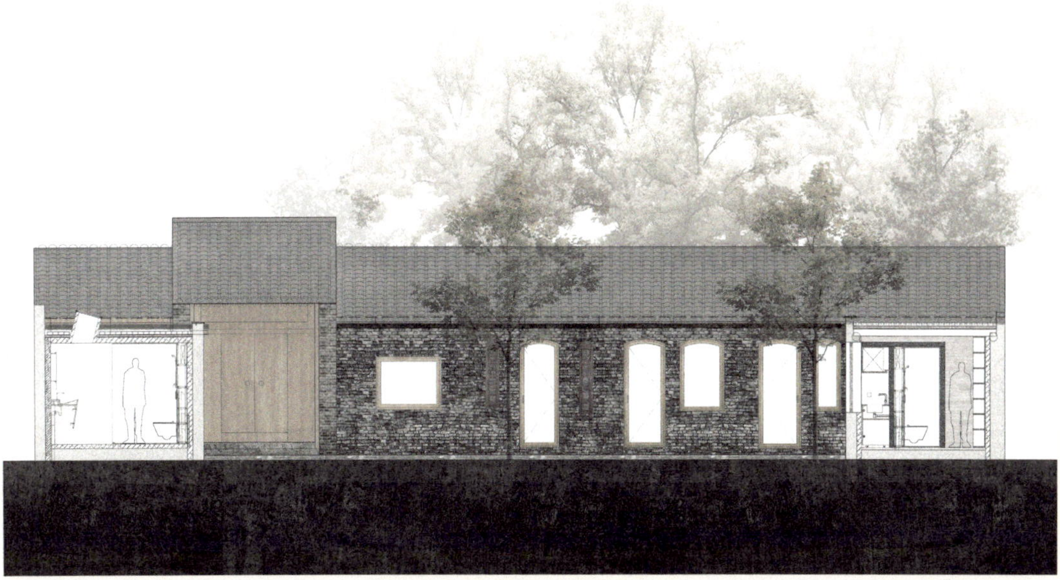

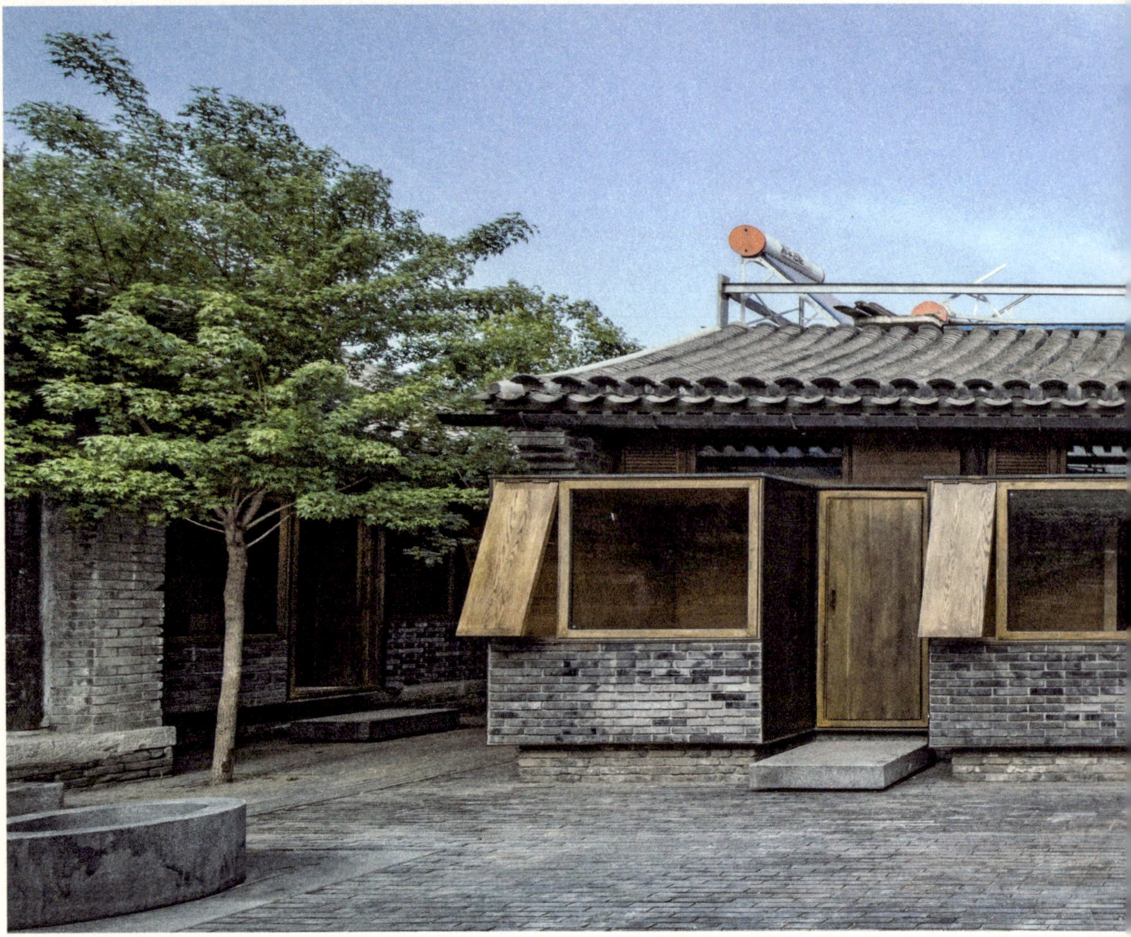

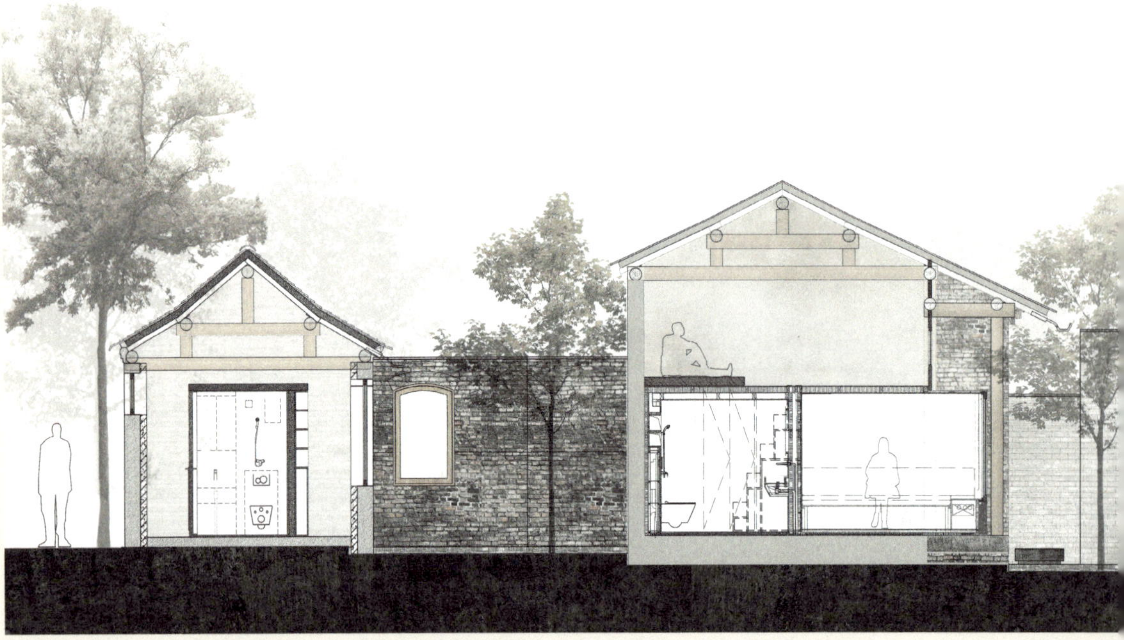

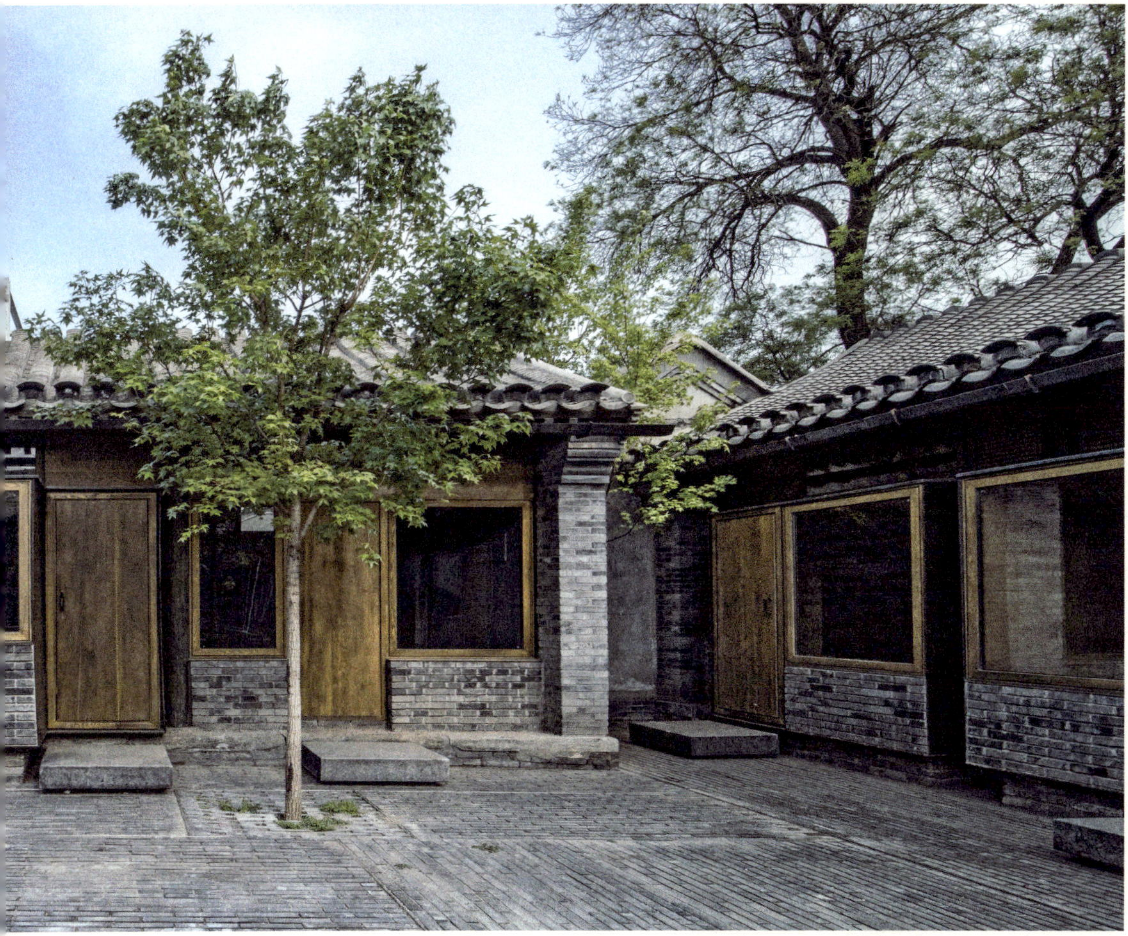

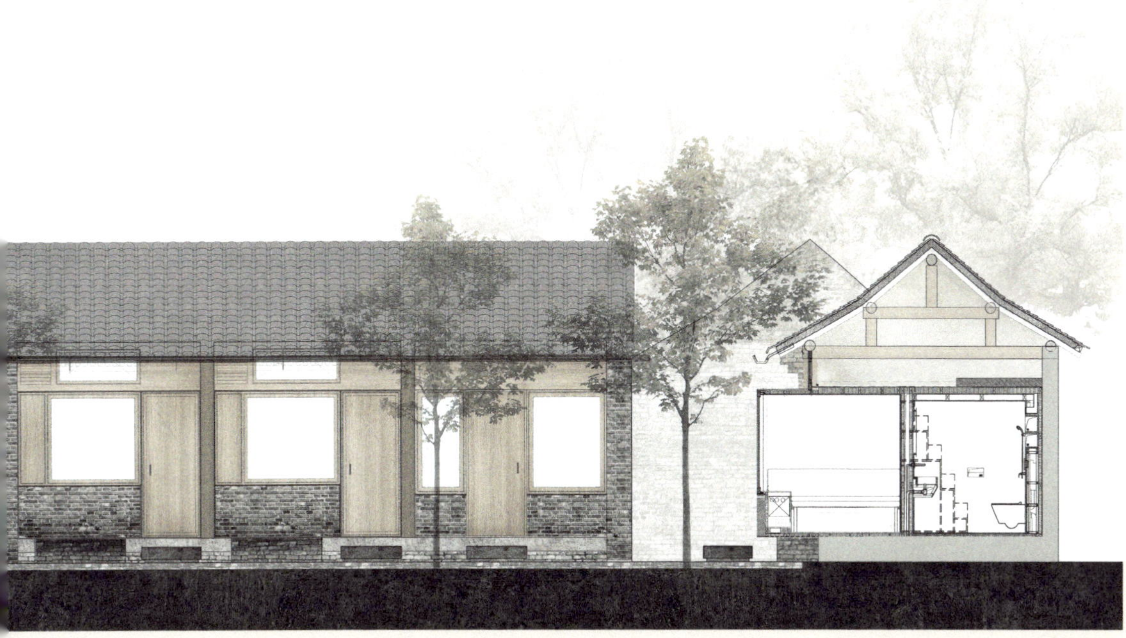

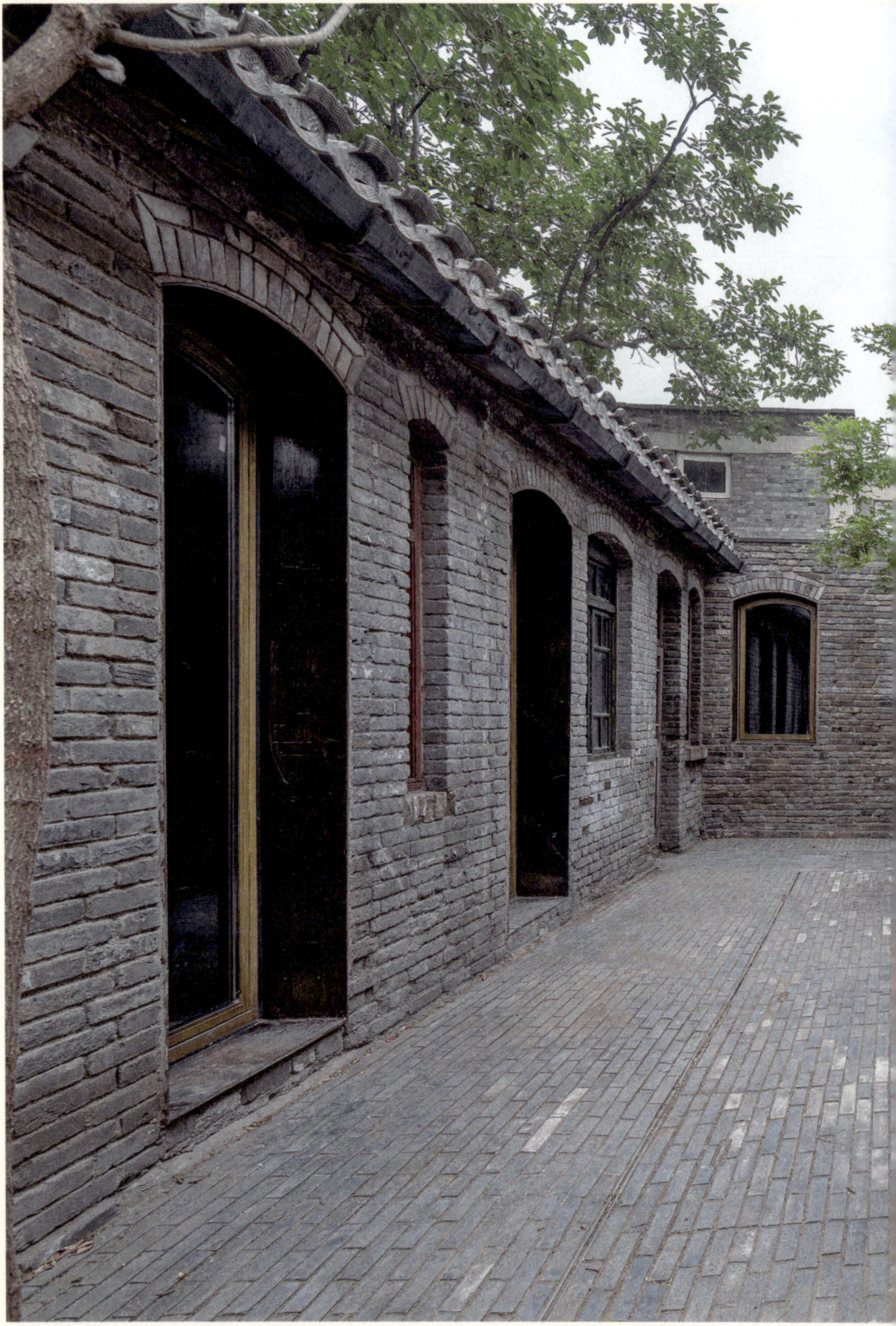

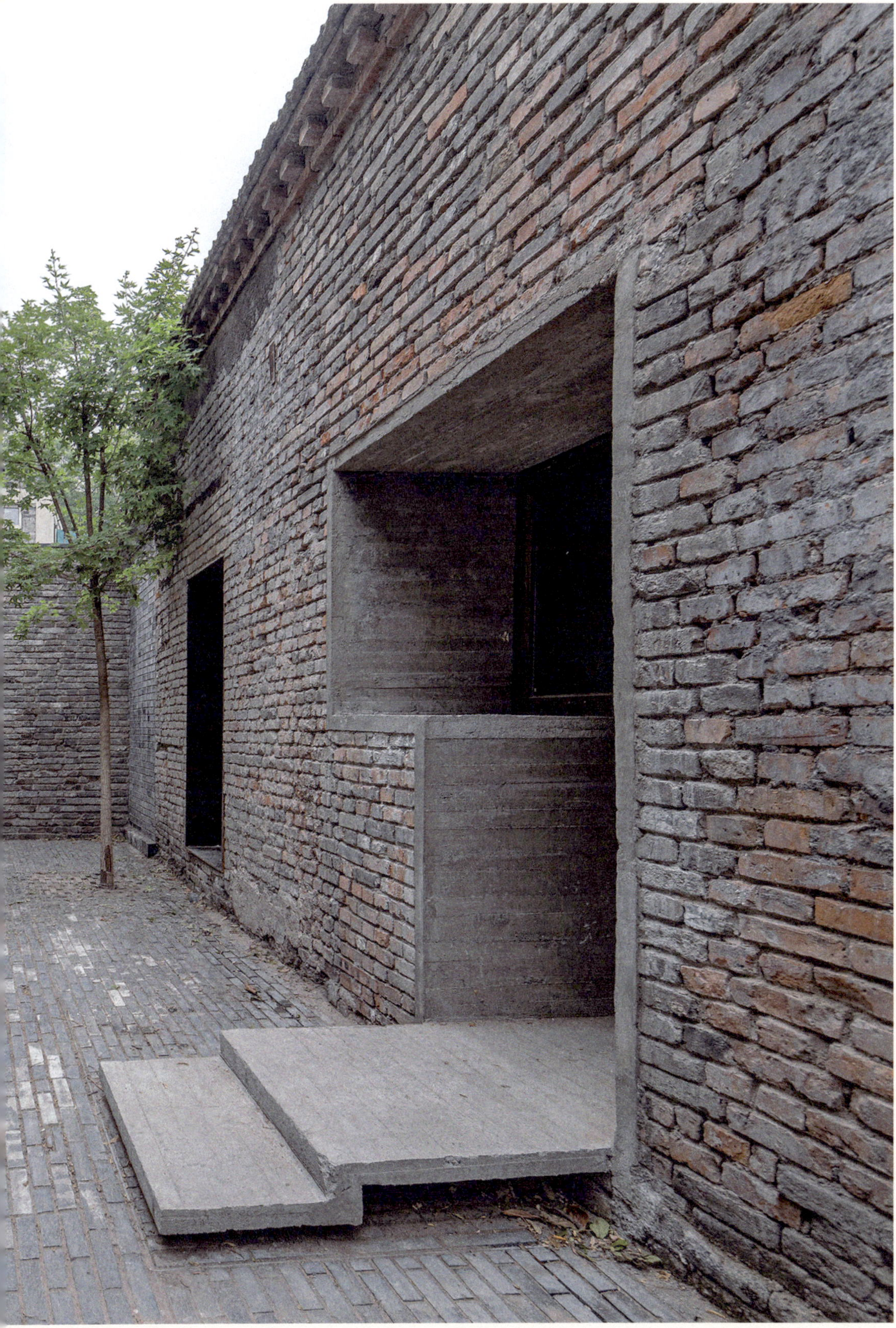

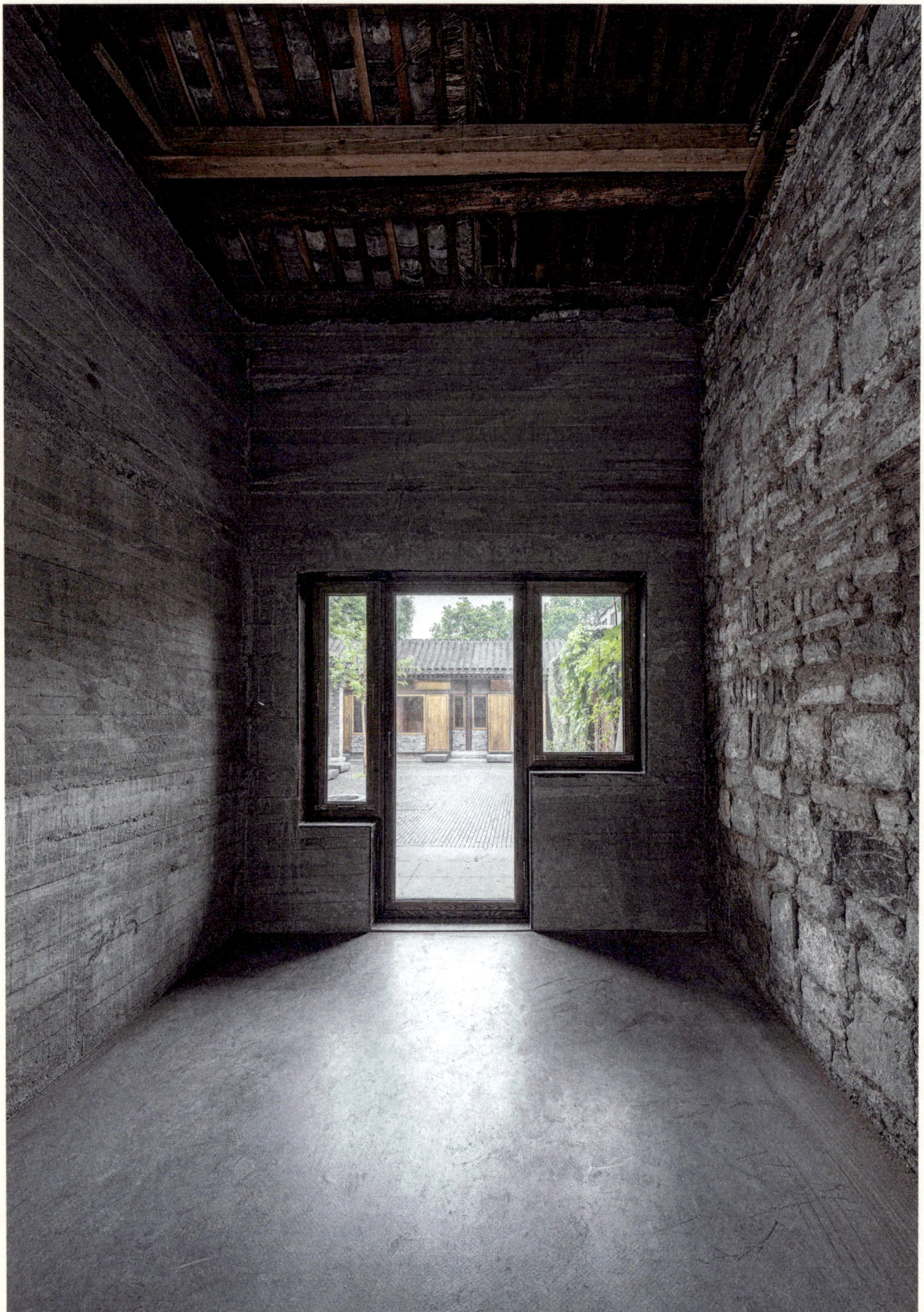

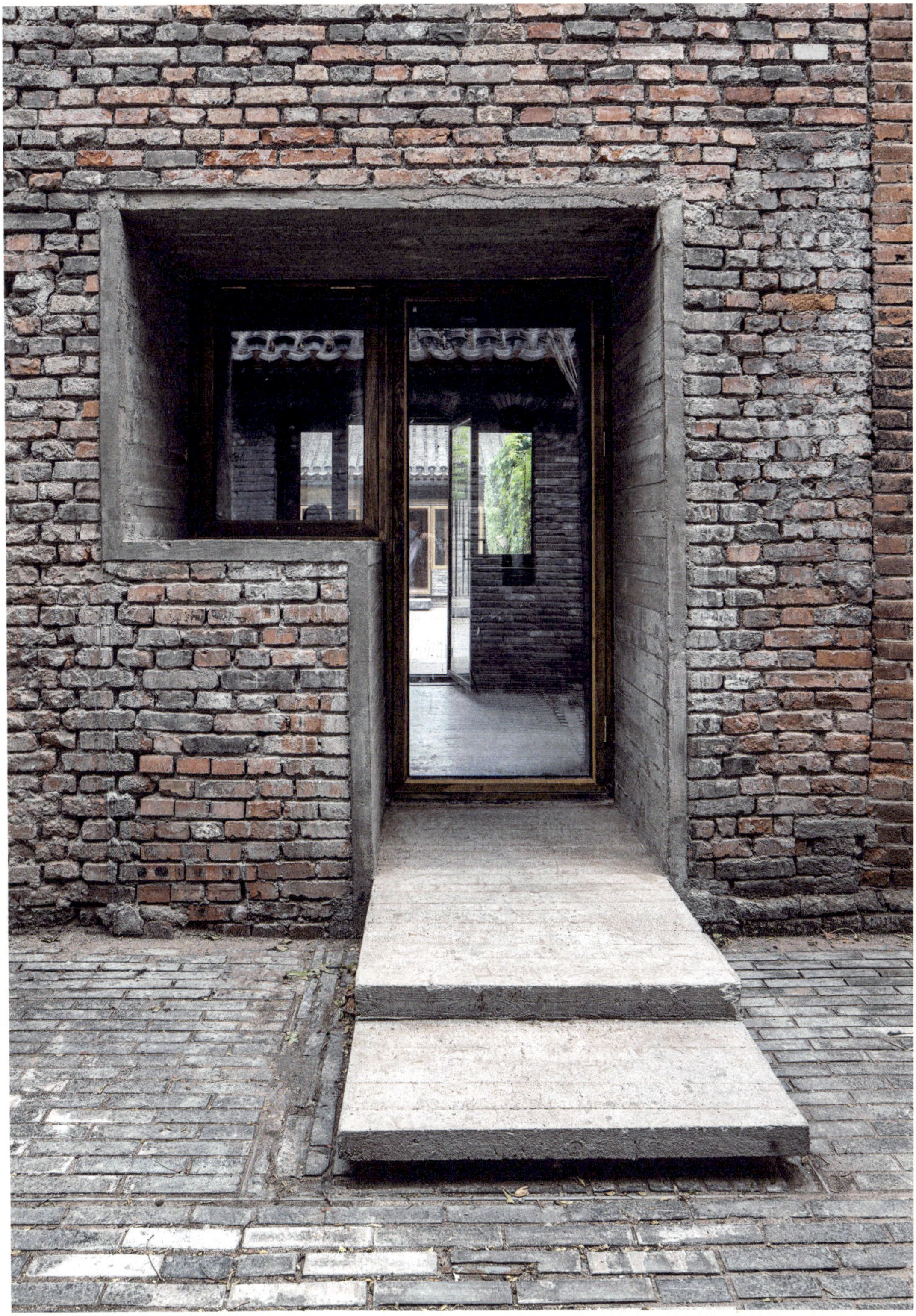

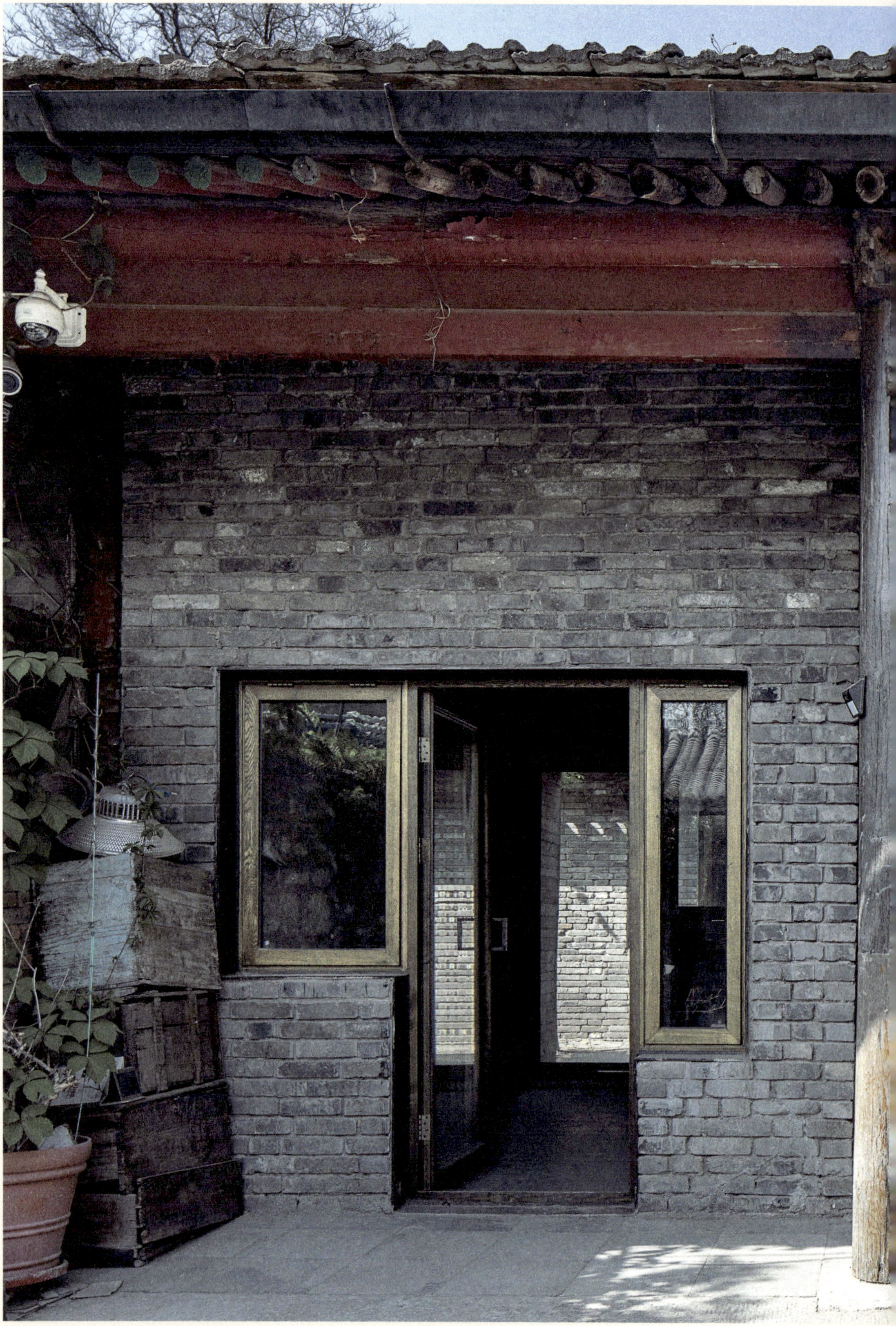

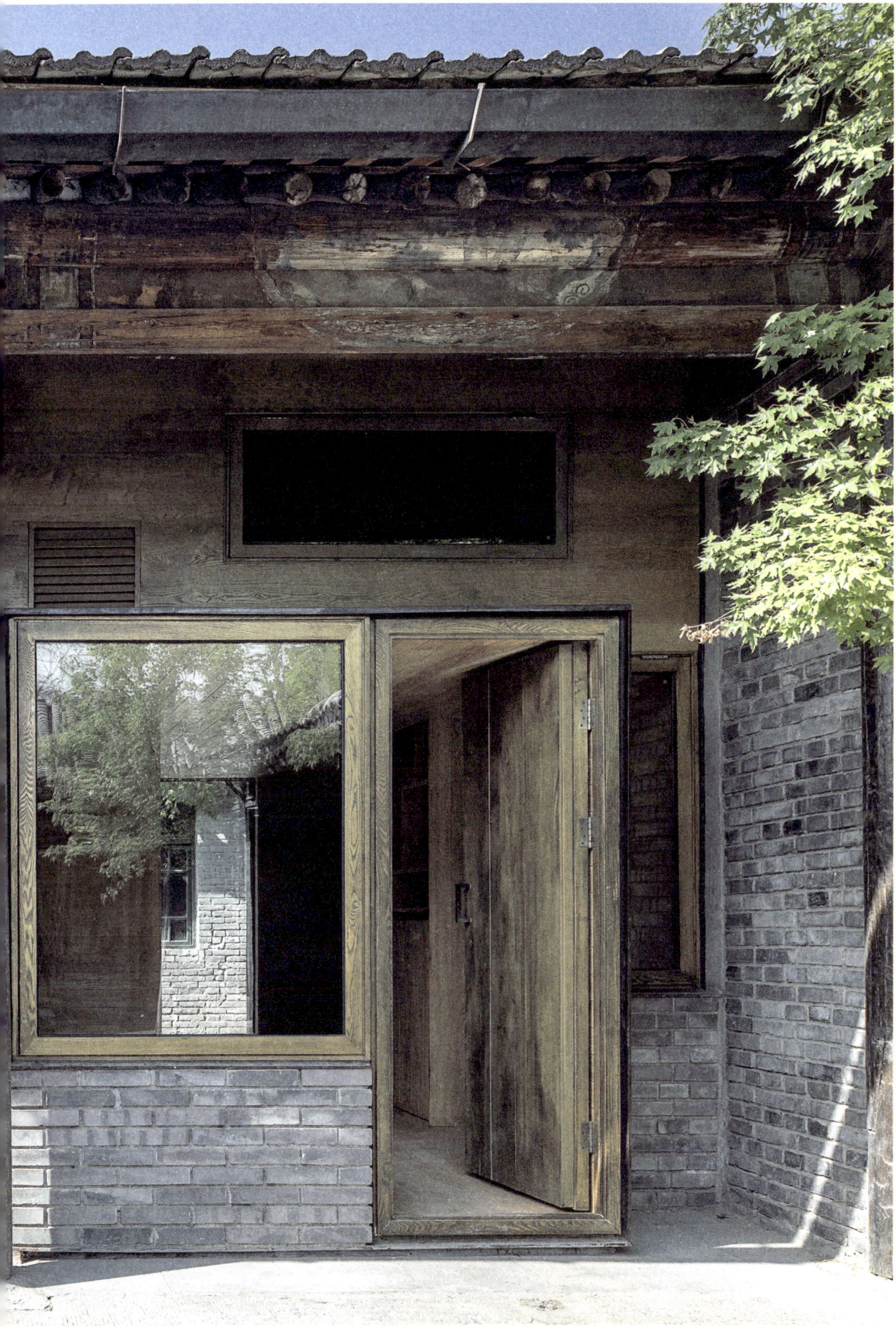

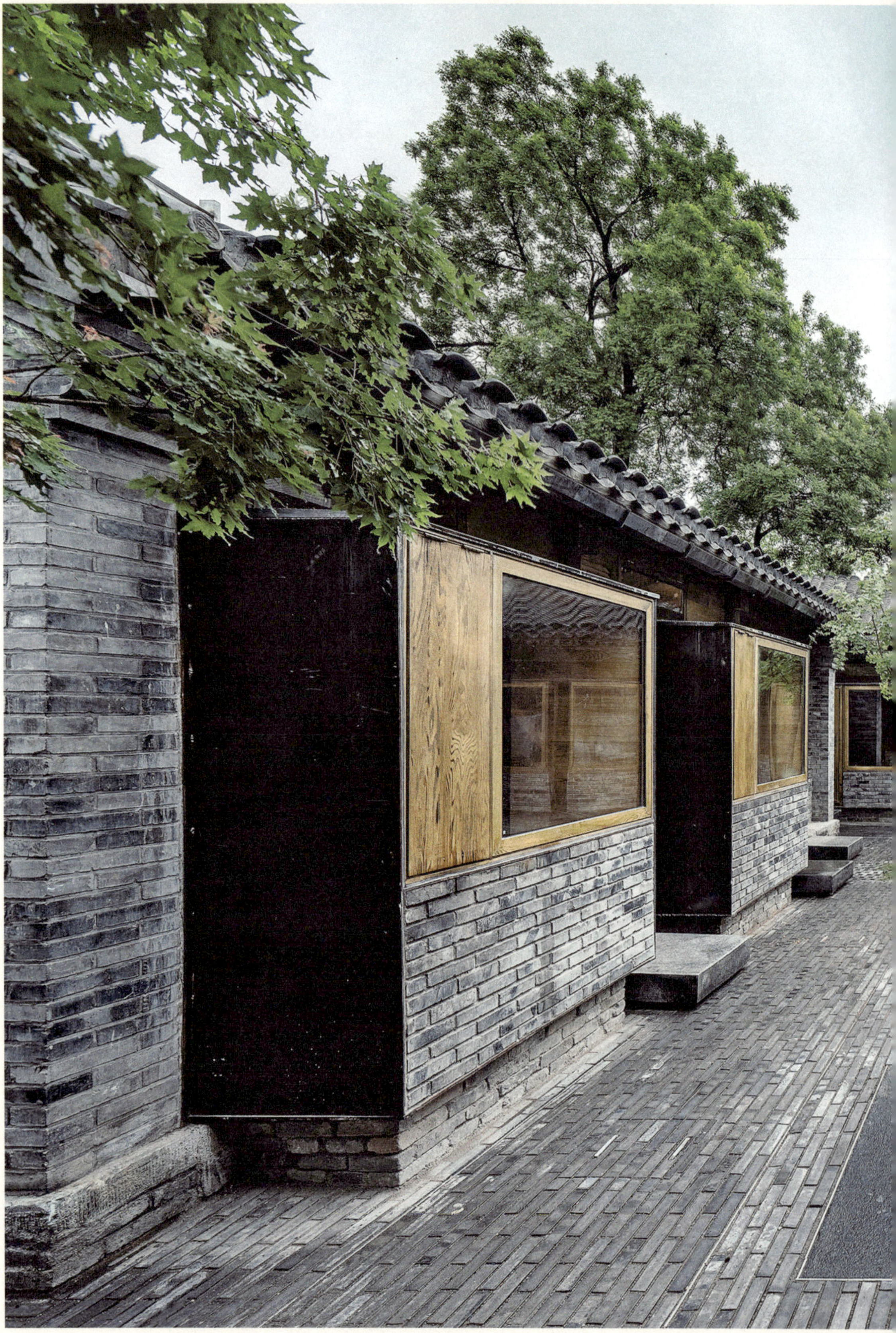

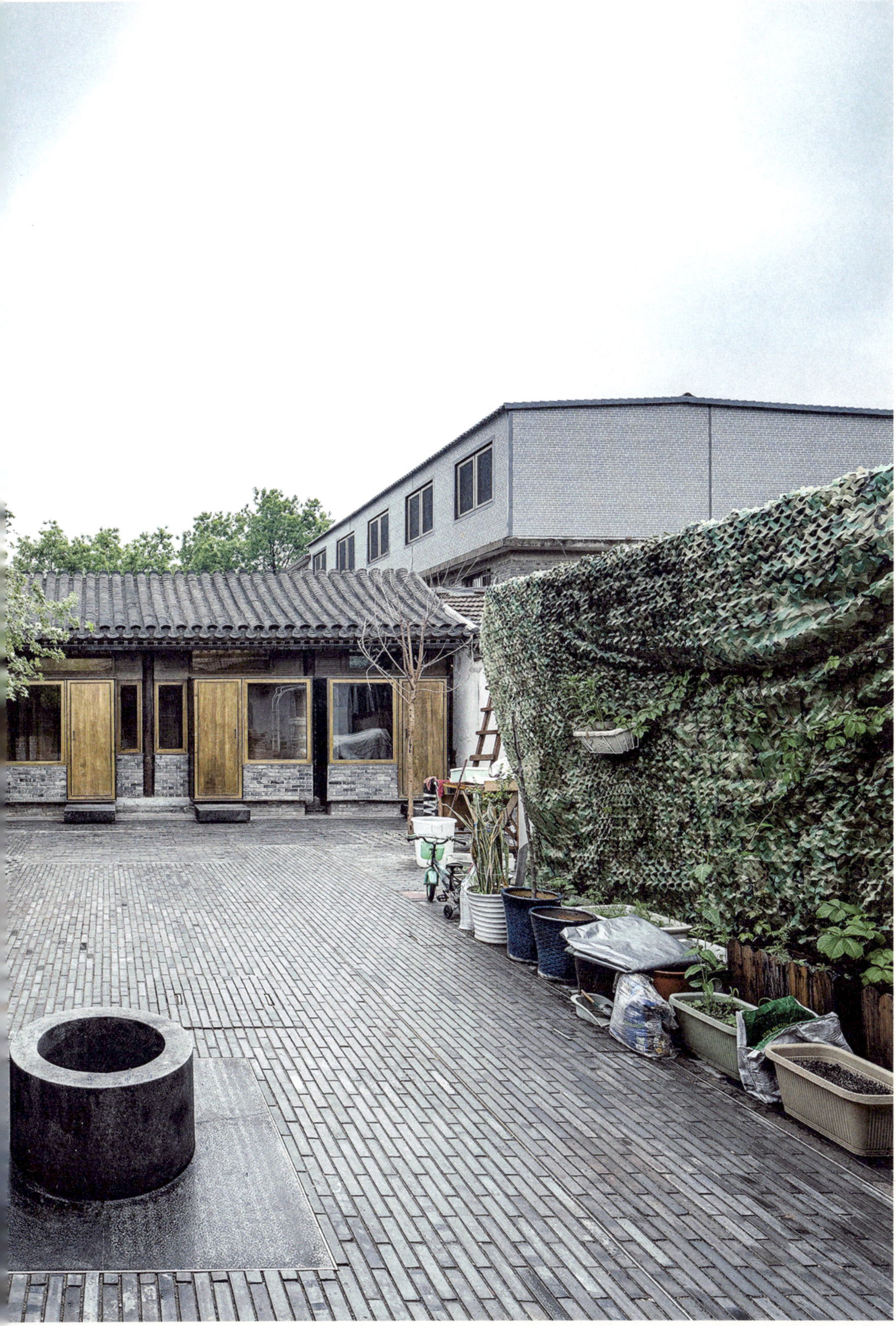

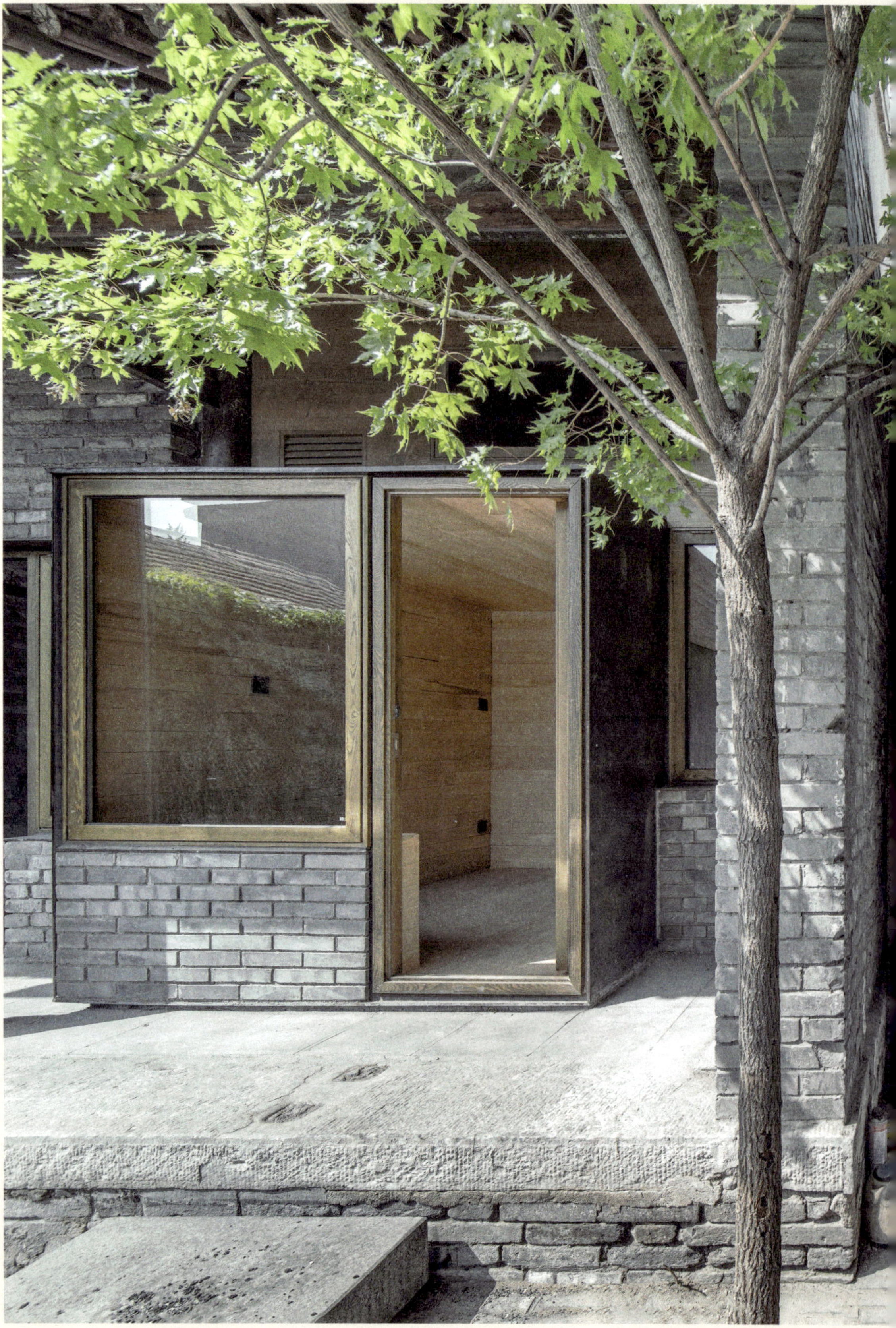

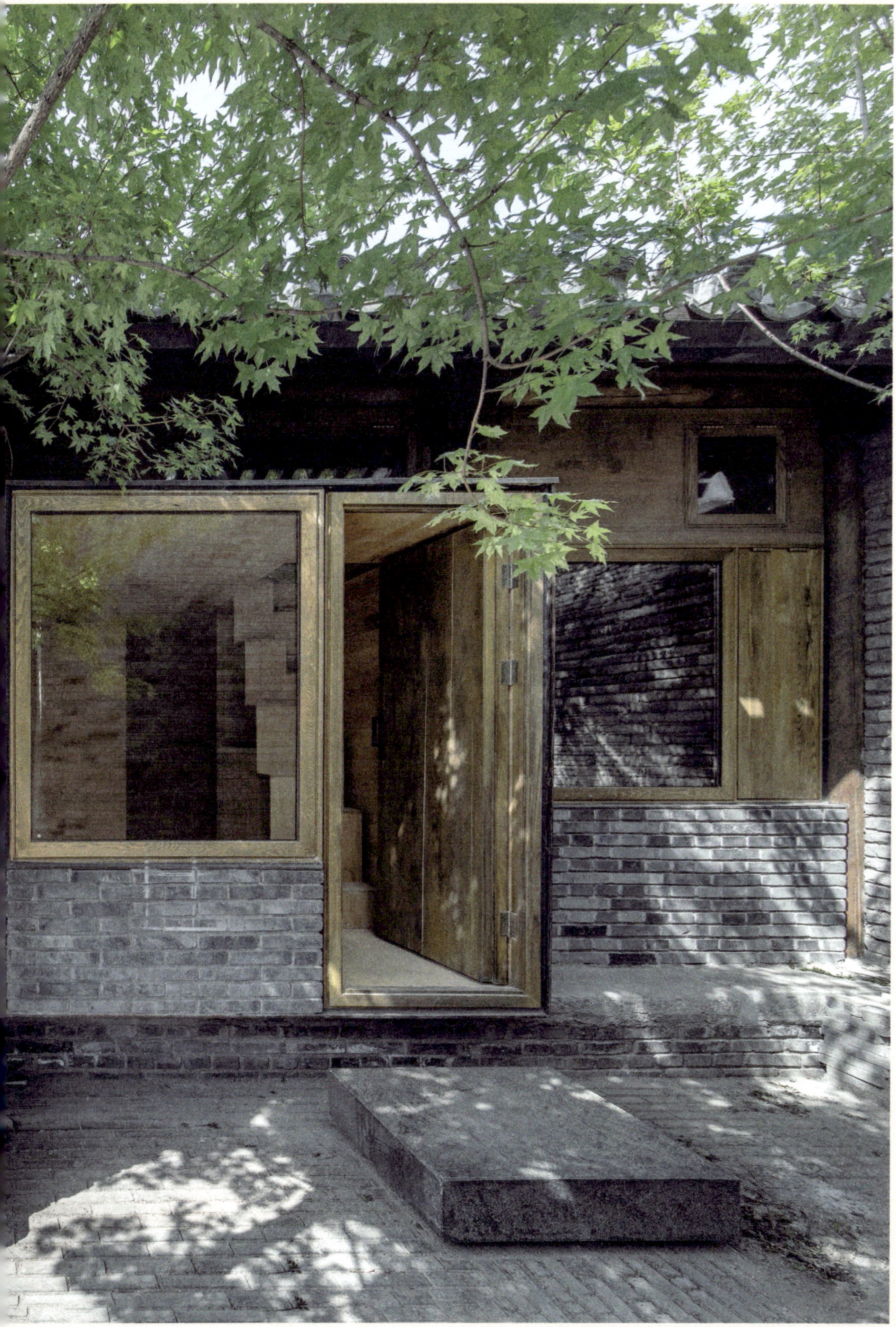

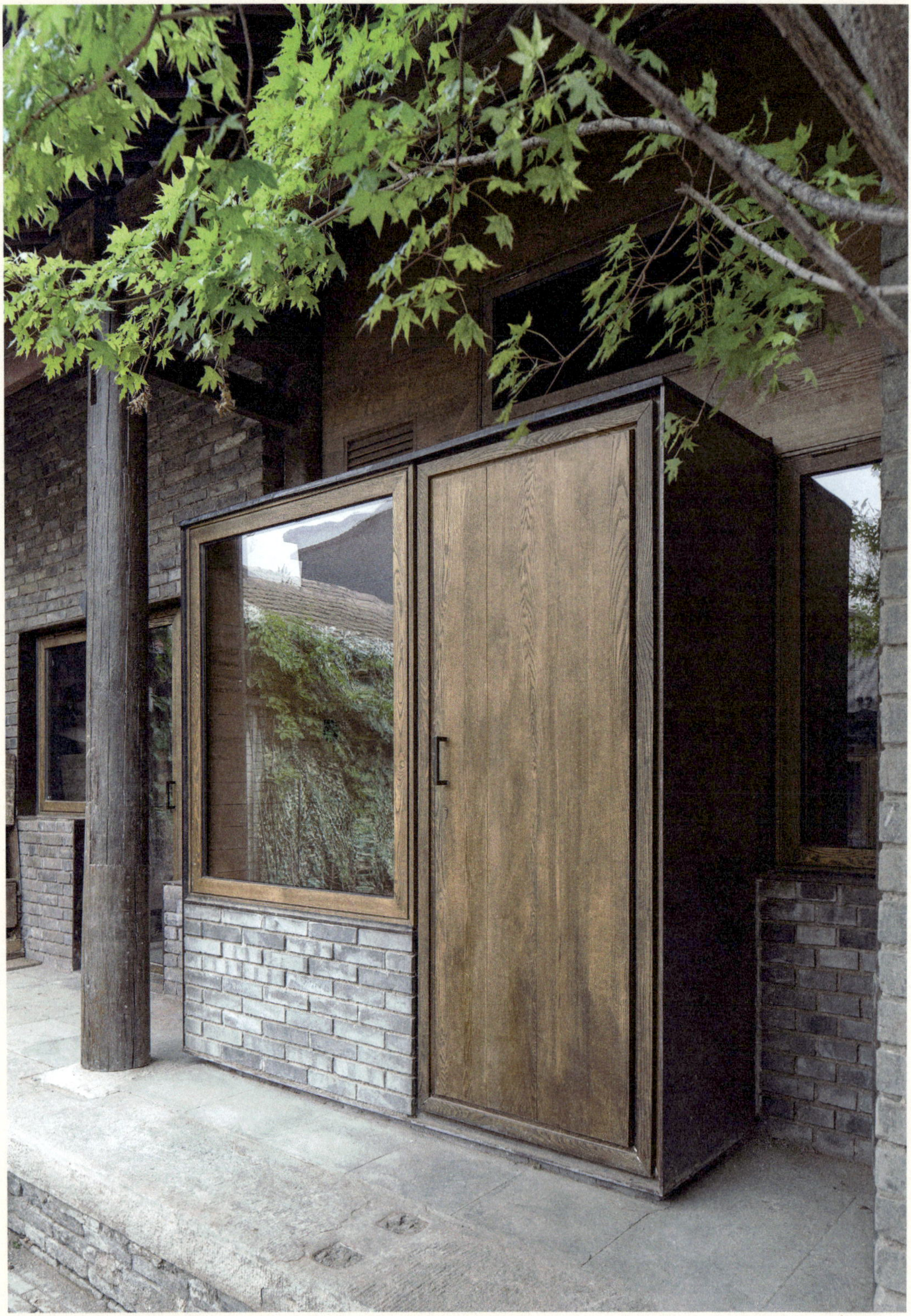

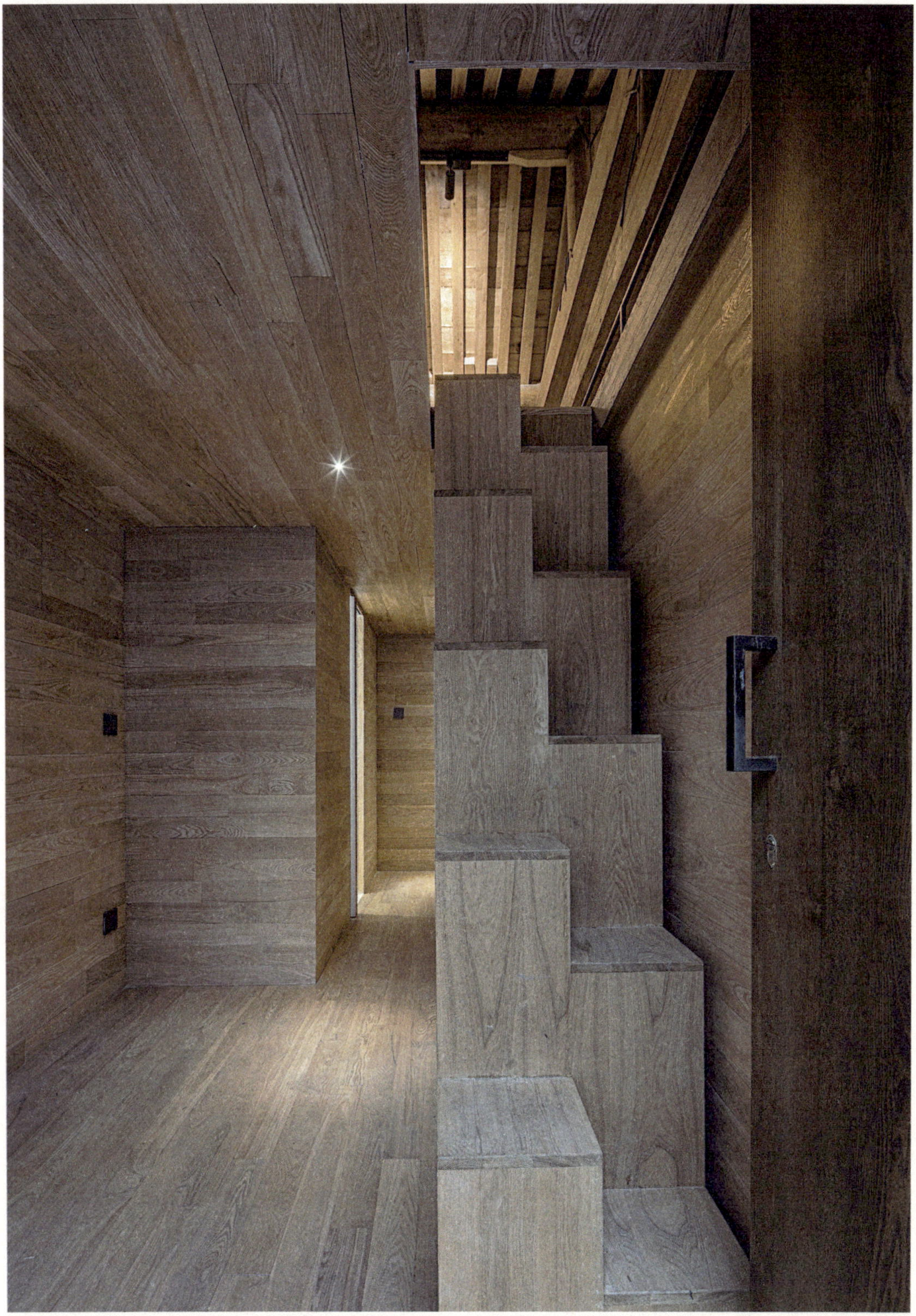

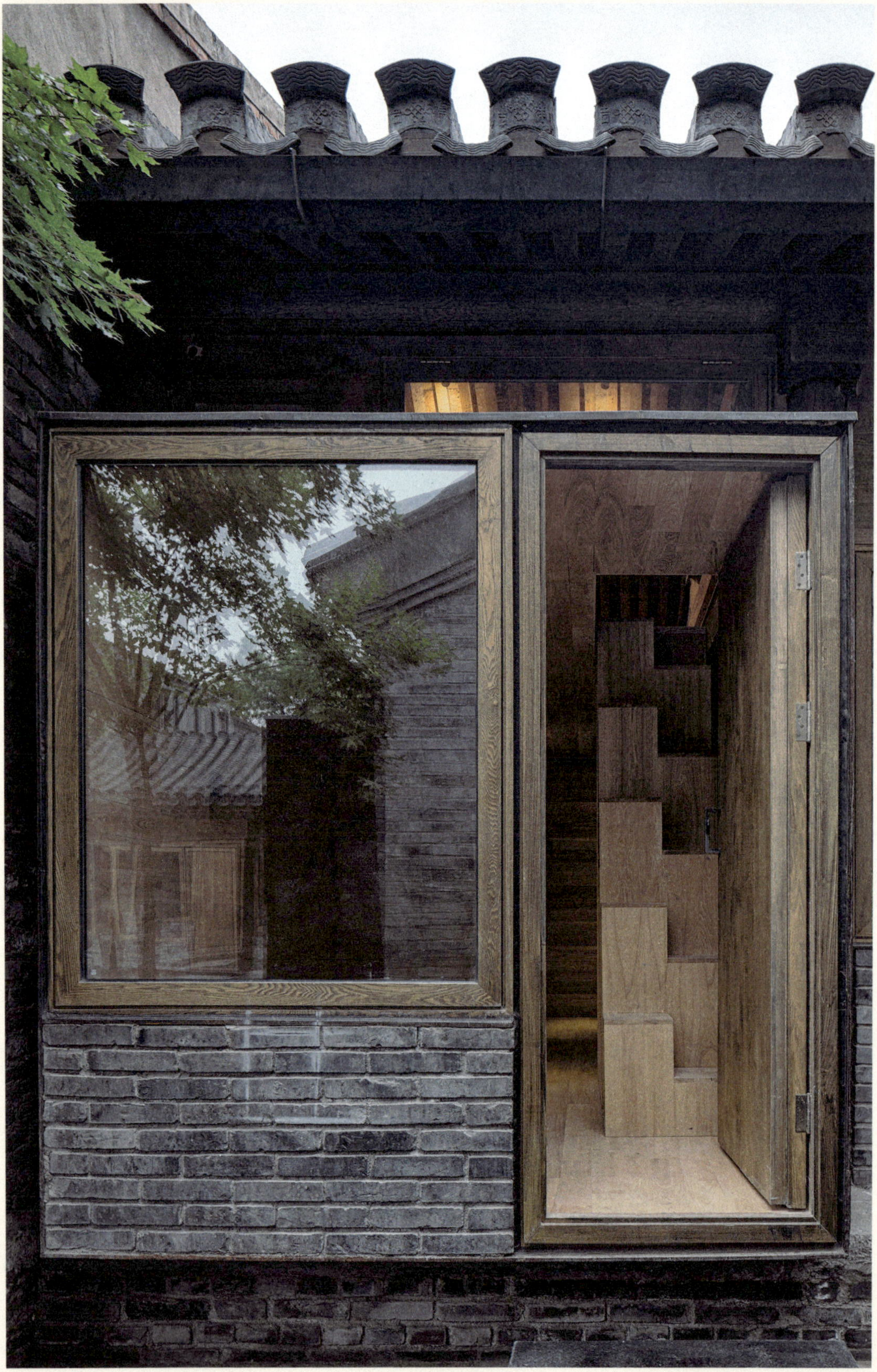

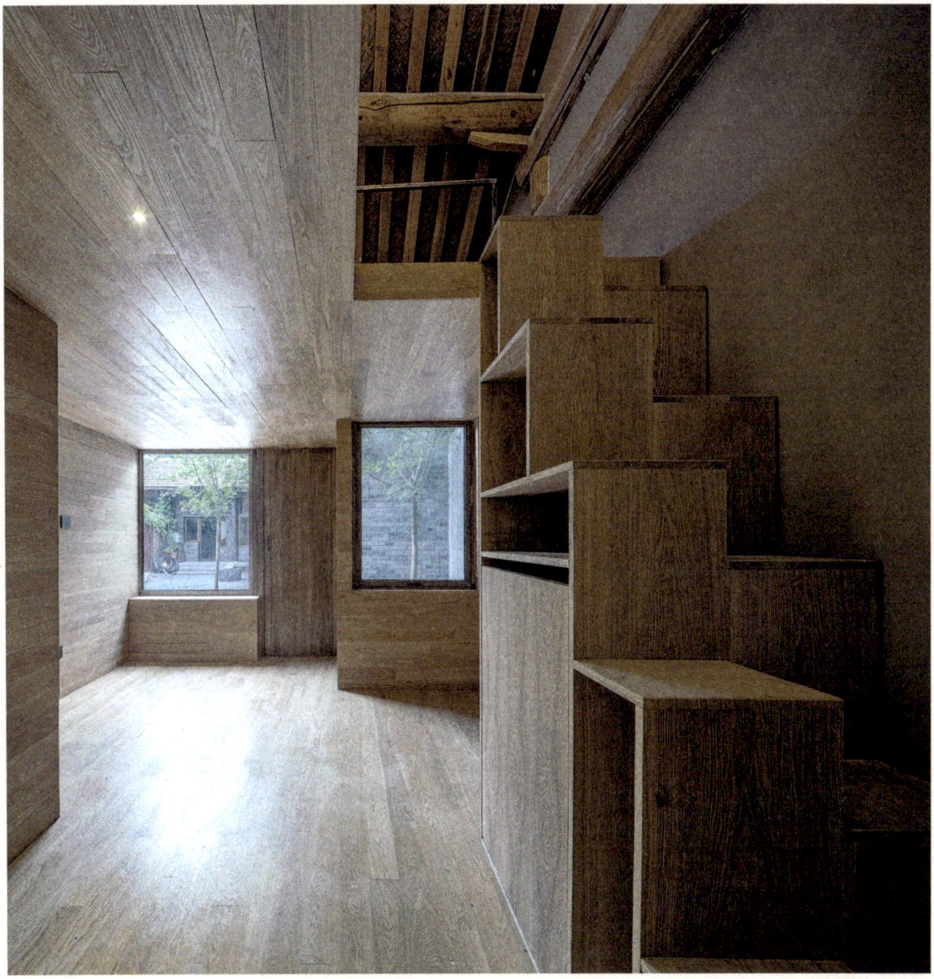

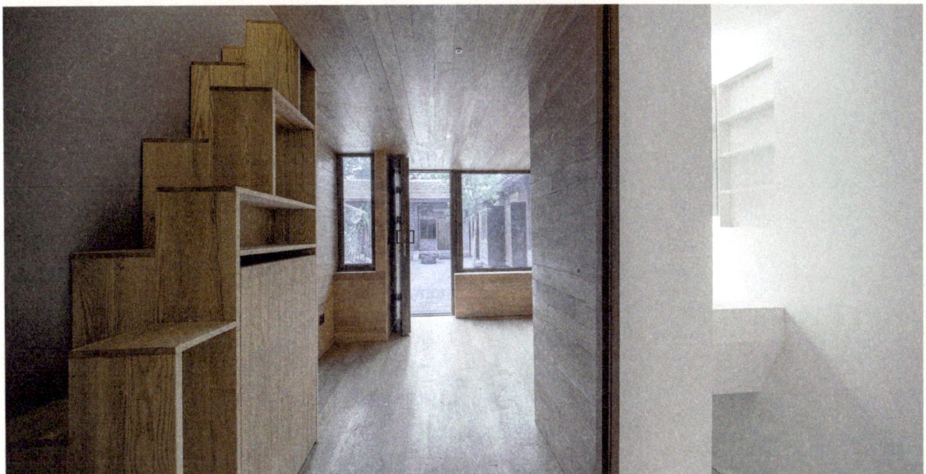

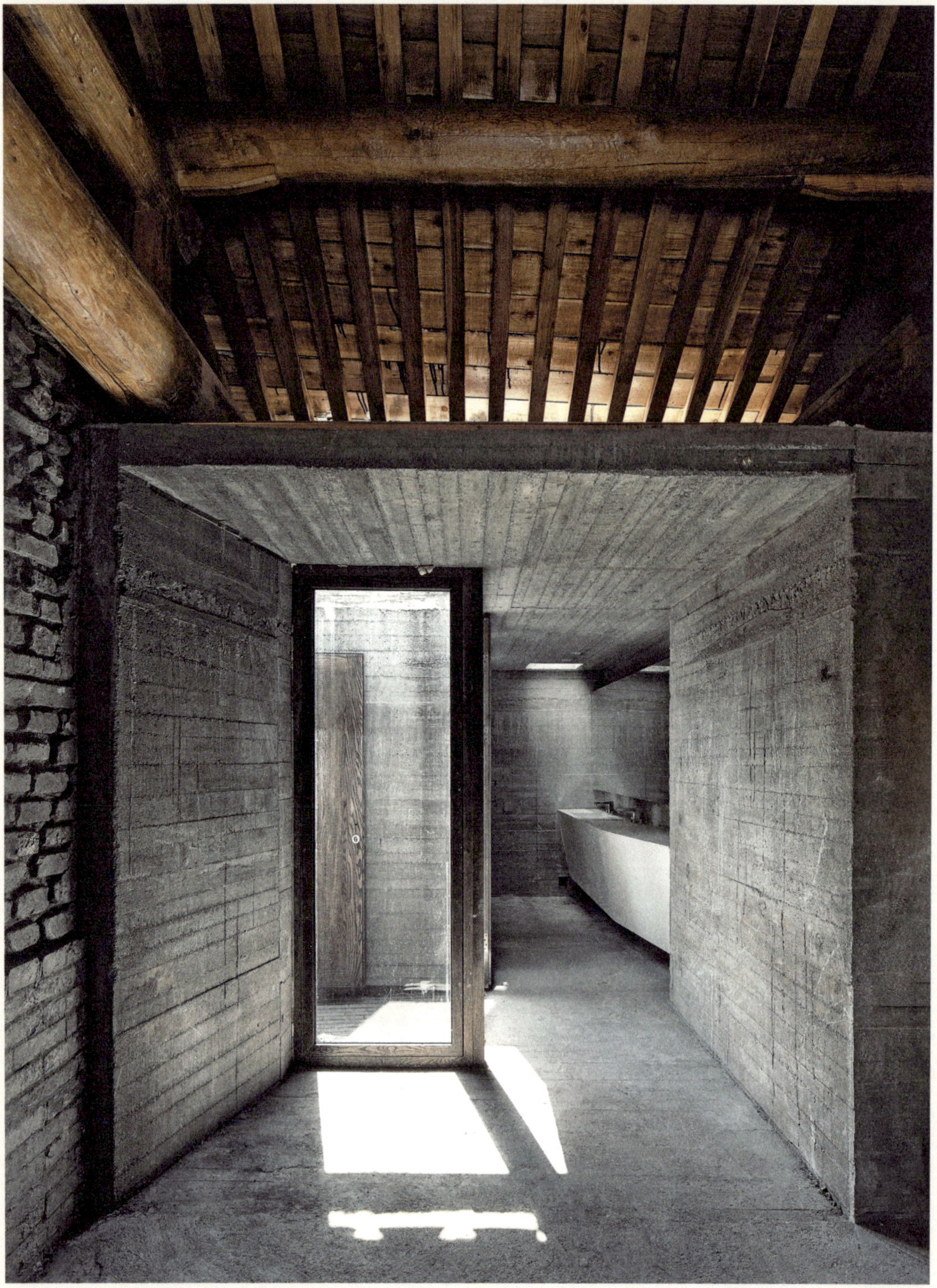

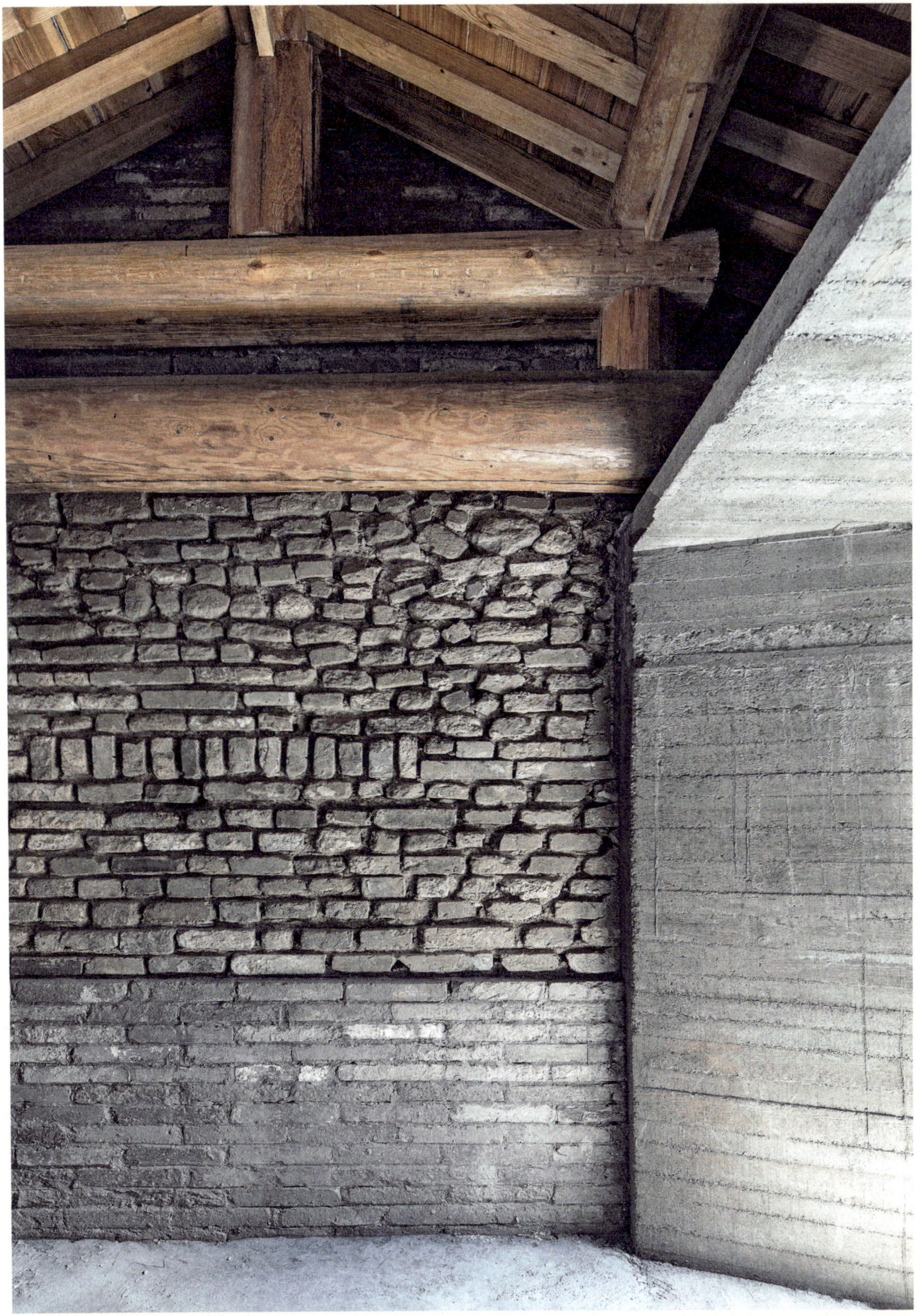

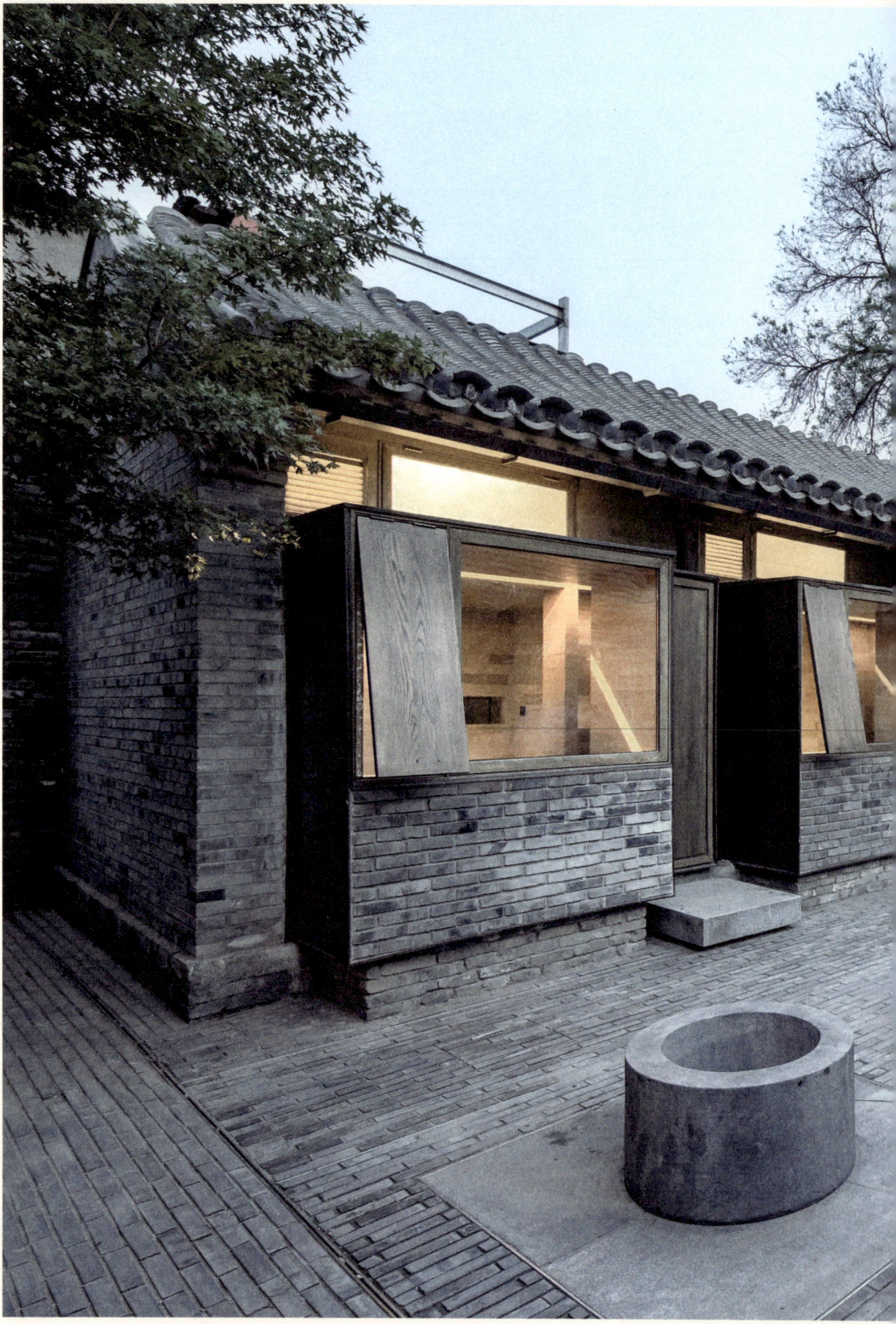

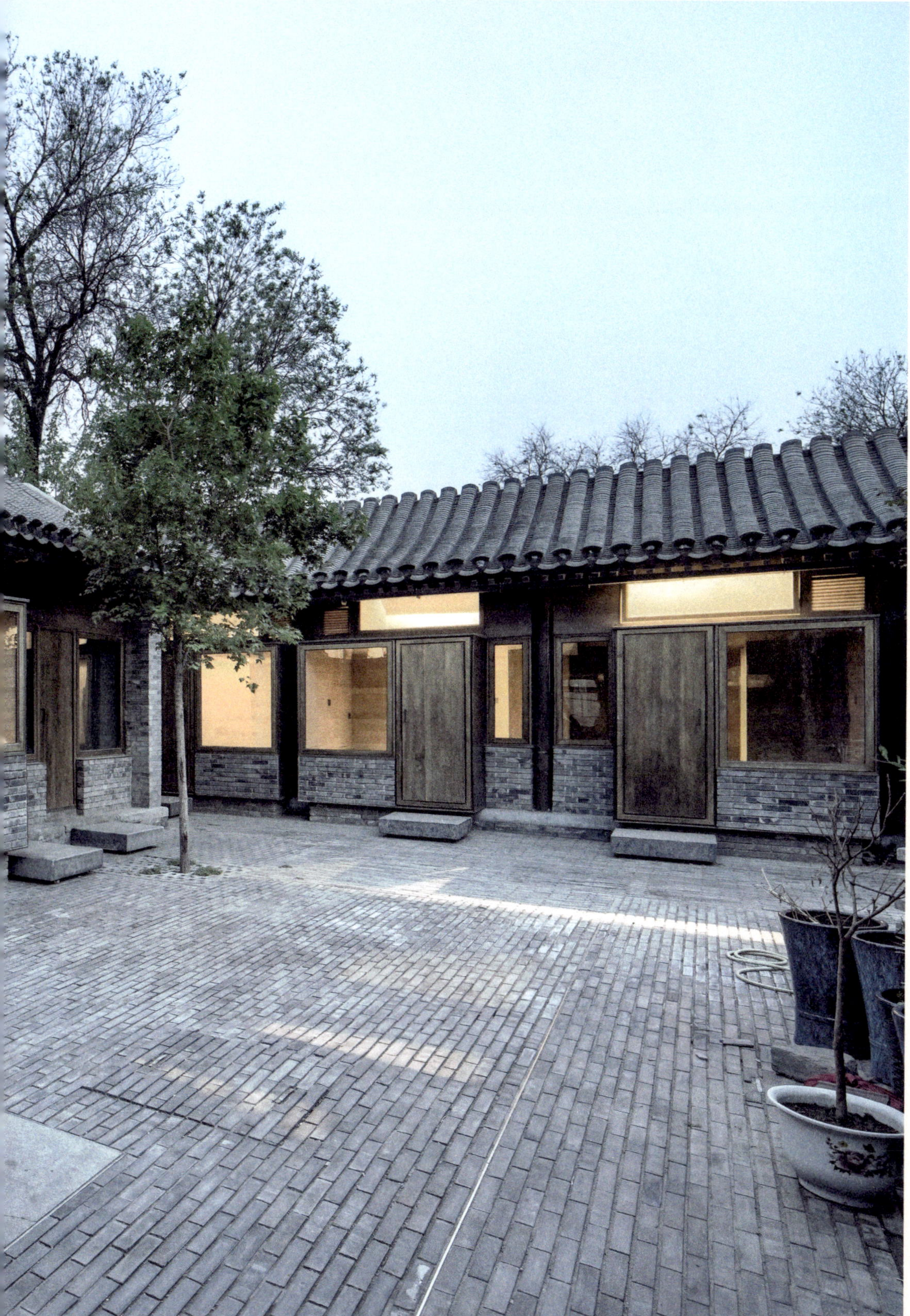

Zhang Ke is the founder and principal architect of ZAO/standardarchitecture 标准营造. Zhang Ke received his Master in Architecture from the Harvard University Graduate School of Design (GSD) in 1998 and his Master and Bachelor in Architecture from Tsinghua University in Beijing. He has been teaching Design Studios at Harvard GSD since 2016.

With a wide range of works realised over the past 20 years, his studio has emerged as one of the most critical and innovative protagonists among the new generation of Chinese architects. Recent works include the Novartis Campus Building in Shanghai, the Community Art Center in Rizhao, the Camerich R&D Campus in Beijing, a number of hutong transformation projects in the historic centre of Beijing and various buildings embedded in the landscape of Tibet. Zhang Ke was awarded the Alvar Aalto Medal in 2017 and the Aga Khan Award for Architecture in 2016. Other notable awards include the International Award Architecture in Stone, Verona, Italy (2011), Design Vanguard by Architecture Record (2010), China Architecture Media Award (CAMA), Best Young Architect Prize (2008) and the WA Chinese Architecture Award, Winning Prize (2010 and 2006).

Contributor Biographies

Hans-Jürgen Commerell is a photographer, curator and publisher who has been the co-director of the Aedes Architecture Forum, in partnership with Kristin Feireiss, since 1994. He studied social and business communication at Berlin University of the Arts. Since the early 2000s Commerell has diversified the programme of the Aedes Architecture Forum by looking more closely into the East-Asian cultural space. With *TU MU Young Architecture from China,* the first exhibition on young architecture from China worldwide, Commerell started an intensive and fruitful inquiry and exchange with the Chinese built environment, urban culture, rural development and architectural masterpieces which continues still today. In 2009, together with Kristin Feireiss, he conceptualised and established ANCB The Aedes Metropolitan Laboratory, an international (networking and) operating cultural platform focused on innovation in global urbanism with its reciprocal socio-economic and ecological effects.

Nondita Correa Mehrotra is an architect working in India and the United States. She studied architecture at the University of Michigan and the Harvard University Graduate School of Design (GSD). Correa Mehrotra is principal of RMA Architects, which has offices in Mumbai and Boston. She is also Director of the Charles Correa Foundation, based in Panaji, India, and worked for over two decades with Charles Correa and was Partner at Charles Correa Associates from 1990 to 2014.
She has taught at MIT, the University of Michigan and the Rhode Island School of Design. She was a finalist for the design of the symbol for the Indian rupee, an idea she had initiated with the Reserve Bank of India in 2005. In addition, she has also designed furniture, curated exhibitions and designed several architectural books. Correa Mehrotra served on the Master Jury of the Aga Khan Award for Architecture from 2017 to 2019, where she previously had been a technical reviewer. Correa Mehrotra was a member of the LafargeHolcim Awards jury for the Asia Pacific region in 2020.

Farrokh Derakhshani is the director of the Aga Khan Award for Architecture and has been associated with the award since 1982. Derakhshani trained as an architect and planner at the National University of Iran and later continued his studies at the School of Architecture in Paris (UP1). His main field of specialisation is the contemporary architecture of Muslim societies. He lectures widely and has organised and participated in numerous international seminars, exhibitions, colloquia, workshops and international competitions. He has served as a jury member at various international competitions and schools of architecture and collaborated on a large variety of architecture-related publications.

Kristin Feireiss of Berlin, Germany, is an architecture curator, writer and editor. She studied art history and philosophy at Johann Wolfgang Goethe University in Frankfurt. In 1980, she founded (with Helga Retzer, d. 1984) the independent Aedes Architecture Forum in Berlin as the first private architecture gallery in Europe. Since 1994 Feireiss has led this international platform in partnership with Hans-Jürgen Commerell and presented over 350 exhibitions and accompanying catalogues. Together with Commerell she initiated the ANCB The Aedes Metropolitan Laboratory in 2009. She has received many honours and awards, such as the Cross of the Order of Merit of the Federal Republic of Germany (2001), an Honorary Doctorate from the Carolo-Wilhelmina Technical University of Braunschweig (2007), the Knight in the Order of the Netherlands Lion (2013), and the Austrian Decoration of Honour for Science and Art (2016).

Kenneth B. Frampton CBE is regarded as one of the world's leading historians of modernist architecture. He is a British architect, critic and historian. Frampton is the Ware Professor Emeritus of Architecture at the Graduate School of Architecture, Planning, and Preservation at Columbia University, New York. He has lived in the United States permanently since the mid-1980s.

Frampton studied architecture at the Guildford School of Art, Surrey, and the Architectural Association School of Architecture, London. He has taught at the Princeton University School of Architecture (1966–71) and the Bartlett School of Architecture, London (1980), among other places. He has been a member of the faculty at Columbia University since 1972, and that same year he became a fellow of the Institute for Architecture and Urban Studies in New York and a co-founding editor of its magazine *Oppositions*. Frampton was a member of the Aga Khan Award for Architecture Master Jury in 2001.

The Canadian Centre for Architecture holds Frampton's archive, and in 2015 his library was acquired by the Department of Architecture, The University of Hong Kong.

Frampton was appointed Commander of the Order of the British Empire (CBE) in the Queen's Birthday Honours 2021 for his services to architecture.

Amanda (Xiao) Ju is a PhD Candidate in the Visual and Cultural Studies programme at the University of Rochester, New York. She received her BA in Art History from Barnard College and her MA in Visual and Cultural Studies from the University of Rochester. Her research and teaching interests include modern and contemporary art in China, international socialism, (post-)socialisms and feminist theories. She has written for *Caa.Reviews, Heichi Magazine,* and *InVisible Culture*. Ju has received several awards, such as the Celeste Hughes Bishop Award for Distinction in Graduate Studies, University of Rochester, in 2019 and the Art History Distinctive Senior Thesis, Barnard College, Columbia University, in 2015.

Mohsen Mostafavi, architect and educator, is the Alexander and Victoria Wiley Professor of Design and Harvard University Distinguished Service Professor. He served as Dean of the Harvard University Graduate School of Design (GSD) from 2008 to 2019.

Mostafavi received a Bachelor in Architecture from the Architectural Association School of Architecture in 1976. Prior to teaching at Harvard, he was formerly Dean of the College of Architecture, Art and Planning at Cornell University, where he was also Professor in Architecture. Previously, he served as the Chairman of the Architectural Association School of Architecture in London. Mostafavi has taught at numerous institutions, including the University of Pennsylvania, the University of Cambridge, and the Frankfurt Academy of Fine Arts (Städelschule). Mostafavi served on the Steering Committee of the Aga Khan Award for Architecture from 2001 to 2013 and has served on the design committees of the London Development Agency (LDA) and the RIBA Gold Medal. Mostafavi was a member of the Aga Khan Award for Architecture Master Jury in 2016. He is a consultant on a number of international architectural and urban design projects.

Martino Stierli has been The Philip Johnson Chief Curator of Architecture and Design at The Museum of Modern Art since 2015. Mr. Stierli oversees the wide-ranging programme of special exhibitions, installations and acquisitions of the museum's Department of Architecture and Design.

Stierli has taught at various Swiss universities, including the universities of Zurich and Basel, as well as ETH Zurich. He studied art and architectural history, German, and comparative literature at the University of Zurich, where he received his MA in 2003. From 2003 to 2007, he was part of the graduate programme Urban Forms – Conditions and Consequences at ETH Zurich, where he earned a PhD in 2008.

He has written extensively on contemporary architectural practice, and his scholarship has been recognised with a number of prizes, among them the ETH Medal of Distinction for Outstanding Research (2008), the Theodor Fischer Prize by the Zentralinstitut für Kunstgeschichte in Munich (2008) and the 2011 Swiss Art Award for Architectural Criticism. In 2012, Stierli was a fellow at the Getty Research Institute in Los Angeles.

Image Credits

All copyrights belong to their respective owners listed below, to whom we are grateful for the honor of presenting their works in this book.

Wang Ziling: 12-13, 18, 33, 36-37, 68, 70, 71, 73, 79, 81, 84 top, 84 bottom, 85, 110-111, 114, 117, 125, 126, 135, 140-141, 143, 144-145, 146, 147 top, 147 bottom, 148, 149, 151, 152-153, 157, 158-159, 165, 201, 202-203, 212-213, 215 bottom, 220, 221, 222, 223 top, 223 bottom, 224 bottom, 225, 228, 233, 262-263 top, 268-269, 272-273, 278, 279, 280-281

Wu Qingshan: 19, 21, 66-67, 74-75, 76, 77, 78 bottom, 80 bottom, 136-137, 138-139, 150, 154, 155, 156, 160-161, 169, 171, 185, 190-191, 192-193, 204-205, 206-207, 208, 209, 210-211, 214, 215 top, 255, 258, 264-265, 266, 267, 270-271, 274, 275, 276, 277 top, 277 bottom

Aga Khan Trust for Culture / Christopher Little: 101

BriYYZ on Flikr: 164 https://creativecommons.org/licenses/by-sa/2.0/deed.en

Rob Deutscher via https://commons.wikimedia.org/wiki/File:CCTV_Beijing_(6805979911).jpg: 95 top

Rob Deutscher via https://commons.wikimedia.org/wiki/File:Galaxy_Soho.jpg: 95 bottom

Theo van Doesburg, Cornelis van Eesteren *Contra-Construction Project (Axonometric)* 1923, from the collection of The Museum of Modern Art, New York: 174

EyeEm / Alamy Stock Photo: 113 bottom

Fabioomero on Visualhunt.com; https://visualhunt.com/f6/photo/28086009342/2918f8e422/: 97

Gisling via https://commons.wikimedia.org/wiki/File:Fragrant_Hill_Hotel.jpg: 93 right

Historic Collection / Alamy Stock Photo, unknown photographer: 89

Ismoon / Yang Tingbao https://commons.wikimedia.org/wiki/File:Yang_Tingbao._Peace_Hotel._Heping_fandian,_Beijing_1954._Project.jpg: 93 left

Epp Jerlei: 172, 173

Zhang Ke: 20, 48-49, 50, 51, 52, 54, 56, 59, 60, 128-129, 130-131, 132-133, 134, 199, 200

Ekaterina Kvelidze: 90 left, 167-168 https://creativecommons.org/licenses/by-sa/4.0/deed.en

Jorge Láscar via https://creativecommons.org/licenses/by-sa/4.0/deed.en: 168

Giorgio Lazzaro: 198

Zhang Mingming: 57, 61 top, 61 bottom

Zhu Pei via https://commons.wikimedia.org/wiki/File:03-Shou_County_Culture_and_Art_Center.jpg: 99

Pedro Pegenaute: 98

People's Architecture Office: 108-109

Sun Qingfeng: 22-23

Jakob Schmitt: 55

Su Shengliang: cover, 2-3, 17, 41, 42-43, 53, 62-63, 64, 65, 69, 181

Fang Shujun: 58

Chen Su: 23 top, 23 bottom, 24

Naiji Tian: 239, 242, 246

Tao / SHU He: 106-107

Clorindo Testa. Courtesy of *Fundación Clorindo Testa:* 175

Urbanus / Yang Chaoying: 102-103

Li Xiaodong Atelier / Li Xiaodong: 104-105

Zhang Yifan: 27 top, 27 bottom

ZAO/standardarchitecture: 28-29, 30, 31, 34-35, 38-39, 40, 44-47, 78 top, 80 top, 82, 83 top, 83 bottom, 113 top, 118-124, 127, 142, 170, 182-183, 183 bottom, 186, 187, 188, 189, 194-197, 216, 217, 218, 219, 224 top, 256, 257, 259-261, 262-263 bottom, 284

Hutong Metabolism
ZAO/standardarchitecture

With contributions by Nondita Correa Mehrotra, Farrokh Derakhshani, Kristin Feireiss & Hans-Jürgen Commerell, Kenneth Frampton, Amanda Ju, Zhang Ke, Mohsen Mostafavi and Martino Stierli

Photos by Wang Ziling, Wu Qingshan, Su Shengliang et al.

Editor: Cristina Steingräber

Project management: Epp Jerlei, Tonderai Koschke, Nadia Siméon and Cristina Steingräber

Copyediting: Dawn Michelle d'Atri and Claire Cichy

Art direction: Julia Wagner, grafikanstalt

Reproductions: Eberl & Kœsel Studio, Altusried-Krugzell, Germany

Printing and binding: DZA Druckerei zu Altenburg GmbH, Germany

© 2021 Aga Khan Award for Architecture, ArchiTangle GmbH, ZAO/standardarchitecture and the contributors

Aga Khan Award for Architecture
P. O. Box 2049
1211 Geneva 2
Switzerland
www.akdn.org/architecture

ZAO/standardarchitecture
No.2 Huangsi Street
Dongcheng District
Beijing, 100011
China
www.standardarchitecture.cn
www.z-a-o.cn

Published by
ArchiTangle GmbH
Meierottostraße 1
10719 Berlin
Germany
www.architangle.com

ISBN 978-3-96680-015-0